Memory of Silence

Memory of Silence

The Guatemalan Truth Commission Report

Edited by

Daniel Rothenberg

palgrave
macmillan

MEMORY OF SILENCE
Copyright © Daniel Rothenberg, 2012.

All rights reserved.

First published in 2012 by
PALGRAVE MACMILLAN®
in the United States—a division of St. Martin's Press LLC,
175 Fifth Avenue, New York, NY 10010.

Where this book is distributed in the UK, Europe and the rest of the world,
this is by Palgrave Macmillan, a division of Macmillan Publishers Limited,
registered in England, company number 785998, of Houndmills,
Basingstoke, Hampshire RG21 6XS.

Palgrave Macmillan is the global academic imprint of the above companies
and has companies and representatives throughout the world.

Palgrave® and Macmillan® are registered trademarks in the United States,
the United Kingdom, Europe and other countries.

ISBN: 978–0–230–34024–4
ISBN: 978–1–4039–6447–2

Library of Congress Cataloging-in-Publication Data

Guatemala, memoria del silencio. English
    Memory of silence : the Guatemalan Truth Commission Report /
edited by Daniel Rothenberg.
        p. cm.
    ISBN 978–1–4039–6447–2 (hc : alk. paper)—
    ISBN 978–0–230–34024–4 (pbk. : alk. paper)
    1. Human rights—Guatemala—History—20th century. 2. Political
violence—Guatemala—History—20th century. 3. Guatemala—
History—1985– 4. Guatemala—Politics and government—1985–
I. Rothenberg, Daniel. II. Comisiónpara el EsclarecimientoHistórico
(Guatemala). III. Title.

JC599.G8G7813 2012
972.8105'3—dc23   2011033456

A catalogue record of the book is available from the British Library.

Design by Newgen Imaging Systems (P) Ltd., Chennai, India.

First edition: March 2012

10 9 8 7 6 5 4 3 2 1

Printed in the United States of America.

*For the memory of Guatemala's
many thousands of victims.*

Contents

Part III   Consequences and Effects of *La Violencia*

Part IV   Conclusions and Recommendations

Figures and Tables

Figure

Tables

Acronyms and Abbreviations

AAAS	– American Association for the Advancement of Science
ACI	– *Alianza Contra la Impunidad*, Alliance Against Impunity
AEU	– *Asociación de Estudiantes Universitaríos*, Association of University Students
ALMG	– *Academia de Lenguas Mayas de* Guatemala, Academy of the Mayan Languages
ANACAFE	– *Asociación Nacional del Café*, National Coffee Association
ASC	– *Asamblea de Sociedad Civil*, Civil Society Assembly
AVANCSO	– *Asociación para el Avance de las Ciencias Sociales*, Association for the Advancement of Social Sciences
BANDESA	– *Banco Nacional de Desarrollo Agricola*, National Agricultural Development Bank
CADEG	– *Consejo Anticomunista de Guatemala*, Guatemalan Anticommunist Council
CALDH	– *Centro de Acción Legal para los Derechos Humanos*, Center for Legal Action for Human Rights
CDHG	– *Comisión de Derechos Humanos de Guatemala*, Guatemalan Human Rights Commission
CEH	– *Comisión para el Esclarecimiento Histórico*, Commission for Historical Clarification
CERJ	– *Consejo de Comunidades Étnicas Runujel Junam*, Runujel Junam Council of Ethnic Communities
CIA	– Central Intelligence Agency
CICIG	– *Comisión Internacional contra la Impunidad en Guatemala*, International Commission against Impunity in Guatemala
CIEDEG	– *Conferencia de Iglesias Evangélicas de Guatemala*, Conference of Evangelican Churches of Guatemala
CIEPRODEH	– *Centro de Investigación, Estudio y Promoción de los Derechos Humanos*, Center for the Investigation, Study and Promotion of Human Rights
CIIDH	– *Centro Internacional para Investigaciones en Derechos Humanos*, International Center for Human Rights Investigations
CNR	– *Comisión Nacional de Reconciliación*, National Commission for Reconciliation

CNR   – *Comisión Nacional de Resarcimiento*, National Commission for Reparations
CNT   – *Confederación Nacional de Trabajo*, National Labor Confederation
CNUS   – *Comité Nacional de Unidad Sindical*, National Committee for Union Unity
COMG   – *Consejo de Organizaciones Mayas de Guatemala*, Council of Guatemalan Maya Organizations
CONADEGUA   – *Coordinadora Nacional de Derechos Humanos de Guatemala*, National Human Rights Association of Guatemala
CONAVIGUA   – *Coordinadora Nacional de Viudas de Guatemala*, National Association of Guatemalan Widows
CONTRAGUA   – *Confederación de Trabajadores de Guatemala*, Confederation of Guatemalan Workers
COPREDEH   – *Comisión Presidencial Coordinadora de la Política Ejecutiva en Materia de Derechos Humanos*, Presidential Commission for the Coordination of Executive Policy on Human Rights
CPR   – *Comunidades de Población en Resistencia*, Communities of Population in Resistance
CRAG   – *Comité de Resistencia Anticomunista de Guatemala*, Guatemalan Anticommunist Resistance Committee
CRN   – *Comité de Reconstruccion Nacional*, National Reconstruction Committee
CUC   – *Comité de Unidad Campesina*, Committee of Campesino Unity
D-2   – referencing the army directorate of intelligence and their agents
DIC   – *Departmento de Investigaciones Criminales*, Department of Criminal Investigations
DIGESA   – *Dirección General de Servicios Agrícolas*, General Directorate of Agricultural Services
ECAP   – *Equipo de Estudios Comunitaríos y Acción Psicosocial*, Community Studies and Psychosocial Action Team
EGP   – *Ejército Guerrillero de los Pobres*, Guerrilla Army of the Poor
EMP   – *Estado Mayor Presidencial*, Presidential Joint Chiefs of Staff
ESA   – *Ejército Secreto Anticomunista*, Secret Anticommunist Army
FAFG   – *Fundación de Antropología Forense de Guatemala*, Guatemalan Forensic Anthropology Foundation
FAG   – *Fuerza Aerea de Guatemala*, Guatemalan Air Force
FAMDEGUA   – *Asociación de Familiares de Detenidos-Desaparecidos de Guatemala*, Association of Family Members of the Detained and Disappeared of Guatemala
FAR   – *Fuerzas Armadas Rebeldes*, Rebel Armed Forces
FAR   – *Fuerzas Armadas Revolucionarias*, Revolutionary Armed Forces

FASGUA   – *Federación Autónoma Sindical de Guatemala*, Independent Union Federation of Guatemala
FCG   – *Federación Campesina de Guatemala*, Campesino Federation of Guatemala
FECETRAG   – *Federación Central de Trabajadores de Guatemala*, Central Federation of Guatemalan Workers
FENOT   – *Federación Nacional de los Obreros del Transporte*, National Federation of Transport Workers
FERG   – *Frente Estudiantil Robin García*, Robin García Student Front
FIL   – *Fuerzas Irregulares Locales,* Irregular Local Forces
FLACSO   – *Facultad Latinoamericana de Ciencias Sociales*, Latin American Faculty of Social Sciences
FONAPAZ   – *Fondo Nacional para la Paz*, National Fund for Peace
FRG   – *Frente Republicano de Guatemala,* Guatemalan Republican Front
FRMT   – *Fundación Rigoberta Menchú Tum,* Rigoberta Menchú Tum Foundation
FUNDAPI   – *Fundación de Ayuda para el Pueblo Indígena*, Foundation for the Assistance of Indigenous People
FUR   – *Frente Unido De La Revolución,* United Revolutionary Front
G-2   – Also known as "Las Dos" ("The Two") referencing military intelligence and their agents
GAM   – *Grupo de Apoyo Mutuo*, Mutual Support Group
IACHR   – Inter-American Commission on Human Rights
ICCPG   – *Instituto de Estudios Comparados en Ciencias Penales de Guatemala*, Guatemalan Institute for the Comparative Study of Criminal Law
INTA   – *Instituto Nacional para Transformacion Agraria*, National Institute for Agrarian Change
INTCAP   – *Instituto Técnico de Capacitación y Productividad*, Technical Institute for Training and Productivity
IRCA   – International Railways of Central America
LRN   – *Ley de Reconciliación Nacional*, Law of National Reconciliation
MANO   – *Movimiento de Acción Nacionalista Organizado*, Movement of Organized Nationalist Action
MINUGUA   – *Misión de Verificación de las Naciones Unidas en Guatemala*, United Nations Verification Mission in Guatemala
MLN   – *Movimiento de Liberación Nacional*, National Liberation Movement
MP   – *Ministerio Publico*, Public Prosecutor
MR-13   – *Movimiento Revolucionario 13 de Noviembre*, Revolutionary Movement of November 13
NOA   – *Nueva Organización Anticomunista*, New Anticommunist Organization
ODHAG   – *Oficina de Derechos Humanos del Arzobispado de Guatemala*, Human Rights Office of the Archbishop of Guatemala

ORPA	– *Organización del Pueblo en Armas*, Organization of the People in Arms
PAC	– *Patrullas de Autodefensa Civil*, Civil Defense Patrols
PGT	– *Partido Guatemalteco del Trabajo*, Guatemalan Labor Party
PID	– *Partido Institucional Democrático*, Democratic Institutional Party
PMA	– *Policía Militar Ambulante*, Mobile Military Police
PN	– *Policia Nacional*, National Police
PNR	– *Programa Nacional de Resarcimiento*, National Reparations Program
PR	– *Partido Revolucionario*, Revolutionary Party
PRAHPN	– *Proyecto de Recuperación del Archivo Histórico de la Policía Nacional*, Project for the Recovery of the Historical Archive of the National Police
RNVP	– *Registro Nacional de Victimas*, National Victims' Registry
S-2	– referencing military intelligence working out of army bases
SAMF	– *Sindicato de Acción y Mejoramiento Ferrocarrilero*, Union for Railway Worker Action and Improvement
SEDEM	– *Asociación Seguridad en Democracia*, Security in Democracy
SEGEPLAN	– *Secretaría de Planificación y Programación de la Presidencia*, Presidential Secretariat for Planning and Programming
SEPAZ	– *Secretaría de la Paz*, Peace Secretariat
STIGSS	– *Sindicato de Trabajadores del Institute Guatemalteco de Seguro Social*, Union of Workers of the Guatemalan Institute for Social Security
UFCo	– United Fruit Company
UNDP	– United Nations Development Programme
UNHCR	– United Nations High Commission for Refugees
UNOPS	– United Nations Office for Project Services
URNG	– *Unidad Revolucionaria Nacional Guatemalteca*, Guatemalan National Revolutionary Unity
USAC	– *Universidad de San Carlos de Guatemala*, University of San Carlos
USAID	– United States Agency for International Development

Foreword

Christian Tomuschat

Lead Commissioner, Commission for Historical Clarification

Whenever a nation has experienced a dark chapter in its history, the question arises whether the past should simply be forgotten or whether it should be recalled and recorded for the benefit of the current generation and for the future. Guatemala took the courageous decision to establish a truth commission, the *Comisión para el Esclarecimiento Histórico* (Commission for Historical Clarification, CEH), in order to create the foundations through which different social groups could achieve new understandings of harmonious coexistence. This was not an easy course to choose.

Both negotiating partners attempting to craft the terms of a peace agreement—the Guatemalan government on the one side and the guerrilla forces, the *Unidad Revolucionaria Nacional Guatemalteca* (Guatemalan National Revolutionary Unity, URNG) on the other—knew perfectly well that they had committed grave violations of human rights and international humanitarian law, the rules that determine the permissible use of methods of warfare. Eventually, at a meeting in Oslo in June 1994, the two parties agreed that, after the end of the conflict, their conduct should be investigated by an impartial commission. The report of this commission would then become part of the nation's collective memory.

There were two main reasons behind the decision to create a process to address the horrendous occurrences of the internal armed conflict that haunted Guatemala from the middle of the 1960s to 1996. First, a tradition of truth commissions had already been established in Latin America through prior independent commissions in Argentina, Chile, and El Salvador. Second, precisely because of this situation, civil society in Guatemala was eager to investigate and clarify what occurred in the recent past and identify those responsible for the atrocities that were committed. These demands did not find an unreserved positive response as can be clearly seen in the limitations on the commission's operation.

After the final peace agreement in December 1996, the CEH was created and began its work in September 1997, after months of careful preparations. In principle, the commission was given only six months to complete its work with the possibility of extending its time frame for an additional six months. This short period was all that was provided to investigate a civil war that had lasted more than thirty years and claimed more than 200,000 lives.

The commission's report was submitted to the Guatemalan people, the government of Guatemala, and the United Nations in February 1999. Its twelve volumes provide a well-documented account of the most atrocious aspects of the fratricidal war. Of course, the report could not possibly provide a complete picture of all that had occurred. In general, the country's conservative elites, who also had victims to mourn, decided to distance themselves from the CEH, viewing it as a "left-leaning" institution. The report is, therefore, mainly presented from the perspective of the nation's victims who were forced to endure violence, death, and destruction for decades without receiving any assistance or support from public authorities.

This is not a weakness but, in fact, it is one of the great strengths of the work of the commission. Volumes VII to XI of the commission's full report, in particular, are dedicated to the suffering of the common men and women of Guatemala. In these volumes, the tragic events that took the lives of thousands of human beings are described in great detail. The CEH deliberately chose to present its findings not only through statistics, but also through victims' experiences, to ensure that their suffering would not be lost in the anonymous stream of history. The commission's report helps restore their dignity by recalling their lives as human beings.

For the common citizen perhaps the most devastating feature of those years was the climate of total lawlessness. The state had abandoned its functions as the guardian of law and justice. The military regimes that followed, one after another, focused on the objective of fighting "subversion," which often consisted of simple acts seeking "social justice." Thus, political claims that in Western Europe would have been characterized as belonging to a social-democratic perspective were stigmatized as endangering the security of the state. And, there was no limit to the persecution of perceived dissent. During this time, the judicial system proved ineffective; it was as if it did not exist. And, as the CEH noted, in some parts of the country systematic repression took on a racial character that met the legal definition of genocide.

The expectation on the part of the commission was that in the new era of peace, the Guatemalan judiciary would take on cases of genocide, attempting to prosecute perpetrators as it was compelled to do under domestic law—the *Ley de Reconciliación Nacional* (Law of National Reconciliation, LRN) of December 18, 1996—and international law, in particular, the 1948 United Nations Convention on the Prevention and Punishment of the Crime of Genocide. Unfortunately, once again, the attorney general was not able to perform his duty. Thus, the genocidal acts committed during the armed conflict remain without sanction to this day. It then fell to the Inter-American Court of Human Rights to remind Guatemalan authorities that they failed to comply with their duty to punish these acts.

The commission's report has received a great deal of support and praise within Guatemala and among the international community. In addition, it should be noted that its findings have never been challenged. In fact, the commission's conclusions largely mirror the findings of *"Nunca Más!"* (1998), the report sponsored by the Catholic Church of Guatemala, whose representatives originally feared that the CEH report would not yield significant results, given its many limitations.

Indeed, there was one stipulation of the Oslo Agreement that was severely criticized by human rights organizations, namely the requirement that responsibilities would not be "individualized." These groups were concerned that a report that failed to present the names of the perpetrators would be of little value. In the course of the commission's work, it turned out that this restriction was not a significant obstacle to providing a meaningful account of what occurred in Guatemala.

Given the long time span covered by the CEH's mandate as well as the large numbers of victims, it would have been impossible to identify the perpetrators in each and every violation documented by the commission. For this reason, names could only have been presented in a partial, if not random, manner. In addition, the CEH would have been obligated to provide those individuals named with the opportunity to defend themselves according to the procedural guarantees provided by the International Covenant on Civil and Political Rights. This could not have been accomplished with the modest means at the disposal of the CEH and the limitation of having only three commissioners.

However, it is important to note that the CEH report clearly establishes institutional responsibilities for human rights violations based on the documentation and analysis of material gathered through rigorous field research. It then fell to the responsible Guatemalan governmental authorities to draw the requisite conclusions. In this regard, there has been a marked lack of political will in the years following the presentation of the report.

Despite its substance as a text containing valuable lessons for all countries that are called upon to reckon with the legacy of governmental injustice and crime, the CEH report has found relatively few readers outside the Spanish-speaking world. This is deeply unfortunate, but can be partially explained by the fact that the majority of material remains available only in Spanish. To make the important work of the commission accessible to an interested public around the world, Daniel Rothenberg—who worked as my assistant in the early stages of the CEH— has had the felicitous idea to prepare and publish this condensed volume. While it is clear that a reduced text of this type cannot fully reproduce the wealth of information and reflection contained in the full report, this book is well-structured and provides a valuable representation of the commission's work.

This book explains the philosophical rationale behind the work of the CEH. The chapters covering the main patterns of violent crime and other injustices provide summaries that succeed in capturing the essential points of interest. The text also presents excellent selections of the so-called "paradigmatic cases" that reflect in a few pages key patterns of violence and criminal wrongdoing. The report concludes with the recommendations that the commission was charged with formulating and to which it gave its utmost attention. These recommendations balance the need to provide justice for the country's many victims with an understanding of the nation's limited resources, respecting at the same time the legislative powers of the Guatemalan Congress. While recommendations of this kind cannot transform the nature and the practices of a society, they remain benchmarks against which the performance of Guatemala's system of governance can be measured.

It is my hope that this book will help Guatemalans and others better understand the work of the CEH and the suffering of the Guatemalan people during a terrible period in the nation's history. It is only by courageously facing the truth of the recent past that Guatemala and the larger world can honor the nation's victims, prevent the recurrence of government atrocities, and build the foundations for lasting peace.

Introduction

Facing *La Violencia*: The Importance of the Guatemalan Truth Commission

Daniel Rothenberg

This book presents a one-volume edited version of the final report of the Guatemalan Commission for Historical Clarification (CEH), commonly known as the Guatemalan Truth Commission. The report is the definitive account of one of the most brutal cases of government repression in the Western Hemisphere, a thirty-four year conflict forged by the Cold War, strongly influenced by U.S. foreign policy, and so severe that the commission determined that the state committed genocide against its own indigenous people.

Despite its scope, significance, and impact, the conflict remains largely unknown outside the country and inadequately understood by the majority of Guatemalans. One reason for this is the difficulty of accessing a readable version of the commission's work. Until this publication, the CEH report was largely unavailable in English and only available in Spanish in an unedited form that is over 4,400 pages long and fills twelve volumes. This book significantly expands access to the commission's important and sobering analysis of the conflict. Its goal is to ensure that the tragedy of the nation's recent history is more fully understood and acknowledged within Guatemala, in the United States, throughout the region, and around the world.

Facing *La Violencia*

The Guatemalan conflict produced some of Latin America's most shocking instances of political terror, including massacres, extrajudicial executions, rape, and torture. The suffering in Guatemalan is known locally by a term revealing in its brutal simplicity—*la violencia*—"the violence." The systematic abuses that defined daily reality were part of a decades-long internal conflict between the government and an insurgency known as the *Unidad Revolucionaria Nacional Guatemalteca* (Guatemalan National Revolutionary Unity, URNG). The fighting came to a negotiated conclusion through a series of peace agreements, one of which—the Oslo Accord of June 1994—mandated the creation of the commission, which was to be implemented shortly after the conflict ended.

The agreement explained that the CEH was needed because "the people of Guatemala have a right to know the whole truth" regarding the conflict and that the commission's task was "clarifying with complete objectivity, equanimity and impartiality" the "grave acts of violence, disregard for fundamental rights of the individual and suffering of the population connected with the armed confrontation." The CEH was designed to formally link peace, democratic transition, and national reconstruction with a process of documenting and analyzing past atrocities. It began its work in 1997 and submitted its report in early 1999. In documenting and analyzing past abuses, the commission tried to explain how Guatemala came to experience the longest armed insurgency in Central America and the most violent conflict in recent Latin American history.

As the CEH found, understanding *la violencia* requires a consideration of a number of factors within Guatemalan society and history, particularly the nation's severe poverty and profound structural inequality. While Guatemala is rich in natural resources, a small elite identifying itself as ethnically and culturally distinct has long controlled most of the country's land and wealth. From the colonial era on, Guatemala's social and political system has supported gross inequality, linking the economic dominance of a minority with systematic discrimination against the majority, especially the nation's indigenous Mayan population. The country long relied on a series of repressive laws and regulations that, when challenged, were backed up by state violence.

Even now, more than a decade after the negotiated peace, the nation is among the poorest and most unequal in the hemisphere. Over half of all Guatemalans live below the poverty line, with 15 percent living in extreme poverty. More than 40 percent of children under five are chronically malnourished, and the country has some of the region's worst social statistics regarding health, housing, and education. Although the peace process created substantial improvements in legal rights and basic protections for its Mayan population, Guatemala remains ethnically divided between indigenous people—representing between 40 and 60 percent of the total population (including small groups of Xinkas and Garifunas)—and the nation's Ladino population, a local term used to refer to a mixed Spanish, immigrant, and indigenous heritage. Poverty and marginalization are substantially worse among the Maya, over 75 percent of whom live in poverty and over 25 percent live in extreme poverty.

While racism, inequality, and marginalization have produced enormous suffering for the Guatemalan people, these conditions alone did not create the conflict. Instead, as the commission concluded, structural inequality defined a general social context maintained through authoritarian rule, with the conflict resulting from escalating levels of state repression in response to movements for social change. In the mid-1950s, a successful ten-year democratic process that challenged the status quo was overthrown with support from the United States. This led to decades of military rule, fraudulent and restrictive elections, and the systematic use of repression to protect empowered interests. During the 1960s and 1970s, social movements led by students, the Catholic Church, unions, and community groups sought alternatives to the dominant socioeconomic structure. While these efforts often achieved significant gains at the local level, the state reacted with threats, intimidation, attacks, and assassinations, making it difficult, and ultimately impossible, for these groups to continue their work and for their reforms to advance.

Inevitably, the opposition turned toward armed insurrection. The first stage of the insurgency began in the early 1960s and operated largely in the capital and in eastern Guatemala. The army responded with brutal repression that relied heavily on a violent and increasingly intrusive intelligence service, which ultimately crushed the movement. The next stage of the insurgency grew over time and peaked from the late 1970s through the early 1980s. In response, state repression became totalizing, leading to the period of the most intense and sustained abuses.

The U.S. government played a key role in Guatemala's domestic politics during this time, providing substantial economic assistance as well as significant military support and training for successive regimes. From the mid-1950s on, through overt and covert means, the United States significantly influenced domestic Guatemalan politics as part of a regional foreign policy defined by the Cold War. These efforts linked economic development with military aid, creating a broad political alliance to combat the spread of communist beliefs. While ostensibly favoring democracy, the rigid nature of this approach led the United States to support governments, in Guatemala and elsewhere, that viewed virtually any organized opposition to dominant social and political interests as a fundamental threat to national security.

These factors ultimately led to a tragic twentieth century case of how state terror came to define national politics. In part, the conflict can be seen as an example of a larger, regional phenomenon; Guatemala was one of a number of Latin American regimes that relied on systematic human rights violations as a key element of governance and a focused policy response to movements for social change. From the 1970s through the 1980s, the majority of Latin Americans lived under authoritarian, often military, governments linking nationalism, centralized bureaucratic management, and a Cold War-era vision of national security. Many of these governments committed widespread human rights violations against those seen to be challenging the state. The subsequent revelation of the severity and brutality of these acts played a key role in delegitimizing authoritarian rule and enabling Latin America's transition to democracy.

However, state repression in Guatemala was especially brutal and widespread and stands out within a region that, at the time, was known for government sponsored abuse. The commission determined that over 200,000 Guatemalans were killed in the conflict, the vast majority of whom were Maya civilians unaffiliated with either the military or the URNG. State repression was so severe and overwhelming that the CEH determined it met the legal definition of genocide.

In any conflict or civil war, all sides bear responsibility for violence and destruction, and the CEH concluded that both the state and the URNG committed serious violations. Nevertheless, in the case of the Guatemalan conflict, the army and state institutions committed the vast majority of serious violations. The CEH found that the state and institutions under its control were responsible for 93 percent of recorded violations, including virtually all of the massacres and most cases of torture, rape, disappearance, and killing. The CEH concluded that the URNG committed 3 percent of recorded violations, including killing, kidnapping, and various forms of abuse.

The systematic nature of *la violencia*, its cruel and brutal management of power, is difficult to describe and overwhelming by almost any measure. During the most violent period in the conflict, the army and paramilitary groups committed hundreds of massacres, destroying thousands of villages, and forcing 500,000 to 1.5 million Guatemalans to flee their homes. Torture, rape, mutilation, and brutal punishments were commonplace. Many rural areas were heavily militarized through policies of surveillance, forced resettlement, and the mandatory participation of all rural men in groups known as the *Patrullas de Autodefensa Civil* (Civil Defense Patrols, PAC).

The repression was not a collection of isolated cases or the result of occasional military excess, but rather an expression of carefully planned government policies. Guatemala's brutal counterinsurgency was managed within a hierarchical structure led by the *Estado Mayor* (Joint Chiefs of Staff), which developed general strategies that were implemented within a complex chain of command within the army and related security services, including: military intelligence (G-2 and S-2), *Kaibiles* (Special Forces), militarized police services, death squads, *comisionados militares* (military commissioners, civilians linked to the army), networks of *orejas* ("ears," or spies), PACs, and others. As the commission concluded, "The majority of human rights violations occurred with the knowledge or by the order of the highest authorities of the State" and "the responsibility for a large part of these violations…reaches the highest levels of the Army and successive governments."

One of the commission's primary concerns was to explain how, over three and a half decades, Guatemalan society, especially the government, became so reliant on violence and repression, so predatory and tragically destructive. By the late 1970s, institutionalized human rights violations had become the central mechanism of daily rule and the key manner in which the government interacted with citizens, especially in the majority Maya *altiplano*, or highlands. The state's use of violence radically reconstituted life for rural indigenous residents and defined governance as a function of brutal, impulsive, and often unpredictable repression. Human rights violations were so pervasive that, in much of the country, almost every Guatemalan could tell terrifying stories of abuse and cruelty, as evidenced by the thousands of testimonies gathered by the CEH.

State terror in Guatemala went beyond killing and destruction to reconfigure the very nature of social reality. Through violence and the militarization of daily life, the state established a culture of fear and intimidation. Simple conversations were transformed by the possibility that those listening could be *orejas*, passing information, whether real or invented, to state authorities or paramilitary groups. During the worst period of *la violencia*, ordinary social relations became inherently uncertain and infused with sudden and often inexplicable acts of brutality.

Throughout the conflict, the state bound severe repression with a near-complete denial of responsibility, linking a dysfunctional judiciary with institutionalized impunity. It was dangerous and often fatal for Guatemalans to draw attention to atrocities or to try to find out what happened to loved ones detained by the authorities. Those responsible for human rights violations at every level—from soldiers on the ground to the military officials that designed repressive strategies—were shielded from accountability for their acts. The total-izing nature of impunity made dissent and discussion impossible, as the CEH concluded, "Terror has been the goal of…the counterinsurgency policy" whose "objective was to…silence society."

In this way, *la violencia* was an assault on truth. And, in retrospect, the domi-neering, silencing nature of terror succeeded in concealing much of the country's tragic truth. Many within the country—especially those living in Guatemala City or other areas where the repression was selective—were unaware of the severity of state's brutal policies. This lack of understanding and acknowledgment con-tinued long after the acts of violence had ended.

However, Guatemalan society's failure to engage its repressive past was not simply the result of a lack of available information. In fact, from the mid-1980s on, a number of civil society groups gathered testimonies and related data—at first, partial and later more comprehensive—on political terror in Guatemala. They documented the existence of systematic human rights violations and presented their findings domestically and internationally. As a result of partial awareness of the Guatemalan government's atrocities, the nation came to be viewed as a pariah within the global community.

Nevertheless, the full scope of *la violencia* was not understood for years as Guatemalan society generally avoided a full engagement with what occurred and its profound implications. This resulted from a number of interconnected demands and pressures, including ongoing fear of repression; the fact that the vast majority of victims were poor, indigenous, rural residents; and, the widespread belief that those targeted had become involved in *babosadas* ("foolishness") and deserved their fate. The nation was deeply affected by decades of conflict, and claims about past repression were read through a divisive and highly politicized lens. The CEH was created within this context to address years of silence and broad social denial and, "to place on record Guatemala's recent bloody past" as an essential part of the process of rebuilding the nation.

"Never Again"—The CEH and the Role of Truth Commissions

The Guatemalan Commission for Historical Clarification is a truth commission, a formal investigative body charged with documenting and analyzing past politi-cal violence. Truth commissions are a relatively new global phenomenon and rep-resent an important development within international human rights theory and practice. They build on the claim embodied in the words "never again" (the title of a number of truth commission reports), which provided the moral foundation for creating the international human rights system following the mass killing and destruction of the Second World War. Truth commissions seek to provide an objective account of severe political repression, giving voice to victims, memo-rializing suffering, and establishing mechanisms through which the public can engage the past as a necessary ground for rebuilding devastated societies.

Truth commissions have become a key element of what is known as transitional justice, a collection of practices—including domestic and international prosecutions, reparations, memorials, and policy reforms—that reflect on and respond to past atrocities in the wake of authoritarian rule, war, and internal conflict. Within this framework, truth commissions play an essential role by outlining the nature, scope, and mechanisms of past repression. They collect and analyze large numbers of victim statements in order to understand what occurred, determine patterns of repression and develop policy recommendations to assist victims, support peace, and prevent the recurrence of widespread political violence.

The first commissions were created in South America in the 1980s and early 1990s by emerging civilian governments facing recent military regimes that committed systematic human rights violations. They gathered information on characteristic violations, particularly a pattern of illegal detention, torture, and execution known as disappearance in which the bodies of those killed are hidden and certainty about their fate remains unclear. The efforts of these commissions built on emerging domestic, regional, and international human rights movements that "spoke truth to power" by gathering objective proof of violations in the face of official denial. They presented the public with personal testimonies of suffering, revealed the locations of secret torture centers, and through these efforts played a key role in delegitimizing prior authoritarian governments.

Truth commissions are sometimes criticized because, while they document atrocities, they are not courts and lack the authority to hold perpetrators accountable for their actions. This idea results from a misconception that these investigative bodies preclude or replace legal action. In fact, many commissions have existed alongside tribunals or played a significant supporting role in the development of criminal and civil cases. Nevertheless, there are situations where truth commissions have been created in countries that have passed blanket amnesty laws protecting perpetrators from prosecution.

In reviewing the contributions of truth commissions, it is important to understand that they play a different social role than prosecutions and provide different understandings and insights. Truth commissions are broad inquiries into decades of repression involving thousands of cases and the complex, often interconnected, roles of multiple state institutions, various insurgent groups, and distinct domestic and foreign actors. Trials seek truth in a more focused manner, determining criminal responsibility based on specific legal definitions and generally focusing on a small number of perpetrators and a select set of facts and incidents. It is also important to note that truth commissions cost a fraction of what is required for trials, especially those conducted by international tribunals, and have an expressly communicative mission to present the public with an overview and general analysis of past atrocities to support political transition and national reconstruction.

Truth commissions have become common mechanisms for ending conflicts and responding to the legacy of past political repression. From the mid-1990s on, these investigative bodies became increasingly institutionalized such that most peace negotiations and political transitions from authoritarian rule either included truth commissions or involved discussions of possible commissions.

There have now been dozens of truth commissions around the world, organized in different ways and with varying levels of success. Within Latin America and the Caribbean alone, truth commissions have been created in Argentina (1983), Brazil (1985), Chile (1990), Ecuador (1996), El Salvador (1992), Haiti (1995), Panama (2001), Paraguay (2004), Peru (2001), and Uruguay (2000).

These commissions have evolved over time, shifting in relation to local context and in response to the work of other investigative bodies. The Argentine commission produced the most widely read and influential report, but offered only a few pages of general policy recommendations. The Chilean commission led to the creation of a significant national reparations program, yet only documented cases of those killed by the regime, failing to gather data on survivors of illegal detention, torture, and rape. The Salvadoran commission was run by the United Nations, composed entirely of foreigners, and its stern recommendations were soundly rejected by the government, which passed a blanket amnesty five days after the report was released.

South Africa's commission is by far the most well known. It was created in 1995 following the nation's transition to democracy and charged with investigating human rights violations committed under the apartheid regime. Whereas prior commissions conducted their research in private and kept the identities of those presenting testimonies confidential, South Africa's Truth and Reconciliation Commission became a national sensation by holding public hearings presented live on radio and television. Victims and even some perpetrators told their stories publicly before millions of South Africans, connecting the truth-seeking process with the larger society. The commission was also empowered to provide direct reparations to victims and included a controversial policy of offering perpetrators amnesty in exchange for testimony regarding their responsibility for past human rights violations.

These investigative bodies—in Latin America and around the world—have transformed the way in which the global community responds to sustained political violence and atrocities. Truth commissions present the revelation of painful, traumatic reality as an essential form of justice and as a prerequisite for peace and democracy. The development of these investigative bodies from the 1980s on defines a key stage in the maturation of the human rights movement, linking the complex nature of postconflict reality with a formal, national encounter with victims' stories and an analysis of a country's reliance on mechanisms of terror.

The CEH is widely viewed as among the most successful truth commissions in terms of the quality and rigor of its work and the comprehensive nature of its report. The commission built on the experiences of prior investigative bodies and substantially expanded the focus of truth commissions, especially by linking the documentation and analysis of key violations with an investigation of the structure of repressive institutions and the social, economic, and political development of the conflict. Ultimately, the goal of the CEH was to connect the a rigorous review of *la violencia* with a process of national transformation, "Knowledge of the truth, as terrible as it may be, places the people of Guatemala on the right path, preserving the memory of the victims, supporting a culture of mutual respect and engagement with human rights and, in this way, strengthening the democratic process."

"A Violent and Dehumanizing System"—Historical Clarification and the Guatemalan Conflict

The CEH is formally defined as a "historical clarification commission" (it is the only truth commission with this name) indicating a focus on investigating the underlying causes and evolution of the conflict. While the CEH's documentation of specific cases started with the events of January 1962, when the armed insurgency began, and continued through December 1996, when the conflict came to a formal end, the commission's analysis extended to a consideration of the historic and structural roots of *la violencia*.

The CEH grounded its overall analysis in an acknowledgment of Guatemala's profoundly unequal and repressive economic, political, and social system, tracing it back to the Spanish colonial period and on through the modern era. From the country's independence in 1821, the CEH determined that it established "an authoritarian State which excluded the majority of the population" and "was racist in its precepts and practices." Guatemalan society was based on an agricultural economy that concentrated valuable land in the hands of a minority and relied on large numbers of disempowered workers.

The nation's structural inequality was supported by laws, regulations, and other mechanisms of governance that were backed up by violence and designed to protect the interests of a privileged elite. The exploitative nature of the system was especially clear in late nineteenth century as the nation's economy became dependent on large-scale coffee production. This export industry relied on *fincas* (plantations) that removed poor Guatemalans—both Maya and Ladino—from lands on which they had lived and farmed for years and then subjected them to various forms of forced labor. These mechanisms created "a violent and dehumanizing system" as "the State gradually evolved as an instrument for the protection of this structure, guaranteeing the continuation of exclusion and injustice."

The antidemocratic nature of Guatemalan society was supported by a series of autocratic leaders whose exploitative policies continued into the twentieth century. At that time, U.S. companies, particularly the United Fruit Company (UFCo), gained control of much of the rural economy, especially within the rapidly expanding banana industry as well as other forms of export agriculture. The UFCo owned enormous areas of productive land while also managing significant elements of nation's infrastructure, such as railroads and ports. The company's growth was substantially enabled by its strong ties with powerful political interests within the U.S. government.

In 1944, while much of the world was consumed with the wars in Europe and the Pacific, a broad coalition of Guatemalans including reformist military officers, students, intellectuals, and professionals overthrew the military dictatorship of General Jorge Ubico who had come to power in 1930. The coup was followed by elections won by Juan Jose Arévalo, a nationalist leader whose government initiated a ten-year period known as the "democratic spring." President Arévalo challenged the economic control of the nation's elites as well as the dominant role of foreign companies. His government set up a social security system, a minimum wage, and new labor laws providing workers with various rights, including the right to organize unions. Although the Catholic Church hierarchy, landowners, and empowered elites criticized these reformist actions (many modeled on the New Deal legislation of the Roosevelt administration) the military was held in check by the support of key officers and a general reformist orientation within the ranks.

In 1950, Jacobo Arbenz succeeded Arévalo as president in a landslide election. He continued the progressive tradition of the previous government, passing an agrarian reform designed to address structural elements of the country's social and economic inequality. The agrarian reform targeted a relatively small group of *finqueros* (plantation owners)—including UFCo, the nation's largest landowner—that controlled the vast majority of productive land. The law did not allow the state to confiscate large *fincas*, but rather required plantation owners to sell the government portions of their land not under cultivation in exchange for bonds at the price owners used for calculating taxes. The land was then distributed to individual *campesinos* (rural residents/workers) and cooperatives.

UFCo appealed to the U.S. government for assistance to oppose the "communist" tendencies of the Arbenz regime. The Eisenhower administration viewed Arbenz through the lens of Cold War ideology, understanding his policies as an affront to an economic system that served national interests and an example of the growing influence of Soviet ideas in the region. In response, the relatively new Central Intelligence Agency (CIA) engineered a coup in 1954 that overthrew Arbenz and ended the "democratic spring." The coup unleashed a reign of terror, involving multiple assassinations. Declassified documents later revealed that the U.S. embassy provided direct assistance to the military regime that replaced the Arbenz government as it arrested over 15,000 people and forced thousands to flee the country.

To this day, many Guatemalans view the "democratic spring" as a symbol of a lost alternate history for the country, one in which a series of popularly elected governments might have, over time, addressed the country's profound inequalities through rational policy reform so that *la violencia* would never have occurred. However, after 1954, Guatemala was ruled by a series of military officers—or civilians strongly backed by the military—that continued to support the dominant social and economic system and increasingly relied on violence to control the population. National politics in Guatemala were structured within a larger context of U.S. regional hegemony and increasingly defined by Cold War ideology. This led to mounting divisions expressed in social movements that were subjected to waves of repression as the government was unable to manage the multiple and divergent claims of its citizens. As the CEH explained, "The State was incapable of achieving social consensus around a national project to unite the whole population."

Following the 1954 coup, Colonel Carlos Castillo Armas took control of the government only to be assassinated in 1957. He was followed by Miguel Ydígoras Fuentes, a conservative president who supported the U.S. government's emerging anti-communist ideology. On November 13, 1960, disaffected military officers inspired by Arbenz staged a coup with the goal of reestablishing a progressive nationalist government. While the uprising was quickly repressed, its leaders—many of whom were inspired by the 1959 Cuban Revolution—went into hiding, later establishing armed opposition movements that would eventually develop into the URNG.

In 1962, some of these officers formed the *Frente Rebelde Alejandro de León Aragón 13 de Noviembre* (Alejandro de León Aragón Rebel Front of November 13, MR-13). According to the commission, this act that defined the start of the armed conflict. In late 1962, the *Partido Guatemalteco de Trabajadores* (Guatemalan Labor Party, PGT) helped bring the MR-13 and other groups together to form the *Fuerzas Armadas Rebeldes* (Rebel Armed Forces, FAR). In 1964, MR-13 separated from FAR, although both groups were committed to leftist revolutionary ideologies similar to many insurgencies developing throughout Latin America.

In 1966, Julio César Méndez Montenegro of the *Partido Revolucionaio* (Revolutionary Party, PR) a center-left party was elected president. Initially, the PGT, the FAR as well as various liberal interests hoped that the new government would address key structural issues within Guatemalan society and enable a more democratic social order. However, the newly elected civilian government heightened repressive practices, leading to a series of military governments that lasted until the mid-1980s.

In 1966, the Guatemalan military initiated a brutal counterinsurgency campaign against the MR-13 and the FAR who had gained support in the eastern part of the country. During this time, the U.S. government provided financial support and training to the Guatemalan military, including assistance in developing an increasingly powerful and sophisticated system of military intelligence. The counter-insurgency was managed by Colonel Carlos Manuel Arana Osorio (who later became president in 1970) and involved tactics developed by the U.S. military in Vietnam. From the mid-1960s to late 1960s, state repression targeted civilians, killing thousands of rural *campesinos* and establishing the country's first *aldeas modelos* (model villages), forced resettlement communities in which Guatemalans were required to live under military control and surveillance. During this period the role of military commissioners expanded significantly, as they passed intelligence to authorities and were often responsible for disappearances and other violations. These brutally repressive policies succeeded in defeating the insurgency and set the stage for the totalizing violence that followed. To this day, the number of civilians killed during this military campaign remains poorly documented and the CEH acknowledged the difficulties of gathering accurate information about the impact of repression during the 1960s.

As the CEH concluded, these state's counterinsurgency policies were justified and enabled through a collection of ideas known as National Security Doctrine which defined combatting communism and "subversion" as the primary focus of government policy. This Cold War–era ideology envisioned Guatemalan society as facing constant and serious internal threats. The conception of national security was so broad that virtually any act that questioned the dominant social and economic system—union organizing, student movements, church activities, community development projects—was viewed as subversive. As a result, those participating in these activities were considered enemies of the state and subjected to arrest, detention, and interrogation, as well as possible torture and extrajudicial execution.

At various stages in the conflict, especially in urban areas, state repression targeted specific individuals and organizations. This was seen in the rise of death squads in the 1960s, which used various names—such as the *Movimiento de Acción Nacionalista Organizado* (Movement of Organized Nationalist Action, MANO); or the *Nueva Organización Anticomunista* (New Anticommunist Organization, NOA)—which were supported by right-wing political parties and directed and staffed by the intelligence services. Targeted repression during this period led Guatemala to become the first nation in Latin America where the verb *desaparecer* ("to disappear") took on a new, brutal meaning; linking illegal detentions, torture, and execution with a denial of responsibility and a process of hiding victims' bodies, often in clandestine cemeteries. Disappearances were commonly committed by the *Policía Militar Ambulante* (Mobile Military Police, PMA), the *Guardia de Hacienda* (Treasury Police), the *Policía Nacional* (National Police) and the police detective corps known as *judiciales* (judicial police), all of which operated in close coordination with military intelligence.

Many popular movements arose in the 1960s and 1970s in Guatemala. Through the work of catechists, lay workers, and groups such as *Acción Católica* (Catholic Action), the Catholic Church adopted the principles of liberation theology, linking religious practice with demands for social justice. *Campesinos* formed movements such as the *Comité de Unidad Campesina* (Committee of Campesino Unity, CUC) that organized indigenous and Ladino workers to address a variety of demands from increased wages on plantations to land rights. Students from the *Universidad de San Carlos de Guatemala* (University of San Carlos, USAC) pressured the government to investigate acts of political violence, mobilizing marches and popular protests. Labor unions organized workers, often successfully, in state enterprises and private factories.

These efforts were often interconnected as members of one social movement coordinated efforts with other groups. In addition, some activists established ties with the underground insurgency and others chose to become guerrilla combatants. As popular movements were violently repressed, the political space for debate and discussion was reduced. The state's reliance on repression negated the possibility for compromise, negotiated settlements, or other means of peacefully addressing political divisions and societal conflict. Alongside its reliance on repression, the state did little to address the fundamental structural inequalities within Guatemalan society, leading to heightened demands for change followed by increased violence. As the CEH stated, "Thus a vicious circle was created in which social injustice led to protest and subsequently political instability, to which there were always only two responses: repression or military coups."

By the late 1970s, the country had reached a crisis point. The state's repressive activities were directed against virtually all social movements and political activities that challenged the status quo. As a result, many involved in social change movements were forced to abandon their work or flee the country. Others joined the growing armed insurgency that was composed of four groups: the PGT; the FAR; the *Organización del Pueblo en Armas* (Organization of the

People in Arms, ORPA); and, the *Ejército Guerrillero de los Pobres* (Guerrilla Army of the Poor, EGP). As repression increased, these groups gained popular support, particularly among poor Ladino workers and Maya residents of the *altiplano* as well as among laborers working on the large plantations of the *Costa Sur* (Southern Coast).

The situation in Guatemala was one element of a larger political context defined by Cold War divisions that, from the late 1970s through the early 1990s, created violent internal conflicts throughout Central America. National security services came to dominate domestic politics in the region, supporting inequitable social and economic systems in opposition to popular movements seeking political change and challenging U.S. regional hegemony. In 1979, a broad popular effort linking revolutionaries, middle-class interests, intellectuals, and others overthrew a military dictatorship in Nicaragua, eventually leading to a leftist government. In 1980, civil war broke out in El Salvador between a coalition of armed leftist insurgents and the government.

Within this general context, the Guatemalan insurgency gained support and appeared as part of a general challenge to the region's dominant and unequal social structures. In response, the state expanded its repressive activities, which rapidly grew to devastating levels. The CEH found that 81 percent of all serious violations were committed between 1979 and 1982, including the vast majority of massacres. It was during these years that the CEH concluded that the state committed genocide against the nation's Mayan peoples.

The government at this time was run by two military regimes. From 1978 to 1981, General Romeo Lucas García led the country, until he was overthrown in a coup by General Efraín Ríos Montt, an Evangelical minister, who controlled Guatemala from 1981 to 1983. The army developed a policy of "scorched earth" tactics that destroyed thousands of *aldeas* (rural villages) within a broad policy of militarizing the nation, especially the rural *altiplano*. The army established bases throughout the country and forcibly recruited tens of thousands of indigenous men into the armed forces, subjecting them to brutal forms of training.

In an effort to reduce support for the insurgency, the military sought to "drain the water from the fish" through indiscriminate killing and mass repression. The commission documented 626 massacres, and there were likely many more. These coordinated attacks commonly followed a set pattern in which soldiers, Kaibiles, military commissioners, and PACs would surround a village and then abuse, rape, torture, and kill the entire population, through spectacles of violence that sometimes lasted for several days. In this way, *la violencia* transformed rural Guatemala. As the residents of entire communities were killed, their homes and fields burned, other communities fled into the mountains. Many became internally displaced persons and lived in the countryside for months and even years. Others became refugees, fleeing Guatemala for other countries, with around 150,000 crossing into Mexico. Some refugees continued farther north, beginning a pattern that led, over two decades, to the migration of hundreds of thousands of Guatemalans to the United States.

Military repression came to define state power as thousands of Guatemalans were arrested in their homes, at checkpoints along roads, on market days in main towns, and during patrols. Many were detained on the basis of reports by *orejas* and *confidenciales* (spies) some of whom used their power to settle personal disputes. Others were selected based on statements from torture victims. Those detained were commonly beaten and abused and then brought to military bases, where they were interrogated by intelligence agents (from the G-2, the "Dos", or the S-2), commonly tortured, and often killed. The CEH determined that over 50,000 people were disappeared, their whereabouts unknown and their corpses buried in clandestine cemeteries throughout the country.

In an effort to undermine support for the guerrillas and to control the population, the military forced all men living in rural Guatemala to participate in the PAC. Its members, *patrulleros*, were required to engage in continual patrols in and around their communities. At their height, the army estimated that there were over 1 million *patrulleros*, which the CEH found represented almost half of all adult Guatemalan men. Some *patrulleros* were unarmed and tasked with manning roadside guardhouse or overseeing their *aldeas*. Others participated directly in killings, torture, rapes, and massacres against their neighbors and residents of nearby communities. The CEH determined that 18 percent of serious violations were committed by the PAC, representing a key mechanism through which the civilian population was forced to become complicit in state terror.

Through scorched earth policies that destroyed villages, makeshift homes, and crops, and ongoing army and PAC patrols, the state made survival difficult for internally displaced populations. By combining this ongoing repression with a series of amnesties, the army convinced thousands of Guatemalans to come down from the mountains and live under military control. They were processed, subjected to "re-education" programs, forced to join PACs, and resettled in *aldeas modelos* and other communities under the constant surveillance of the army and the supervision of military intelligence and its network of informers. The military's policies linked formal mechanisms of control, including restrictions on movement, with various forms of social assistance. These programs included food aid, employment and development policies, some of which were financed by the U.S. government and various international assistance agencies. In this way, social relations among the nation's rural, largely indigenous, population were radically transformed through constant surveillance, forced complicity in violations, and a domineering ideology of silence and submission.

In 1982, the country's four guerrilla movements—EGP, FAR, ORPA, and PGT—joined together to create the URNG. These groups often had substantial local support and hoped that, by joining together, they could overthrow the government. The Guatemalan insurgency was inspired by the Nicaraguan revolution and the military success of neighboring Salvadoran guerrillas. They imagined that they would gain control of large areas of the country and even planned a national strategy for controlling key regions and then marching on to the capital to overthrow the government. However, in reality, the URNG lacked adequate arms, training, and logistics. The CEH concluded that the guerillas never controlled enough combatants, weapons, or territory to militarily challenge the Guatemalan state.

Under the Carter administration, in response to the country's terrible human rights record, the U.S. government stopped providing direct assistance to the Guatemalan military. This suspension continued through the worst years of *la violencia.* As a result, U.S. support for the country's armed forces was provided covertly and through the assistance of key allies such as Israel (for example, the standard assault weapon of the Guatemalan Army was the Israeli *Galil* and not the M-16, as in El Salvador and elsewhere in the region). Declassified material reviewed by the CEH has revealed that U.S. government was aware of widespread massacres, torture, and other atrocities and generally supported the country's counterinsurgency efforts. Nevertheless, the full extent of the U.S. involvement in *la violencia* is still not known.

In 1983, Ríos Montt was overthrown in a military coup led by General Oscar Mejía Víctores. While the government continued the country's brutally repressive policies, it also led Guatemala to a democratic transition in 1985. This process involved drafting a new constitution and ending formal military rule in response to domestic calls for change, a devastated economy, and substantial international pressure. Elections were held and, in 1986, Vinicio Cerezo became the country's first popularly elected civilian president in many years. Nevertheless, the military remained in control of the nation and the repressive actions of military commissioners and PACs continued to operate alongside ongoing surveillance and systematic human rights violations. The political transition in Guatemala was gradual. It took over a decade to negotiate a formal end to the conflict, reduce the influence of the military, and establish the foundations, however fragile, of a more substantive democracy.

The CEH and the Peace Process

From the late 1980s on, there were substantial pressures to end the armed conflict in Guatemala and throughout Central America. The regional accords of 1987 set the stage for peace in Nicaragua and created a tentative plan for ending the wars in El Salvador and Guatemala. The collapse of the Soviet Union in 1989 reconfigured global politics, ending the Cold War and redefining the significance of National Security Doctrine and prior justifications for mass repression. In 1990, the leftist government in Nicaragua lost the national elections and, in 1993, neighboring El Salvador formally ended its conflict.

Preliminary meetings between the URNG and political parties led the guerrillas to agree not to disrupt the country's 1990 elections, which were won by Jorge Serrano. He was the first democratically elected civilian leader in fifty years (since the democratic spring) to succeed another democratically elected civilian leader. In 1991 and 1992, preliminary meetings were held to define basic principles for the peace negotiations. However, the two sides were unable to agree on key issues and the process stalled until mid-1993 when President Serrano tried to suspend the constitution, dissolve Congress, and seize control in what was known as an "*auto-golpe*" or "self-coup." The attempted coup was rejected through the coordinated efforts of the military, the business elite, and civil society, indicating broad support for democracy and suggesting the possibility for ongoing negotiations among previously opposing forces. Serrano fled the country and was replaced by Ramiro de León Carpio, the country's human rights ombudsman.

Later that year, the United Nations took on a more prominent role and, by early 1994, the "Group of Friends" was assembled, linking Colombia, Mexico, Norway, Spain, the United States, and Venezuela to the peace process. In Guatemala, a collection of domestic groups, from business associations to indigenous organizations, joined together to support the peace process through the *Asamblea de la Sociedad Civil* (Civil Society Assembly, ASC). Despite their diverse and competing interests—it included representatives of the far right *Frente Republicano Guatemalteco* (Republican Guatemalan Front, FRG) led by General Ríos Montt as well as business leaders and members of human rights groups—the ASC managed to work together and outline key national goals related to the negotiated peace.

The first major peace agreement was signed in March 1994, establishing a commitment to international human rights and authorizing the creation of the *Misión de Verificación de las Naciones Unidas en Guatemala* (United Nations Verification Mission in Guatemala, MINUGUA), to monitor human rights conditions in the country. In June, the Oslo Accord was signed, establishing the mandate for the CEH and linking the peace process with a commitment to documenting and analyzing past political violence.

What followed were a series of agreements linking formal peace with a reconceptualization of Guatemalan society, including promises to address many of the root causes of the nation's unequal and repressive social structure. In November 1995, the government and the URNG signed an agreement outlining a commitment to defend indigenous rights and to create a more inclusive and respectful society. In May 1996, they signed an agreement outlining broad policy reform on social and economic issues including improving access to land for the poor (although avoiding comprehensive land reform); expanding education, health, and social services; strengthening labor protections; and, increasing tax collection to enable the state to cover the costs of social reform.

In September 1996, the parties agreed to support civilian control of government by restructuring the police, demobilizing the PAC, dissolving key elements of the security forces, significantly reducing the size of the army, and redefining its mission to address external rather than internal security. Later that year, the PAC was disbanded through the demilitarization of over 270 thousand *patrulleros* and the recovery of thousands of weapons. The PMA and the *Estado Mayor Presidencial* (Presidential Joint Chiefs of Staff, EMP)—an intelligence unit working out of the Presidential Palace responsible for many violations—were also dismantled, as part of a broad restructuring of the security services. Following the formal end of the conflict, the remaining URNG combatants were also demilitarized. These efforts were supported by substantial international economic and technical assistance.

In December 1996, on the eve of the formal end of the conflict, several operational agreements were negotiated, including key constitutional reforms and legal mechanisms to allow for the reintegration of members of the URNG. That month, the Guatemalan Congress passed the *Ley de Reconciliación Nacional* (Law of National Reconciliation, LRN), which provided amnesty for certain political crimes, yet specifically denied legal protection for those who had committed torture, genocide, and other serious violations. The LRN was not a general amnesty, but rather created a mechanism for individually reviewing the case of each alleged perpetrator seeking protection from claims. On December 29, 1996, peace between the Guatemalan government and the URNG was formally signed at a public ceremony in the main plaza in front of the Presidential Palace.

Taken together, the peace accords presented an extensive set of promises linking a broad commitment to human rights with a series of substantial reforms that, if implemented, could refashion Guatemalan society. While these policy reforms did not envision dismantling existing power structures, they presented transformative ideas to expand basic rights, combat institutionalized racism, and address social inequality. The accords provided for significant expansions of education, health, and social security, an increase in tax revenues, shifts in access to land, the reconfiguration of security services, and institutional support for democracy and basic rule of law principles. Interestingly, the Guatemala envisioned by the peace accords was similar to the policy vision of the "democratic spring" and embodied many of the progressive goals of social movements from the 1960s onward.

Just as the conflict was defined by brutal human rights violations and sustained state repression, the peace agreements began with a focused commitment to human rights through the establishment of the commission. Nevertheless, when the accord was signed, the CEH was viewed critically by many sectors of Guatemalan society. Some objected—as is common with virtually every truth commission—that an inquiry into past abuses would open old wounds, create social discord, and stimulate renewed violence and repression. Others viewed the United Nations–mediated process as serving a leftist agenda, or as an element of a larger international campaign to criticize or even humiliate the nation.

However, the most serious and sustained criticisms of the commission came from Guatemalan civil society, especially local human rights advocates that had struggled courageously for years in the face of sustained and brutal repression. These criticisms were grounded in the fact that the CEH was created through a political compromise between the parties and signed by high-ranking army officials and URNG commanders, precisely those responsible for the very human rights violations and acts of violence that the commission was tasked with investigating.

National and international human rights advocates worried that the commission was designed to be ineffectual or to serve as a formal mechanism of minimizing the impact of *la violencia* or misrepresenting the nature of past atrocities. For some, the term "historical clarification" sounded like a way of avoiding accountability, perhaps suggesting that structural issues—not actual people and institutions—were the primarily responsible for the conflict, or by directing attention to external factors or foreign influences. These concerns were not unreasonable given the ongoing repression of human rights defenders, the continuing power of military and intelligence services, and the institutionalized impunity that protected virtually all perpetrators.

The concerns of civil society groups were highlighted by the fact that they were not formally included in the development of the CEH's mandate despite the fact that their efforts were crucial to drawing attention to the abuses of *la violencia*.

They also pointed out that the agreement specified that two of the commissioners were to be selected by the parties, but made no provisions for review by civil society groups. Others questioned whether the time given to the CEH—six months, with a possible additional six-month extension—would be adequate to document and analyze three and a half decades of complex and devastating violence.

However, the most contentious aspect of the Oslo Accord was the mandate that the CEH could not "individualize responsibility" that is, it was barred from presenting the names of perpetrators. To many in the activist community, this signified that the CEH was designed in advance to present a disengaged inquiry into past atrocities, divorcing documentation from accountability, providing truth telling, but no justice.

Before the CEH began operation, these concerns were so significant that the *Oficina de Derechos Humanos del Arzobispado de Guatemala* (Human Rights Office of the Archbishop of Guatemala, ODHAG) created a special project to document past atrocities as an alternative to the official commission. This initiative, the *Proyecto de Recuperacion de Memoria Histórica* (Recovery of Historical Memory Project, REMHI), began in 1995 and used networks of local parishes to gather thousands of first-person narratives from victims. It was designed to ensure that the suffering of Guatemala's victims would be recorded out of a concern that the CEH would fail to seriously reflect on past atrocities. In the end, these concerns proved unnecessary as the ODHAG and other Guatemalan human rights and civil society groups worked closely with the commission. Over time, these groups embraced the CEH and came to view its report and conclusions as the foundation for ongoing advocacy.

Mandate and Functioning of the CEH

The full name of the Oslo Accord is the Agreement on the Establishment of the Commission to Clarify Past Human Hights Violations and Acts of Violence That Have Caused the Guatemalan Population to Suffer (The text of the Oslo Accord is presented in Appendix 3). The terms "human rights violations" and "acts of violence" reference a key distinction within international law between the responsibilities and obligations of state and nonstate actors. "Human rights violations" reference abuses committed by formal state actors—such as the military, police, and intelligence services—as well as nonofficial or quasi-official actors operating under the command or control of the state, such as death squads and the PAC. "Acts of violence" reference abuses committed by nonstate actors, particularly the URNG guerrilla insurgency. The significance of this language is twofold: first, it highlights the CEH's clear grounding within established principles of international law; and, second, it specifies the commission's commitment to investigating acts committed by both the state and the URNG.

The agreement required that the CEH begin its work immediately following the end of the conflict and provided six months for formal operations, with a possible six-month extension. In early 1997, the three commissioners were appointed. Christian Tomuschat, a German law professor and former United

Nations independent expert on Guatemala, was appointed by the secretary general of the United Nations. The state and the URNG selected the other two commissioners: Otilia de Lux Cotí as a Guatemalan "of irreproachable conduct" and, Alfredo Balsells Tojo, a Guatemalan academic selected from a list presented by university presidents. Two of the three commissioners were Guatemalan and one was an indigenous woman.

Soon after being selected, the commissioners began holding meetings with the Guatemalan government, the URNG, and civil society organizations, particularly human rights and indigenous groups. They outlined a budget and worked with the Guatemalan government and the international community to obtain financial support. The final budget was around $9.8 million, with 10 percent provided by the Guatemalan government and 90 percent by the governments of Austria, Belgium, Canada, Denmark, the European Union, Germany, Italy, Japan, the Netherlands, Norway, Sweden, Switzerland, the United Kingdom, and the United States.

The CEH's legal status in Guatemala was established through negotiations between the government and the special representative of the secretary-general of the United Nations. This process was finalized by the Guatemalan Congress, which approved the commission and provided specific immunities and privileges for the commissioners and their mission.

While technically the commission was composed solely of the three commissioners, the CEH's work involved a substantial research, analysis, and support staff of 269 professionals, including 127 internationals and 142 Guatemalans. While the CEH was not a United Nations managed truth commission (as in neighboring El Salvador), it is sometimes referred to in this way. This is because many CEH staff were drawn from United Nations missions, particularly MINUGUA, and because its logistics and finances were managed by the United Nations Office for Project Services (UNOPS).

The CEH began its preliminary work in mid-1997 and formally started operations at the end of July 1997, working out of a central office in Guatemala City (The CEH's methodology is presented in Appendix 2 "CEH Mandate and Methodology"). In September, the CEH opened four regional offices in Guatemala City, Cobán, Santa Cruz del Quiché, and Huehuetenango as well as ten satellite offices in Barillas, Cantabal, Escuintla, Nebaj, Poptún, Quetzaltenango, San Marcos, Santa Elena, Sololá, and Zacapa.

Commission staff interviewed victims and witnesses in these offices whose locations were widely publicized on the radio, in newspapers, and in other media. In addition, the CEH staff met with local government officials, traditional leaders, and civil society groups to ensure that victims knew about the commission, its mission, and its various offices. Since many Guatemalans had trouble visiting the CEH offices, researchers traveled to over 2,000 communities, often multiple times, to gather testimonies and related information. These efforts included over 500 collective testimonies in which community residents jointly presented their stories.

The field offices operated for around eight months, closing in mid-April 1998. By that point, most field research had been completed, although the CEH continued to receive testimonies in the main office until the end of July and research teams traveled around the country gathering testimonies and engaging in fact-checking.

The CEH also gathered material from over a thousand "key witnesses" including politicians, former and current military officers, former guerrillas, union leaders, activists, and others. These statements were used to understand state security institutions, URNG strategies and operations, social movements, and different aspects of the country's social and political context during the armed conflict. With the assistance of various nongovernmental organizations, the CEH gathered testimonies and material in Canada, Mexico, the United States, and several European countries.

In addition, the commission collected a large number of documents—including material presented by victims, key witnesses, submissions from various organizations such as business associations and Mayan groups, clippings from Guatemalan newspapers, court filings, etc.—that were organized and analyzed in the Documentation Center. The CEH requested documents and information from the parties, including the army, Guatemalan courts and other Guatemalan government institutions, as well as the URNG and each of its member organizations.

The commission found the army's responses were "inadequate and unsatisfactory." The army provided limited documentation, no reports for events occurring before 1987, and also "did not provide the CEH with a single operational plan for the military zones in regions most affected by the armed confrontation." Many requests were met with claims—later found to be false—that documents never existed or had been lost or destroyed. The CEH determined that the URNG responded more positively in providing many, though not all, key documents and reports.

The CEH also requested material from a number of foreign governments, including Argentina, Cuba, Israel, Nicaragua, and the United States. Of these, only the United States responded with substantial documents. The material provided by the United States was used alongside cables and reports from the embassy, the CIA, and others declassified through Freedom of Information Act requests by the National Security Archive, a Washington D.C.–based group, in preparation for the start of the commission's operations. These documents were supplemented by large amounts of material from the Guatemalan press as well as many secondary sources.

The commission also reviewed forensic evidence from exhumations of mass graves and clandestine cemeteries. Much of this material came from prior exhumations, but the CEH specifically supported the *Fundación Antropologico Forense de Guatemala* (Guatemalan Forensic Anthropology Foundation, FAFG) to conduct exhumations of four sites.

Central to the work of the commission were substantial submissions documenting and analyzing human rights violations that had been gathered by Guatemalan human rights and civil society groups. In particular, the CEH integrated the work of two major, large-scale data collection projects into its analysis of past atrocities. The first was a quantitative analysis of data collected by the

Centro Internacional para Investigaciones en Derechos Humanos (International Center for Human Rights Investigations, CIIDH) based on field research by a number of Guatemalan civil society organizations. The second was the REMHI project in which ODHAG staff trained local Guatemalans who collected over 6,000 testimonies documenting many of the same abuses highlighted by the CEH. ODHAG presented the REMHI report in April 1998 just as the CEH was closing its field offices. Two days later, Bishop Juan Gerardi, the driving force behind the project, was assassinated.

While all of these materials were integrated into the final report, the core of the CEH's work research was its extensive fieldwork. The CEH gathered 7,338 individual and collective testimonies involving the experiences of over 20,000 people. This material was entered into a secure database managed in the central office. The database allowed for qualitative analysis of the testimonies found throughout the report, including direct quotations and thematic analysis. The database also facilitated a quantitative review of key information on dates, places, victims' names, perpetrators, and types of violation (some of the commission's tables are included in this volume). Also, to facilitate more detailed statistical analysis, particularly estimations of the total number of victims and related data on victims and violations, the CEH contracted the American Association for the Advancement of Science (AAAS). Their report also reviewed data from various Guatemalan human rights groups, linking CEH database with information from the CIIDH and the REMHI project.

The testimonies were evaluated for their coherence and relation to the commission's mandate to develop specific "registered cases," indicating a violation or cluster of violations that could be determined to have actually occurred. To count as a registered case, the CEH reviewed the data gathered to ensure that it met one of three degrees of certainty—complete certainty, well-founded probability, or reasonable likelihood. This process involved multiple levels of review by field investigators, database analysts in the central office, a team of legal experts, and, finally, by the commissioners. The CEH finalized 7,517 registered cases that were listed in one of the appendixes to the CEH final report.

By July 1998, the field research was completed. Then, CEH staff focused on reviewing the data collected, developing thematic analyses, and preparing policy recommendations. The data review process involved a number of teams focusing on specific issues and the thematic analysis was divided into three teams whose focus became the basis for the first three chapters of the CEH report: "causes and origins," "strategies and mechanisms," and "consequences and effects" of the conflict. The work on the roots of the conflict was prepared with the assistance of a group of distinguished Guatemalan academics. By August, many of the teams had completed their work, including nearly one hundred case studies. The remaining CEH staff drafted the final report.

On February 25, 1999, the CEH formally presented its key findings and recommendations to the Guatemalan government, the URNG, and a representative of the secretary general of the United Nations. The event took place in the National Theatre in front of a crowd of thousands and was widely covered by all local media.

Structure of this Book

In editing the original CEH report for this book, the overarching goal has been to present the commission's research, analysis, conclusions, and recommendations as accurately as possible. The material was selected to highlight the emotional and documentary significance of the testimonies while preserving and respecting the focus, tone, and vision of the commission's work.

The edited material is divided into four sections that generally follow the original structure of the CEH report. The book begins with a series of poems and statements followed by the commissioners' prologue. The first section presents a detailed analysis of the most serious violations committed by both of the parties during the conflict including: state responsibility for extrajudicial executions and disappearances, torture, forced displacement, massacres, rape and sexual violence, and genocide; followed by URNG responsibility for killing, kidnapping, looting, and other violations. The second sections presents material from the CEH's analysis of key actors within the conflict beginning with a review of state institutions and groups associated with state policy, followed by a review of the different organizations that composed the guerrilla insurgency. The third section reviews the consequences and effects of *la violencia* with a consideration of how decades of conflict impacted Guatemalan society, including a review of how human rights groups, indigenous organizations, and other social movements confronted repression, often at great personal and institutional cost. The fourth section reviews the CEH's key conclusions regarding the conflict, its causes, impact, and significance and includes the complete text of CEH's recommendations. These present a set of detailed plans for responding to the legacy of the conflict through policies to honor victims, provide reparations, combat impunity, prevent the recurrence of violence, and build the foundations for sustainable peace and social justice.

While the overall structure and focus of the material presented mirrors that of the final report, it is important to note a number of key changes. The book presents an ellipsis (...) to indicate where sections have been cut from the CEH's original text. In some cases, the ellipses reference a short edit—a word, a sentence, or several sentences—and, in other cases they indicate where lengthy sections have been removed. The order of the material within specific sections generally follows the structure of the original report, but some adjustments have been made such as moving paragraphs and sections for clarity and coherence.

The original report included a separate volume with fifty-two *casos ilustrativos* ("case studies") presenting detailed descriptions of characteristic violations, historical events, or particular patterns of violence. This book integrates the case studies within the main body of the text by presenting corresponding case studies following most sections. So, for example, the section on massacres is followed by an edited version of the CEH's case study of the massacre at *Las Dos Erres*.

The book includes a number of stylistic edits. The original commission report used numbered paragraphs as is common for United Nations documents and other formal reports. In this book, all paragraph numbers have been edited out to improve the clarity of the text and to reduce its bureaucratic tone. Also, the original report used many footnotes referencing textual clarifications as well as references to multiple primary and secondary sources. This book uses endnotes and only includes references for direct quotations, whether from interviews, documents, historical material, or secondary sources.

In some parts of the text, new titles for subsections have been inserted and some of the original subsection titles have been italicized or placed on separate lines to ensure consistency. Some lengthy sections have been divided into separate paragraphs, and grammatical changes have been made for consistency, verb coherence, and to meet the publisher's style guide. In addition, some long sentences have been divided into shorter, multiple sentences for clarity. In general, quotations from testimonies have been left more or less as in the original, with some grammatical adjustments. American English spellings are used throughout and some Spanish terms are italicized. Where names of organizations, groups, government bodies, and other formal entities are presented they appear first in the original Spanish, followed by an English translation and the acronym, where appropriate (a review can be found in Appendix 1, "Spanish terms, acronyms and abbreviations").

Most of the material presented here was translated specifically for this book. However, the conclusions and recommendations were translated by the CEH and these English versions are used with minor edits (information on the translation process can be found in "Notes on the Translation").

The process of editing twelve volumes into several hundred pages was complex and took several years to complete. The editing and review was assisted by an extraordinary group of Guatemalan and international consultants, including Roddy Brett, Michelle Bellino, Iduvina Hernandez, Gustavo Meoño Brenner, Victoria Sanford, Arturo Taracena Arriola, Christian Tomuschat, Edelberto Torres Rivas, and Manolo Vela Castañeda. These consultants read, reread, and commented on various versions of initial and subsequent edits. They provided detailed suggestions regarding the structure, focus, and orientation of the book. In addition, over two dozen informal consultants reviewed the project providing many helpful suggestions and comments. Despite the exceptionally sensitive and valuable comments by these individuals, responsibility for these edits and this book is that of the editor.

The one-volume version of the report of the Guatemalan Truth Commission is presented in both English and Spanish. It has been designed for scholars, journalists, students, travelers, and anyone interested in understanding *la violencia*, the recent history of Guatemala, truth commissions, and the defense and protection of human rights within Latin America and around the world.

"So That Future Generations May Be Aware"

The commission was given the difficult mandate of establishing the factual and interpretive ground for ongoing debates regarding *la violencia*. The commissioners described their work as a service to Guatemalan society, "So that future generations may be aware of the enormous calamity and tragedy suffered by their people." In the end, the CEH was motivated by the belief that engaging and acknowledging the truth of past political violence was essential for achieving peace, democracy and reconciliation in Guatemala.

The commission's extraordinary collection of thousands of individual and communal testimonies and its detailed database remain confidential. The final report—whether the full twelve volumes or the selections presented here—are the only publicly available documents of the CEH's work. This material represents the most comprehensive inquiry into *la violencia* and its work provides great insight into an especially painful and violent period in Guatemalan history.

The commission's presentation of systematic violence committed over three and half decades by the state against its people—and, to a far lesser degree, by the insurgents against civilians—is overwhelming. The CEH's detailed descriptions of brutality, cruelty, and systematic repression are difficult to process, raising questions about how it was possible for people to commit such terrible acts against their neighbors and fellow citizens. This is true for Guatemalans who lived through the conflict, those born after it ended, as well as those encountering *la violencia* for the first time.

The CEH's greatest accomplishment is that it managed to fulfill its mandate under very challenging circumstances, breaking through decades of silence and fear and naming and thereby legitimizing the suffering of thousands of Guatemalans. As the commissioners suggest, acknowledging *la violencia* is itself a form of justice and an essential means of rebuilding a traumatized society.

The CEH report demands our attention. It embodies the global aspirations of the human rights movement to courageously face terror and abuse, even as this process requires an encounter with the darker side of politics and the human capacity for cruelty and abuse. The work of the CEH, in its rigorous commitment to presenting the voices of victims and analyzing decades of repression, is of great historical and moral significance. It provides insight into a brutal period of recent history that devastated Guatemala and linked the nation to a global political struggle in which severe, even genocidal, violence was justified on the basis of national security. While the events documented here occurred some years ago, they provide lessons for both the present and the future. The Guatemalan Truth Commission reminds us of our capacity for terrifying destruction, the fragility of human dignity, the importance of engaging with the past, and the necessity of imagining and creating a better and more just world.

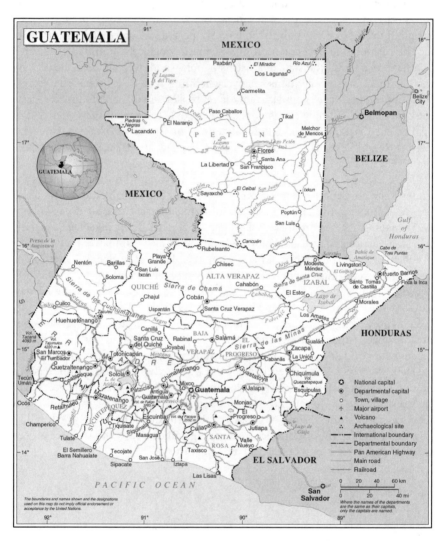

Figure 1   Map of Guatemala, Map No. 3834 Rev. 3, May 2004. Courtesy of the United Nations.

Memory of Silence

The Guatemalan Truth Commission Report

As we consume life's quota,
how many truths elude us?
—Augusto Monterroso, "Movimientoperpetuo"

Silence lost its way
when a hand
opened the doors to the voice.
—Francisco Morales Santos, "Al pie de la letra"

Let the history we lived
be taught in the schools,
so that it is never forgotten,
so our children may know it.
—Testimony given to the CEH

cease to do evil
learn to do good;
seek justice,
correct oppression;
defend the fatherless,
plead for the widow
—Isaiah 1:16–17

Prologue

Christian Tomuschat, Otilia Lux de Cotí, and
Alfredo Balsells Tojo

Guatemala is a country of contrasts and contradictions. Situated in the middle of the American continent, bathed by the waters of the Caribbean and the Pacific, its inhabitants live in a multiethnic, pluricultural, and multilingual nation, in a state that emerged from the triumph of liberal forces in Central America. Guatemala has seen periods marked by beauty and dignity from the beginning of the ancient Mayan culture to the present day; its name has been glorified through its works of science, art, and culture; by men and women of honor and peace, both great and humble; by its nobel laureates for Literature and Peace. However, in Guatemala, pages have also been written of shame and infamy, disgrace and terror, pain and grief, all as a product of the armed confrontation among brothers and sisters. For more than thirty-four years, Guatemalans lived under the shadow of fear, death, and disappearance as daily threats in the lives of ordinary citizens.

The Commission for Historical Clarification (CEH) was established through the Oslo Accord on June 23, 1994, in order to clarify with objectivity, equity, and impartiality, the human rights violations and acts of violence connected with the armed confrontation that caused suffering among the Guatemalan people. The commission was not established to judge—that is the function of the courts of law—but rather to clarify the history of the events of more than three decades of fratricidal war.

When we were appointed to form the CEH, each of us, through different routes and all by life's fortune, knew in general terms the outline of events. As Guatemalans, two of us had lived the entire tragedy on our native soil, and in one way or another, had suffered it. However, none of us could have imagined the full horror and magnitude of what actually happened.

The commission's mandate was to provide answers to questions that continue to be asked in peacetime: why did part of society resort to armed violence in order to achieve political power? What can explain the extreme acts of violence committed by both parties—of differing types and intensities—in the armed confrontation? Why did the violence, especially that used by the state, affect civilians and particularly the Mayan people, whose women were considered to be the spoils of war and who bore the full brunt of the institutionalized violence? Why did defenseless children suffer acts of savagery? Why, using the name of God, was there an attempt to erase from the face of the earth the sons and daughters of Xmukane, the grandmother of life and natural creation? Why did these acts of outrageous brutality, which showed no respect for the most basic rules of humanitarian law, Christian ethics, and the values of Mayan spirituality, take place?

We received thousands of testimonies; we accompanied the survivors at such moving moments as the exhumation of their loved ones from clandestine cemeteries; we listened to former heads of state and the high command of both the army and the guerrillas; we read thousands of pages of documents received from a full range of civil society's organizations. The commission's report has considered all the versions and takes into account what we have heard, seen, and read regarding the many atrocities and brutalities.

The main purpose of the report is to place on record Guatemala's recent, bloody past. Although many are aware that Guatemala's armed confrontation caused death and destruction, the gravity of the abuses suffered repeatedly by its people has yet to become part of the national consciousness. The massacres that eliminated entire Mayan rural communities belong to the same reality as the persecution of the urban political opposition, trade union leaders, priests, and catechists. These are neither perfidious allegations, nor figments of the imagination, but an authentic chapter in Guatemala's history.

The authors of the Oslo Accord believed that, despite the shock that the nation could suffer upon seeing itself reflected in the mirror of its past, it was nevertheless necessary to know the truth and make it public. It was their hope that truth would lead to reconciliation, and furthermore, that coming to terms with the truth is the only way to achieve this objective.

There is no doubt that the truth is of benefit to everyone, both victims and victimizers. The victims, whose past has been degraded and manipulated, will be dignified; the perpetrators, through the recognition of their immoral and criminal acts, will be able to recover the dignity of which they had deprived themselves.

Knowing the truth of what happened will make it easier to achieve national reconciliation, so that in the future Guatemalans may live in an authentic democracy, without forgetting that the rule of justice as the means for creating a new state has been and remains the general objective of all.

No one today can be sure that the enormous challenge of reconciliation, through knowledge of the truth, can be successfully faced. Above all, it is necessary to recognize the facts of history and learn from the nation's suffering. To a great extent, the future of Guatemala depends on the responses of the state and society to the tragedies that nearly all Guatemalans have experienced personally.

The erroneous belief that the end justifies the means converted Guatemala into a country of death and sadness. It should be remembered, once and for all, that there are no values superior to the lives of human beings, and thereby superior to the existence and well being of an entire national community. The state has no existence of its own, but rather it is purely an organizational tool by which a nation addresses its vital interests.

Thousands are dead. Thousands mourn. Reconciliation, for those who remain, is impossible without justice. Miguel Angel Asturias, Guatemala's nobel laureate for Literature, said: "The eyes of the buried will close together on the day of justice, or they will never close."

With sadness and pain we have fulfilled the mission entrusted to us. We place the CEH's Report, this Memory of Silence, into the hands of every Guatemalan, the men and women of yesterday and today, so that future generations may be aware of the enormous calamity and tragedy suffered by their people. May the lessons of this report help us to consider, hear, and understand others and be creative as we live in peace.

Part I

Human Rights Violations and Acts of Violence

This book...presents an analysis of the painful events of the internal armed confrontation as revealed through testimonies and other sources of information gathered by the commission...Confronting this material is difficult because it presents an almost endless series of acts that were not only illegal but also express inhuman brutality. However, this is the reality that the commission was mandated to investigate, above all, so that the people of Guatemala know what occurred and remember, so that it will never happen again...

Despite efforts to ensure that the research would fulfill its mandate, the commission understands that it was impossible to reveal each and every human rights violations or act of violence committed during the internal armed confrontation. Nor was it possible for the commission to clarify in depth all of its ramifications, especially regarding actors other than the army and the guerrillas...In light of this situation, the commission does not pretend that this...is a complete account of the human rights violations and acts of violence committed during the internal armed confrontation in Guatemala. Nor should one consider this report to be the final word on the history of the armed confrontation...In the future, generations of scholars will struggle to explain, in its depth and complexity, all the factors and mechanisms of terror that were used to brutalize the people of Guatemala for over three decades.

It is necessary to gain a more precise explanation of why those responsible for the confrontation committed such extraordinarily immoral acts that shock civilized sensibilities. Why was the desired goal understood to be an authorization to use any method, including torture and forced disappearance? Why up until the present has there been no expression of repentance? Why, as these pages reveal, was the violence especially cruel toward women, children, and the elderly? Why was violence directed toward the most intimate aspects of the people's moral core, disrespecting and attacking the beliefs and symbols of Christianity as well as Maya spiritual beliefs?...

Ultimately, the *Comisión para el Esclarecimiento Histórico* (Commission for Historical Clarification, CEH) can attest that what is described here...actually occurred. The commission fulfilled its mission in an objective, equitable, and impartial manner, believing that knowledge of the truth, as terrible as it may be, places the people of Guatemala on the right path, preserving the memory of the victims, supporting a culture of mutual respect and engagement with human rights, and, in this way, strengthening the democratic process.

I

Extrajudicial Executions and Forced Disappearances

According to the CEH's analysis of the many testimonies collected through fieldwork, the right to life was among those most consistently violated... International human rights law, based on conventions as well as custom, international humanitarian law as well as all constitutions guarantee the right to life... Article 3 of the 1948 Universal Declaration of Human Rights establishes that "all individuals have the right to life, liberty and security of person." The right to life is the most fundamental right and, it is for this reason, that the international community considers respecting and protecting this right to be a general obligation as well as a key element of international customary law...

Extrajudicial Executions

Based on the information gathered by the CEH, the army was responsible for 86 percent of extrajudicial executions during the internal armed confrontation. The *Patrullas de Autodefensa Civil* (Civil Defense Patrols, PAC) were responsible for 21 percent, military commissioners for 11 percent, and other security forces—National Police, *Guardia de Hacienda* and others—for 4 percent. Although in a large percentage of cases the army was the only responsible party, collaboration with the PAC and commissioners was common.

In some cases, state agents perpetrated arbitrary executions based on general directives and enjoyed certain autonomy. In others, the execution was of someone that had been clearly identified. The decision to execute a particular individual could have two possible sources. First, military units would receive orders from a superior authority, whether the commander of a unit or military base in a specific area or from the Army Joint Chiefs of Staff...

A local S-2...would receive an order from his commander to kill someone and he would do it because the local S-2 would never think, would not even consider, questioning an order that came from above...[1]

Second, the zones, bases, task forces, and military units deployed in the field operated according to the general guidelines set by their superiors, leaving specific decisions to commanders of these units. However, the decisions to execute certain nationally known or internationally known people were made at the highest levels...

Throughout the internal armed confrontation, the army carried out thousands of arbitrary executions, many of which were committed against people accused of having ties to the guerrillas. In many cases, victims were executed by the army without any prior verification as to whether the accusation of being a member of the guerrilla or a collaborator was true. For example, beginning in 1980, the army ordered all of the municipalities in Cotzal to have a Guatemalan flag that they would provide. The *aldea* (rural village) Chisís was one of the last of the *aldeas* to pick up its flag at the Cotzal base. When several members of the community came to retrieve their flag, four *campesinos* were accused of being members of the guerrilla. They were interrogated about their links to the insurgency and told to hand in their arms or they would be executed. It appeared that one of the victims had collaborated with the guerrillas. All the victims were then brought to the edge of a pit inside the base and killed so that they fell in. This took place in front of all the people from the *aldea* who had come to the base. After the execution, the officer in charge told the people, "Now you can pick up your flag and see how you have been freed from the guerillas."[2]...

Many times people were accused of collaborating or being guerrillas as a result of personal conflicts with members of their community or residents of other *aldeas*...When faced with accusations of this type, the army did not corroborate the truth of these charges and would summarily execute those accused, even members of the PAC and military commissioners.

Vicente Alvarez Contreras, a military commissioner from the *aldea* El Pitorreal, in Dolores, Petén, had problems with a commissioner in the neighboring town who had accused him of being a guerilla at the military base in El Chal. On the night of January 22, 1982, soldiers from the El Chal base went to Vicente Contreras' home, shot at it, entered the house and took him, his wife, and his oldest daughter to the home of the military commissioners that had denounced him...Four days later, his body...was found while the bodies of his wife and daughter never appeared...

During regular military operations by the army, uniformed soldiers committed arbitrary executions. In covert operations, executions were carried out by soldiers wearing civilian clothes or dressed as guerrillas...

In the *cantón* Hamaca, in the municipality of San Ildefonso Ixtahuacán in the department of Huehuetenango, in the middle of the night, a group of men dressed as civilians and known to be members of the G-2 of Huehuetennago

> entered the home of his brother Marcos Domingo Díaz and these men took him away beating, pushing and kicking; in the middle of the road they were punching him all over his body and then they took his life with a bullet...[3]

The army's patrols were a routine tactic that was driven by several objectives: sometimes gathering information and locating guerrillas and other times engaging in combat. During these patrols, members of the army carried out many arbitrary executions:

> We went out on patrol again, really, destroying the little houses…and every once in a while, we would find one or two guys out there. The officer would order us to kill them and leave them there and we'd move on[4]

> I said, "My lieutenant, here is part of what we found, a woman" [she was around 19 years old and had a baby around 8 months old], "Bring her over," he said. "Truthfully, now, what are you doing here" he said, "Really, you're a guerrilla." She said, "Truthfully, no." He said, "Good, kill her" "Son of a bitch," I said, "Really? And the child too?"…They killed her…They shot off three bullets, and then [they killed] the child.[5]

Death Threats

From the 1970s on and throughout the armed conflict, individuals and groups received death threats of various kinds, especially in Guatemala City and the departmental capitals. Some were direct, through personal threats and telephone calls. Others were indirect: through notes left at school and at work; lists distributed by death squads sentencing individuals to death for being guerrillas or communists; and messages painted on the walls of houses and offices.

The threats sometimes occurred alongside open or secret surveillance by operatives…

> Starting in November 1978, Ricardo Adolfo Juárez Gudiel began to be harassed and receive death threats. At that time, he was shown a flier that arrived at the Department of Political Science stating that he had been sentenced to death for being a member of the *Partido Guatemalteco del Trabajo* (Guatemalan Labor Party, PGT). From then on, he noticed that on certain days there were several people inside a car monitoring his house for a number of hours. When he left for the university, these unidentified individuals would follow him at close range and bump his car lightly or place themselves so that he could see them while they made fun of him. This situation continued until 1981. Later, he received a second anonymous note indicating it was his turn to be executed. On August 4, 1981, while he was walking in the street, an unidentified individual approached him and shot him, killing him instantly.[6]

The appearance of these lists and materials not only created terror among those whose names were mentioned, but also affected their relatives and the groups and institutions to which they belonged. Although those [who participated in social movements] were generally aware of the risks they faced, the appearance of death lists made the danger more clear and the terror more palpable.

Once it became widely known that the threats would be carried out and that those whose names appeared on a list would be executed the sense of fear increased…This led potential victims to respond seriously, by going into exile or giving up their [political] activities. Some chose to go underground and others committed suicide. Arbitrary execution resulting from death threats served the double function of physically eliminating some dissidents while dissuading others from getting involved...

The main goal of arbitrary execution as a component of the strategy of terror was to suppress various forms of political opposition, even peaceful opposition, by physically eliminating members of these movements or causing their "voluntary exile."...

The assassination of well-known leaders heightened the general sense of terror achieved through threats and subsequent executions. This sense of vulnerability and uncertainty increased following the death of the political leader Manuel Colóm Argueta who was murdered...on March 22, 1979. This planned, public execution seriously impacted his political party, the *Frente Unido de la Revolución* (United Revolutionary Front, FUR) as well as the general population...His organization was left without a leader and without direction as other members were executed or fled the country into exile...

The arbitrary execution of well-known professionals not involved in militant acts was another mode of generalizing terror. In 1980, at the University of San Carlos, staff that had never participated in politics, either inside or outside an academic setting, were assassinated. One example was Luis Felipe Mendizábal, the director of the Office of the Registrar:

> No one has been able to understand why they killed him. But there was a goal, terror in and of itself as a form of counterinsurgency. Many people must have said, "If they'd kill Felipe Mendizábal, who wouldn't they be willing to kill?" And that created the terror that still exists in Guatemala...[7]

The impact of these modes of urban terror was heightened by the frequent discovery of bodies showing signs of torture and mutilation that were widely covered up by the press. The diffusion of these images created a constant reminder of *la violencia* even among those who were not directly involved in the political struggle...

Terror Techniques in Rural Areas

In rural areas the same techniques of terror were used, including arbitrary executions, although they were adapted to the situation in the countryside. In the nation's interior, communities were left in a state of uncertainty, vulnerability, and disorder through the systematic elimination of traditional leaders, catechists, and members of cooperatives:

> The *Alcalde Rezador*... is the highest leader of all...The *Alcalde Rezador* that was there [in Huehuetenango] in 1980 was a little old man and with four or five of his [friends], I mean, all of them, the Army came and decapitated them right there by the ceremonial center...They knocked off their heads in front of everyone, like a lesson that everyone would end up decapitated.[8]

The symbolism expressed in the way leaders were killed can be seen in the...case of the arbitrary execution of Antonio Hernández, a Maya leader and director of the *Comité de Unidad Campesina* (Committee of Campesino Unity, CUC) and *Acción Católica* (Catholic Action) in the Xesic *cantón* of Santa Cruz del Quiché. Beginning in 1977, the victim began to receive threats because of his activities. On October 17, 1980, his wife and daughter were detained and interrogated about him. On January 21, 1982, Antonio Hernández was captured in the Xesic Center IV. A gun shot was heard, when he was captured, he yelled, "*Muchá, muchá*, be careful." Later his corpse appeared in a ravine. He had been tortured:

> They crowned him with a blackberry bush. They gave him a crown of thorns and left him with a Bible. They pulled down his pants. They nailed him down like on the cross.[9]

Neighbors pulled him out of the ravine and a wake was held in Xesic. The army arrived at the wake and those that were there ran away, leaving the corpse. His relatives returned at around three in the morning. The burial was on January 22 and almost 5,000 people attended from Chimaltenango, Chichicastenango, and Totonicapán. The army was on alert and was there watching. After the burial, once night had fallen, the army took the body out of the grave. For eight days, they left him unburied. After the soldiers went away, the community reburied him.

In rural areas, a common practice was to leave corpses abandoned on the roads so that neighbors would later find them…another common practice was the public exhibition of corpses at strategic points and in places that held clear social significance or symbolism, such as by the doors of public institutions, in parks, churches, or schools…

> We found José in the center [of town]. His body was badly beaten. We could see him well because the soldiers had left him naked and tied to a post in the very center [of town]…[10]

Leaving bodies exposed on posts, displaying the severed heads of victims on poles or hanging from trees, cutting off their tongues or their hands, mutilating their breasts or genitals, these were practices that became common and were committed either before or after a victim's death…

> That night we found four women and the officer said that we would sleep with them on a hill. After making use of them, the officer gave the order to make some stakes and plant them there. There they were placed there and their bodies left lined up along the mountain.[11]

On February 8, 1989, in the municipality of Río Bravo, Suchitepéquez, the corpses of Melecio Darío de Léon Régil Gamboa and his son Melecio Aarón de León Régil Rosales appeared with signs of torture. Their bodies had been bound. They had been strangled with barbed wires that wrapped around their necks, wrists, and ankles. Their faces were burned with a flammable liquid. They had bayonet and weapon marks on their legs. They had no clothes, only underwear…

The isolation of many rural communities allowed the army, military commissioners, and *patrulleros civiles* (civil patrollers) to act overtly and covertly exercising control over the entire population, holding forced meetings, requiring residents to be present at and participate in acts of violence designed and implemented to create terror in communities.

> [The Head of the *Estado Mayor de la Defensa Nacional* (National Defense Joint Chiefs of Staff)] travelled by helicopter...he arrived in communities and gathered the people. In this speeches he said, "The guerrillas are here and you are helping them." Then, as an example, he would choose a few people and have them shot in front of everyone, saying, "This is so that you don't keep supporting the guerilla, because even if you haven't started working with them yet, you certainly won't do so now"...[12]

In the majority Maya rural areas, executions were cruel and were often committed publicly...It was common not to kill someone with a gun, but instead to choose to cut them with a machete to cause great pain before their eventual death. One night in November 1982 in the municipality of El Naranjo, Petén, Roberto Castillo Manzanero was captured. He was tortured by cutting off his toes and fingers, then his feet and hands, proceeding little by little, until all that remained was his body and head, and he died, bloodied...

The majority of arbitrary executions were committed by state agents alongside actions and methods designed to make it difficult or impossible for judges to investigate [the case], intensifying the sense of impunity. The mood of terror...created a situation of intense intimidation such that it was virtually impossible for there to be an investigation of the actions of the counterinsurgency forces. Victims' families were overwhelmed by fear and didn't approach the proper authorities to investigate arbitrary executions...and, in the few cases where cases were filed, the officials failed to conduct serious investigations...

Many people were buried in clandestine cemeteries immediately after being killed, preventing the identification of the victims and the reconstruction of what occurred. When soldiers patrolled in the mountains or were involved in clandestine actions in urban areas they often buried their victims where they were killed.

> After we killed them, we threw them in a pit that we dug...The officer ordered us to cover them with dirt there, really, and we threw down the dirt, covering up the graves and there they lay.[13]...

The CEH documented a total of 23,671 victims of arbitrary executions committed by state agents, of which 81 percent were identified either individually or in groups, and 19 percent remained unidentified...

Forced Disappearances

The CEH documented...6,159...cases of forced disappearances during the armed conflict. The practice of forced disappearances increased significantly between 1979 and 1983, the most intense period of the conflict...

Forced disappearance was an element of the state's implementation of a counterinsurgency strategy in Guatemala using the army, the PAC, military commissioners, the *Guardia de Hacienda* (Treasury Police), the *Policia Nacional* (National Police), the *Judiciales* (detective corps of the National Police) and death squads. There were victims of this type of human rights violation throughout the entire period of the armed conflict. . Out of the total number of forced disappearances documented by the CEH, 80 percent were perpetrated by the army, 12 percent were committed by the PAC, and 8 percent were committed by other security forces, mainly the National Police.

The army committed disappearances on its own mainly in the countryside, where they engaged in individual and mass actions committed in both a selective and indiscriminate manner…The army worked together with the PAC in 11 percent of the forced disappearances and with military commissioners in 6 percent [of the cases]…There is evidence that this violation began in 1954. Nevertheless, the first registered detentions followed by forced disappearance in Guatemala occurred in 1966. This represents the first-known use of mass forced disappearances in the region…

At its core, the goal of forced disappearance was to dismantle or destroy political organizations, unions, and popular associations by capturing or removing their leadership, or supposed leadership individually and en masse…It also allowed the intelligence services to obtain information about the plans and activities of insurgent groups and the opposition by using torture and rape. In addition, these actions punished victims and, through them, their families, communities, and organizations, and spread terror by hiding those detained and threatening anyone seeking to discover their whereabouts…

> After six in the evening cars with tinted windows and Jeeps with armed men arrived. They knocked on the door, entered and then one heard a lot of noise as if they were breaking things. [The victim] was raped in front of her relatives and then they took her from the house in one of the vehicles and that was the last we heard of her.[14]

The ultimate goal of forced disappearance was the destruction of "something"—an organization, the development of an idea—through "someone"—the victim. As a strategy of the counterinsurgency war, it represented one of the main mechanisms of getting rid of the leaders of social organizations. This goal, which defines the essence of forced disappearance, defines it as different from arbitrary execution. While the former has an immediate effect on society and the victim's organization, in forced disappearance the impact continues over time.

Concealing the victim's whereabouts and physical condition—whether or not he was still alive, whether or not he was being cruelly tortured, and whether or not he was passing on information about his organization or community—created an atmosphere of uncertainty that remained among those that had not been captured and were part of the daily lives of the victims: their family, their political party, their union, social, or cultural organization as well as the residents of their community. The impact of forced disappearance was the persistence of doubt, fear, and insecurity resulting from the uncertainty generated by concealing the fate of the disappeared detainee. The group to which the victim belonged then became vulnerable and acted to protect itself, it stopped its activities, its members went into hiding, its families sought refuge, and the community fled or was dispersed...

In urban areas in the 1960s and 1970s, security forces detained people in public places, victims' homes, or workplaces...

> We were standing on the corner on one of the streets in the neighborhood waiting for a bus. He was going to town and the children were going to school...And then, just as the bus came through the intersection, a car cut in front of the bus and stopped and when I looked up after first saying goodbye to the children I saw that they had grabbed him by the arms. He said, "What's going on?" Then, a man said, "Get in!" And, then another said, "It's done!"...I said to the man, "Oh my God why are you taking him and where are you taking him?" And the man pulled up his hand and shot him, I think in the leg; then, he cried out, a cry of pain. And, then they tied up his hands and feet and threw him in the car and took him away.[15]

In rural communities detentions occurred during military operations involving dozens of soldiers...

> It was in '82 when it got worse. The army arrived and took them out of the houses one by one, they were all very frightened, and only the women stayed in the houses...On the night of June 27, 1982 the soldiers took Alberto from his house and he never reappeared...[16]

During the most intense phase of the armed confrontation...many detentions that led to forced disappearances occurred at temporary army and *Guardia de la Hacienda* checkpoints. These sites for control and registration were generally located on bridges and along roads. According to victims' statements, these places became sites of terror for people because soldiers would detain people passing by, stopping public and private buses and reviewing those who were traveling based on lists. Often, those whose names appeared on the lists or those without an identification card (including those too young to have one) were separated from the rest of the people, detained, and were never heard from again...

> It was nine when the Army soldiers stopped the bus that had lots of people and forced them to come out. They inspected them to see if they had arms or secret papers and they took only one man. On Monday, his wife went to look for him at the army base near the cemetery in the municipality of Patzún because the people had said that on Sunday soldiers had taken four men to the base, prisoners who had their hands tied behind their backs...The man never reappeared...[17]

Many of the cases gathered by the CEH document how forced disappearance was used to punish not only the victim and the social or political organization to which he belonged, but also his community and family...

> On July 24, my brother Carlos came to see me and we talked...I remember the clothes he wore. The next day I saw on television that there was a big battle in

Vista Hermosa. I didn't know that my brother lived in that house and in one of the newspapers I saw a picture of my brother's body. Two months later, on September 11, the PMA and the Judicial Police came to my father's house in zone 11. They kidnapped my father, my stepmother, my sister-in-law, and my sister who was eighteen months old and my two daughters who were nine and ten years old. They never reappeared...[18]

In the first stage of the armed confrontation, the state tried to destroy political organizations, such as the PGT, the FAR, and the MR-13. However, as the conflict continued and grew more intense, the state not only pursued these groups, but also targeted virtually every organized group, even those that had no defined political position...because from the state's perspective, they represented a threat to the established order...

The state used forced disappearances in its campaign against workers' right to organize as it faced a strong union movement...

> It was in 1964 when my *compañero* (comrade), a union organizer in Escuintla, active member of the union at the *finca* (farm) Torolita, member of FASGUA and supporter of many worker struggles in rural areas and in factories in Escuintla, was taken in the middle of the night by the Judicial Police. They took him and he never reappeared...[19]

After being targeted for repression, the union movement began a process of steady rebuilding during the 1970s. Between 1977 and 1980, during an intense struggle to receive back wages, eight leaders of the Coca-Cola union were assassinated. In this context, the *Comité Nacional de Unidad Sindical* (National Committee for Union Unity, CNUS) was formed as a solidarity organization to support the Coca-Cola workers. The committee was composed of various unions and popular organizations supporting the defense of fundamental rights, all of whom were victims of state persecution...

In the 1970s, the Catholic Church began intensely working to support *campesino* (rural worker) organizations within a national campaign to support *delegados de la palabra* (representatives of the word) and catechists. In the department of Izabal, one of the earliest responses of the state [to these actions] was the forced disappearance of four *campesinos* that were *delegados de la palabra*...

> We were members of a cooperative and the cooperative bought some land...the big landowners said that we were communists. The cooperative had five *caballerías* (a measurement of land)...good for coffee. There were twenty-five plots for twenty-five families, with twenty-five titles properly registered. We had an organization with committees...On January 6...at six in the morning, two months before the coup, 150 people arrived. They were Army, military commissioners and civil defense. The Army was from Puerto Barrios and the Los Amates military base and were armed with shotguns, rifles, machetes, and pistols. They wanted to take possession of the land. They gathered all the people. They forced the women to lie face down in the little school. They tortured the men, putting black bags filled with lime over them...They beat them. Of the five victims, four were disappeared...[20]

University groups played an important role in the social and political life of the country and represented another sector of society subjected to repression. As a result of the 1978 assassination of Oliverio Castañeda, secretary-general of the *Asociación de Estudiantes Universitarios* (Association of University Students, AEU) of *Universidad San Carlos* (San Carlos University, USAC), and the forced disappearance of Antonio Ciani, vice-president of the group, USAC students decided that the AEU leaders had to go underground to protect its members.

Then, in May 1988, "when the student movement began to reestablish itself,"[21] four members of the board—Carlos Ernesto Cuevas, Marilú Hichos, Gustavo Adolfo Carías, and HéctorInteriano Ortiz—were disappeared.

Again, the student organization had to rebuild itself, but its leaders remained underground until 1989 when an edition of the magazine *Estudiante* (Student) published the names of the entire association board. The decision to present their names was inspired by political opportunities promised by the start of the peace negotiations as well as the need to open a new legal space to address the movement's marginalization. Then, in 1989, during a political context of intense repression that came to be known as "Black August," ten university leaders were illegally detained, five of whom were disappeared...

The denial of justice and lack of rule of law were other violations among many associated with forced disappearance. These violations were the result of a failure on the part of state institutions responsible for the administration of justice.

The institutions that could have been called upon to end forced disappearances actively supported the process by providing false information, confusing relatives regarding the whereabouts of those detained, and threatening victims' families so that they would give up their search. They also acted by omission, refusing to receive complaints, failing to engage in investigations of what occurred, and denying the administration of justice.

This issue has special relevance for understanding the presence of state institutions throughout the country...in Guatemala, there were two realities. In urban areas, the state was represented by various institutions such as the civil government, National Police, military bases, judges, and the Public Ministry. However, in rural areas there were practically no civilian state institutions. So, the only state authorities active in rural areas were those that were specifically responsible for violations. As a result, relatives were afraid even to ask for information about the whereabouts of victims, "How could one go to the military base to ask what happened to him when they were the ones that took him?"...[22]

Fear was the most powerful obstacle preventing relatives from initiating actions regarding the whereabouts of those disappeared:

They took him to the base in Nebaj...the wife followed and saw them take him into the base...she saw many women in front of the base crying and complaining that they had taken their husbands. The soldiers laughed and didn't care. Later they asked them if they wanted to come inside to see, but the women refused because they were afraid that they would be detained.[23]

Fear was a common denominator in rural areas as well as in the capital. Based on the many testimonies received by the CEH, it is clear that this fear was the result of direct and indirect threats by state agents to victims' families when they presented a complaint or tried to find out about the status of a prisoner.

> "*Señora*, did you see that it was the police?" "Yes," I said, "it was the police, only dressed in civilian clothes"... "So, they identified themselves?" he said. "Those scum didn't identify themselves," I said. "Do you have children?" He said. "Yes," I said. "In that case, don't say that it was the police," he said.[24]

State functionaries responded with a dismissive attitude. It was difficult to file formal complaints and it was assumed that those responsible would benefit from complete impunity. The general feeling within the country was one of resignation resulting from the impossibility of presenting any action before the state to address the abuse of fundamental rights. .

Forced Disappearance of the Members of the Confederación Nacional de Trabajo (National Labor Confederation, CNT) in Guatemala City and at the "Emaús Medio Monte" Ranch

The CNT was founded in 1968 through the unification of three worker organizations: the *Federación Central de Trabajadores de Guatemala* (Central Federation of Guatemalan Workers, FECETRAG); the *Federación Nacional de los Obreros del Transporte* (National Federation of Transport Workers, FENOT); and, the *Federación Campesina de Guatemala* (Federation of Guatemalan Peasants, FCG)...From its inception, it was composed of industrial unions, *campesino* organizations, and cooperatives.

During the 1970s, the CNT was at the center of union activity and was the largest of the worker organizations. In 1974, it included seven associated unions. By 1979, it included a total of sixty-nine unions. Given its important role in social mobilization, the CNT gained significant influence among union movements at the time as well as with the FAR and the PGT, which exercised political influence within this sector...

Through the application of National Security Doctrine, the state considered the union movement to be part of the insurgency. A former trade unionist who was detained and tortured in one of the military barracks described how security agents showed him a detailed organization chart of the CNT-FAR that presented the two groups as one. State agents and businessmen had information about union activities obtained through the infiltration of the CNT by the state security apparatus. For this reason, the CNT expelled many of its members. One witness recalls that one of the watchmen at the headquarters was part of "*la judicial*"...

CNT members were subjected to various repressive acts. For example, in January 1979, a bomb exploded at their headquarters. That same year there were a number of raids. In one, a security guard was beaten and in another, the CNT's files were taken. On February 22, 1980, the National Police arrested seven leaders. Anonymous threats were found in the mailboxes and bathrooms, and there was even a list circulated of those "sentenced to death" that included the CNT's leaders and advisors. They were followed when they left work. One witness remembers "beige Toyotas" with as many as four people carrying pistols and threatening them.

Facing these growing threats, the trade unionists were afraid, so much so that some considered abandoning the movement...Because of internal problems within the organization, the leadership called an emergency meeting for June 21, 1980. At that meeting, they hoped to resolve ideological differences about the direction of the union movement and strategies for its survival, as well as the expulsion of three CNT members, and support for the Coca-Cola union, which was subjected to intense repression.

In the early hours of Saturday, June 21, Edgar Aldana Ruano, a union member, was murdered. As a result of the murder and ongoing security problems at the CNT headquarters, those responsible decided, at eleven in the morning, to cancel the meeting that was scheduled for that afternoon...However, since it was impossible to notify all the delegates in time, from two in the afternoon on, some began to arrive.

In the words of one survivor:

> At ten to three, I passed by a store [close to the CNT's office] and saw some armed men, not with pistols, but with machine guns...They wore bandannas and were dressed in street clothes. There were around three uniformed officers and, based on their insignias, they were high ranking [officers].[25]

The group was made up by more than sixty armed men, belonging to the Judicial Police, the National Police, and the army.

> I felt that they were going to raid it. I arrived at the CNT and the door was open. I closed the door. I went up the steps and said to my *compañeros*, "Let's go. Let's go. There's going to be a raid." Just as I finished saying these words, the doorbell rang. One of my *compañeros* opened up and then they pushed in the door. There was already a jeep parked in front of the door, so none of us could leave.[26]

At that moment, there were about thirty people there. Ninth and Tenth avenues were surrounded by troops that had stopped traffic and were pointing their weapons. Those posted on the street were dressed in street clothes and wore masks. There were also three or four soldiers that could be identified by their insignias, caps, olive green uniforms...

Three people managed to escape. One of them recounted:

> ...We heard our *compañeros'* screams. I could hear that they were being abused. It sounded as if they were being thrown against the walls. You couldn't hear shots, just beatings...The operation lasted between three and five minutes; it was a "lightning operation."[27]

Another witness who arrived later for the meeting recalled the scene about ten minutes after the military operation.

> The block was empty. The union's watchman wasn't out front...there wasn't anybody there. There were blood stains in the hall and the filing cabinets were open...When I went back out to the street, around six people came over and told me what had happened, while two *compañeros* from the union were crying...[28]

Two months later, union leaders and members of the University of San Carlos' School for Union Studies organized a seminar outside the capital at the Emaús Medio Monte Ranch in Escuintla...On August 24, 1980, army soldiers and National Police forces under the direction of the second-in-command of the detective division detained and disappeared sixteen people...

On September 2, 1980, the ranch administrator, José Luis Peña, was captured, tortured, and executed...According to the Inter-American Commission on Human Rights (IACHR), those kidnapped were taken to garages belonging to the National Police's investigative division in zone 6 in the city where they were tortured under orders of the new chief of investigations.

The government denied responsibility for the disappearance of the trade unionists. The Minister of the Interior stated that the disappeared leaders could have been kidnapped by extremist groups with the goal of creating problems for the state...

According to declassified U.S. government documents:

> ...the police deny having any knowledge of the whereabouts of the trade unionists, but the strike, like the prior one (the April 29, 1980, raid on the headquarters) has all of the characteristics of an operation by the security forces. With apparent impunity, the attacking group even rerouted traffic on the city center's crowded streets during the operation...[29]

On June 25, 1980, the Supreme Court received a habeus corpus petition for the disappeared. On July 1, the request was granted by the criminal court, with a hearing scheduled for the following day...On July 7, the criminal court declared the petition baseless because state officials reported that those kidnapped were not detained and the file was sent to the Sixth Judge of the lower court in Guatemala City's criminal branch, to investigate the whereabouts of the kidnapped men. The court ordered, "Carry out whatever review is necessary to best clarify the matter under investigation."[30] According to information provided by the general court archives, this was the last judicial action in this case...

2

Torture

The CEH documented 11,598 victims of torture. Of that number, 54 percent of the victims survived...Due to the frequency of torture in Guatemala, it is likely that it was used in many cases of forced disappearance and that if it were possible to count these cases, the number of torture victims would be much larger...

Torture was applied in various stages. Following detention there was personality "softening," followed by interrogation where different techniques were used. In the end, victims were generally executed or turned into army collaborators. In some cases, torture ended with the release of the victims. At times, prisoners were forced to sign documents declaring that they had not been tortured or to present legal confessions in which they admitted to committing a crime. They were also threatened so that they wouldn't engage in any type of legal action and were sometimes advised to leave the country...

Torture Methods

The "softening" involved several days of brutal and systematic violence in which victims were forced to spend many hours hooded or standing. Often, these detainees were beaten and kicked. They were not allowed to sleep for a period of several days and were given nothing to eat or drink...

The goal was to humiliate the victim, to psychologically and physically weaken him so that when he was interrogated his personality would be completely destroyed, thereby aiding the work of the torturer. The victim was left completely disoriented, without a sense of time or place.

The interrogation centers at military installations included sites specially created for these purposes. There were holes, wells with water, toilets, pits with bodies...

I was in my house when a group of men arrived with their faces covered in balaclavas. They knocked on the doors of my house...They beat me. They threw me on the ground. They blindfolded my eyes and tied my feet and hands...In the base they threw me in a pit. There, they accused me of being a guerrilla. They told everyone that was detained there, "You know your guerrilla buddies." They wanted us to tell them where the guerillas we knew were living. I tried to be serious and strong and I never lost faith that I would go free...

Of course I was scared. That morning, they took me out of the pit where they held me and brought me to a dark room made of wood and old aluminum. They started torturing me. They electrocuted my feet. They jabbed me in my stomach and back. Some of them were smoking and they put out their cigarettes on my body.

I didn't say anything. On the contrary, I lied through my teeth. They put my face in a bag of lime. They returned me to the pit but this time it was filled with shit and every half hour they would come to the pit, take us out and interrogate us. They said, "Son of a bitch, Tell me where your guerrilla friends are."... [1]

The most common methods of physical torture were systematic beatings, cuts and wounds, sleep deprivation and denial of food, forcing people to watch the torture and killing of others, burns, suspension and hanging, asphyxiation or immersion as well as sexual torture, torture with electricity, torture with pharmaceuticals, and dental torture...

They took me away. They removed my shirt and took off my pants and they grabbed one of the officer's sweaters and put one of the sleeves of the sweater in my mouth and tied me with it... "Here, you'll tell us the truth"... Then I saw that they grabbed a cable and put it in a socket... and they began to give me electric shocks... I didn't know what electric shocks were, but I felt everything. It's not like being beaten. I thought that I was dying little by little... [2]

They took him to the military base... Once he was there, they began to beat him and interrogate him about his *compañeros*, continually hitting him in the head and he lost consciousness various times... They threatened him with a knife saying... that they would slit his throat. When he didn't respond, they put a rope around his neck and hung him, and when he was about to die they let him down, giving him time to recover... One of the soldiers offered him money if he would tell them who the other guerillas were. He responded saying how could he tell them if he didn't know? They put a plastic bag over his head and tied it at the neck until he asphyxiated. They continually changed the two soldiers that tortured him and each one used his own means of torture... [3]

They began beating Jesús in the mouth until his teeth broke. And, then they pulled out a knife and they made him swallow them, one by one, while they were interrogating him about the names of his guerrilla *compañeros*. Finally the officer, who was angry because he hadn't told them anything, grabbed his tongue and told Jesús that he would cut it out as he repeated his order to tell them the names... [4]

In many cases victims of torture were killed. Once the victim no longer had any more valuable information, refused to cooperate or when the person had been captured by mistake, he was executed...

A high-ranking soldier at the Choatalúm base, in the September 9 neighborhood, Chimaltenango saw:

many of those detained who had been kidnapped from their homes and *aldeas*, they were killed and buried in the patio at the base. They put down soil and then planted beans and vegetables so it looked like a field so that no one visiting would suspect a thing...[5]

In this way, the clandestine cemeteries and crematoria were an integral part of the interrogation centers and served as a means of dealing with those that were tortured and then killed...

Responsibility for Torture

According to the testimonies received by the CEH, 88 percent of the reported cases of torture were carried out by the army. Other bodies of state security committed torture, usually in coordination with members of the army, especially members of the intelligence services. Other groups that acted with the army, based on their orders or with their consent, included PAC, military commissioners, and other security forces....

Military intelligence was responsible for compiling and recording information and was the element within the army most responsible for acts of torture. Describing interrogation methods, a high-ranking former soldier in Playa Grande explained:

> Those from intelligence were responsible for getting the truth out of people. They covered them with a hood filled with glue, spooned out their eyes, cut out their tongues, hung them by their testicles. Those people were criminals. The group was divided into those responsible for torture to obtain information (the investigators and jailers) and those responsible for killing (the butchers)...[6]

In the usual interrogation procedure, those detained were quickly asked about their company or battalion to obtain information of immediate strategic value. The more detailed interrogations took place in military zones...A declassified document from the U.S. Department of State stated:

> ...Clandestine prisons have always existed in Guatemala...when insurgents are captured by the Army, they are held incommunicado in isolated places in different military zones, interrogated and once the Army feels that it has extracted all of the relevant information, they are assassinated and their bodies are disposed of...[7]

Interrogations [often] began at a base and later continued after transfer to a military zone based on the apparent importance of the detainee...

> Around seven in the morning when I was about to have breakfast, I was taken right in front of my wife by a group of six men who were wearing balaclavas over their faces. The neighbors saw how they handcuffed me and put me in the back of my car. Various men guarded me. Some said that they'd been watching me since the day before, waiting for the moment to take me.
>
> For three days, I was at the base at San José Ojetenam located in the school. There, they beat me and asked, "So, you're a guerrilla?" And, I answered, "No." Then they said, "You'll tell the truth when we run electricity through you." They

tied my thumbs with some wires and the rest of my body with rope. In the room, there was a generator for the lights, I had a wire connected to my left thumb and they put another wire coming from the device on my right thumb. Then, the electricity ran through me and made me fall out of my chair. It shocked me and dragged me across the floor. I lost consciousness during one of the many electrocutions. One of them said to another, "If we leave him one second longer, he'll die."…

Then, they took me in a helicopter to the brigade in Quetzaltenango where they put me in a place with eighty men. They kicked, beat and punched me and interrogated me saying, "You're a guerrilla." And, I answered, "No I sell snow cones." Those who said that they were guerillas received food, cigarettes, bananas, and were free, not tied up like me. It was always filled with prisoners, some left, and then the next day others would arrive to take their place. I don't know what happened to the ones [who left].

One day a major arrived accompanied by a woman. The major asked her if I was a guerilla. Then, she answered, "No, he sells snow cones. I know my *compañeros*."

Then, the officer turned to me and said, "My apologies, little brother. There has been a mistake."

They gave me a tortilla, a piece of fish, and a glass of water. Then, they let me return to the other detainees. Four days after having returned to Quetzaltenango, they told me to leave the country and not to say where I would go because if I did, they'd come and kill me…[8]

In most of the bases, prisoners that were to be disappeared were held for one or two days before they were killed… The most important detainees were taken to Guatemala City where they were brought to secret sites at the [buildings of the] *Estado Mayor* or the *Escuela Politécnica* (Polytechnic School)…

The commanders of the military zones were aware of and definitely authorized the torture committed by the intelligence officials and teams of interrogators in their installations… Similarly, they were informed that those tortured were killed and they approved the methods of dealing with bodies: burning, clandestine cemeteries, thrown in the streets, and so on…

Officers in military intelligence were responsible for training and educating agents and for providing basic instructions to participants in the surveillance networks. The training regarding torture was explicit. A high-ranking officer told his soldiers:

"After capturing a guerrilla, you have to torture him," and he would tell us how, cutting off his tongue, poking out his eyes, cutting off his fingertips, "Whoever isn't brave enough to do it, I'll do it to you."[9]

Military commissioners were the eyes and ears of the army within communities. A commissioner who worked for one of the local landowners in the Cahabón region explained the way he used torture:

I ripped out their toenails and then I hung them. In Chiacach and Chioyal, we tortured by taking the soldiers' bayonets and scraping the bottoms of the men's feet…nails were ripped out with pliers…I stabbed their chests with a bayonet. People cried and begged me not to hurt them…but the lieutenant and the commissioner arrived…and forced me when they saw me taking pity on people…[10]

The PAC also committed acts of torture to ensure discipline among its members, to punish people who refused to join them, and against anyone suspected of being a subversive.

> About twenty *patrulleros*, among them San Bartolo's patrol leader and the patrol leaders from Molubá, los Cimientos, Sinchaj, surrounded Micaela's house where her children were. The *patrulleros* were armed with Galil rifles and with sticks covered with nails to be used for beatings. At Micaela's house, they found her children. They were looking for Francisco, the oldest son, but he wasn't there. Then, they began to interrogate Micaela. They threatened to burn down her house. They beat her. They hit her hard with the stick with nails. With one punch they knocked out a tooth…The *patrulleros* continually patrolled the *cantónes,* checking them house by house. Five days later, the *patrulleros* returned to Micaela's house. That time they captured Francisco. The tied him up, put him under their control, covered him in gas and lit a fire, burning him alive…[11]

The National Police and the *Guardia de la Hacienda* worked for military intelligence. These armed groups also committed torture…On December 19, 1981, Quirino Pérez Hernandéz, a council member of the municipality of Tacaná, San Marcos, was detained in his home several days after receiving a death threat. He was taken by men wearing *Guardia de la Hacienda* uniforms with their faces covered by balaclavas…Two days later his body was found near the municipality…

> He has been tortured, he was missing two fingers, he had been strangled and it was clear that lime had been put on his face. They removed his testicles. It was barbaric. I hope to God that these things never happen again…[12]

Secret Prisons

In Guatemala, torture was systematic and widespread and relied on special illegal detention centers popularly known as secret prisons. These illegal centers were found in public buildings such as police stations, military zones, and other security forces' facilities…The CEH assumes that most bases had secret detention centers. These interrogation centers were designed so that the prisoners and torture victims were kept hidden. They tried to hide the existence of these clandestine centers, even from soldiers not affiliated with military intelligence. These sites included many places that were specially prepared for the "softening" of detainees from the conflict, such as well or pits with water, naturally occurring or man-made caves and ditches, small improvised cells covered with aluminum sheets…

One of the most important interrogation centers of the Intelligence Division of the Joint Chiefs of Staff was popularly known as *La Isla* (The Island) or *La Hielera*

(The Cooler) and was located next to the headquarters of the *Policia Militar Ambulante* (Mobile Military Police, PMA) where it operated until 1992...After its existence was made public, the secret prison known as *La Isla* was moved to a site near the La Aurora airport...

In the sixties, among the most infamous torture and detention centers was *La Tigrera* (The Little Jaguar), located at the National Police barracks at the corner of Seventh Avenue and Fourteenth Street in zone 1 in Guatemala City and in the catacombs and cloisters of the nearby San Francisco Convent.

On the day of his inauguration, President Méndez Montenegro told the press that "torture will be definitively eradicated," adding that police detention centers and torture sites would be closed including *La Tigrera* at the police barracks and the cells known as *Las Cuadras.* The new chief of the Judicial Police said:

> ...the agents of the Judicial Police will protect honorable citizens...torture and the abuse of authority will not take place. Those problems are over...[13]

In the city and country, many privately owned facilities were also used as centers for detention, interrogation, and torture. These places were owned by Guatemalan Army officers or provided by military commissioners, leaders of the *patrullas civiles*, or army collaborators. Given their clandestine nature, their secrecy was jealously guarded...

Several army units took over civilian sites such as churches, empty buildings, and abandoned mines, where they set up centers for detention, interrogation, and torture. These sites were used for a few weeks, months, or years depending on the army's needs...

Where torture victims managed to survive and were released, one of the effects was fear of any involvement with security forces or state agents...Torture created terror among victims, discouraging subsequent political or social activities and formal charges regarding these human rights violations.

> I was afraid for a long time. I never thought of filing a complaint because the Army was all-powerful and they would have killed me. Besides, my nerves are shot, I think for the rest of my life...[14]

Torture in the Military Zone of Playa Grande, Ixcán,
Department of Quiché

The case here refers only to the events that occurred at the military base at Playa Grande, Ixcán, between 1981 and 1983...Detentions took place in communities or along the road. They were carried out by various groups of armed, uniformed soldiers that prevented witnesses from responding out of fear of suffering the same fate as the victims. Once captured, the victims were transferred to military installations...

Many people with no connection to the armed confrontation were tortured merely on the basis of rumors, jealousy, or out of personal revenge. Community leaders, catechists, leaders of cooperatives, family, friends, and neighbors of members of the guerillas were all subjected to torture.

A victim's disappearance began when he entered the Playa Grande military base...Soldiers systematically refused to provide information to relatives who dared to ask about those captured and threatened them with the same fate:

> On January 14, 1982, a group of women went to the Playa Grande base to file a complaint about their husbands and sons. A soldier who was at the entry gate told them, "If you don't leave at once, I'll leave you piled up in the street" Because of the death threats they received, that was the only time those relatives tried to file a complaint...[15]

Before being interrogated, victims were held in very small cells:

> Then they took us out of the pit and stuck us in a building inside the base and then in a very small jail. There, we couldn't even move.[16]

They were placed in "holes" or pits...Placing those detained into holes was very common in the region, and it was also used against PAC members who didn't follow set rules...

A former army *confidencial* (spy) stated:

> They put you in a pit full of water. If you were short, it covered you completely, but if you were tall, it came up to your neck...They tried to keep your nerves on edge. Also, there was a metal sheet on top and when it warmed up the heat above your head was terrible. You had to urinate and defecate there in the hole. Two or three men were sometimes placed in the same hole. It was the width of the pipes used on the highway. There were many in the base, by the soccer field. There were three behind the offices belonging to the "*dos*" [G-2, military intelligence]. Beyond the officers' house, there was a hill with a gas tank. There were several holes there where people were held and tortured.[17]

According to survivors, they were asked questions like: How long have you collaborated with the guerrillas? Where are the guerrilla camps? How did you support them, with information or logistics? Who in the community are members of the guerrilla? How many and what kind of weapons do they have? These questions were repeated over and over in the different sessions to which the victim was subjected. Sometimes, the interrogators covered their faces so they couldn't be identified.

One of the most common forms of torture used in the cases investigated was known as "the hood." It consisted of covering the victim's face with oilcloth or a plastic bag, sometimes filled with agricultural chemicals...until it caused asphyxiation. When the person passed out the hood was removed, only to repeat the process various times.

> They beat me. They hit me with a pistol and many times they put a plastic hood on me to suffocate me. They asked me a lot of questions about the guerrillas and about types of weapons. I didn't know anything about it and they let me go the next day.[18]

Another method of torture used to suffocate the victim involved placing the victim's head in a container (sink, barrel...) full of water. When the torturer decided that enough time had passed, he took him out and continued asking questions, repeating this action several times.

> They stuck our heads in a sink full of water and when you felt like you were about to die, they pulled us out. Two men held me by my arms. I felt like I was dying. I couldn't breathe. They did this several times so that you would tell them where the guerrillas were.[19]

They also used electricity.

> They lay me down on a bed of wires, turned on a generator and connected some wires. Afterwards, I only felt pain. I twisted and screamed.[20]

It was very common to repeatedly burn the victim's body with cigarettes...

> The commander interrogated him. Because we didn't know a lot about the guerrillas, he burned his face with the tip of a cigarette. And, in the middle of the night, they were interrogating him as soldiers stood on his chest and pressing down on his stomach, torturing him so he would say that he was one of the guerrillas.[21]

Sometimes, they lay victims down on beds of barbed wire.

> Helicopters arrived all day long, with two or three people. They tortured them. There was a bed with barbed wire. They threw them on there and the soldiers got on top of them. Others were put in barrels...[22]

In addition to physical torture applied from the first moment of detention, they also used psychological torture throughout the period of captivity, even after the interrogations and physical brutality had stopped...

Most of the time victims were eventually executed.

> They covered their faces and mouths and bound their hands. Then they took them to the beach and there, they were killed in the Río Chixoy. What I saw was terrible, I haven't told anyone here in the village.[23]

> I saw how eighteen or twenty people from San Pablo died. They didn't give them anything to eat. They had them out in the sun with their hands tied behind their backs. They killed them…[24]

Executions were carried out inside the Playa Grande military base where there were people specifically designated to kill the victims.

> There were two or three that specialized in eliminating the patients [detainees]. Most of those went crazy or disappeared or aren't around to talk about it. I knew many of them. They were soldiers. They didn't stay very long. They were rotated…so that they didn't know too much…[25]

Some victims were released so that they would tell their neighbors, relatives, and friends about the torture and torments that they suffered.

3

Forced Displacement

The scope of the institutional violence to which Guatemalan civilians were subjected during the armed confrontation is clearly demonstrated in the phenomenon of displacement. It is estimated that between 500,000 and 1.5 million Guatemalans were forced to flee as a direct consequence of repression, especially during the early 1980s...

Some of those displaced sought to escape death by crossing the border, while others tried to survive without leaving the country. Some migrated to urban centers or to other departments and some found refuge in the mountains or jungles near their homes, where they were forced to endure subhuman conditions. Through the CEH's investigation, it is clear that many people died during their flight and displacement, generally as a result of hunger, cold, illness, fear, and exhaustion.

From the moment they were forced to flee their communities to save their lives, the army relentlessly pursued and harassed people, trying to kill them. Those displaced suffered many massacres and executions during the time they spent in the mountains. The army also systematically destroyed stored food, agricultural fields, and homes, making it very difficult for those displaced to survive in the mountains.

The persecution of the displaced population was not limited by the country's borders...In an attempt to control refugees and those displaced, the Guatemalan Army entered Mexico and Honduras, violating the international agreements and covenants regarding refugees as well as the national sovereignty of other countries...

From its start, the armed conflict created forced displacement among individuals and groups that feared attacks from the army and its related organizations...Mass displacement was first documented in the late 1970s and reached its climax between 1981 and 1983, the years in which *la violencia* was most severe. During this period, it is estimated that around 80 percent of the population in the departments most affected by institutionalized violence—such as Quiché, Huehuetenango, Chimaltenango, and Alta Verapaz—were forced to abandon their communities for at least some period of time. During the same time, there were also substantial displacements in other departments, such as Baja Verapaz, Sololá, San Marcos, Petén, and Izabal.

Given their desperate situation, many of those displaced crossed the border to escape *la violencia* by becoming refugees in Mexico and, to a lesser degree, in other neighboring countries. According to the United Nations High Commissioner for Refugees (UNHCR), in 1984 there were 46,000 Guatemalan refugees living in camps in southern Mexico, the majority of whom originated from departments near the border such as Huehuetenango and Quiché. It is estimated than another 100,000 refugees lived dispersed near the border or in other parts of Mexico. In Honduras, there were 800 officially recognized refugees, and it is estimated that many thousands sought refuge in the United States, mainly in Florida, California, and Texas.

Selective Repression Leads to Mass Displacement

The rise in violence in rural areas increased the movement of those displaced from *aldeas* and villages to urban centers. These shifts first became noticeable in the early 1980s, when selective repression began to significantly impact local social organizations. Military operations, alongside the activities of commissioners and *confidenciales,* created a climate of terror within communities. During this period, there were disappearances at night and along roads, captures during market days, "black lists," and threats. This led some of those involved in civic and religious organizations to decide that they had to abandon their homes.

> We could no longer sleep in the house because the army would come. They burned a house, killed someone and it was only possible to enter one's home in the daytime. We had to go sleep in the hills at night. In that way, little by little, the people began to flee to the mountains.[1]

Before *la violencia* became widespread, the majority of the victims of repression were men involved in social or political activities. As a result, within the communities, women, the elderly, and children were not believed to be the targets of military attacks. So, they would stay at home while the men would leave, either temporarily or permanently. During those times when the army's soldiers would come to check on the husbands, father, sons, or daughters, the families would not flee their homes.

However, beginning in 1981, the repression became indiscriminate. This started with cases where soldiers who couldn't find those they were looking for would kill their relatives, paying no attention to their age or situation.

This arbitrary selection of victims had a profound communicative impact on the population. Those participating in social or political movements faced the consequences of their activities on their relatives. And, the constant nature of threats to families forced them to flee as part of a general, collective process...

The initial acts of violence instilled terror in the heart of the affected communities. This terror increased with each of the army's successive operations until it reached its height with the campaign plan *Victoria 82* (Victory 82). This plan started the scorched earth operations used as a strategy for destroying the social base of the insurgent movement. In this way, hundreds of communities were razed in a systematic manner.

The widespread nature of *la violencia* led to mass displacement as the only means of survival. Many communities abandoned their homes, sometimes warned by local leaders or by members of the guerrilla, and at other times, after hearing that the army was destroying nearby communities:

> Because we knew what the Army did when it arrived, killing people and burning houses, it was better to go to the mountains. We already knew that the Army's plan was to capture and kill and do away with all of our people.[2]

Even when the army invaded communities without their prior knowledge, some still managed to escape. The communities lived through periods of generalized panic and terror. Families were commonly separated when they fled and many were killed as soldiers often pursued those who tried to escape, shooting at them and throwing grenades...

> At six in the morning, we heard a lot of noise. People were running and shouting. We heard lots of shots, as if it was a war. Then we understood that something bad was going on. When we left our house, one of the neighbors yelled, "Run, they're coming to kill us." Without thinking, we started running, taking our children as best we could. When we were leaving, we realized that the community was full of *pintos* (soldiers), there were also armed civilians...who fired on us when they saw us running.
>
> Lots of people were falling as they fled. I could see that next to me or in front of me. People were falling as if they had tripped, but no, they were falling because they were shot or because grenades landed near them. When this happened people flew up in the air and fell like rag dolls...
>
> I ran away, taking my two children. When the soldiers realized this they started shooting at us. A bullet struck my left arm, but this didn't stop me. I kept running even as I saw my arm bleeding...There came a point where I couldn't keep going. I felt like my heart was giving out. Then, I stopped to see if the soldiers had stopped following me. I sat down to rest...my daughter's face was covered in blood...She was dead. She took a bullet in the back and that prevented the bullet from killing me...[3]

Fleeing their homes was only the first phase of the suffering of those displaced, who faced inhuman conditions as they escaped with their communities. They had to survive in a hostile environment to which they were unaccustomed, without food, with no safe haven, carrying children and the elderly, as daily life became an enormous struggle...hundreds of those displaced died of hunger, sickness and *susto* ("terror")...

> We never counted those who had died because we could only think of saving ourselves from death, but it was around 200 or so. Some because they were caught and killed, others died of hunger because they cut down the fields. They stole

everything. They destroyed our *piedras* (stones for cooking) and we couldn't pre-pare food...We had to stay in the mountains eating only herbs without salt and wild plants, without clothes, unable to light a fire during the day...[4]

From the moment that the people were forced to flee their communities to save their lives, the security forces engaged in operations to pursue, harass, and kill them.

Controlling the Population

From 1983 on, the army's strategy focused on trying to regain control over the displaced population by urging them to return to areas under their command by luring them with amnesties and subsequently imposing military structures to ensure long-term control of the conflict zones...

After the March 1982 coup, the high command determined that violence alone would not be enough to defeat the insurgency. Out of this reevaluation, the army created new position, known as the developmentalist philosophy, which recognized that

> ...one had to fight a war on all fronts: military, political, and above all, social and economic. Our objectives are the hearts and will of the people...[5]

This led the army experts to design new strategies that sought to improve the basic living conditions of the population through social and economic projects alongside military actions. This signaled a new phase of the conflict redefining the war as involving the physical, social, and ideological rebuilding of the areas devastated by the scorched earth operations.

This counterinsurgency strategy of "pacification," in other words, of control-ling the civilian population in the areas of conflict, was designed to be imple-mented in three phases...In the first phase, they sought control through the combination of repressive measures and emergency aid. This phase was known as *fusiles y frijoles* (rifles and beans)...

The second phase was called *techo, tortillas y trabajo* (housing, food, and work) and involved forced resettlement of the displaced in places where they could be easily monitored, such as model villages, which were built with this goal in mind. This phase also included deepening and strengthening militarized structures such as the PAC and, creating construction and infrastructure proj-ects supported by the food-for-work program. This phase fit into the strategy of *polos de desarrollo* (development poles).

The third phase was known as *paz, segurida y desarrollo* (peace, security, and development), an attempt to involve national and international institutions and organizations in the creation of sustainable production and socioeconomic development projects. In practice, however, this phase was never fully realized in the way that the army had planned. The goal of this phase was to keep the civilian population under control by minimizing their reasons for supporting the insurgency and thereby denying them logistical support.

During the implementation of each of these different phases, there were continual violations of fundamental human rights. From moment the displaced civilian population arrived...they were systematically abused both physically and psychologically, and denied freedom of movement, action, and expression...

Amnesty and Reception

In the first phase, the army used different tactics to regain control over the displaced population. They declared consecutive amnesties that were designed and publicized to attract the displaced and overcome their fear and mistrust. They also continued policies of harassment and persecution, sweeping through the mountains to capture those displaced, destroy their fields, and make survival in the mountains ever more difficult...When their suffering in the mountains became overwhelming, when death was ever-present, turning oneself over to the army became the only viable option...

After accepting amnesty, the displaced faced rejection and stigmatization by military authorities. Despite the fact that the decrees explicitly guaranteed their status as noncombatant civilians, many that returned were accused of collaborating with the insurgency and held responsible for the violence. In some cases, these allegations and accusations built on of the deep sense of popular religious belief naming them "demons" or denying their dignity...

> President Ríos Montt had said that all the people who had left their homes should return...Then our brothers, women and children who were in the mountains appeared before the officers, but the officers severely abused them, saying, "You're all thieves. You're the ones that kill the Army. You're like cats that hide in the mountains. You're animals..." There were between nine and twelve or families there. The rest changed their mind halfway there and refused to appear.[6]

Accepting amnesty was difficult for those displaced, not only because of the challenge of overcoming their mistrust and fear, but also because they faced multiple types of psychological and physical humiliation. In light of what it meant to turn oneself in to the army, many of those displaced made this decision because it was the only way to survive:

> We spent two years [in the mountains], but since we didn't have money, clothing, food, we decided to turn ourselves in...There were about two hundred of us from various communities. The first to turn themselves in were from Sechinapemech. When we came down, the soldiers in Semuy met us. They surrounded us and told us not to be afraid, because they weren't killing people anymore. They took us down in trucks and left us at the Catholic church. Every day we were afraid because we didn't know if they were going to kill us. "Perhaps tomorrow," we said.[7]

In fact, the CEH documented various cases in which those displaced, upon coming down from the mountains to accept amnesty, were arbitrarily executed by state security forces. This flagrantly violated the safety guarantees outlined in the amnesties.

> Some neighbors were killed, after trusting the amnesty, by *patrulleros* who were waiting on the roads and who accused anyone moving without permission of being a guerrilla. Others were killed because their land had been occupied by Army collaborators...[8]

The mechanisms of control were implemented immediately upon the return of those displaced...

> You had to listen to speeches. They were always about the same topics, the ones that they wanted to get into our heads... "You're groups of communists, but later those same communists are going to kill everyone. The men are going to bring people from other countries and they're going to keep your daughters, your wives, your land, and everything you have"... "but now we'll protect you and now you won't accept anything from them because if you resume taking things from them, we'll return again to kill you. Your lives are in our hands"...They also beat it into us that if someone from outside came to advise us to involve ourselves again in *babosadas* that we should immediately tell them so that they would be captured.[9]

The army used various methods to gain complete control over those that accepted the amnesties and to disempower their leaders. Sometimes, they tried to draw them closer to the army or assigned them positions of responsibility within the PAC. In some cases, after capturing and severely torturing them, they were forced to discredit and delegitimize the insurgency while also urging the displaced to accept amnesty...

The displaced populations as a whole were regarded with suspicion, because of the alleged relations that they had established with the guerrillas...They were subjected to intelligence operations, such as interrogations and subsequent reviews, because it was assumed that they had information about the location and activities of the insurgency. They were seen as potential guerrilla collaborators, even after their return, and had to be "reeducated"...

The receiving centers were located in various places, inside military installations, in occupied churches, and in public buildings in main towns. At times they were truly concentration camps...where people were held surrounded by wire fences. The reeducation process was not always the same, varying by location, its implementation, and the duration of stay in the centers, from several weeks to a year...

All of the centers had the same goal, to ideologically train and prepare people for reintegration. First, they were forcibly indoctrinated with the idea that the army was the defender of the nation and that everything they did or had done was for their own good and for the good of the country. Then, they were bombarded with a psychological campaign against the "subversives." And, finally, they were severely threatened so that they would never again "oppose" the army by collaborating with the guerrillas or fleeing to the mountains.

> They taught us that we had *shuca* (useless) minds and that we had to change. They warned us not to listen to anyone outside of Acamal, not to pay attention to anyone who talked about social struggle. If someone spoke about these things or if anyone of us complained about life in that *aldea*, we had to inform on him. We couldn't have meetings among ourselves, that there was no need, that if we had any doubts, we should ask those in charge in Acamal...[10]

The reeducation process involved constant abuse during interrogations and throughout the overall reintegration process. Whether through direct accusations or physical or psychological abuse, the message of state agents to the displaced that had turned themselves in was that they were responsible for *la violencia* and that they should pay for their sins...

Polos de Desarrollo

The time displaced people spent in receiving centers was designed to prepare them for resettlement, either in the *aldeas* where they originated or in the so-called model villages. In the rebuilt areas, all resettled communities were subjected to daily social militarization, whether or not they lived in officially managed villages. The difference was based on the quality of institutional support, which in some cases involved access to basic services such as roads, clean water, schools, electricity, and public meeting halls.

The design and construction of the model villages was part of the counterinsurgency strategy institutionally positioned within the *polos de desarrollo* program... Two *polos de desarrollo* projects existed in the department of Quiché. One was in the Ixil triangle, covering seventeen communities, the most well known being Acul; Another was in Playa Grande, covering nine communities, including Xalbal and Cantabal. In Alta Verapaz, they placed a *polo de desarrollo* in Chisec that covered seventeen communities, including Acamal. Finally, in Chacaj in Huehuetenango there were model villages...

The *polos de desarrollo* were one of the clearest expressions of...the developmentalist philosophy that combined military action with economic growth activities in the affected areas. This was not new for the country. Beginning in the 1960s, U.S. advisors had introduced the idea of civic action into eastern Guatemala through which soldiers carried out humanitarian and development projects.

The objectives of the four *polos de desarrollo* were clearly political-military in nature. The program allowed the army to mobilize the state's resources to quickly dominate and control some of the areas previously considered to be the guerrillas' strategic base by creating programs that, on the one hand, gained the trust of the people, and on the other hand, created a dependency on the army...

Various state institutions...played key roles in implementing the counterinsurgency policies of the *polos de desarrollo*. The most prominent was the *Comité de Reconstruccion Nacional* (National Reconstruction Committee, CRN), created by the army...From 1982 on, it was charged with the task of implementing the development components of the *Plan Nacional de Seguridad y Desarrollo* (National Plan for Security and Development). The CRN's main function was to administer food aid within the *polos de desarrollo* through the food-for-work projects managed by the United Nations World Food Program and largely financed by the United States.

The *Instituto Nacional para Transformacion Agraria* (National Institute for Agrarian Change, INTA) was another institution that played an important role in government policies of resettlement in the "pacified" areas, particularly in the Ixcán. INTA's policy of canceling property rights under the principle of "voluntary abandonment" created serious conflicts both at that time and up until the present. This achieved various key objectives for the military government. On the one hand, it resettled people sympathetic to the army in these areas, helping to consolidate their control and influence. On the other hand, it encouraged the displaced and refugee population to return so as not to lose their land...

Many other institutions—such as *Dirección General de Servicios Agrícolas* (General Directorate of Agricultural Services, DIGESA), *Banco Nacional de Desarrollo Agricola* (National Agricultural Development Bank, BANDESA), *Fundación de Ayudapara el Pueblo Indígena* (Foundation for the Assistance of Indigenous People, FUNDAPI), and the *Instituto Técnico de Capacitación y Productividad* (Technical Institute for Training and Productivity, INTECAP)—as well as different national and international NGOs participated in the creation and operation of the *polos de desarrollo*. It is worth noting that various U.S. NGOs played a significant role in the first phase of these policies such as CARE, financed by the United States Agency for International Development (USAID) as well as groups linked to extreme right-wing evangelical churches, such as Gospel Outreach and Christian Broadcasting Network. The work of all of these organizations and institutions was managed by interinstitutional coordinators that, in turn, were under the firm control of the army...

The *polos de desarrollo* presented the outside world with an image of the army as a helpful force committed to the progress and well being of the civilian population. This improved the institution's image within international circles, increasing financial support that was administered by the military. International funds, particularly from the United States, were necessary for construction and maintenance. Still, it was, to a large degree, a failure in that the *polos de desarrollo* never achieved self-sufficiency and collapsed from 1985 on, as the army focused its energies on other goals.

Model Villages

In principle, model villages were communities that were built or rebuilt with the specific purpose of controlling the population in the areas of conflict that had already been "pacified" through the scorched earth operations...While the first model village, Choatulum, in Chimaltenango, was created in 1982, the most significant construction of model villages occurred in 1983 and 1984 as the *polos de desarrollo* policy was implemented.

During the peak of the *polos de desarrollo*, between 50,000 and 60,000 people lived in the model villages, that is, around 6 percent of the displaced population that had returned between 1982 and 1984...

In exchange for food, they were forced to work building model villages, roads, and other activities that allowed the military to access strategic places within the areas of conflict. The control of food was a key element of the army's strategy in the model villages. The distribution of food, as well as various types of humanitarian assistance (clothing, blankets, and medicines), was carefully controlled by the army to create dependency that reinforced their power over the population...

The army...required the people resettling in those places to build houses following a predetermined pattern of parallel and perpendicular streets with houses located close together. This urban-styled plan was most commonly seen in the Ixil area and was designed to maximize control over the population. Over time, it was not only dysfunctional, but also conflicted with the traditional modes of settlement of rural indigenous people. In addition, in some model villages, two unrelated families, including some who did not get along, were randomly selected and placed in the same house...

> The Army forced us. So, in order to control ourselves, each one had to buy a lot, a short distance from every other family because that was for the best. When we were all together, they could control us, which was for the best. "You have to be close together so that you can easily monitor each other because if you're separated it is harder to control and the guerrillas might return."...[11]

The indoctrination process that began at the reception and reeducation centers continued in the model villages. In addition, the population was kept under rigorous control including a growing militarization of daily life through the PAC. For this reason, all model villages were located near military installations, whether bases, military zones, or buildings occupied by the army...

> We were constantly under surveillance. We couldn't leave without permission. If we returned late from an authorized leave, they wouldn't give us permission to leave again. They were always criticizing us. For example, when we went out on Sundays, they constantly insulted us, saying that we were going to see our *compañeros* in the mountains...one could leave but never all the members of the same family, that is, you always left members of your family inside, in case you chose not to return.[12]

> In Sacol as in Acamal...you had to line up at six in the morning and six in the evening, sing the National Anthem, the *Patrulleros'* Anthem. If you didn't want to sing, if you made any mistakes or you didn't want to go out on patrol, you were punished...[13]

In the resettlement areas, freedom of movement, action, and expression were restricted in a completely disproportionate manner, especially given that these were "pacified" areas. The strict military control over all aspects of life and corresponding restrictions on personal freedoms in these reconstructed areas coupled with ongoing repression ensured that there was a constant fear that "the past" could return at any time.

Río Pixcayá Massacre, Village of Estancia de La Virgen, San Martín Jilotepeque

In 1976, the *Ejército Guerrillero de los Pobres* (Guerrilla Army of the Poor, EGP) began its political work in Chimaltenango. Its presence in the area increased from mid-1981 on, especially in San Martín Jilotepeque...

In a series of actions, they took Sololá on October 28, Tecpán, on November 16, and Patzún on December 17. Civilians participated in these actions by cutting telegraph lines, obstructing highways, and placing barricades on the Inter-American highway from Chimaltenango to Santa Cruz del Quiché with the goal of preventing soldiers from reaching the villages occupied by the guerrillas. This made the army believe that all of the inhabitants of the region supported the insurgents...

On November 18, 1981, the army launched a mass offensive against the area of Quiché and Chimaltenango, marking the start of the large massacres in Chimaltenango and especially in the municipality of San Martín Jilotepeque...

In 1982, terror reigned in San Martín Jilotepeque. There were repeated violations of human rights including massacres, forced disappearances, and torture, the burning of corpses, homes, animals, crops, looting, and other abuses...

March 1982... saw the worst violence in an area including the *aldea* of Estancia de la Virgen and neighboring communities. There were three documented massacres: one on the Catalán ranch, and the others in the villages of San Miguel and Santa Teresa... The surviving population crossed either the Motagua River or the Pixcayá River to take refuge in nearby communities where they believed there would be less danger.

From March 8, 1982, on, entire families displaced from the community of Estancia de la Virgen began arriving. They had very few belongings with them. They came from various neighboring communities and were fleeing the army's persecution.

Since the group was large, between 1,000 and 1,500 families, it was very difficult to find refuge. In Estancia de la Virgen, "they asked for shelter" but couldn't find it because the population of that *aldea* had also started to flee and... there wasn't enough space for everyone... Their only alternative was to stay on the banks of the Pixcayá River, about an hour's walk from Estancia de la Virgen...

Around eight in the morning, after the soldiers surrounded the area, they began to shoot at a large group of men, women, and children. The soldiers "used grenade-launching rifles and the shots came down like rain."[14] From the other side of the river, forces from Polytechnic School machine-gunned people. The ground forces were supported by a helicopter from which soldiers fired on those that were desperately trying to escape.

Few were able to save themselves. Since those displaced were from other villages, they were unfamiliar with the area and didn't know where to run. Then, the army started a fire... "They set fire to the forest... many died in the mountains, because of the fire."[15]; "The Army burned the whole mountain, to force the people out and kill them as they ran."[16]

Even newborns were killed, "suckling babies and one-year-olds were thrown into the river and there they drowned."[17]

One of the soldiers throwing the children in the river said, "Adiós niños. (Good bye, children)"...[18]

By ten in the morning, no more gunfire was heard. And, by the time the operation was over, the fire had gone out.

The Pixcayá River, which represented the possibility of survival for those displaced from San Martín, became a tragic scene of destruction and death, "The river turned red with the blood of the dead."[19]

Between 300 and 400 unarmed civilians died on March 18, 1982, as a result of the Guatemalan Army's massacre. The displaced families, who fled the soldiers' attack, had all been killed. After the massacre, some of the soldiers went on toward the village of San Antonio Las Trojes de San Juan Sacatepéquez... They gathered the men in the village and forced them to go down to the Pixcayá with them, to bury the dead that had fallen along the banks of the river...

On March 30, the inhabitants of the village met and decided to send people to the capital to report what had happened. They went to the U.S. embassy and also to the Guatemalan government, where they were received by Jorge Serrano Elías, who presided over the State Council in the time of Ríos Montt, "...As a result, a foreign commission came and this calmed the situation a little."[20]...

It is common to hear the inhabitants of Estancia de la Virgen speak about those buried in the legal cemetery, on private land, in a common grave, and in a clandestine cemetery, as well as those eaten by dogs and birds of prey. Those who know the locations of the remains of their dead, visit them, and adorn those places with flowers. Some are anxious to have them buried in an appropriate way, clearly identified, so that, at last, their loved ones can rest in peace...

4

Massacres

The CEH documented a total of 626 cases of massacres committed by the Guatemalan Army, security forces, and paramilitary structures, such as the PAC and military commissioners...In addition, 69 percent of the arbitrary executions documented by the CEH were committed during massacres as well as 41 percent of rapes and 45 percent of torture. The massacres represented the most intense expression of the state's repressive power.

In 63 percent of the massacres documented by the CEH, the army acted alone, while in 27 percent it forced members of the PAC or military commissioners to participate. Around 3 percent of massacres were attributable to members of the PAC acting without the army present as well and 1 percent of massacres were committed by military commissioners acting without the army present.

The massacres during the first fifteen years of the armed conflict were generally committed against the *campesino* and Ladino populations in the departments in the eastern part of the country where the earliest guerrilla units operated. In contrast, during the deadliest period, from 1978 to 1984, military operations following the counterinsurgency plan were mainly concentrated in Mayan communities in five of the departments in the *altiplano*. During this time, 95 percent of all the massacres...were committed...

These statistics reveal the magnitude of the massacres as part of the army's military operations to destroy the internal enemy. Through the application of counterinsurgency strategy, hundreds of communities were destroyed in different parts of the country during the armed conflict. The methods used in these mass killings reveal the level of cruelty with which perpetrators mercilessly treated their victim, all of whom were unarmed civilians.

It is not possible to understand the impact of the massacres through statistics alone. Understanding requires a qualitative analysis of this ruthless violence that reveals the logic of the strategies and military tactics used as well as the terror caused to the targeted population.

Selective and Indiscriminate Massacres

One of the key elements of selective massacres was a specific method for identifying individual victims. Perpetrators used various mechanisms of selection including lists of names carried by the perpetrators and the use of a "signaler," a person that was generally hooded and identified alleged guerrillas or their collaborators to the perpetrators...

It is important to note that in many of these cases, the "signaler" had been previously captured and then tortured to ensure his participation in these types of operations...

> That day, the soldiers arrived with a guerrilla who was masked and tied up. He had a sort of hat on his face...they gathered the women in one place and the men in another. They put them in five lines, then the guerrilla walked among the men five times...saying "This one, yes. This one, no"...The guerrilla walked like a crazy man. He couldn't walk well and could barely hold himself up. We saw part of his face and it was swollen and bruised. Perhaps he had been tortured...After he had identified thirty-seven or thirty-eight, the Army forced us to sharpen sticks like those you use to plant corn...The lieutenant said to us, "You know how to use machetes" and they forced us to attack our own brothers with machetes. We cut the heads off of some the arms off of others. Some withstood a lot and experienced a great deal of pain. In the end, some were nothing but pieces, others didn't die. "Why didn't this one die?" the lieutenant asked. "Don't you know how to use this type of weapon?" and then he shot those who hadn't yet died...Then, they forced the men to dig a big hole for the bodies. The corpses are still there.[1]

The cases of selective massacres are of particular interest to the CEH, because they reveal with great clarity the prior work of the intelligence services in the planning and objectives of these operations...

In the indiscriminate massacres...there was no specific selection of victims. They were committed while residents were in their communities going about their daily activities, working in the corn fields, walking from one place to another, buying things in the market in town. The state forces killed whomever they found, in their homes, on the road, or at places of work, often after surrounding a location...

> The soldiers entered the community on October 20, 1982 and carried out the massacre on the 22nd. They killed everyone they found there, except for one person who managed to escape and is the only survivor. Before starting the executions, the women were separated from the men and raped. Everyone was denied food for two days. On the day of the massacre the soldiers in the unit woke up the men and forced them to dig a ditch. Once this task was completed all of the members of the community were forced to line up around the ditch and each one was asked where the communists and guerrillas were. When they didn't respond, a lieutenant gave the order to kill each of the victims with a machete, even the children. After the bodies fell in the ditch, the lieutenant gave the order to finish them off with a burst of a machine gun. Then the troops looted the houses, burning them afterwards and eating all of the animals left behind. Before leaving the place, they hacked up the corn and bean fields with machetes and set them on fire...[2]

This type of massacre is important because it demonstrates state planning in targeting groups of people as the objective of these criminal acts. That is, people were targeted simply for belonging to a group identified as the enemy, regardless of the particular characteristics of individual members of the group. These repressive patterns are one element of the determination that genocidal acts were committed...

Military Tactics

In general, soldiers entered communities in a rapid and unexpected manner, making the most of the element of surprise. In many cases, the army arrived in the community in the early hours of the morning, surprising people in their homes while they slept or were getting ready to leave for work...

In other cases, the army not only used the element of surprise, but also engaged in deception, taking advantage of people's naiveté to prevent their possible escape. Early on, they took advantage of people's trust in the military as well as their fear of the terrible consequences of disobeying the army's orders...

The CEH has shown that, in many massacres, the army entered on important days for the communities, such as holidays and market days when they knew that the people would be gathered together.

> One Sunday in May 1981, it was market day at the San Francisco de Cotzal *finca*. As on every Sunday, there were many people gathered from several villages close to the *finca*... At midday, one hundred armed men in plainclothes arrived by truck, under the command of the leader of the Cotzal military base...They surrounded the main plaza and the leader ordered everyone to form a big line...[3]
>
> It was Holy Thursday, the population of Cocob was getting ready for the holiday. In the morning, the community was surrounded by, "nothing but *Kaibiles*, nothing but soldiers, big and strong"...They said, "It's clear you're guerrillas, which is why you're all gathered here." The community was destroyed.[4]

According to the information gathered by the CEH, the PACs participated in one out of every five massacres involving state agents. Whether they were from surrounding communities or from the victimized community, the PACs were forced to follow the orders of commanding officers, under the threat of losing their own lives.

> We all know what the men did in the massacre at the cemetery, forced by the soldiers. All of them had some family members and they killed their families, their brothers. But, we know that they were forced to do it and, at the time, we knew that you had to do what the soldiers said because if not, we were all going to die. But, the pain always remains, the suffering that they killed their own brothers. The fear has deep roots, it is brutal to see how our own people killed each other...only bad ideas brought *la violencia*, ideas of stealing, taking, abusing...[5]

There were also cases in which the PAC acted without the army. In these massacres, the patterns were similar to those followed by the armed forces. Most likely this is because they previously participated in similar operations or received military training for that purpose. Generally, *patrulleros* explained that they were carrying out the army's orders. However, even in those cases where the PAC acted alone, they were never punished for the acts that they committed and, in some cases, perpetrators received commendations from the authorities...

In almost all of the operations that led to massacres, the army used a variety of mechanisms to instill terror...Once a community was surrounded or placed under control, the people were often gathered in one place, usually a meeting hall, or in front or inside of a public building, like a church, government office, court house, or school...The massacre then became a spectacle of killing that the public was forced to watch...

The participation of the PAC and military commissioners was an important factor in generating terror. By forcing them to commit torture, kill, mutilate corpses, and destroy communities, they involved civilians in the massacres, converting victims into victimizers. This allowed terror, humiliation, and feelings of guilt to continue after the massacre, especially in those cases where perpetrators remained in the same community with their victims...

> They made us kill our brothers. That we can never forget. We continue living with that burden. It is worse than if the soldiers had killed us. We have that painful memory in our thoughts forever...[6]

The different tactics that the army used to generate terror revealed that there were no limits to the severity of punishment for collaborating with the insurgency, or simply, for participating in local development projects or Catholic Church programs. These acts were viewed as crimes that justified an absolute disregard for people's lives and dignity. The systematic criminalization of victims through the army's discourse emphasized that people and their leaders were responsible for the massacres as a result of "their crimes" or perhaps that the guerrillas "had put ideas in their heads"...

Destruction of Communities

The army destroyed what they considered to be the potential sources of the insurgency's support and sustenance, also...making it impossible for those that managed to escape to return and rebuild their lives following a massacre.

> The Army forced us to destroy what the neighbors had planted, because they said that with the corn the guerrillas could eat well.[7]

> On that day, July 2, the Army burned down the entire town, the houses, our crops, animals, everything. That was deeply sad and it left us poor. Those from the Army killed our people...[8]

The destruction of communities should not be understood solely in terms of material devastation and includes other types of harm. It is important to recognize the impact of the mutilation and desecration of victims' corpses, the ban on burying relatives by their surviving families, and the impossibility of conducting mourning and burial ceremonies used by Mayan communities to honor the life cycle. Out of fear, survivors often did not return to their homes or did so days later, little by little, finding corpses decomposing or eaten by animals.

> One saw it all, the dogs were eating the cadavers, the women's braids were sticking up out of the ground, a dog carried a piece of a child in its mouth, there were vultures eating bodies…[9]

In this way, the army systematically attacked cultural, spiritual, and religious elements of life that held deep meaning for the people. There were many cases of contempt and cruelty directed against Mayan community's elders who played a central role in cultural and spiritual life. The army also destroyed crops, especially corn which has profound spiritual significance within Mayan beliefs. And, they desecrated temples, religious imagery, and sacred sites.

> They destroyed our sacred places, destroyed our sites and offended us by killing our guides, our priests, our elders.[10]

> On August 25, at six in the morning, a platoon of soldiers arrived and started grabbing ten of the elders [all Mayan priests]. They took them away and killed them…They kicked them. They brutalized them. They took them naked, wearing only underwear. They tied them with chains. They made their arms swell. They broke open their cases, they ripped apart their papers, and they stole their money…[11]

The majority of the massacres were committed in regions where the insurgency had established itself, was gaining support, and had intensified its military activities. The army considered many communities in those areas to be guerilla collaborators or potential supporters, since the ideology of the insurgent groups addressed the peoples' experiences of extreme poverty, marginalization, and injustice.

Faced with this situation, the army high command decided to conduct a strategy of mass killing against the civilian population in order to destroy the threat of insurrection and regain control over these communities. They did this with the clear knowledge that the guerrillas lacked arms and had limited military capacity and with an understanding of the partial or total defenselessness of the people they attacked.

Massacre at Las Dos Erres

On December 5, they received orders to go to Las Dos Erres, a community that military intelligence considered to be sympathetic to the guerrillas...

At around five-thirty in the evening, the troops gathered and were ordered to dress themselves as guerillas, with olive green shirts and pants and carry the types of arms commonly used by the insurgents...The objective of dressing like the guerillas was, "so the people would be confused and think that it wasn't the Army committing the killings, but the subversives."[12] They identified themselves with a red cloth tied on the right arm so as not to get confused during the attack...

At around nine at night two civilian trucks left in the direction of Dos Erres, carrying fifty-eight *Kaibiles*...At eleven at night...the group arrived at the "entrance" to Las Dos Erres, leaving their trucks and walking six kilometers to the village, reaching the place at around two-thirty in the morning on the following day, December 6, 1982.

As soon as the *Kaibiles* arrived, they violently removed people from their homes. They went from house to house. They gathered the women and children in two churches and locked the men in a school. The men were interrogated one by one and they searched all the homes, but found no weapons or propaganda and did not discover any guerillas. Between four-thirty and five in the morning one could hear

> ...some screams for help; a young girl or an adolescent, about fourteen years old, was screaming...they raped this girl behind the church.[13]

After having gathered the entire population together, at around six in the morning, the patrol leaders consulted their superiors over the radio and, once they received their orders they informed the rest of the group that they were going to "vaccinate"[14] the inhabitants after breakfast...At two in the afternoon, they threw a newborn, three or four months old, into a dry well. That is how the massacre began...

All of the minors were executed with blows from a sledgehammer to the head, while the smallest ones were held by their feet and smashed against walls or trees. Then, they were thrown down a well.

Meanwhile, the men, women, and some children remained "locked up in the churches and the school, you could just hear their prayers and cries."[15] In addition, "some of the specialists began to rape the young girls."[16]

Then, the *Kaibiles* took charge of the men, women, and the elderly. These were taken, one by one, blindfolded, out of the school and the churches and led to the edge of the well, where they were forced down on their knees. They were asked if they were part of the insurgency and who was the head guerrilla in the village. If they didn't answer, or claimed they didn't know, a *Kaibil* instructor beat them with a sledgehammer. Just as they had done with the children, they hit them on the skull and later threw the corpses in the well. This went on all day long on December 6.

According to an ex-*Kaibil* who participated in the massacre, on the nights of December 6 and 7, the soldiers again raped the girls that were still alive as well as various women that they had divided among themselves, "I could see how they fought for the minors to rape them..."[17]

On December 7, the *Kaibiles* began indiscriminately killing men and women. Some were executed by smashing their heads with a sledgehammer and others with firearms...

> ...one of the men managed to remove the blindfold after falling into the well. He survived the blow to the head and, on seeing himself on top of the rest of the corpses, he insulted one of the Kaibiles who was at the edge of the well. He fired at him with his Galil rifle and, when he saw that he hadn't died, he threw a fragmentation grenade at him.[18]

The last victims of December 7 were not killed right away. According to the statements documented by the Public Ministry of an ex-*Kaibil* who participated in the massacre:

> When the well was almost full, some people were still alive. They raised themselves up, trying to get out of the well, but they couldn't. They asked for help and called out to God. Afterwards, while they were covering it over, you could still hear the victims' cries and tears.[19]

Those that were still alive were held in the churches and the school. On the nights of December 7 and 8, they pointed their weapons at the women and made fun of them. Again, they raped of them, just as with the girls. They started beating the men.

> They grabbed them by force...They put them in a line. There was also a line of men with weapons to the left, right, in front, and behind. Then they told the people in the church, "Come out." When they entered the churchyard, you could hear machine gun fire. They said, "Listen, those are sons of bitches...we don't want them and we're going to do away with all of them. We'll kill them..." Then they started taking the women by force, kicking and beating them, grabbing them by their hair, they took them to a place below the school...Around two minutes later, they said, "Leave them here." They left them and shots were heard, gunfire, and then a single scream. You could hear the cries of children, older people, women. With the gunfire you could hear how they killed them, another fifteen or twenty shots as if they were finishing off whomever was left...Then the men came back, taking out their cartridges and putting in new ones...They were laughing, as if nothing was wrong.[20]

The men who were still alive were taken to the mountain, where their throats were slit and they were shot. In this way, "the people of Las Dos Erres were finished, there was no one left."[21]

The group of *Kaibiles* had finished killing all the inhabitants of Las Dos Erres except a boy who had hid in the bushes and managed to save himself. That night, the troop of *Kaibiles* celebrated the massacre, "...they were happy with the way they killed a particular person and how there was no one left."[22]

In the morning of December 8...

> ...A group of people arrived at Las Dos Erres. There were about fifteen of them counting the children, including a child that was only a few days old. When the soldiers saw them arrive, they thought of killing them and throwing them into the well since there were so few. But, when they went to see if people could still fit in the well, they found a hand sticking out as if perhaps there was someone was still alive and was trying to get out. So, the soldiers began filling up the well with more earth.[23]

Since no more people could be put in the well, they led them to a place a half hour up the road and they shot them there, leaving the bodies strewn about.

Once the group of *Kaibiles* had finished, they left Las Dos Erres and went through the mountains in the direction of San Diego, La Técnica, close to the border with Mexico.

The soldiers took two girls, ages sixteen and fourteen from the last group of victims and they dressed them the same to make it look like the rebels and not the army were responsible for the massacre, since "the guerrillas always carry women along."[24] They kept them for three days, raping them repeatedly and "when they became bored with them,"[25] they strangled them...

In February 1994, the *Asociación de Familiares de Detenidos-Desaparecidos de Guatemala* (Association of Detained-Disappeared Relatives of Guatemala, FAMDEGUA) requested an exhumation from the lower court judge of San Benito, Petén. In July of that year, the work began under the direction of the *Equipo Argentino de Antropología Forense* (Argentine Forensic Anthropology Team)...They managed to exhume the remains of ten people...The investigative work restarted on May 2, 1995...

On November 24, 1995, the prosecutor in charge of the case asked to be relieved due to the threats that he had received, and the supporting plaintiff (FAMDEGUA) asked that a special prosecutor be named. The case was transferred to the Public Ministry's Office of Special Cases...Later, a special prosecutor was named for the case. In September 1996, faced with the slow pace of the investigation, the representatives of FAMDEGUA decided to submit the case to the Inter-American Commission on Human Rights (IACHR)...

The destruction of the Las Dos Erres community was not an isolated act, but rather the culmination of combined acts of intelligence, displacement, and control of the population that could not have occurred without the knowledge and approval of the army's high command...

5

Rape and Sexual Violence

Rape was committed in a systematic and widespread manner by state agents within the framework of the counterinsurgency strategy. Rape became a weapon of terror in serious violation of international human rights and humanitarian law...Sexual violence caused suffering and profound long-term consequences for direct victims as well as for their families, partners, and communities...

Documenting the sexual violence that women suffered presented various challenges...One of the main difficulties that the CEH faced was women's silence regarding the violations they experienced. In most cases, this silence had lasted for years and extended to the victims' closest relatives:

> I have never spoken about how the soldiers raped the women, much less that they had also abused me...I am going to the grave with this...No one can know...My children don't know, *el señor* doesn't know...No one knows...[1]

> It is not easy for a woman to dare to mention that she was raped and even more difficult for an indigenous woman.[2]

According to the testimonies gathered, few of the indigenous women who were victims of sexual violence shared their pain with other women who were also victims of this type of violence, increasing their isolation and sense of guilt. In fact, the pain they suffered has not generally been acknowledged as such. This is evident in the use of qualifying euphemisms to refer to rape. The victims or witnesses used the verbs *"pasar"* ("to pass") or *"usar"* ("to use") instead of *"violar"* ("to rape") as in "the soldiers *pasaron con ellas*" ("the soldiers passed time with them"), *"las usaron"* ("they used them")...

In most cases, the suffering of women who were rape victims is not known even among their relatives—children, partners, or parents—and in those cases where the community knows about what occurred it is silenced and denied, a factor that creates a sense of great shame among surviving victims and their communities...

The fact that state agents were the perpetrators of these violations, mainly army soldiers...creates mistrust on the part of indigenous women toward institutions identified with the state which exists apart from their culture and community. This further contributed to the fact that the victims do not file complaints regarding what occurred. In addition, the absolute impunity that protects those responsible for sexual violations increases women's sense of insecurity, especially when those who committed these acts, such as former members of the PAC or former military commissioners, continue to live in their communities.

The stigma that Maya women victims of rape face creates intense fear of rejection by families and communities. Some survivors of sexual aggression fled to other communities to avoid living with the shame of being marked as a "raped woman." These women have had to live with the fear of "being discovered" and the anxiety that others will blame them.

The main interest of the women who spoke about the sexual violence they suffered is seen when they explain that they have told their stories "so that it doesn't happen to others" and so those responsible will be punished. In addition, the lack of possibile reparations contributes to the ongoing silence...

Despite the difficulties in receiving testimonies regarding human rights violations committed against women, the CEH registered 9,411 female victims...and 1,465 cases of rape...Rape was committed alongside other human rights violations. According to the testimonies received, sexual violence was systematically linked with violations against women's freedom and massacres. Based on the database, in 25 percent of rape cases, victims were arbitrarily executed...The testimonies suggest that many women that were detained...were also raped.

> The soldiers would say, "we're getting fresh meat." All the women were raped day after day. The truth is that every woman who was captured, no matter the age, was raped. At all times of the day. Soldiers lined up to abuse them. Later, they executed them and those responsible laughed about the way they died.[3]

Regarding ethnicity, 89 percent of identified victims of rape documented by the CEH...were Mayan, 10 percent were Ladina and, 1 percent belonged to other groups. The ethnic groups most affected were K'iche', Q'anjob'al, Mam, Q'eqchi', Ixil, Chuj, and Kaqchikel...Two-thirds were adult women (between eighteen and sixty years old), a third were girls (newborns to seventeen years old), and 3 percent were elderly...

Based on an analysis of the testimonies, the CEH has established that...members of the army carried out massacres against indigenous communities that involved sexual violence against the women...On March 13, 1982, members of the army and members of the PAC of a neighboring community carried out a massacre of Achí women, boys and girls in Río Negro, Rabinal, Baja Verapaz.

> They gathered the women. They played marimba and forced them to dance...they accused them of dancing at night with the guerrillas. They took the younger women aside and raped them. Then they forced them to walk...up into the hills...They hit the women a lot. They told them they were cows. They treated them as if they were cows being taken to pasture...the majority of the women were there naked, raped...[4]

Women and girls that were captured in areas of displacement or whose families had accepted amnesties were raped by soldiers...This violence was committed and designed to destroy the will of those captured by heightening feelings of guilt, weakness, impotence, and failure...

> A woman was systematically raped by the soldiers, sometimes in front of her husband. The man couldn't bear the pain and rage about what they were doing to his wife as he watched and couldn't do anything.[5]

The CEH also learned of...cases that occurred at the military bases in Lancetillo and San Miguel Uspantán and in reception centers for those who accepted the amnesties.

> At night they came in to rape, usually the ones who had only one or two children, the young ones. But, one night, they played marimba and raped everyone...I will never be able to forget that. The soldiers were going to kill us if we didn't let them and I had to protect my daughter's life who was very young. I didn't want to and the soldier forced me...[6]

In the few cases where women who were victims of these violations by state agents dared to file a complaint, officials either blamed them or refused to receive them:

> There was a state of terror. Neither the judge nor the mayor nor the police could be trusted because the people that worked there were the same ones who forced the women, saying that what happened to them was their fault...The courts were not independent...Also, at that time, doctors were prohibited from treating these cases, whether they involved those wounded or women that had been raped...[7]

Women were used as a means of punishing men that the security forces had decided were enemies, thereby extending abuse beyond activists to their partners. In this way, women from families with men accused of collaborating with the guerrillas were victims of sexual violence. Mothers, wives, companions, daughters, sisters and even neighbors were indiscriminately raped...

> When they arrested her husband, the soldiers forced her to cook for them. She agreed so that they would free her husband. Fifteen soldiers raped her in front of her husband who, at that moment, was hanging from a tree. She was seven months pregnant...[8]

Rape was also used as a method of intimidation against women that went to the military bases to file complaints regarding the disappearance of their relatives...

> A woman entered the church to ask about her husband. Her daughter went with her. They told her, "He's here." They let her in and they raped them in front of all the soldiers and detainees.[9]

According to the information collected by the CEH, the army used sexual violence systematically and with absolute impunity as part of the counterinsurgency strategy. Sexual violence was ordered by superior officers and occurred within a context that ensured impunity for this violation, demonstrating its use as a weapon of war...

Selective rape was used against alleged female guerrillas, as well as against women who were leaders or members of social, political, student, or rural organizations, unions, or were human rights activists. These rapes were typically committed while the women were detained and occurred alongside torture. These acts were often followed by the death or disappearance of the victims... A significant number of selective rapes occurred in urban areas throughout the armed confrontation...

Despite all the difficulties in documenting the gender-based violence women experienced during the internal armed confrontation... It is important to recognize the courage of those women who dared to tell their stories, despite the fact that this forced them to relive their suffering.

Maya K'iche' Women Victims of Rape in the Department Of Quiché

In the department of Quiché, *la violencia* began with the persecution of community leaders, priests, and Catholic activists, creating a general atmosphere of terror.

In 1980, the army intensified its efforts to dismantle the community organizing of *Acción Católica* (Catholic Action) and the *Comité de Unidad Campesina* (Committee of Campesino Unity, CUC), believing that those organizations were linked to the guerrillas.

As a result of this repression, the Catholic Church left the department in mid-1981. At that time, the army occupied Catholic churches and convents in almost every municipality, establishing military bases and using these facilities as centers for detention, torture, and execution, ensuring increased control over the population. The army also occupied other public buildings, such as schools and municipal halls. From that moment on, the population of Quiché experienced ongoing human rights violations. Rape was one of the most significant violations suffered by women and it was often followed by the execution of the victim…

In one military operation, a group of soldiers surprised a woman and a girl with insurgent propaganda. The witness recounts:

> Then the captain gave the order. That son-of-a-bitch ordered two soldiers to grab the young girl and he raped her, just like that. He kneeled down, calmly removed his gear, lowered his pants and he said, "Hold that girl down, *muchá*" and he raped the poor woman…He raped the younger one too. Then, he let the rest of them rape her…[10]

Girls who were out working also became rape victims. A nine-year-old was surprised by soldiers next to the stall where she sold things by her house at the edge of the highway in Xepol, Chichicastenango. They took her home, locked her parents in a room and the girl in another. They raped her and then tossed her aside, severely injured…

In the municipality of Chinique:

> …following the interrogation, the wife [of the murdered man] was raped consecutively, about fifteen times, by the soldiers as well as by the men dressed in plain clothes…[11]

The army and the PAC detained women. The data suggests that this was often done in order to rape them…This practice was frequent in the military bases and other places used as prisons, "The civil patrols raped her for eight days at the base."[12]

On Sunday, March 15, 1981, soldiers coming from the San Miguel Uspantán base entered the community of Macalajau and captured a young K'iche girl who was sixteen years old. They took her to the base and tortured and raped her.

In San Bartolomé Jocotenango, some women were illegally detained for over a year. Besides suffering all types of sexual abuse, they were forced to cook and clean for the soldiers and members of the PAC.

In March, 1982, at the base set up at the convent in San Andrés Sajcabajá, various women from different communities were detained for around three months. During their captivity, they were repeatedly raped. They were also forced to serve the soldiers and the *patrulleros*. They had to wash their clothes, cook their food, and take care of all sorts of cleaning...

In many cases, women were raped because they were accused of collaborating with the guerillas, either as members of the insurgency or as relatives of insurgents...In March 1981, a sixteen-year-old girl was brutalized:

> They accused her of collaborating with the guerrilla, because her brother had been burned in the Spanish embassy. Her father had already been tortured and disappeared. She had a sewing machine in her house because she worked for the cooperative...It was very easy to accuse her of making clothing for the guerrillas...The family was in the CUC which is where she worked...She was raped and tortured. She gave out the names of CUC *compañeros* without knowing anything about the guerrillas...[13]

Various women accused of being guerrillas spent six months in detention at the Uspantán convent that was occupied by the army, "At night, the soldiers came in to rape the young women."[14]

When the women were alone and defenseless in their homes, they were sometimes accused of being guerrillas and were called on to turn in their husbands...Others were removed from their homes by force and raped in the countryside. Even minors suffered these rapes.

In other cases, members of the PAC, relying on accusations, demanded that women have sex with them and, at times, when they resisted, they raped and killed them. There were times when the *patrulleros* accused entire villages of collaborating with the guerrillas. Based on this, they locked the women in their homes, raped them, and immediately set the houses on fire...

According to some witnesses of the massacres, sexual violence against women occurred with the acquiescence of the troops' commanding officers. The soldiers knew that they would be allowed to commit rape. The women were considered as the spoils of war and were sometimes offered as an incentive or gift to the troops:

> Then I called another one, a private first class soldier... "Soldier," I said to him, "Take care of the lady"... "She's a gift from the second lieutenant"... And, he called the other guys saying, "There's meat, guys." That's what he said and then they came, grabbed the girl, and took that young thing. They all raped her. Truthfully, it was a mass rape.[15]

There are many testimonies from direct victims and relatives that describe the cruelty of these acts:

> The soldiers gathered many women and children and they locked them up and burned them. Also, they raped the women before killing them. They cut off their breasts, ears and hands...[16]

Women who were wounded as they fled were at risk of becoming prisoners and being raped. There are many documented cases of this practice...

> At five in the morning the PAC surprised them as they slept in a hidden place. So, they started running away. The PAC caught up to them at six in the morning because they were tired from running through the countryside. The PAC shot Doña Petrona and her little girl and another young daughter stopped running and stayed there where her mother was killed. They used machete strikes and left them in pieces where they were captured. The oldest daughter was tortured and raped until twelve noon and they killed her with a machete. Her name was Petrona Ramos...[17]

The shame that women who have been raped are subjected to by society has prevented victims from denouncing these acts. In addition, the dominant climate of impunity has made victims' complaints useless, and it has been impossible to initiate criminal cases against perpetrators.

The trauma of rape survivors is a legacy of ongoing suffering.

> The evil can't be cured. You carry it with you and try to get over it. The damage done by rape cannot be fixed...After the rape, you feel so empty, as if you're less than nothing...[18]

6

Genocide

Guatemala ratified the Genocide Convention on January 13, 1950, and...it was in force during the time of the armed confrontation. The CEH used this international instrument as the legal reference for its investigation and analysis of genocide.

Article II of the convention defines the crime of genocide and its elements as follows:

> In the present Convention, genocide means any of the following acts committed with intent to destroy, in whole or in part, a national, ethnical, racial or religious group, as such:
>
> a)   Killing members of the group;
> b)   Causing serious bodily harm or mental harm to members of the group;
> c)   Deliberately inflicting on the group conditions of life calculated to bring about its physical destruction in whole or in part;
> d)   Imposing measures intended to prevent births within that group;
> e)   Forcibly transferring children of that group to another group.

The acts defining genocide have remained constant up until the present day. For example, the Statute of the International Criminal Court, adopted at an international conference in Rome on July 17, 1998, describes the crime of genocide in exactly the same terms.

The convention outlines several objective elements of the acts described in Article II that define the crime of genocide as well as a subjective element requiring that the action be carried out with "the intention to destroy in whole or in part."

...The convention establishes that the protected groups or potential victims of genocide must be national, ethnic, racial, or religious groups...It is very important to distinguish between "the intent to destroy a group in whole or in part," that is, the positive determination to do so and the motives behind such intent. In order to prove the crime of genocide, it is only necessary to demonstrate that there exists an intent to destroy the group regardless of motive. For example, if the motive to destroy an ethnic group is not pure racism but rather a military objective, one would still define the crime as genocide.

An act meets the requirements of the crime of genocide as defined by the convention even if it is part of a larger policy that is not strictly aimed at physical extermination. In this sense, it is significant to distinguish between a genocidal policy and acts of genocide. A genocidal policy exists when the final objective of the actions is the extermination of a group, in whole or in part. Acts of genocide exist when the final objective is not the extermination of a group, but rather other goals of a political, economic, military, or other nature, while the means used to achieve these objectives involves the extermination in whole or in part of the group…

Methodology

In order to determine if the acts that were committed were indeed genocide, the CEH used the legal framework of the convention and…jurisprudence for the following types of analysis: Analysis of the general policies of the state, particularly the National Security Doctrine that guided the Guatemalan State's counterinsurgency strategies and provided support for understanding the context in which the acts occurred and the intent with which they were committed.

- Diachronic analysis linking time with acts and places, as well as synchronic analysis linking acts and places with perpetrators and victims. This analysis was based on the acts described in sections "a," "b," "c," "d," and "e" of Article II of the convention. The analysis was carried out chronologically, examining links between the acts outlined in the convention and the intent underlying those acts, followed by a review of the sequence of acts and their common characteristics with the goal of establishing whether or not the acts of violence committed by the state and its agents occurred in a structured manner that was directed in a discriminatory way against a specific group or groups within the population.
- Analysis of those acts that violate, or that the perpetrator considers to violate, the integrity of the group, occurring simultaneously with acts of physical destruction within the same operations. This form of analysis included acts that, based on a review of the means used, indicated an attack on the integrity of the group, such as rape and sexual mutilation, torture, public executions, the exhibition of cadavers, the destruction of material elements of culture, and so on.

The period of analysis, between 1981 and 1983, is when the greatest amount of violence was documented. Similarly the analysis focuses on set regions and certain ethnic groups. The CEH determined that these groups and regions were where the majority of human rights violations were concentrated. Based upon these criteria and available analytical methods, it was possible to conduct an investigation of what took place among four selected ethnic groups in four regions of the country:

- Maya Q'anjob'al and Maya Chuj, located in northern Huehuetenango in Barillas, Nentón, and San Mateo Ixtatán;
- Maya Ixil located in Nebaj, Cotzal, and Chajul, in the department of Quiché;
- Maya K'iche' in Zacualpa, department of Quiché;
- Maya Achi in Rabinal, Baja Verapaz

The selection criteria were the following:

- Intensity of violence (largest number of victims);
- Patterns of violence (indiscriminate violence);
- Composition of victims (identifiable groups)
- Quantity of information

Of course, this investigation was limited by the circumstances in which the CEH operated. The CEH was only able to document a portion of the human rights violations that occurred during the internal armed confrontation. This has made it necessary to correlate quantitative data regarding levels of destruction or extermination with other sources, such as the REMHI project and the database of the *Convergencia por la Verdad* (Alliance for Truth).

To ensure the greatest accuracy of the sources, analysis, and statistical review, a system of control and fact-checking was created specifically for these investigations. The system involved random checking of samples from the CEH database, and the use of other databases as references to evaluate the work of the CEH.

For quantitative analysis, the CEH database established the percentage of the human rights violations by comparing the intensity of violence in each region to its demographic base. At the same time, there was a comparative analysis of the violence against the indigenous and nonindigenous population in each region in order to establish if discrimination existed. In this way, the CEH examined whether there was a substantial difference between the quality and severity of human rights violations suffered by members of one group in comparison to another.

The CEH analyzed its sources exhaustively. For each region, there was a careful examination of the cases presented as well as the case studies, individual and collective testimonies, declarations by key witnesses—including agents and ex-agents of the state—and contextual reports. Maps were produced, including those related to military operations and the presence of the guerrillas in the regions. This information was compared with other sources such as army and guerrilla campaign plans, press reports, declassified documents from the U.S. government, and field investigations.

In principle, this process allowed those factors that caused human rights violations to be distinguished from those that were noncausal, eliminating the possibility that the CEH was only analyzing consequences. At the same time, this process allowed for the use of independent analytical variables as controls, guaranteeing objectivity regarding the data gathered. The independent variables included, among others, the command structure of the armed forces; the guerrilla's political and military interest in the regions analyzed; recognized norms of international humanitarian law; and, the conditions of the noncombatant, civilian population...

Victim Group

The convention identifies the protected groups as ethnic, national, racial, and religious. There are subjective and objective elements in the definition of these groups. A racial, national, religious, or ethnic group is one that identifies itself as such—a subjective element of identity—which, at the same time, is viewed by the rest of society as distinct, based on particular common elements such as history, language, physical characteristics, religious practice, location within a specific territory, or particular norms of behavior. In other words, national, racial, religious, and ethnic groups possess social, cultural, and economic elements that distinguish them from other sectors of society...

Of the various understandings of group referenced in the convention, the CEH used the notion of an ethnic group. Among these, it was possible to investigate what occurred among...the Maya Ixil, the Maya Achí, the Maya Kaqchikel, the Maya Q'anjob'al, the Maya Chuj, and the Maya K'iche'. In some of the selected regions, two or more ethnic groups live together. The Maya Q'anjob'al and Maya Chuj live in Huehuetenango in the northern part of the municipality of Nentón, the municipality of San Mateo Ixtatán, and in Barillas. The K'iche', Q'anjob'al, and Q'eqchi' live alongside the Ixil, who are the majority in the areas of Nebaj, Cotzal, and Chajul, in Quiché.

In these cases, the CEH understands indigenous people as a group through which ethnic groups identify themselves as part of a larger entity and are perceived as such. That is to say, they understand themselves and each other to be indigenous as does the larger Guatemalan society, including state institutions that recognize this status. In those cases where two or more ethnic groups live within the same region, they are understood to be members of a single Maya group.

For an act to qualify as genocide, the convention requires that the act be committed with intent to destroy a group in whole or in part. The phrase "in part" is understood as "a reasonably significant number relative to the total of the group, such as all or a significant section of the group, such as its leaders"[1], that is, a substantial part of the group is required. In order to determine if one is dealing with a substantial part of a group, one must recognize perpetrators' destructive capacity as directed toward the possible extermination of a group.

The destructive capacity of perpetrators was determined, in each case, by the area of control over which they were able to engage in acts of extermination. For example, acts of genocide committed by a military unit operating in a specific region would only be analyzed in relation to the particular ethnic group found in that region. To determine if a substantial part of the group there was affected, the CEH's analysis reviewed what proportion of the ethnic group was in the area under the perpetrators' control.

General Policies

The human rights violations described below, occurred within the framework of the "counterinsurgency" war, also called the "counter-subversive" war as defined by National Security Doctrine. The fundamental principle of this doctrine was to prevent the transformation of existing social, political, and economic systems. According to the doctrine, strategies were to be implemented in all areas of society, including "the political sector," the "socioeconomic sector," and the "psychosocial sector."

In accordance with National Security Doctrine, the army defined the "annihilation of the internal enemy" as a strategic objective of the counterinsurgency war. The army understood the internal enemy as composed of two categories of individuals, groups, and organizations: those who tried to overthrow the established order through illegal actions and represented "revolutionary communists" and those that, while not being communists, still sought to overthrow the established order.

This doctrine also affirmed that the "counter-subversive" war defined the population as its "objective" because it considered the war to be one of "subversion," in which the guerrillas tried to achieve their goals through the population's active participation. In this sense, the general population was "the environment in which their activities took place."[2] Thus, according to the doctrine, it was necessary to recover or maintain that population's support and force them to actively participate in the war in favor of the government.

From the 1970s on, when the guerrillas operated in the eastern region of the country where the majority of the population is Ladino, the army began to conflate the Maya population of the *altiplano* and the enemy. The 1972 Manual of Military Intelligence G-2 expressed this clearly, "The enemy has the same sociological characteristics as the inhabitants of our *altiplano*."[3]

In the 1980s, the army came to identify indigenous people as the internal enemy. The army believed that the guerrillas had succeeded in addressing the historical grievances of the *altiplano's* majority indigenous population by appropriating their demands regarding poverty and the lack of available land.

> The great indigenous masses of the nation's *altiplano* have found their interests addressed by the subversive's claims which have become their issues such as the lack of available land, immense poverty and after many years of consciousness-raising they view the Army as an invading enemy...[4]

The army believed that "the great indigenous masses" of the *altiplano* constituted the social base of the guerrilla movement.

> Having succeeded in winning over the great masses of the population, especially indigenous people, the subversive factions were able to declare liberated zones in the *altiplano*...[5]

The armed forces' perception was shared by civil servants in the government. In this way, Francisco Bianchi, secretary of president Efraín Ríos Montt, not only identified the indigenous people with the guerrilla, but stated that the result of this identification would be elimination:

> The guerrillas won over many Indian collaborators, therefore the Indians were subversives, right? And how do you fight subversion? Clearly you had to kill Indians because they were collaborating with subversion.[6]

One aspect that enabled the army's identification of indigenous people with the enemy was

> …the de facto discrimination, exploitation, and injustice which the indigenous people of Guatemala suffered by virtue of their origins, culture, and language.[7]

Racism polarized Guatemalan society, dividing it into two major groups: indigenous people and Ladinos. Racism played a central role in the ideas and practices of Guatemalan society's dominant classes in relation to "the *indios.*" … [8]

In this way, racism was an ideological element of the general social context that enabled the army to link the indigenous people … with the insurgents. Moreover, racism heightened the sense of indigenous people as distinct, inferior, almost less than human, outside the world of ordinary moral obligations, making it less difficult to kill them …

Analysis of the Regions

The following sections analyze events in regions that the CEH investigated. All these events took place in the context of the "counterinsurgency war." During this war, the state implemented a plan, one of whose objectives was "annihilating the guerrilla and parallel organizations"[9] to achieve "the reestablishment of law and order, gaining the support of the population to become citizens."[10] An analysis of human rights violations reveals that military operations took place in three stages.

The first was characterized by selective repression, that is, violence directed against individuals or specific sectors. Selective repression also continued in later stages alongside other forms of violence. The second stage was characterized by mass repression including policies of destroying *aldeas* and persecuting displaced survivors. In the third stage, human rights violations continued through the imposition of mechanisms of reorganization and control of the population that survived the prior stages, with the goal of preventing the resurgence of those social structures that existed before the conflict and ensuring that all civilian activity occurred under complete military control.

The three stages formed part of a general strategy aimed at annihilating the enemy. For this reason, it is necessary to analyze them together. Clearly, it was during the second stage when most of acts were perpetrated that fall under the definition of international crimes specified in the convention. These include indiscriminate massacres, mass sexual violations, public torture, bombings, and killing refugees and displaced people. The first stage helped the army obtain information on those places where they later chose to institute mass violence as a counterinsurgency strategy. The third stage completed the work of "pacification" by placing survivors under military control to prevent the resurgence of any type of organized opposition. Violence continued to increase until it peaked in 1982. Violence continued in 1983, but underwent a transformation. Acts of "annihilation" were gradually replaced by actions designed to "capture, organize, reeducate and incorporate into society people who had recognized the amnesty."[11]

Region I (Maya Ixil People): Municipalities of San Juan Cotzal, Santa María Nebaj, and San Gaspar Chajul, Quiché

...The army viewed the Ixil people as different and distinct from Ladinos. The distinction between Ixil and Ladinos is clear throughout the military document "Appraisal of Civil Affairs for the Ixil Region," which reviews regional characteristics and contains a series of claims that express value judgments on the nature of the Ixil population. For example:

> Attitude of the population: as a result of their historical and ethnic characteristics, the Ixil population rejects cooperating with ladino authorities...as a result of their particular sociological characteristics, they have always been mistrustful, especially towards anything related to ladinos.[12]

The perception of the Ixils as a population with "special characteristics" derives...from an interpretation of the Ixil people's acts of resistance in the country's recent history...The Ixil ethnic group was not only perceived as distinct, different from the Ladino group, but also as antagonistic to authority, to economic power, and to Ladinos in general...

The army expanded the use of the label "insurgents" to specifically reference the Ixil people as the enemy without distinguishing between the civilian population and combatants...In a 1982 document, the United States Central Intelligence Agency reviewed the army's perspectives and actions regarding combat in Quiché as follows:

> The belief, well-documented, of the Army that the Ixil indigenous population is totally in favor of the EGP, has created a situation in which one can expect that the Army will leave no survivors equally among combatants and non-combatants...[13]

Members of the military high command made similar claims during that time:

> The idea regarding the other *aldeas* was that those who were not with the guerillas went to [the municipal seats of] Nebaj, Cotzal or Chajul. The rest were with the guerrillas.[14]

The army's determination that the population of the Ixil area were the guerrillas' social base—providing food, recruitment, places for refuge—was clearly a factor in unleashing the repression, since one of the army's strategic objectives was to deny the guerrillas' access to the population that constituted their base of support...

Through this identification, all Ixil were considered to be subversives and, during the course of military campaigns, there was no attempt to distinguish between members [of the group]. In other words, the Ixil became targets as a result of their identity, as such, even though the motivation may have been primarily that of a strategic-military nature...

The definition of the Ixil ethnic group as the enemy led to the creation in 1981 of...Operation Ixil. This military operation used a specific strategy that took into account the sociocultural characteristics of the Ixil people and emphasized the importance of an

> ...intense, profound, and carefully prepared psychological campaign to impact the Ixil mentality and make them feel part of the Guatemalan nation...[15]

Material expressions of Mayan identity such as *traje* (traditional dress) and language led to threats and abuse. In Guatemala, *traje* expresses a strong identification with a specific ethnic group. The use of particular *traje* identifies women with their communities of origin. Ixil women were identified and persecuted for wearing their *traje*...

> She and her family were able to make it to the *Costa Sur* to work, but other people couldn't because they would be killed between Santa Cruz and Sacapulas. They would be killed when the soldiers recognized they were from Nebaj. [Also] in Patulul, Suchitepéquez they killed people who were identified as Ixiles by the women's *cortes* (traditional skirt). They were accused of being guerrillas. In order to survive, a woman had to change her *traje* to K'iche *traje*...[16]

At the beginning of the 1980s, the army identified the Maya Ixil people with the insurgency and consequently with the internal enemy...As a result...the army engaged in acts to partially annihilate the Maya Ixil people. The military campaign plans explained that there were three possible courses of action to follow with respect to the enemy: "elimination," "annihilation," or "extermination."...

From 1980 to 1983 the army perpetrated acts of violence against community leaders...Formal authorities such as mayors and auxiliary mayors were attacked...Members of the Catholic Church were especially victimized...Traditional Maya authorities were also victims of repression...Such acts constitute premeditated attacks deliberately aimed at the leadership and, through them, at the group itself...The actions against the leadership had an enormous impact on the community, and materially and morally weakened traditional, organizational, and conflict-resolution structures:

> Then the Army heard...that they coordinated among various families. That's why the Army began to control that too. That's how they cut relationships among

families. That's when they destroyed traditions, the way of life...that existed among the people. Because people always knew how to defend themselves, how to provide justice for certain problems. But, the war started, *la violencia*, and that is where this was forgotten...[17]

The specific targeting of community leaders for repression reflects...the intent to partially destroy the group that is a subjective element of the crime of genocide. As indicated, the leaders are those in charge of guiding the group, and executing them destroyed the groups' organizational structure. This is especially true in the case of the Ixil, where religious authority coincided with political authority...

To date, there have been fifty-two massacres documented by the CEH and other sources in Nebaj, Cotzal, and Chajul, where 88 percent of the population was Maya Ixil. However, 96 percent of the victims belonged to this ethnic group. This means that almost all of the victims from the region were Maya Ixil...None of the massacres were directed against the Ladino population...

Indiscriminate massacres were a form of aggression directed against entire *aldeas*. This mechanism of repression expressed an understanding that the Ixil people in their entirety were in favor of the EGP. Actions were not taken against individuals, whether supporters or not, but against the group...It did not matter what people did or did not do. They were considered enemies simply for being members of a particular group...

The CEH only recorded three massacres in which the [targeted] villages were not burned. All of the other *aldeas* where massacres occurred were physically destroyed, either during or after the massacre. In addition, many other *aldeas* were burned and destroyed where no massacres occurred because the population had fled...

One of the aims of the scorched earth operations was to "clear" the area of its population. Those who were not killed were forcibly displaced to other regions...However, the intent went beyond the metaphorical objective expressed by the phrase "drain the water to kill the fish." Once the goal of depopulating areas was achieved, persecution continued against the population in the places where they sought refuge, and again they suffered massacres and destruction of their crops. In other words, the acts of destruction and persecution defined and expressed an intent to exterminate.

According to the data gathered by the CEH...between 70 and 90 percent of the communities in the Ixil area were destroyed. When communities managed to recover, the army would attack them again, destroying their homes and food to make it impossible for them to survive. In some places the army returned as many as three times to burn houses and farms, as the community of Xoloche explained:

How many times did they burn [the community]? The first time was 1981. Then, in 1982, they returned to burn our house, just like this wooden house with roof tiles, a good house...In 1983 we built our house, but they burned it again. When we returned again, we made small huts, very small ones...We heard when they were coming and we hid outside. When we came back our houses were gone. They burned them and we rebuilt them again because if not, where else would we live?...[18]

During indiscriminate massacres carried out in the Ixil area, the army victimized the most vulnerable members of the community, especially children and the elderly...Such acts could not have had any military purpose...

Oh, lots of people died, since '82, so many people. There were massacres, everything. There were women who had just given birth, they were burned. Children, too, were burned...How could a baby possibly be to blame? It was the most difficult time, the most difficult...[19]

The CEH determined that the combination of violent actions perpetrated by the state against the Maya Ixil population during the period from 1980 to 1983 constituted acts of genocide...in that one of the objectives of the military counterinsurgency campaign was the partial destruction of the victim group as a means of defeating the enemy. The state adopted this position based on its determination that the Maya Ixil population had a historic propensity for subversion and were, or could be, a base of support for the guerrilla movement in this region. This perception equated the identity of the entire Maya Ixil population with that of the guerrilla and led, during a period of the armed confrontation, to a campaign oriented toward the partial destruction of the Maya Ixil population...

Region II (Maya Achí People): Municipality of Rabinal, Baja Verapaz

Rabinal was not a combat zone. Although some guerrilla actions occurred, these were mainly for propaganda purposes. The region was used for passage, for obtaining supplies, recruiting members, and as a rearguard. Geographically, the municipality is located on the border of areas where different ethnic groups live—Achís, Ki'ches, and Pocomchis—and in a corridor that provides access from Guatemala City to Alta Verapaz and the area of Ixcán, Quiché. For these reasons, the army viewed the entire area to be of strategic importance and decided that it must be under its complete control...

In the period between 1981 and 1983, military or paramilitary groups assassinated at least 4,411 people in Rabinal which represented 20 percent of the population. The level of violence in the region cannot be explained by the prevalence of combat since...this was not a zone of conflict and all of the victims were civilian noncombatants. The brutality with which the area was attacked supports the conclusion that the army considered it to be a strategic area and, at a certain point in the conflict, identified the region's population as an internal enemy.

Nearly 100 percent of the victims identified by the CEH were members of the Maya Achí people. The high percentage of Maya Achí victims, much higher than the distribution within the population (82 percent Maya Achí and 18 percent

Ladinos) demonstrates that...violence was specifically directed against the Maya Achí population...

The main targets of selective repression were community leaders. In Rabinal, they executed catechists, health promoters, and auxiliary mayors. Detentions or executions were based on accusations that they were guerrilla supporters or guerrillas...When they weren't executed, leaders were tortured until they collaborated with the army...The authority of the traditional leaders and auxiliary mayors was supplanted by that of the military...Targeting the leaders of different sectors of the group for repression increased the group's vulnerability and threatened its continuity since previously, these leaders were in charge of managing and resolving conflicts within the group.

In the Rabinal area, the CEH recorded twenty massacres, although as is true for all information in this report, those massacres documented by the CEH represent only a portion of the actual total. According to one witness, "There was no village where there was not a massacre."[20]...In these situations, there were deliberate efforts to increase the number of victims, such as taking advantage of a market day, as in Plan de Sánchez; or surrounding and cordoning off the community, as in Río Negro...In no case did massacres occur simultaneously with or as a consequence of confrontations between the army and the guerrillas...

Massacres were accompanied by the destruction and burning of property. In the north of Rabinal, the region near the Chixoy dam was completely razed...ten communities were destroyed: Río Negro, Los Encuentros, La Laguna, Agua Fría, Comalmapa, Jocotales, Chitucán, Los Mangales, Pacaal, and Hacienda de Chitucán...

The intentional destruction of homes, tools, harvests, and domestic animals caused hunger, exposure, and illness. Killings and the destruction of property were carried out simultaneously or in succession within the same communities. Both actions were part of a common pattern of acts directed against the group...There were two choices for communities: rapid death by a machete or bullet or probable slow death from hunger or illness...

As a result of the repression, especially the massacres, many communities abandoned their villages...Generally, people stayed in the mountains near their *aldea* with the goal of returning to their community once the army had left...

> Every time the Army arrived I would hide in the mountains with some thirty Achí families. This went on for two whole years. We would plant and the soldiers would destroy the crops. We couldn't survive living like this. So, I had the idea of going to live in Trinitaria to save my life...[21]

During the mass repression, children, women, and the elderly were the direct victims of violence. In 1982, the killings in at least four massacres were aimed at these groups, "They kicked the children to death. The children screamed and screamed, and then they were silent."[22] In some cases, massacres were predominantly directed against children, like the second massacre in Río Negro, in which 107 children died, or the massacre of Agua Fría, where thirty-five children that had fled the massacre in Los Encuentros were executed...

In communities such as Río Negro or Pacux, children were forcibly trans-ferred to other communities, where they were given new identities...the children suffered serious psychological trauma by being forced to live with those who they had seen kill their parents and siblings...

The CEH determined that the array of human rights violations carried out by the state against the Maya Achí population during the years 1980–1983 con-stituted acts of genocide...The goal of the military campaign carried out in the Rabinal area was the partial destruction of the Maya Achí people. This was seen as a necessary prerequisite for maintaining absolute control over a militarily strategic area and for separating the guerilla forces from their presumed social base...

Region III (Maya K'iche' People): Municipality of Zacualpa, K'iché

The army labeled the population in Zacualpa as the enemy and a target for elimi-nation because of the municipality's strategic location and as a result of guer-rilla presence in the area. According to the CEH's findings, at least 1,215 people were subjected to human rights violations, representing almost 12 percent of the municipality's population.

However, the army did not label the entire population as the enemy, but only the Maya K'iche' population. Over 99 percent of the victims were Maya K'iche' and less than 1 percent were Ladino (around 10 percent of the population is Ladino)...

In Zacualpa, repression was directed against religious, political, and rural development leaders. Among the main victims of the selective repression were the members of Acción Católica, Mayan priests, CUC members, and participants in community development groups and cooperatives. Victims were identified on the basis of their leadership and, in many cases, leaders were executed at the same time or together with their families...

The disappearances of leaders deeply impacted community life...The leaders were replaced by military commissions and heads of the *patrulleros*. The army named functionaries to replace democratically elected authorities. By attacking leaders and repressing all forms of communal organization, the army attacked the foundations of the Maya K'iche' community of Zacualpa...

The first selective massacres were directed against members of the CUC and Acción Católica. Later, after the *patrullas* were created...massacres against entire families began. The army executed men, women, children, and the elderly, often by burning them inside their homes...Soldiers would arrive in the morn-ing, surround the community, search from house to house, rape the women, and then kill them with everyone else...In some cases they tortured victims before executing them...

It was a Sunday, at four in the morning when they arrived...The Army came to destroy the *aldea* of Piedras Blancas. They burned the people in their houses while they were asleep; men, women, children, everyone together...They stabbed them and then threw them into the flames while they were still alive...in other houses, the soldiers tortured the victims by cutting off their tongues before killing them...[23]

The massacres were committed as part of a military plan that targeted the non-combatant civilian population. In all cases, military attacks were carried out without facing any form of resistance or combat...

There were torture centers in almost every community...Under threat of death, the army would force *patrulleros* to torture and execute people...

With everyone together, they would call out those that were on the list. They separated the victims and took them to a wooded area and tied them up. Then the soldiers ordered the *patrulleros* from Tunajá to give a machete blow to each of the people that were tied up. One *patrullero* refused to torture his neighbors. He was kicked and badly beaten by those from Cruz Chich.[24]

This pattern was followed in Turbalá, Trapichitos, Pasojoc, Tunajá, and San José Sinaché...By forcing civilians, neighbors, and relatives to abuse each another, the army engaged in acts directed against the group's core beliefs. The acts were carried out in front of many people, which heightened the sense of terror...

The CEH finds that the crimes committed by the military against the Maya K'iche' from 1981 to 1983 constituted acts of genocide...The objective of the military campaign in the Zacualpa region was the partial destruction of the Maya K'iche' people...The CEH did not document any indiscriminate massacres in Zacualpa targeting the Ladino population. In fact, in some cases, Ladinos were warned so that they could flee the community before the killing began...

Region IV (Chuj Maya and Q'anjob'al Maya Peoples): Municipalities of Nentón, San Mateo Ixtatán, and Barrillas, Huehuetenango

The Maya Chuj and Maya Q'anjob'al live in municipality of San Mateo Ixtatán, to the north of the municipality of Nentón, and in the municipality of Barillas...Conditions of extreme poverty and the need to migrate to the *Costa Sur* created a state of ongoing tension in the north of Huehuetenango...The Maya Chuj-Q'anjob'al group was perceived as rebels and distinct from the Ladino group, as well as antagonistic to authority and particularly skilled at organizing to pursue their interests...

Military intelligence viewed the indigenous people of Huehuetenango as "very difficult to infiltrate"[25]...Statements by military intelligence described how the indigenous people from the north of Huehuetenango were especially dangerous enemies, describing how the population had been influenced ideologically:

The people [have been] changed by the insurgency in their ways of thinking, feeling, and acting...Our units have encountered great difficulty in reaching the population as understanding and communication between our people and the indigenous people is extremely difficult as a result of language, background, and customs which present an insurmountable barrier to our efforts to approach them.[26]

The reference to background, language, and customs describe what being an ethnic group means to its members...What the army called "background" was linked to a history that, in the case of indigenous Maya groups, is associated with an oppressed culture dominated by the state and capable of rising up "at any moment." "Language" was seen as a marker of social cohesion. The perceptions of "us" and of "custom" describe specific ways of living that define a group. In this way, military intelligence identified and clearly defined this group as inaccessible and characterized by insurmountable barriers that were key elements of its identification as an enemy group.

In defining the enemy, the analysis of military intelligence was especially stark, dividing the country into two regions: those areas inhabited by indigenous people, "the problem is even more serious where the percentage of indigenous people is higher as they have openly expressed their opposition to the Army"[27]; and, those areas inhabited by Ladinos..."the situation is a bit more favorable where Ladinos live as they have demonstrated support for the Army."...[28]

Military intelligence refused to acknowledge the historical causes of the dissatisfaction of indigenous people, such as Guatemala's agrarian problem and its extreme poverty. [Instead] they suggested that the guerrilla movement's increasing success in mobilizing [the Maya population north of Huehuetenango] was because of the the indigenous people were "easy to manipulate"...rather than recognizing them as a "mass" capable of rebelling in unison. Still, the army viewed the guerrilla movement as so vast that it included a total of 20,111 members in the area of Huehuetenango. This belief contrasts starkly with information provided by the EGP, specifically from ex-combatants of the Ernesto Che Guevara Front that affirmed they never had more than fifty-two armed men...

Political violence [in this area] unfolded in three stages. The first was characterized by selective repression directed primarily against community leaders, members of the Catholic Church, and deputy mayors. This type of violence began in the 1970s. The second stage, from 1981 to 1983, was designed to destroy the communities and "eliminate their population." Political violence in this phase was massive and indiscriminate. The third stage began in 1983 when abuse was more selective and was characterized by persecution, displacement, population control, social and political reorganization, and "reeducation" and psychological campaigns to "reclaim" the population...

In 1981, a chief priest named Mamín was publicly decapitated, along with four other people.

On July 19, 1981, the soldiers of the Army killed my father in Chimban. My father was a Maya Chief Priest. He was eighty years old and had been living in Chimban for two years. Some 150 soldiers arrived in Chimban, coming from Soloma and Jacaltenango. Some forty soldiers arrived at my father's house. They brought out a hooded man and that is how the soldiers took my father from the house. I followed the soldiers to the place where they killed him. First they interrogated him, saying that it was clear that he was a guerrilla. Then they started stoning him, and they split open his head. Afterwards they chopped him with machetes until he died. They cut off one of his arms and the soldiers took the arm in all the neighboring villages to teach the people what happened to "subversives." ... [29]

Between 1981 and 1982 in Chuj and Q'anjob'al area in the north of Huehuetenango, the CEH recorded nineteen massacres ...

The Army entered the municipal capital of San Mateo from Barillas. They got out of vehicles behind the town in the *cantón* of Yoltán and from there they entered, setting fire to the first houses of the town, machine-gunning men, women, and children, massacring thirty-five people. They also killed the municipal treasurer and stole money from the city hall, painting the letters "EGP ARE ASSES." The next day the same military men returned to the municipal center to investigate what occurred, registering them in the municipal books as natural deaths ... [30]

The vast majority of communities in the region suffered forced displacement ... [often] lasteing from four to six weeks although, in some cases, continuing for two years or more. By 1983, there were 43,000 officially registered [Guatemalan] refugees, 53 percent of whom came from Huehuetenango ... The Guatemalan Army persecuted those who fled ... In 1983 alone, there were fifty-two incursions by the army registered in refugee camps in Chiapas, Mexico ...

During the massacres carried out in the north of Huehuetenango, the army victimized the most vulnerable members of the community, especially girls, boys, and the elderly ... Forcing people to witness abuses created permanent trauma for many people, especially children.

What we have seen has been terrible. Burned bodies, women with their bodies pierced by stakes and buried as if they were animals ready to be cooked ... children massacred and stabbed with machetes, and women killed like Christ. [31]

The CEH recorded at least seven massacres where all of the children were executed ... Killing children was not an excess or accident; these were premeditated assassinations ...

Acts of sexual violence were committed where women, especially young women, were present. The CEH registered cases where soldiers specifically went to look for women from communities to rape them ... Collective rapes were committed during most massacres ...

The CEH finds that the crimes perpetrated by the armed forces against the Q'anjob'al and Chuj Maya populations of northern Huehuetenango constituted acts of genocide ... Testimonies from various sources and an examination of official documents reveal the repetitive and mass nature of these operations and their logical and coherent execution leading the CEH to conclude that these acts were committed with full prior knowledge, participation, and backing of the military ...

Conclusions

In the four regions studied regarding genocide, the CEH found that the violence was massive and overwhelmingly impacted the Maya people. In the Ixil and Rabinal areas, 15 percent of the population were killed, while in the north of Huehuetenango and Zacualpa 4 percent and 9 percent were killed... The proportion of Maya victims was much greater than the proportion of Maya in the general population relative to Ladinos. In the Ixil area, 98 percent of the victims were Maya. In the northern Huehuetenango, the proportion of Maya victims was 99 percent, while in Rabinal it was nearly 100 percent, and in Zacualpa 98 percent.

These overwhelming percentages indicate that human rights violations were directed in a purposeful, discriminatory manner against the Maya population in these areas. Generalized discrimination against the Maya people can also be seen in the way that the army systematically executed leaders of the Maya community. In 1981 and 1982 in the four regions analyzed, the army executed the majority of... religious leaders such as catechists, Mayan priests, representatives of *cofradías,* and members of Acción Católica [as well as] development workers, participants in community-based organizations such as CUC, members of cooperatives, and political leaders such as deputy mayors...

After analyzing the data from the four selected geographic regions, the CEH determined that during a specific stage of the internal armed confrontation—1981 and 1982—the army identified the Maya people as an internal enemy. It did so because it believed that they constituted or could constitute a base of support for the guerrillas... Inspired by National Security Doctrine, the army expanded the concept of internal enemy beyond guerrilla combatants, militants, or sympathizers, to include membership in certain ethnic groups.

The CEH concluded that, taken together, these destructive acts were directed in a systematic manner against groups of the Mayan population. Among these acts, the elimination of leaders and criminal acts against minors, cannot be understood to serve a military objective, demonstrating that the only common factor among all victims was their membership in an ethnic group. These acts were committed "with the intent to destroy in whole or in part" the [Maya] groups (Article II, first paragraph, of the convention).

Among those acts directed toward the destruction of the Maya groups identified by the army as the enemy, the most significant was "killing" (Article II, subsection "a" of the convention), most powerfully expressed in massacres... involving the participation of regular and special forces of the army, *patrulleros civiles,* and military commissioners. In many cases, survivors identified the perpetrators, such as the officers who commanded the operation, as being from the nearest military base.

Careful analysis has allowed the CEH to conclude that, in almost all of these cases, the perpetrators' objective was to kill the maximum possible members of the groups... In studying what occurred in the four regions, the CEH has established that alongside mass killings—which on their own were adequate proof of an attempt to eliminate groups defined as enemies—army units or *patrulleros civiles* systematically committed acts of extreme brutality, including torture and other cruel, inhuman, and degrading actions. The effect of these acts was to terrorize the population and destroy the basic elements of social cohesion between members, particularly when they were forced to witness or commit these acts themselves. Army units or *patrulleros civiles* engaged in collective sexual violations against women, often committed in public and designed to…harm the social reproduction of the group over time.

The CEH concluded that…perpetrators committed numerous acts "causing serious bodily or mental harm to members of the group" of the affected Maya populations (Article II, subsection "b" of the convention)…These acts corresponded with the intention to physically and spiritually destroy the groups.

The CEH's investigations proved that mass killings…were accompanied by the destruction of communities. The most notable case was the Ixil region where between 70 percent and 90 percent of rural communities were destroyed. Also, in the north of Huehuetenango, Rabinal, and Zacualpa, perpetrators razed entire communities…

The CEH concluded that among the acts previously described…some were "deliberately inflicting upon the group conditions of life calculated to bring about its physical destruction in whole or in part" (Article II, subsection "c" of the convention)…The CEH's analysis shows that committing these acts required coordination of the military system at a national level, which enabled the "efficient" actions of soldiers and *patrulleros civiles* in the four regions…

All of these issues have convinced the CEH that these…were not isolated acts or excesses committed by troops out of control or improvised actions by mid-level army officers. With great dismay, the CEH concludes that the massacres and other human rights violations committed against these groups reflected high-level policies. They were strategically planned, as is manifested by acts that express a coherent and logical plan…

In considering all of the available options to combat the insurgency, the state chose the one with the highest cost in terms of the lives of noncombatant civilians…The state made this decision despite the fact that they had adequate sources of information to identify insurgent combatants, analyze their military capacity, and distinguish them from civilian noncombatants.

As a result, the CEH concluded that agents of the Guatemalan State committed acts of genocide against the Maya people that live in the Ixil region, Zacualpa, northern Huehuetenango and Rabinal during the counterinsurgency operations conducted in 1981 and 1982…

Based on the basic conclusion that genocide was committed…the CEH affirms that that the intellectual and material authors of the crimes are, unquestionably perpetrators [of genocide]. The genocidal acts committed in Guatemala were also the responsibility of the state. This is because these acts were the result of policies established by high-level commanders, rather than the material authors of these acts…the military authorities knew about the massacres committed by their agents. These acts were never investigated or sanctioned to ensure that they would not occur again. The failure to investigate these acts is the responsibility of the military authorities, competent judicial bodies, and political authorities.

The state of Guatemala has never taken any action to investigate or sanction those responsible for these acts, despite the fact that many of them were well known publicly. This is evidenced by the multiple petitions presented before international bodies such as the IACHR, which required that the government investigate serious violations to the right to life in their visit to the country in 1982.

Finally, in relation to the crimes of genocide, the CEH concluded that the state of Guatemala...has violated Articles IV and VI of the Convention for the Prevention and Punishment of the Crime of Genocide. The convention requires that those persons who have committed genocide—whether they are government leaders, functionaries or private citizens—should be tried by a competent court of the state in whose territory the acts were committed or before a competent international criminal court...

Massacre at the *Finca* San Francisco, Nentón, Huehuetenango

On July 17, 1982, at ten in the morning, a large group of soldiers and a helicopter transporting a captain and four other officers belonging to Huehuetenango's military zone 19, arrived at the *finca* San Francisco. There was no guerrilla presence there...

They proceeded to gather the women and children in the church and the men and the elderly in the office of the auxiliary mayor. All of the men were searched, "at that time, I had a watch and money in a bag and they took it all."[32] A group of soldiers entered all the unoccupied homes and took many of the things they found including food, money, tape players, radios, and watches.

A survivor recalls that, around noon, they forced two of the residents to bring

> ...a pair of oxen that they were going to eat. They were going to have a party. That's what the leader told us, "But [the animals] have to be yours and not those of the boss."[33]

At around two in the afternoon, they took the women out of the church in groups of ten and twenty, although some escaped to their homes. Thirty soldiers followed them...The women were raped...then, they set fire to the houses. The women were burned alive.

They took the children out of the church...

> After having killed our women, they brought out our children, kids who were ten, eight, five, and four years old. They grabbed their legs and spun them around and killed them on the wooden posts of the houses. Those kids' brains were left in pieces like corn meal. I had six children, they all died...as did my wife. None of them survived.[34]

They moved on to the elderly...

> They started taking out the elderly. They lay them down on the floor and took a dull machete to their necks. The old men yelled. What had they done to suffer such pain? About fifteen old people died that way...[35]

Finally, they killed the men in groups. Pointing at them, they said, "Come on outside"...

> We were very afraid because we knew that they were going to kill us, just as they had done with our wives and children. We talked among ourselves. The soldiers said, "What are you thinking about? Why are you talking so much in there? We're not going to do anything to you." Some of us prayed to God to save our lives. There was nothing more to be done...I saw how they stripped my *compañeros*, taking off their shirts and using them to cover their eyes and tying their hands behind them and laying them face up and with a soldier to shoot each one...The rest of the soldiers grabbed people the way you would pull at a dead dog, dragging them

like animals, and taking them to the church, and leaving them laying there. They left the people in piles.[36]

At five in the afternoon, there were only around twenty *campesinos* at the office of the auxiliary mayor that were still alive. Four of them escaped through a window when the soldiers weren't watching. One of those who fled was caught and shot...but the other three managed to escape...

> ...I started to run and heard the soldiers say, "There goes another one." There was a stream of bullets behind me that sounded like stones being thrown. I hid...I ran back and forth and that's how they didn't kill me. Then as it was getting dark, I left and went under a macoya tree. I stayed there and thought, they might kill me here, but I was so worn out by the fear and the shooting...

Finally, they managed to find each other:

> We found each other halfway through the journey, a league from San Francisco. We went toward the Mexican border, arriving between four and six in the morning on the 18th. All night, we went through the rain and the mud, without any light, sometimes crawling, sometimes walking...[37]

One of the ones sent to get the oxen didn't want to return and he watched what happened from a distance. This witness confirmed that once the soldiers finished the massacre, they roasted the meat of the oxen that they had taken and ate, drinking and dancing to the music of the radio-tape players that they had stolen from the houses.

Before leaving, they set fire to the village.

In San Francisco, approximately 350 civilians died...The people in the neighboring *aldeas* knew what had occurred at the San Francisco *finca*. News spread across the region and this was one of the main causes for the displacement of the residents of the *aldeas* toward Mexico...The majority belonged to the Maya Chuj ethnic group.

Between July and August of 1982, almost 9,000 people fled to Mexico. The *aldeas* of Yolambojoch, Yuxquén, Santa Elena, Yulaurel, La Ciénega, Yolacatón, Buena Vista, Yaltoyá, and El Quetzal were completely abandoned...In 1984, forty-five *aldeas* and *fincas* were abandoned in the municipality of Nentón. Most of these *aldeas* disappeared...

7

Acts of Violence

The Guatemalan guerrillas had an obligation to comply with the laws of war and to extend humanitarian care, under all circumstances, to those not involved in hostilities as well as to victims of armed confrontations. Nevertheless, the insurgent groups often failed to respect these basic principles...

Of the five main violations, the majority of acts committed by the guerrilla groups were arbitrary executions... Most of the cases... were attributed to the EGP and the FAR. This is because both organizations provided important documents to the CEH including their "war reports" in which they admitted responsibility for many acts, thereby demonstrating their commitment to fulfilling the CEH's mandate.

The CEH did not receive many complaints against the ORPA. While this could mean that the armed group did not commit significant violations of humanitarian law, the CEH cannot be certain especially because the organization did not submit its "war reports."

In many cases, victims accused "the guerrillas" for acts without specifying the name of the organization, either out of fear or simply because they were unsure of who was responsible. While respecting the testimony of each of the victims, the CEH used other evidence to determine the actual responsible parties based on the admission by an organization of participation in particular actions, as well as the region and time period when the acts occurred.

Ajusticiamientos

The term *ajusticiamientos* is used by the guerrillas to reference executions of people outside of the insurgent organizations based on the pretext of applying "revolutionary justice"... During the conflict, the *ajusticiamientos* committed by guerrilla organizations were not isolated cases nor were they acts of rogue operatives. Rather, they were tactical acts with clear and defined strategic objectives documented in the organizations' writings and confirmed by their members and commanders in interviews with the CEH...

Ejército Guerrillero de los Pobres (Guerrilla Army of the Poor, EGP)

The EGP's first public actions were *ajusticiamientos*...From 1975 on, the EGP committed executions of "all those who oppress the people," in the different departments where its fronts operated. These were known within the organization as acts of "revolutionary justice,"...

> Don Chepe Sosa, was killed [in early 1980 in the department of Suchitepéquez] by the guerillas because he was abusive. They killed him near his plot of land...He was from the East...and when he was drinking he would to say that he would shit on an *indio*, wipe himself with him and toss him aside and, when he felt like it, he would shit on an *indio* again, wipe himself again and so on. He always boasted while drinking and carried a. 38 at his waist, saying that he would be ready for the day they came to kill him...He looked down on indigenous people...He treated the people of Santo Domingo badly...When they came for him, they told him to take out his gun and defend himself because *los indios* of Santo Domingo were going to kill him. And, they killed him...[1]

In the department of Chimaltenango, local leaders and municipal mayors were the victims of the political violence on the part of the army as well as the guerrillas...Gabino Tubac, a Kaqchikel, won the race for mayor of San José Poaquil in 1980 as the candidate of the *Movimiento de Liberación Nacional* (National Liberation Movement, MLN). His mandate lasted only three months, until March 3, 1980, when he was executed by members of the guerrilla in the town's main square.

Catarino Galindo Marroquín, Ladino, a native of Tecpán, was mayor of the municipality two times, from 1960 to 1962 and from 1978 until his death. He was known as "a Ladino from the town, powerful, who was abusive to indigenous people and discriminated against them."[2] He was executed by members of the EGP on November 16, 1981.

Filiberto Osorio Marroquín, was a Ladino and ex-military commissioner and the mayor of Patzún between 1981 and August 1982. He had a room with weapons at city hall and expressed his desire to "do away with the people of Chipiacul and turn the place into his own pasture."[3] He was recognized by some people when he accompanied the army during one of massacres in Chipiacul. He was executed by EGP members on August 31, 1982...

At some of these executions, the guerrilla asked the people's opinions in order to involve them in the decision and gain their trust.

> In April 1981, I was in Ixcán and I heard about the death of the mayor and the justice of the peace. It was an EGP *ajusticiamiento* because they were the ones who went around avenging crimes against the people [such as those] that forced people to bring water and firewood to their homes. The community asked for the *ajusticiamiento*. Many people decided on it and the EGP agreed to the *ajusticiamiento* at the right time. All of this was planned, prepared and happened in the month of March or April...[4]

In some parts of the *altiplano* the population informed the EGP who were oppressors and army informants by creating lists using a system similar to that used by the army to identify alleged guerrillas…At times, people's denunciations were linked with longstanding local conflicts between families over land or with other types of revenge…

According to representatives of the guerrilla organizations an *ajusticiamiento* was always preceded by an investigation of the complaints received from the population about the alleged collaborators:

> So as not to make the mistake of eliminating people who could eventually be convinced of the need for revolution…[5]

At times, they talked to those who had been identified to convince them to stop their activities.

> In some cases, before a collaborator carried out any massacres, he had to be eliminated so that he would be the one to die and not a lot of the *compañeros*. Other times, he would just be threatened, you would go to his house and warn him, "Look, man, you're doing this job, but stop it. The people you're killing are your neighbors, your people." Many saved themselves in this way by no longer acting as Army collaborators…[6]

Once a death sentence had been decided, the condemned person was not provided with an opportunity to defend himself. He was simply told the reasons for the decision, sometimes in private and sometimes before the people.

> The judgments were conducted during the meetings…They met with him and talked about everything, but there was absolutely no possibility of defending oneself. Once the decision was made, there was no escape. They didn't allow anyone to come to his defense. In every case, a meeting was arranged to explain the reasons why. And, it was often conducted in front of the entire population. They would say, "Here is this man and we're going to execute him because of this, this, and this." They didn't accept questions and even said, "No one from the audience should speak because we've already gathered all the information in the town and the majority of people wanted him to be shot."…[7]

Fuerzas Armadas Revolucionarias (Revolutionary Armed Forces, FAR)

The FAR's strategy involved *ajusticiamientos* of military commissioners and army collaborators. These actions were conducted along with their first military actions in the capital as well as in the eastern part of the country…

Many cases were reported in Captain Santos Salazar's war reports from the Southern Region:

> August 18 [1982], *aldea* of Chulate, Suchitepéquez, *ajusticiamiento* of two commissioners, recovery of two weapons.

> May 12 [1983]: at 20:00, in the *aldea* of El Semillero, Tiquisate, Escuintla, the head of the military commissioners of the place, Pedro Mexicano, was *ajusticiado*. Our forces didn't have any problems...[8]

Throughout the conflict, the FAR's strategies included the *ajusticiamiento* of army collaborators, called *confidenciales, orejas,* or *esbirros* (thugs). In June 1981, a FAR war report stated:

> At the El Salto ranch, at 8:00 PM, in front of the bus stop of the ranch near the city of Escuintla that goes to the capital of that department, the *esbirro* known as Salomón was *ajusticiado*. The reason for this *ajusticiamiento* is that he was an enemy of the union members. He participated in the handing over of a union leader of the previously mentioned *finca* and also participated in the massacre of the *Radio Tropicana* newscasters in Escuintla, an act that was known nationally and internationally...[9]

In some cases, prior to being executed, the victims received warnings:

> We didn't always arrived with our rifles and kill a commissioner just to kill him. Rather, what we did was warn him, "You're doing this and that, and making this mistake, and look, because of you people are dying." Then, instead of killing him, what we would do was make it clear that he shouldn't offer his assistance to the Army and continue committing crimes against his own people... Then, if those people didn't understand the warning, we would have to say, as a last resort, "Look, get out of here, go away because, if you stay here, you're going to have some problems, some very serious ones"...[10]

In some cases, the victim was tried by a "revolutionary court." On June 20, 1980 the FAR executed an ex-lieutenant of the army... who was the head of personnel for Coca-Cola. The FAR claimed responsibility for this action through a public communiqué:

> On the 20th, at 14:10 hours, a military unit of our Revolutionary Armed Forces engaged in an *ajusticiamiento* of the Army lieutenant and member of the G-2 Francisco Javier Rodas Flores, after he was tried by a revolutionary and people's tribunal and found guilty of serious repressive acts against the Guatemalan working class...[11]

Organización del Pueblo en Armas (Organization of the People in Arms, ORPA)

Since ORPA did not provide their war reports, the CEH has inadequate knowledge of its use of *ajusticiamientos,* making it difficult to present an accurate analysis of what occurred. Nevertheless, based on some of the cases presented to the CEH, it is possible to identify some common elements regarding ORPA's use of *ajusticiamientos...*

Military commissioners and army collaborators, *orejas,* and *confidenciales* were the most frequent targets…Sometimes, community members developed lists of army collaborators that were later turned over to ORPA members with the goal that they would later be executed:

> Note that we would say to them, "Look, we want a list of the Army's main collaborators, because we want to tell them that they have to leave because if they've caused a lot of harm this is what has to be done." Then, it was common for us [to receive] a long list with thirty, forty, fifty names and at the top, "This is the list of the *orejas* that have to be *ajusticiado*." In other words, they asked us to take care of them…[12]

According to a leader of the ORPA, the decision to execute someone was planned in advance:

> It was a very delicate situation, [the decision] was made at the command level of the front and on many occasions the commander-in-chief of the organization was informed. It was based on detailed and meticulous research of the testimonies of many of those affected…[13]

There were times following an *ajusticiamiento* when ORPA would leave an explanatory note, as in the case of the military commissioner Rufino Asunción Mejía y Mejía, who was executed by ORPA on June 12, 1985 in Santa Rosa in the Dos Marías *finca,* municipality of La Reforma, department of San Marcos:

> After executing him, ORPA left some typewritten papers in his pants pockets that said, "for collaborating with the rich"…He was killed with a bullet through the roof of his mouth.[14]

Ajusticiamiento of Patrulleros—Guerrilla Organizations' Policy against the Patrullas De Autodefensa Civil (Civil Defense Patrols, PAC)

From the second half of 1981 on, the army began to organize people into PACs…The guerrilla organizations were taken by surprise, facing a new phenomenon that involved turning their social base against them. At first, there was no clear directive regarding the actions they should take in response to the new situation…

ORPA's policy from the beginning was,

> "Not to consider the PACs as either political or military opponents, but to try to win them over politically."[15]

The rule was not to attack the civil patrols:

> It was our policy not to confront them, but rather, to communicate with them and to try to convince them politically that we weren't enemies.[16]

And, according to ORPA's leaders:

> The search for a good political relationship with the *patrullas* provided a sense of security because then the combatant felt like he wasn't fighting against the *campesinos* themselves, but was fighting instead against the clearly defined institution of the Army.[17]

At first, the EGP wanted to detain people so that they wouldn't organize themselves into the PAC. However, because of the army's fierce repression, they understood that joining the patrols was a means of survival for the people...

In 1983, the EGP decided to avoid occupying populations where there were civil patrols because the battles

> with these armed groups took place within the community resulting in casualties on both sides in the struggle. Naturally the bullets there in the center of town killed people who were not directly involved in the conflict.[18]

The EGP's ultimate position...was only to attack the army and not to engage with the PAC, even when dealing with "reactionary groups"...

> When they ran into a civil patrol, they asked the *patrulleros*, "Where are you going?" They responded, "We're going to the mountains" and identified themselves. "Don't do anything. We're guerrillas and we have no problems with you. Please understand us." And, we explained our goals. The *compañero* would say to the *patrulleros*, "You're poor, we're poor, and there's no reason for us to fight." They understood and didn't say anything.[19]

> In other places there were *compañeros* who committed real abuses...The only orders were that you had to pull back, that you weren't supposed to shoot at the *patrullas*, that they were *compañeros* who had been forced. For that reason, we couldn't attack them even if they called us cowards...but sometimes we couldn't hold back. Then we'd have to shoot and even to kill some of them...[20]

The perception of some *patrulleros* was that the guerrillas didn't want to kill them, "If they wanted to, they could have killed us"...[21]

The FAR, like the EGP and the ORPA, repeatedly noted that their orders, throughout the confrontation, were not to attack the *patrulleros*.

> Our policy never was to engage in combat against the *patrulleros*, never, never, because we saw it as a policy or main objective, not even a secondary issue. Pure and simple, we avoided combat with them because we were conscious that among the *patrulleros* were our *compañeros* and that they were forced...to carry out the tasks imposed upon them.[22]

Nevertheless, the FAR executed *patrulleros* as seen in their war reports. On August 15, 1982, members of the popular militia and combatants from the Tecún Umán Front executed

> the head of the paramilitary forces (civil patrols) of Quixcayá...together with 5 paramilitaries that accompanied him...[23]

24 of July [of 1983]: at 21:30 hours, commandos from our forces *ajusticiaron* the *esbirro* Oscar Cano Pérez, who led the Patrullas de Autodefensa Civil in the *aldea* Papaturro, department of Santa Rosa. Our forces withdrew with no problems.[24]

Fusilamientos

The term *fusilamiento* refers to arbitrary executions committed by the guerrilla organizations against those within the armed movement, that is, executions of insurgent combatants…

The leaders of the EGP first tried to promote self-criticism through warnings and in some cases, they chose political sanctions, such as expulsion from the organization. However, "in the cases of betrayal and rape, they used *fusilamiento*."[25]

> There was significant emphasis placed on self-awareness, disciplined awareness…Being conscious of discipline provided a lot of moral authority to the *compañeros* regarding warnings or punishments…Punishments were based on the *compañero's* dignity and were, above all, of a constructive nature…Most punishments I knew of involved taking away weapons or complete suspension from a particular position or participation.[26]

According to other testimonies, *fusilamiento* was used as punishment in very serious cases.

> …There were cases in which someone in command did certain things and didn't report them, and as such, without guidance, they went too far. And, when this was discovered, one of two things occurred, they were either expelled or other measures were taken against them…If they were really serious things, some were simply shot…[27]

In 1982, the situation became very difficult for the EGP since, by then, many people had been captured by the security forces. At this time, many detained members of the guerrilla informed on other members. Others were presented in the media where, after publicly admitting their militancy, they tried to convince members of the guerilla to abandon their struggle. As a result, many within the insurgency that were living in the city fled to Mexico and especially to Nicaragua, where they received political and military training.

This time was described by a member of the organization as

> …a period of great uncertainty with mistrust in the air. It was [terrible] for those that had fallen into the hands of security forces and the organization [had serious] internal political problems. In reality, things were in the midst of falling apart…[28]

Within the disciplinary rules of the FAR, the death penalty was used for the most serious violations…

> To impose the maximum penalty [death penalty] the authorization of the High Command is required as well as complete proof of the crime.[29]

The accused had the opportunity to defend himself before a "revolutionary court":

> For these reasons, a military tribunal will be created, allowing the accused full possibility of demonstrating his innocence. The procedures and mechanisms will be determined to ensure an impartial review grounded in reality and located where the crime was committed…[30]

In 1982 and 1983, the FAR was also going through a period of crisis…It was a time when many deserted the ranks of the FAR some of whom were punished through *fusilamiento*.

> They both wanted to leave…one heard the shots…a group went out to find the girl…They brought her to the camp and they said, who else wants to desert?…It was all a disaster because they shot the girl and it turned out that she was three months pregnant…[31]

ORPA also punished desertion through arbitrary executions…

Massacres

In June 1982, there were two cases of massacres [committed by the EGP]: one was carried out by the Augusto César Sandino Front; and, the other by the Ho Chi Minh Front. Their objectives appear to have been punitive and based on a desire for vengeance. In these cases, *patrulleros* and non-*patrulleros* were indiscriminately killed.

The first case was a massacre that took place in Papumay, Xenimaquín *aldea* in the municipality of San Juan Comalapa in the department of Chimaltenango.

Two accounts from the *Informador Guerrillero* (Guerrilla Informer) and the *Comisión de Derechos Humanos de Guatemala* (Guatemalan Human Rights Commission) attributed responsibility to the army. However, two witnesses recognized, albeit in different ways, the EGP's responsibility for the massacre, indicating that a key factor was the significant presence of the *patrulla civil* in the community.

> The PAC of Papumay became bolder, burning some of the houses belonging to the people of Patzaj and destroying some of the EGP's caches on the mountain. Later, during one of the PAC's patrols, they killed two combatants from the EGP patrol…In response, the EGP patrol decided to ambush the PAC. There was a serious battle. Many members of the PAC fell and the guerrillas recovered a lot of weapons…It's possible that the battle extended to the middle of the village and that there could have been victims that didn't belong to the PAC, although no one knows how many people from Papumay died that day.[32]

This first version viewed the massacre as resulting from the expansion of an action directed against the *patrulleros*. However a second version, by an ex-EGP combatant who said he had participated in the acts, indicated the EGP unit's specific intent to carry out a symbolic act to avenge the death of two of their combatants.

> The leader came up with an act of *justicia revolucionaria* and they implemented it. They went from house to house killing people. There were a lot of people there at that time...[a man] was bathing in a *temascal* (a traditional bath)...and they executed him right there, other people were eating or preparing [to eat] and they were also executed. The military objective was the *patrulleros* of the place, who were massacred, but they also killed everyone else so that the general population would learn that they shouldn't act against the guerrillas.[33]

On July 27, 1982, there was another massacre carried out by the EGP in the village of Chex, in the municipality of Aguacatán, in the department of Huehuetenango, where the Ho Chi Minh Guerrilla Front operated.

> About one hundred men dressed in olive green and heavily armed went into Chex and executed twenty-one people, many of them PAC members, but women, children, and the elderly also died. Eight people were injured. The survivors blamed the massacre on the EGP from the *aldea* of Chortíz [Santa María, Nebaj, Quiché] who were avenging the actions of the Army and PAC from Chex.[34]

In early 1982, Chex sought to create a civil patrol before the practice had become obligatory. Apparently, the military responded by suggesting that, in order to receive weapons, the community would have to hand over those that were involved with the guerrillas. At the end of June, soldiers from military zone 19 captured twenty-eight men from the *aldea* accused of being guerrillas. They were never heard from again. With the help of various Chex *patrulleros*, the army destroyed the *aldea* of Chortíz, massacring everyone. This led the guerrilla to take revenge on the inhabitants of Chex...

Kidnapping

Throughout the armed confrontation, the guerrilla organizations...carried out kidnappings for political objectives such as propaganda and prisoner exchanges as well as economic goals, "We needed to take things to that extreme to be heard in this country."[35]

From 1967 on, the FAR defined kidnapping for financial gain as one of their preferred tactics:

> Our enemies are the oligarchy (landholders and bourgeois) and Yankee imperialism and all of its participating agents...We will take advantage of any opportunity we have to tear away from our enemies some of what they have stolen, whether by taxes, in cash or in kind, in the city or in the country, voluntarily or under pressure, as is the case of kidnappings...[36]

On August 28, 1968, John Gordon Mein, the American ambassador to Guatemala, was executed when a guerrilla group tried to kidnap him...On March 31, 1970,...Karl von Spreti, the German ambassador was kidnapped by members of the FAR in the capital...They demanded the release of various detainees that, according to the insurgent's spokesperson, were at risk of being assassinated...also requesting a payment of $700,000. They set a time period [for the government] to meet these conditions...Then, they changed their minds...the body of the ambassador was found near San Pedro Ayampuc, seventeen kilometers from the capital.

A FAR leader told the CEH:

> The Government wasn't agreeing to the pressure...the command in the urban area executed the ambassador to show that they were not playing, that they were being serious.[37]

Toward the end of 1977, the EGP began to engage in kidnappings for economic gain...

> On December 31, 1977, the government advisor and ex-Cabinet Minister Roberto Herrera Ibargüen was kidnapped. To free the kidnapped man, the guerrilla organization asked for money for ransom, the publication of a communiqué in the press, and the release of a combatant from the organization that was in the Army's hands.[38]

On October 7, 1979, members of the EGP kidnapped Jorge Raúl García Granados as a way of impacting the economic elites...He was freed when the family met the conditions demanded by the guerrilla organization...

In 1980, the FAR continued to support kidnappings for economic gain.

> In the first days of June (1980), in the capital city, the businessman Hastedt Villagrán was captured. The prisoner was released after a corresponding war tax was paid.[39]

> At 7 hours 40 minutes on June 16, the businessman José A. de Lima was captured by two members of our organization...The captured businessman is the president of Nestlé-Cindal for Mexico and all of Central America. For his release, a war tax was paid as well as publication of a manifesto.[40]

The PGT also engaged in kidnappings. In March, 1982, Alvaro Contreras Vélez, columnist and owner of *Prensa Libre* was kidnapped.

> A group of armed men arrives at the house of the journalist Contreras Vélez, and told him that they had a message from the president's office and once they were inside they opened fire on one of the bodyguards, who was killed...[41]

A member of the PGT claimed, "The Party had Contreras Vélez in its hands...they were involved in a number of operations of this type."[42]

War Taxes and Other Forms of Extortion

During the armed conflict, the guerrilla movement demanded...material goods through violence, force, intimidation, and blackmail. A report by the *Asociación*

Nacional del Café (National Coffee Association, ANACAFE) recorded 117 cases of extortion were between 1960 and 1996.

According to the FAR's leaders, war taxes were politically valuable during the peace negotiations:

> The war tax was necessary, not to make the guerrillas rich, because we didn't get anything from it, but it was a political weapon to bring the oligarchy to the negotiation table, when they didn't want to participate...[43]

When *finqueros* refused to pay the tax, they took or damaged their property in one way or another:

> I remember for example...when a *finquero* refused to give it to us, then [we'd say], "Look, we'll call the people and you can give us five cows to kill and we'll distribute [the meat] to the *campesinos* and the workers."...In some places...we destroyed machinery...and things like that.[44]

In the years preceding the peace negotiations, according to a member of the guerrilla, there were "more voluntary" financial contributions from the people:

> We would have a meeting and look to these people, "To cover our needs and continue the struggle of the guerrilla forces, we are asking you for a voluntary contribution," and they would give us Q1, Q2, Q50...So, we didn't ask for war taxes at that time.[45]

ORPA was the guerilla organization that most relied on war taxes as a key part of their strategy. They engaged with *finqueros* in relation to the size of their properties and their attitudes regarding the army...

> In general, it was the big *finqueros* that were politically involved, putting bases [on their property and using]...security systems and resources against us, but a large number, the majority, were neutral and...One can now say that there were many *finqueros* that worked with us, as did many of the *finca* administrators and, in the end, that is what guided the strategy.[46]

Forced Recruitment

There are many cases in which the guerrilla forced, pressured and demanded individual civilians and the civilian population to become involved with their organizations.

> At the beginning, participation was voluntary, but this changed when the repression started. That is when recruitment through fraud began by telling the people, "Come join the struggle because we're about to win. We're going to the mountains because we're all already equal." There are testimonies, people who were killed when they tried to get away, because they'd let them leave and then, on the way, they were shot. And sometimes they were shot in front of the entire community to spread fear...[47]

Many of the community testimonies received by the CEH described intimidation and violence by the guerillas to force them to join the armed struggle...

> The guerrillas began to threaten the people that hadn't yet joined them, including punishing people and even killing them. It was at that moment that the people began to be afraid. Little by little the people's participation changed from voluntary to forced. Out of fear that they would kill us if we didn't support them, the majority of the people became organized...[48]

There were frequent threats made against unarmed civilians so that they would join the guerrilla movement...

> When the guerrillas organized us, in their propaganda they said that those who wouldn't join would be killed. This meant that the people under the EGP's control were living under threat, in other words, under constant fear...[49]

> In other *aldeas*...they resisted [participating in the guerrilla organization] and if someone complained to the army, the guerrilla would take him away. That is when they started to pressure the people and it was also when the pressure from the army also increased [and they said] you stay or you go, that is, you work with us or we'll kill you...[50]

During the decade of the eighties the FAR also used forced recruitment...People were forced out of fear to participate in the guerilla organizations, which sometimes led to arbitrary execution.

> The people were under the control of the guerrillas and those that didn't organize were killed by the guerrillas. The people organized so that they wouldn't have two enemies...[51]

ORPA also committed arbitrary executions of civilians who refused to work with them...

Prisoners

The guerrilla organizations sometimes captured soldiers from the army...Each of the groups presented explanations for why they engaged in these acts...

> We didn't get involved in taking prisoners, no way...We simply held them for a few hours or a few days in order to interrogate them...We treated them in such a way that they would understand the difference between how the guerilla treated prisoners and [how the army treated prisoners]...[52]

The CEH received no direct testimonies from victims about being held by the guerilla, but received...testimonies from the guerrilla organizations

> The first prisoners we had were three or four Army officers in 1976 when a helicopter crashed over there in La Shenandoa...There they captured a Lieutenant Colonel

and an Air Force Captain and a mechanic, the only one who was injured…Then they immediately told them they were prisoners of the guerrillas, not to fear any-thing, that nothing was going to happen to them and that the only thing we were going to do to them was interrogate them…the one that was a doctor took charge of caring for the injured man, the two officers were interrogated separately and together. They were very scared because they thought that we were going to kill them…After a couple of hours, they were left right there, free…[53]

Most of the time soldiers that were captured were released. A FAR press release, referred to a case involving many soldiers who surrendered to avoid combat as a result of an ambush carried out in the Northern region on April 19, 1983, in the Palestina sector of the La Libertad municipality, in the department of El Petén, "Six more were injured and surrendered, having been freed after they turned over their military equipment."[54]

Torture and Cruel, Inhuman and Degrading Treatment

Torture was not used in a systematic manner by the insurgents…Nevertheless, the CEH learned of acts that met the definition of torture that that were commit-ted…by a specific guerrilla unit.

The EGP's Commander Ernesto Guevara Front committed torture through-out 1981 and 1982. Some acts [of torture] were carried out before executing the victims and were particularly cruel in nature and other acts were carried out with the sole purpose of causing the victims to suffer…

On April 13 or 14, 1981, in the *aldea* of Tziquiná in Santa Eulalia municipality, Huehuetenango, members of the guerrilla captured Simón García, the head of Santa Eulalia's military commissioners. The victim was hung from a beam in his house for approximately one hour…

On February 19, 1982, Isaac Armas Argueta was executed by members of the EGP in the municipal seat of San Antonio Huista, Huehuetenango. The victim, who was a military commissioner and had been an active member of the MLN, had already been threatened by several neighbors whose involvement with the EGP was publicly known in the community.On the night of the act, the guerril-las took over the town, blocked all access and cut off all communications. The guerrillas looked for the commissioner in several houses until they found him hiding in the center of town. They forced the people in the house to leave and tortured the victim, accusing him of hiding army weapons and demanding that he hand them over. When the guerrillas left, his relatives confirmed that the commissioner had been cut up with a machete and his body had at least sixteen bullet holes, "…there was an arm laying here, an ear over there, his face was disfigured…"[55]

In the middle of 1981, in the El Salvador neighborhood in the *aldea* of Quilén Novillo in the municipality of Aguacatán, Huehuetenango, members of the EGP burst into the home of Epifanio Vicente López. They threatened to kill him. His wife, Julia López Ajanel, who was pregnant, was simultaneously severely beaten in the chest with the butt of a rifle…Afterwards, they entered the house of Santiago López, where they threatened those inside and forcibly removed his oldest son, Valerio López Ixcoy, who they led to a nearby river where he was beaten and later freed to tell his father that they would be back for him. Epifanio was accused of collaborating with the army and Santiago of having refused to join the guerrillas...

Attacks on Public Property, Private Property, and Looting

One of the political-military tactics of the guerrilla organizations were attacks and sabotage of public property. The EGP and the FAR were the two organizations that were most involved in these activities...

> The goal of sabotage, as a form of struggle, is to continually deepen and expand the advance and development of the Revolutionary Popular War. Interrupting free movement along highways, ruining the enemy's communications, destroying bridges, paralyzing factories and mills are all activities that our *compañeros* should engage in.[56]

> Strikes against the enemy should include a full campaign of sabotage and harassment... These strikes will focus on the destruction of all possible types of lines: electricity, telephones, telegraphs, etc. Sabotage of all the roads, mainly those with the most traffic and importance, placing obstacles, rocks, sticks, burned trailers... One shouldn't think this is an anarchic or desperate measure. It is the appropriate response we need to put a stop to the main activities of the enemies of the people in order to end their actions and, ultimately, to inflict upon them a great political-military defeat.[57]

From 1970 on, the guerrilla supported acts of this type. The FAR's National Propaganda Section mentioned the following acts...

> We have destroyed the properties of the bourgeoisie, such as burning Aviateca's Aero Express [the national airline], burning the Central Custom Office and several storehouses... We have placed bombs in the National Palace...[58]

It is not possible to accurately count the number of attacks committed during the conflict. The CEH had access to very different sources and it is worth mentioning two... The ANACAFE report referenced 183 attacks on infrastructure in the country. And, a review of the acts reported by the FAR's four regional units in 1982 referenced 58 acts of sabotage and 37 attacks on mechanisms of production...

The EGP burned municipal centers, especially in the department of Huehuetenango:

> At the end of '81 and the beginning of '82 we burned many municipalities, almost all of them. We determined that we destroyed around 24 of the 31 municipalities in Huehuetenango...[59]

On November 13, 1981, members of the EGP took the town of Zacualpa, Quiché and destroyed the municipal center. On December 16, 1981, the EGP entered the town of Tecpán, Chimaltenango, destroying the municipal center, the post office and telegraph service and the police station. The organization's war reports regarding this act stated:

> Six reactionary members of the local government were *ajusticiado*. We painted [walls] and sabotaged the Inter-American highway...[60]

Beginning in 1975, in the capital, the guerrillas attacked state buildings with bombs, as in the case of the INTA building...

> It was a political objective, because we understood that the problem of land is serious for the country and the INTA takes a long time to resolve land conflicts which is something that has slowed any solution to the agrarian problem in our country. They administrated land issues to serve the rich and the military and that is why we did it...[61]

The other two groups, the FAR and ORPA, also engaged in these types of actions as part of their strategy...

> On November 28 [1983] a group of militants from the same front [the FAR's Lucio Ramírez Front] took the water facility of the Ministry of Communications and Public Works located on the bank of the La Pasíon river [Petén]. The government installations were destroyed and they told the workers about the criminal nature of the government of Mejía Víctores...[62]

The guerrillas also attacked power lines with the goal of impacting the army's military units, although this also affected the civilian population...The insurgency also engaged in other types of attacks.

> On January 27 [1982] we engaged in a sabotage operation that totally destroyed two bridges that linked the towns of San Miguel Uspantán, Nebaj and Chajul in Quiché. In the same department, our forces completely destroyed the El Tesoro bridge...[63]

The three guerrilla organizations justified these actions by arguing that they impacted the economic interests of the state and business sector while also weakening the army...
They also attacked private property, such as farms and machinery...

> Groups of armed workers of our guerrilla front Otto René Castillo engaged in, among other actions, sabotage in the capital directed against the luxury homes used as the base for the businesses and trade organizations of the rich exploiters...our main acts against the great millionaires included the virtual destruction [on December 21, 1981] of three luxury buildings: the Chamber of Commerce, the Pan-American Tower which was the location of the Coffee Bank, and the Financial Center which was where the Industrial Bank operated...[64]

The other guerrilla groups also engaged in attacks in the capital against various targets including airlines and consulates...

The most common acts of sabotage of the three groups were committed against *fincas*...

> From June 25 to July 21 [1982] the guerrilla forces of ORPA burned the *finca* El Matasano, in el Quetzal, the *finca* Panorama, in San Rafael Pie de la Cuesta; two tractors of the *finca* Carolina and the *finca* Platanillo, in el Tumbador, San Marcos. All of these *fincas* were burned for collaborating with the army...

ORPA explained its actions against the property of private individuals in this way:

> *Fincas* were burned. Why? Because there was a certain order to things on the *fincas*...*Finqueros* didn't even pay the minimum wage required by law. Workers lived in terrible conditions, so we began a long campaign of taking over the *fincas* which also had a very specific goal involving three things: payment of minimum wage, better living conditions, and no cheating on recordkeeping or the difficulty of a task...We would impose a rule on the *finquero* that didn't meet these three conditions. Also, those that didn't want to comply almost always called in the Army to threaten or intimidate the neighboring population. Then, we would take the step of burning the *finca* buildings...[65]

During military operations, the guerrillas engaged in acts that impacted the civilian, noncombatant population.

In some cases...civilians were wounded or killed during these hostilities...In other cases, civilians were killed or injured by mines, booby traps, or other arms...It is also worth mentioning that there are cases of civilians who were forced by members of guerrilla groups to migrate from their homes or places of work and who died during their displacement from a variety of causes such as illness and hunger.

Kidnappings of Romeo Augusto de León, Baltasar Morales de la Cruz, and Héctor Menéndez de la Riva by the Rebel Armed Forces (FAR)

In March 1966, various members of the guerrilla groups of the PGT, the FAR, and the MR-13 were captured and their whereabouts were never known, despite the efforts of their relatives. This is known as the case of the "Twenty-eight disappeared."

During that same period, the FAR adopted a new strategy...political kidnappings. In these cases, they did not seek economic benefits, but rather tried to criticize government repression so that the disappeared militants would be presented publicly appear and charged before a court.

In 1966, after three years of military rule, there were presidential elections and a civilian, the lawyer Julio César Méndez Montenegro, was elected president of the Republic. At the same time, FAR leaders decided to carry out kidnappings of high-ranking officials representing each of the state's branches of power: the executive, the legislative, and the judicial.

According to statements made to the CEH, the guerrilla's purpose was to kidnap a member of each of these bodies in order to obtain the freedom of the twenty-eight disappeared, in light of the transition from a military to a civilian government...

On May 4, 1966, at seven-thirty in the evening, Romeo Augusto de León, president of the Supreme Court of Justice, was kidnapped on his way home. The act was carried out by five members of the FAR's urban front and occurred in zone 2 in Guatemala City, just a few blocks from his home. They intercepted the victim and his driver, Coronado Piedrasanta, forcing him to drive the vehicle where they wanted. A few blocks later, they released the driver and continued their escape in the government representative's vehicle...Later, the car belonging to the president of the court was found near the scene of the kidnapping. The victim was taken to a house in the countryside in San Pedro Sacatepéquez.

The information secretary of the government of the Republic, the journalist Baltasar Morales de la Cruz had held various public positions. On May 4, 1966,...he was traveling down a street in zone 1 in a car driven by his chauffeur, Isabel Canizales Poitán, and led by [a car] belonging to his son, Luis Fernando Morales Martínez. After parking, both cars were intercepted by various men from the FAR who came out of a blue Jeep...firing machine guns. Luis Fernando Morales tried to prevent the kidnapping of his father. He was shot and killed. The chauffeur took three bullets and also died.

The kidnappers tried to take the victim in the same Jeep that they had arrived in, but it had an unexpected mechanical failure, so they abandoned it near the scene and escaped by taking the journalists' vehicles. Once these two kidnappings were completed, the FAR gave the government a period of forty-eight hours to present the political prisoners whose whereabouts had been unknown for around two months, or they would execute the two kidnapped government employees.

The pressure exerted by the guerrillas led the judges of the Supreme Court of Justice to respond in favor of the petitions to publicly present the "twenty-eight disappeared" assuring that

> ...if these petitions have not led to the desired outcome, it is not their fault, since the detained have not been brought [before the court] by the police.[66]

The same day, May 4, 1966, the FAR also planned to kidnap Vicente Díaz Samayoa, acting president of Congress. The guerrillas waited for their victim for hours, but could not complete the operation and decided instead to try for the vice president of Congress, Héctor Menéndez de la Riva, who was also the secretary-general of the Democratic Institutional Party (PID). He was eventually kidnapped on the night of May 26, 1966, in zone 10 in Guatemala City and taken to a house in the countryside. His captivity lasted for fifteen days. On the night on June 9...he escaped, appearing before the authorities on the following day...

During this period José María "Chema" Ortiz Vides, head of the FAR's urban commandos, was captured at a checkpoint set up by the security forces. This situation and the knowledge on the part of FAR's leaders that, by this time, the twenty-eight disappeared were dead, changed the conditions for freeing the kidnapped government employees.

> Due to the deterioration of the operation caused by the escape of one of those kidnapped and to save Chema's life, it was decided—based on FAR's needs—to exchange the government employees for the kidnapped guerrilla.[67]

At first, Méndez Montenegro...rejected this exchange...However, in the end, he accepted. For the negotiation of the trade of Romeo Augusto de León and Baltasar Morales for "Chema," a group of mediators was formed including Armando Amado Chacón, a representative of the Red Cross, and Archbishop Casariego...

Based on its review of this case, the CEH determined that Romeo Augusto de León, Baltasar Morales de la Cruz, and Héctor Menéndez de la Riva were kidnapped by members of the FAR based on a decision by their leaders. Likewise, the CEH concluded with certainty that Isabel Canizales Poitán and Luis Fernando Morales Martínez were killed by members of the FAR, thus constituting arbitrary executions.

No situation provides the legal or ethical justification for these crimes. However, the CEH concluded that the acknowledgment of these acts on the part of the current leaders of the URNG is a positive sign for national reconciliation.

Part II

Key Actors in the Conflict and Their Strategies

8

Army, Security Institutions, and Civilians Acting under State Control

The state's goal, as established by the government and implemented by the army was the complete elimination of communism, the armed insurgency as well as all related organizations. National Security Doctrine provided the ideological foundation for these actions. Following the government's 1950s anticommunist decrees, the army began, in the 1960s, to engage in a forceful process of anticommunist ideological indoctrination. The nationalistic right-wing training began with the officers and expanded to the lower ranks and to all sectors of society. The initial ideological focus was provided by the School of the Americas, located in Panama, followed by training in the United States and, later, the education provided in the Guatemalan military academies.

This fact was acknowledged whenthe minister of defense responded to a request from the commission, stating that:

> ...many of the acts that the Commission is investigating occurred in a political-administrative context in which the philosophy and mechanisms of the so-called National Security Doctrine and the counterinsurgency struggle, as an expression of the Cold War in our region, supported completely irregular mechanisms [that were] externally encouraged.[1]

These mechanisms were among the most significant causes of human rights violations committed during the internal armed confrontation. However, despite their "irregular" nature, they were part of a strategy that was carefully planned by the Guatemalan Army. This conclusion is based not only on the concept of National Security Doctrine, but on the testimonies received by the CEH, the analysis of campaign plans provided by the army to the CEH, and a review of the tactics used in counterinsurgency military operations.

The army's strategy during the most intense period of the confrontation was clear from its campaign plans. The military operations were "countersubversive, based on ideological war, internal security, and development"[2] and were conceived alongside a commitment to eliminate the internal enemy:

> Internal enemies are all those individuals, groups, or organizations who, through illegal actions, try to disrupt the established order, represented by elements that use the mottos of international communism, supporting the so-called revolutionary war and subversion in the country... [also] considered an internal enemy [are] those individuals, groups or organizations that without being communist try to disrupt the established order.[3]

Based on this idea, the army acted with extreme severity. Citizens were understood to be either with them or against them; there was no neutral place. In addition to members of guerrilla organizations, the army considered internal enemies to be anyone that identified with communist ideology or belonged to a group—labor, social, religious, student—or who, for whatever reason, was not in favor of the established regime...

Soldiers' Training

During the internal armed confrontation, soldiers' training in the army began with forced, illegal, and discriminatory recruitment that was the primary means of finding men to enter the military. This practice was violent from the start and led to a series of acts of equal or greater severity including ideological indoctrination and physical training for those who became regular soldiers...

The army's procedures consisted of physical punishment, threats, and acts of moral degradation to ensure that the troops were ideologically attuned and willing to follow orders... Many soldiers who were victims of this process told the CEH about their experiences and how they suffered:

> They took me to the military zone in Huehuetenango where I underwent training for three months. It was very hard. The officers constantly abused us. They kicked us, beat us, and treated us as if we were guerrillas. I didn't know anything about the guerrillas but they always accused us of being guerrillas. They didn't respect people and we couldn't demand our rights. If you refused any of the training, you were punished by running for hours and hours in the mud or carrying a backpack filled with stones. At the end of three months of training, we were soldiers. They told us that there would be no more training because of the war. The punishments continued... We soldiers didn't want to go to war but we were all forced into military service and we did it out of fear of being killed by the officers and accused of being guerrillas...[4]

Through the use of illegitimate training practices, the army tried to ensure the troops' blind obedience and a group morale based on mutual complicity guaranteeing impunity for all of its actions. This applied not only to those acts directed against the civilian population, but also to abuses committed among their own ranks within the armed forces. In this way, superior orders, though they may have been clearly illegal, were not discussed by subordinates and any refusal to carry them out was punished. These orders prevailed over the law…

   Military training was particularly violent for the indigenous soldiers that composed the majority of those forcibly recruited by the army, as well as those most vulnerable. These discriminatory practices were bound to a long history of racism and made the conditions of their training much more difficult. It was especially hard for those who didn't understand the Spanish used for giving orders:

> There was a lot of discrimination against indigenous men. They beat the indigenous men, almost for fun, because they couldn't understand a thing. The goal was to teach them Spanish simply through beatings and some asked to be let go… They spoke very little and you could barely understand them. They didn't understand the orders and, since they didn't get it, they said yes without understanding… There were no classes. They had to learn by brute force.[5]

During the training period, a new soldier was subjected to exercises that had little to do with proper military training and including inhuman and brutal practices. These were designed to slowly degrade their values so that later, the soldier would be willing to act in ways completely contrary to the basic norms of respect… the CEH determined that the primary goal of the army's training for a soldier was to enable him to engage in brutal conduct similar to how he was treated. This explains, in part, the magnitude and cruelty of the violations of human rights perpetrated by soldiers… against their own people…

Kaibiles (Special Forces)

"The *Kaibil* is a killing machine for when foreign forces and doctrines attack the homeland or the Army"[6]… This motto can be considered the expression of the *Kaibil* philosophy.

   The U.S. Army's influence on ideological and operational practices in training Guatemalan Army's officers and cadets at courses in Panama was well known. The instructors were high- and low-ranked U.S. officers, the majority of whom had combat experience in Vietnam, were decorated for their war service, and had substantial understanding and training in the techniques of counterinsurgency operations…

   This training was based on survival strategies in extreme combat situations; torture techniques for prisoners of war with the goal of rapidly obtaining information about insurgents; indoctrination in anticommunist ideology; and psychological operations techniques. As part of the training, they simulated attacks and the control and destruction of villages.

   The *Kaibiles'* training was also the influenced by other countries where Guatemalan soldiers attended special forces courses…

> *Kaibil* is a mix of the experiences of the United States Rangers, Colombian *lanceros*, Peruvian commandos, Chilean commandos. These approaches were combined

and formed as a model adapted to our situation, the *Kaibil* course. Later, the *Kaibil* reputation gained its own mystique...[7]

The training encouraged a maximum level of aggression and courage through dehumanizing mental and physical pressure. Killing animals was required, particularly dogs, and then eating them raw or grilled, and drinking their blood as proof of courage...

At first, the *Kaibiles* that graduated were placed in small groups designed to operate independently or to support larger forces. In 1980, as the conflict grew more intense, the *Kaibiles* were distributed among different army units...They provided additional training to the regular troops in various military zones and bases, adding an element of extra aggression to the education of ordinary soldiers...

During counterinsurgency operations, *Kaibil* officers and soldiers acted with regular troops supporting military actions...and independently for special operations...The massacre at Las Dos Erres is one case that reflects the use of these units as an independent military force known for its aggression and barbaric methods...

Policía Militar Ambulante (Mobile Military Police, PMA)

This military unit was created in 1958 through a presidential decree. The *Policía Militar Ambulante* (Mobile Military Police, PMA) was developed, in part, to manage the responsibilities that the *Guardia de Hacienda* had covered in rural areas since 1954, including antinarcotics operations, counterinsurgency actions...and controlling civil disturbances...

The PMA was divided in two main bodies, the *Policía Militar Ambulante Ordinaria* (Regular Mobile Military Police, PMA-O), which was the military police within the regular army structure and the *Policía Militar Ambulante Especial* (Special Mobile Military Police, PMA-E), which carried out security functions for private businesses and ranches. They were paid by these groups and were closely linked with the intelligence services...

This force was most often used to make up for deficiencies within the National Police, with units operating in the capital and linked to the Honor Guard Brigade, the Mariscal Zabala Brigade, and the Army Central Barracks. It worked with these groups in military operations in Guatemala City.

This military unit acted with brutality, supporting larger units and also acting independently...

In mid-1979...an informant carried the news to the base that the guerrillas had taken the municipality of Uspantán. The Captain went with 150 soldiers and went to the *aldea* of Chicamán to interrogate the people and where the guerrillas had gone...He gathered the people together and began to interrogate them...When they didn't respond the way the Captain wanted, they tied them up and began to put needles under their fingernails and they were screaming terribly...The Captain cut the young man's throat and he made a terrifying noise, fell to the ground and blood poured out...the people began to cry...[8]

We had to "break" five dangerous prisoners who had been sentenced, some to twenty years and others to thirty years in prison and who were to be taken to another place with guards. But, there wasn't a problem because the guards knew that we were going to meet them on the road, as strangers, and that we were going to kidnap them and later kill them…The day of the mission, the Lieutenant chose five of us and ordered us to dress in plain clothes…The Lieutenant ordered us to put on wigs and placed the truck across the road so that the other vehicle would stop…We pointed our guns at the guards…and disarmed them…Meanwhile, other members of our group took the prisoners and put them in our truck…We left quickly…upon arriving at the place the Lieutenant had chosen, the prisoners were violently pulled out and placed face-down on the ground…The Lieutenant took out his. 45 pistol and shot them in the head…Later, he said to us, "I want each of you to also shoot these sons-of-bitches, so we can be sure they're all dead…" All of us followed orders. I also had to shoot them. They were left dead at the side of the road…[9]

The PMA was disbanded in 1997 in order to comply with the Peace Accords…

Fuerza Aerea de Guatemala (Guatemalan Air Force)

The *Fuerza Aerea de Guatemala* (Guatemalan Air Force, FAG) was created in the 1920s as part of the army. During the internal confrontation, it used three military air bases in the country…

The FAG was not very well-equipped in military terms. Nevertheless, they had the capacity to meet the needs of the conflict…During counterinsurgency operations, the FAG bombed villages of unarmed civilian populations killing people and destroying crops, homes, animals, and other property…

On August 27, 1982, military planes came to the *aldeas* of Seguamó, Setzacpec and Chactelá and dropped around forty bombs. It was the day of *feria patronal* (local celebration) of Panzós. We had come to play football but they made us go to the *aldeas*… We [the *patrulleros*] went there with guns and burned the houses…as a result of the bombing, around a hundred people were killed, including men, women and children…[10]

The FAG also participated in other operations, such as simulated arbitrary executions and the elimination of victims' corpses by throwing them from planes into the ocean. This mode of eliminating people was also used by other Latin American armies, including those in Argentina and Chile, and sowed terror among the civilian population…

The staff from the D-2 took prisoners and bodies outside to wait for the plane and then put them on board. The pilots were ordered to fly for thirty minutes off of the coast of Guatemala and then to push the prisoners and bodies out of the plane. In that way, the D-2 were able to eliminate the evidence that the prisoners had been tortured and killed…[11]

Estado Mayor (Joint Chiefs of Staff)

The *Estado Mayor de la Defensa Nacional* (National Defense Joint Chiefs of Staff) was the technical and consultative center of the Guatemalan Army [the name of this entity was legally changed several times as it was also known as the *Estado Mayor del Ejército* (Army Joint Chiefs of Staff) as well as the *Estado Mayor General del Ejército* (General Army Joint Chiefs of Staff)—and will be referred to here generally as the *Estado Mayor* or Joint Chiefs of Staff. It supported the minister of defense in all military affairs...Its main functions included advising commanders, planning, coordination, high-level supervision, and control of plans and operations...

The Joint Chiefs of Staff issued the operations orders and campaign plans. While operations were taking place, they engaged in an ongoing review of the situation, allowing for followup on the progress of operations. The official names of the Guatemalan Army's campaign plans and their corresponding years include *Victoria 82; Firmeza 83; Firmeza 83-1; Reencuentro Institucional 84; Estabilidad Nacional 85; Consolidación Nacional 86; Fortaleza 87; Unidad 88; Fortalecimiento Institucional 89; Avance 90; Fortaleza por la Paz 91; Consolidación por la Paz 92; Paz 93; Integración 94; Integración 95;* and *Integración Nacional 96*...

The campaign plans' sections on coordination explained that units involved in operations should prepare their own plans related to their area of responsibility. In this way, military bases received the Joint Chiefs of Staff campaign plan, studied its mission and general directives, and then carried out a review and issued their own plans. These plans could not contradict the general plan, but would contain activities related to the area of operations that they were assigned...

Control over Counterinsurgency Operations

The violations of human rights and international humanitarian law committed during military actions...were not the product of mere chance or the result of excesses, but instead followed operations designed and planned by the army's high command. The Joint Chiefs of Staff exercised continual control over counterinsurgency operations through two mechanisms: formal control through the chain of command; and, the presence of the commanders in all of the areas of operation.

The army's high command was composed of: the president of the Republic as the commander-in-chief of the army; the minister of defense as second-in-command; and the head of the Joint Chiefs of Staff as third in line. Whoever assumed the last position exercised direct command over all army military units and had to be obeyed and informed regarding what took place within his area of operations during military actions. The next level reported directly to the head of the Joint Chiefs of Staff and included military commanders, special military commanders, the services, and training centers,

Within the army, chain of command was completely vertical in terms of military discipline, and its charter establishes that the army "...is unified and indivisible, apolitical, fully obedient and unwavering"...The chain of command and its hierarchical subordination implies a double responsibility. On the one hand,

the heads of units involved in operations on the ground at all levels had the obligation to the superior that commanded them. On the other hand, the superior
that gave the orders had the responsibility to control and supervise compliance
with his orders.

The majority of operational plans that the CEH reviewed established mechanisms of control for the management of operations:

> The units must present punctually every 15 days their IPO (periodic operations
> report) containing the following information: overview of its elements (its base,
> area of operation and other units), combat and overview of results (enemies killed,
> arms and equipment captured and lost)...[12]

The Guatemalan Army's chain of command required that all acts carried out
by a soldier were to be reported to a superior who was required to be aware of all
of his subordinates' actions. Therefore, all of the actions committed against the
noncombatant civilian population were reported to the commander responsible
for that area of operations and, if not, he nevertheless had the obligation to know
about everything that had occurred:

> A massacre was a very obvious act. It was impossible that it could go unnoticed. If,
> in the course of my operations, I, as the head of a patrol, ran into civilians...and
> wiped out ten, twenty, or thirty, and buried them; perhaps I didn't identify them
> or even know who they were. Then, I would call my superior on the radio or send
> a coded message to say, "Ok, look, during such and such patrol, such and such an
> action took place"...[13]

This mode of managing troops in operations made it very clear that...the head
of the Joint Chiefs of Staff as well as any troop commander...always had direct
knowledge of the human rights violations that were committed...

Based on a review of military regulations...the members of the Guatemalan
Army did not act independently when they carried out military actions against
either the guerrillas or unarmed civilians. Instead, they followed previously
received orders. In all cases, these orders, verbal and written (such as campaign
plans), outlined the implementation of previously planned actions designed to
achieve the strategic objectives of the counterinsurgency struggle...

It was clear that within the military establishment there would be no punishment for crimes against humanity, because those responsible were acting
expressly to fulfill orders from the army's high command. As has been pointed
out, the planning of these military operations was developed at this level and the
desired objectives required that human rights violations would be committed...

The army interpreted military discipline as similar to "blind obedience,"
refusing to accept the basic principle that manifestly illegal orders should not be
followed. This led to the systematic disregard [for this principle] and its violation
throughout the armed confrontation...

Military honor was reduced to a concept devoid of moral content, divorced
from ethics, and completely supportive of systematic torture, the extermination
of the civilian population, and the arbitrary execution of women, children, and

the elderly. Group morale was expressed through the institution's closed, defensive position and was directed at assuring impunity for its members.

Intelligence

Guatemala's military intelligence system...was based on National Security Doctrine as applied throughout Latin America within the context of the East/West conflict and under the rubric of a total war of the state against communism.... Intelligence as bound to National Security Doctrine was not a system to gather and analyze tactical information so that the Joint Chiefs of Staff could determine the appropriate countersubversive operations to implement on the ground. Rather, its strategic analysis of the internal enemy included those among the civilian population that "sought to challenge the established order," viewing this information as fundamental for identifying and suppressing enemies of the regime. The system applied a broad and ambiguous notion of the enemy that included everyone who refused to strongly support the dominant political interests.

Under the initial pretext of pursuing communists and later guerrillas, the intelligence services applied the saying "whomever is not with me is against me." What is relevant, and as a result, most serious, is that the intelligence services identified as enemies anyone that failed to support the prevailing goals within the army and, to use a military expression found in the army's campaign plans, they had to be annihilated...

The intelligence services kept their functions, activities, and the information they obtained and analyzed secret from other units in the army... Only the highest levels of the military, the Intelligence Directorate of the Joint Chiefs of Staff, had access to all the information. Other units, such as the intelligence sections of the particular military zones, had only partial knowledge of the information that had been gathered...thereby guaranteeing its compartmentalization.

The division into separate units was used for information as well as for the mechanisms, sources, plans, and operations of the intelligence service. In addition, each level within the intelligence system respected this compartmentalization so that superiors did not demand sources or types of information from their subordinates, but rather clarity regarding its veracity and accuracy.

The planning and implementation of the intelligence service's illegal operations were kept secret...so that the intellectual and criminal responsibility for their acts could not be determined. This protected state agents from accountability and ensured the failure of any police or judicial investigations...

The intelligence services manipulated information against the guerrilla organizations by creating disinformation campaigns as part of psychological operations to destroy the enemy's morale. The intelligence services created and distributed propaganda for these purposes. They even went as far as to develop and pass out material designed to make it seem like it was created by the guerrillas. According to a former member of the Judicial Police, a significant portion of the guerrillas' political propaganda that was distributed during the government of Lucas García was passed out by the G-2.

The intelligence services exercised significant control over the media through censorship, blackmail, the manipulation of media professionals, managing information provided to journalists, and infiltrating the media.

The intelligence service always had substantial resources available for their use including offices, vehicles, weapons, and other support necessary to achieve its objectives. It is worth noting that among other technical resources, the intelligence services received the first computer systems installed in the country and could always rely on...the most modern radio equipment, fixed and mobile surveillance, and wireless listening devices.

The intelligence service's economic support was provided by a unit housed in the Ministry of Finance. They received considerable sums of money from the army's budget and also diverted funds from the budgets of other state bodies. In addition, they received additional funding from private contributions and the appropriation of goods captured from guerrilla organizations...

Intelligence operations in Guatemala were designed and directed by two particular entities: the Intelligence Section of the Joint Chiefs of Staff, known as the G-2, and a unit within the *Estado Mayor Presidencial* (Presidential Joint Chiefs of Staff, EMP), popularly known as *La Regional* ("The Regional") or *El Archivo* ("The File"). Both structures consistently operated without limits and in a dangerous and illegal manner...

From the beginning of the 1960s on, the EMP guaranteed the safety of the president of the Republic while also providing intelligence services through a special unit. This was the intelligence body most closely linked to the country's highest authorities and it compiled and analyzed information useful to those within the president's circle.

During the military governments, this unit provided direct information to the president for the implementation of military operations and counterintelligence that served his interests. It also worked closely with the Intelligence Directorate in counterinsurgency efforts. Beginning with the civilian governments, the unit expanded and enjoyed greater autonomy from the Intelligence Directorate, including using its personnel to spy on the president...

One of the essential components of the intelligence system was the creation of a network of agents that provided information to the state. The intelligence network can be understood as having two main levels...First, there was a formal level composed of members of the G-2 in the military zones, the S-2 in other military units, and members of the National Police and the Treasury Police. Second, there was an informal level involving a large network of collaborators and informants, which included *confidenciales* and *orejas* that infiltrated public and private organizations, as well as military commissioners and members of the PAC...The broad range of agents and units carried out multiple functions within the machinery of the intelligence system. Although all of the levels were involved in seeking information and had operational capacity, each played a specific role during the armed confrontation...

Each formal intelligence network worked with its own informal network. That is, the Intelligence Directorate, the military zones, every other military unit, the National Police, the *Guardia de Hacienda*, all relied on a wide informal network of informants. The intelligence unit of the EMP also had its own informal net-work...The links between [state entities] and informants varied widely...[for example, one informant] began being harassed by members of the G-2. Afraid of what might happen, he told the G-2. A captain told him that they were looking for him because two commissioners had told them that he was working with the guerrillas.

> Then, the Captain asked me if I would be an *oreja* for the army. To prove my loy-alty to the armed forces, every Monday of every week I had to bring information to the military zone in San Marcos. Over three years I brought lunch and drinks to those in army...In that way, I gained credentials as a *confidencial* of the Chiefs of Staff provided by the G-2...I spent the entire time under terrible psychological pressure that still affects me. Being forced to be an *oreja* was the only means of survival.[14]

The intelligence services had substantial confidential resources that they could use to pay for the information that they received...All of the information collected was evaluated and reviewed at formal and informal levels to determine its accuracy...

The heads of intelligence of the Joint Chiefs of Staff designed strategic plans for rural and urban areas. Since they represented the highest operational level, they had more resources than any other section within the intelligence services. This allowed them to develop clandestine operations, especially in urban areas...

On January 25, 1979, the politician and congressman Alberto Fuentes Mohr was executed on La Reforma Avenue in the capital in an operation involving a vehicle and two motorcycles. On March 22, 1979, the politician Manuel Colom Argueta was also executed...in the capital in an operation involving at least three cars, two motorcycles, and a helicopter. Fuentes Mohr was killed just days after registering the *Partido Socialista Democrático* (Social Democratic Party, PSD), and Colom Argueta was killed a week after registering the political party *Frente Unido de la Revolución* (United Revolutionary Front, FUR)...The goal of these acts was to limit political options and increase the level of polarization. Both political movements disappeared after the execution of their leaders...

The intelligence in the military zones and units deployed throughout the nation relied on conventional structures for military operations and clandestine structures for activities that violated human rights. The conventional methods for obtaining information included, for example, when the G-2 and S-2 gath-ered information from their sources and then evaluated and disseminated their findings through the military command responsible for operations on the ground...

The nonconventional procedures were when the G-2 or the S-2 directly or indirectly engaged in interrogations and torture committed in the military bases:

> Those from the Section 2...were in charge of torture, to get information and then kill. To be selected and recruited for the Section 2, you had to be someone with

a record that was well known by the officers. They were very smart people, they knew all the files and were well prepared...They almost never mixed with the troops, they used civilian clothes and only sometimes wore uniforms...[15]

From the start of the armed conflict, the intelligence services in the military bases were associated with repression...

We, as soldiers, detained the people. That was the order, "grab those ones," and so we grabbed them...Later, it was the 2 [G-2] that interrogated. The real soldier only killed during combat, it was the 2 that were the ones in charge of killing. The soldiers only had to detain them and then hand them over...[16]

Intelligence personnel have been described as the most dominant and influential personnel within the army. Members of the G-2 always carried an identity card that guaranteed them immunity and the freedom to travel anywhere...Even the commander of a military zone could not overrule the orders of an intelligence agent...

The Intelligence Directorate did not always act under orders of the army. On various occasions, sectors linked to extreme right-wing ideology and wealthy elites used the intelligence service for their own interests...

Just as occurred in other Latin American countries, various U.S. government administrations were involved in disseminating National Security Doctrine and supporting the development of intelligence services in Guatemala...Some of the high- and lower-ranking Guatemalan officers attended basic and advanced intelligence and counterintelligence courses at the School of the Americas of the Southern Command of the United States. In addition, sometimes officer training used U.S. manuals. The CEH gained access to some of these, which were written in Spanish. For example, the manual *Terrorismo y guerrilla urbana* (Terrorism and urban guerrillas) stated that

another function of the CI [counterintelligence] agents is to recommend CI targets to be neutralized...examples include targets such as government officials, political leaders..."[17]

The *Centro Regional de Telecomunicaciones* (Regional Telecommunications Center), later known as *La Regional* (The Regional) was created in 1964...with support from the Public Safety Division of USAID Guatemala, a U.S. government agency. Its goal was to coordinate security through telecommunications connections in Central American countries by supervising and restricting its use...by those suspected of being communists.

La Regional facilitated communications between distinct police and military units and operated as a system to coordinate and manage the transfer of information on people viewed as enemies of dominant political interests. This would then be analyzed and used by the police and the military for both conventional and secret operations...*La Regional* became one of the primary intelligence units during the armed conflict...

At the end of the 1970s, following the suspension of military aid on the part of the U.S. government of Jimmy Carter, the governments of Argentina, Colombia, Chile, and Taiwan provided support to the Guatemalan Army by training intelligence officers. In Taiwan, officers were trained in strategic intelligence; in Colombia, officers attended courses for analysts and interrogators; and Argentina advised the Guatemalan Armed Forces on intelligence, working with Chilean and Israeli soldiers. In 1981, about 200 members of the police and army were sent to Buenos Aires where they received training in advanced intelligence techniques, including the use of interrogation methods...

Death Squads

In mid-1966, the first death squads appeared in the capital. The *Movimiento de Acción Nacionalista Organizado* (Movement of Organized Nationalist Action, MANO) announced its existence on June 3, 1966. Its symbol was

> ...a white hand over a red circle and beneath it, the warning, "This is the hand that will eradicate the nation's renegades and traitors of the homeland."[18]

This death squad was supported politically and economically by elements of the extreme right under the pretense of eradicating communism. The MLN political party contributed basic ideological support and backed this organization, a fact that was publicly acknowledged by its leader Mario Sandoval Alarcón... Nevertheless, this group [also known as *La Mano Blanca*, the White Hand] was quickly taken over by the army. The soldiers linked to this death squad were a group from military intelligence associated with the General Justo Rufino Barrios barracks...

In the 1960s, other death squads also appeared which were apparently operating as a front for *La Mano Blanca* including *Comité de Resistencia Anticomunista de Guatemala* (Guatemalan Anticommunist Resistance Committee, CRAG); *Nueva Organización Anticomunista* (New Anti-Communist organization, NOA); and *Consejo Anticomunista de Guatemala* (Guatemalan Anticommunist Council, CADEG). "Those were just names used to carry out operations, but it was the same group..."[19]

In 1967, death squads created terror through various communiques in the capital. On April 1, 1967, NOA published a list of twenty-three students and trade unionists along with the photos of three others that had been killed for being alleged communists. Their slogan was, "A known communist is a dead communist." In June 1967, CADEG published a list of ninety people that they considered "arch communists and anti-patriotic."[20] In August, it released another list with 117 names and in September another one with seventy-eight names. The organization publicly declared war on "the fearsome unions": *Federación Autónoma Sindical de Guatemala* (Independent Union Federation of Guatemala, FASGUA); *Sindicato de Acción y Mejoramiento Ferrocarrilero* (Union for Railway Worker Action and Improvement, SAMF); *Confederación de Trabajadores de*

Guatemala (Confederation of Guatemalan Workers, CONTRAGUA); *Sindicato de Trabajadores del Institute Guatemalteco de Seguro Social* (Union of Workers of the Guatemalan Institute for Social Security, STIGSS); and CTS...

The CEH determined that the majority of the death squads were neither autonomous organizations nor independent from the army, but rather were clandestine elements of the intelligence system disguised by "a name." This was a method of psychological warfare whose goal was to spread terror among the population. In this way, these groups hid the participation of soldiers so that human rights violations would not be attributed to the government or state agents. The army supplied personnel, weapons, financing, and operational instructions... A declassified U.S. government document referring to these organizations highlighted that:

> they serve, apparently, as a cover for clandestine commando units of the Army that act as death squads for the armed forces...[21]

The groups carried out secret counterinsurgency operations involving psychological warfare, propaganda, financing, and human rights violations:

> *La Mano Blanca, Jaguar Justiciero,* and *Nueva Organización Anticomunista* were Army creations.[22]

> They have many names...It is all a fabrication of the military leadership. They use different names and some say that there are many civilians supporting the soldiers, but it's a lie. It's the soldiers themselves that try to look like other groups to engage in crimes...[23]

Related to this, a former member of the intelligence services in a military zone said:

> Look, the truth is that the members of the death squads are members of the Army...They are killers...killing people like animals. They do that to intimidate people so that nobody talks, to silence people, because...the government doesn't want them to air their dirty laundry or to let them tell the truth. You know, our Lord Jesus Christ died for the truth and has to be revealed...[24]

Up through the end of the presidency of Julio César Méndez Montenegro and under the government of Arana Osorio the intelligence services used death squads to spread fear in the capital. [For example], in the first half of the 1970s, the death squad *Ojo por Ojo* (Eye for an Eye) tortured and executed various people linked to the PGT as well as supporters of the FAR...

During Romeo Lucas' government, death squads again played an important role in political violence, mainly in Guatemala City. These groups were composed of members of intelligence services and *judiciales*...The human rights violations committed by these organizations were mainly directed against political, union and student leaders, journalists, and university professors...

Death squads reemerged in 1988...with reports of the return of *Mano Blanca* and of the *Ejército Secreto Anticomunista* (Secret Anticommunist Army, ESA)...

National Police

In 1954...the National Police were created as a civilian state institution charged with overseeing the security of people and their property, maintaining public order, and preventing and combating crime...The detective corps was created with responsibility for investigations and finding and apprehending criminals as well as preventing crime. The members of this corps were popularly known as *judiciales* ("judicials" as well as *la judicial*, "the judicial," or Judicial Police)...

From 1954 on, with the creation of the *Comité de Defensa National contra el Comunismo* (Committee of the National Defense against Communism), the *judiciales* were given the responsibility of capturing people that were

> clearly known communists from the previous regime who constitute a danger for the proper development of the country...[25]

Beginning in the mid-1960s, the army increased its oversight and control of the police. This control was expressed through militarization, which had always been characteristic of the police. The majority of police were former soldiers. For example, in the time of General Chupina, director of the police in the Lucas García government, only former soldiers were able to become policemen...

The police sent copies of their daily reports to the Intelligence Directorate of the Joint Chiefs of Staff and regional police did the same with their respective military zones....

A testimony collected by the CEH in San Juan Comalapa, Chimaltenango, explained the way in which the *judiciales* operated at that time:

> The *judiciales* were those that kidnapped people...When the ones from Comalapa went after people, they always covered their faces with balaclavas so that they wouldn't be recognized. They used black leather jackets and were always in vehicles. They used a pickup and a car with tinted windows. It was always *la judicial*... [26]

Regular members of the National Police also committed human rights violations. On August 21, 1984, the body of Domingo Sicay Cuá was found on a path in the rural cantón of Tzachaj in the municipality of Santiago Atitlán, Sololá. According to a direct witness...agents of the National Police stopped him at a bend in the road; they took off their uniforms, put on civilian clothes, hid their motorcycle in the coffee field, and took him into the bushes...they executed him point blank. They then put on their police uniforms and returned with the motorcycle to the highway towards Atitlán...

Guardia de Hacienda (Treasury Police)

The *Guardia de Hacienda* was created on November 13, 1954,...[and in] 1969...was given the responsibility of policing areas within the country with the goal of preventing, repressing, and pursuing crimes and violations...They used uniformed and nonuniformed personnel. Uniformed personnel were assigned to border posts. Nonuniformed personnel were assigned intelligence functions and thepursuit of drug traffickers...

The *Guardia de Hacienda* were always a more discreet and secretive organization than the National Police. They were known as the *cuartelito* (little barracks) because they exhibited a type of discipline associated with the military...In most cases, its members were former soldiers from the army's special forces (ex-*Kaibiles* or ex-parachutists), former members of the PMA, or ex-officers. They were a group similar to the PMA.

Some cases of human rights violations received by the CEH reveal that this group was less interested in hiding its identity than other state agencies and that they sometimes committed violations while wearing uniforms displaying their institutional affiliation. On January 14, 1977, in the village of Xoncá, in the municipality of Nebaj, Quiché, three hooded men wearing *Guardia de Hacienda* uniforms illegally detained Rafael Bernal Chel and two others, both named Domingo. On January 21, in a place known as Boquerón, in the same municipality, the corpses of these three appeared with signs of torture and various gunshot wounds...

The army also used members of the *Guardia de Hacienda* to commit human rights violations...On March 25, 1985, a couple, Humberto Escobar Saldaña and Margarita Elena Méndez, were detained by armed men using a *Guardia de Hacienda* vehicle who were accompanied by soldiers. Initially, the operation was directed only against Ms. Méndez, but when her husband protested, they took them both...Up until the present the couple's whereabouts remain unknown.

One of the most publicized cases of human rights violations committed by members of the *Guardia de Hacienda* was that of Paniagua Morales and others. This was known as the case of the *panel blanca* (white van), in which a series of people were detained, tortured, and executed in the capital between 1987 and 1988. The case was heard by the Inter-American Court of Human Rights, whose March 8, 1998, judgment unanimously held the state of Guatemala responsible...

Military Commissioners

Military commissioners were created in 1938 to

> act as agents of military authority, carrying out administrative functions, and organizing and controlling citizens in accordance with military laws and regulations...[27]

With Julio César Méndez Montenegro's rise to the presidency in 1966, military commissioners began to actively participate in the repression of their political adversaries, mainly the leaders of the *Partido Revolucionario* (Revolutionary Party, PR)...

> The military supported 3,000 to 5,000 agents [commissioners]...Many were members or supporters of the MLN and were violently anticommunist. In areas where

the commissioners were active, supporters of the *Partido Revolucionario*...were
systematically persecuted and terrorized...[28]

With the escalation of the armed confrontation at the end of the 1960s, the roles
of these groups began shifting they started committing human rights violations
associated with counterinsurgency operations.

The commissioners were armed under the orders of Coronel Arana, probably
through an agreement with the Minister of Defense, and they were quite successful in capture and assassination operations, which reduced the capacity of the FAR
as a guerrilla force. Unfortunately, the commissioners were undisciplined in their
actions and they killed many innocent people...[29]

During the 1970s, the internal armed confrontation expanded to the north
and west of the country where military commissioners worked closely with the
army, assisting with forced recruitment, especially of young indigenous men,
"they were functionaries of the Army...they forced everyone to join..."[30]

At the beginning of the 1980s, as the armed internal confrontation reached
its most intense period, commissioners were forced by the army to actively participate in counterinsurgency military operations. As agents of the local military authorities, the commissioners enjoyed total impunity before the people.
Commissioners often used their authority to further their own individual economic and related interests.

In testimonies gathered in the field, they are remembered as those closely
allied with the army and who informed on and executed many of their neighbors...People generally viewed the military commissioners as responsible for
having committed all types of crimes:

The military commissioners...began to kill and force us from our homes...That's
when the massacres began.[31]

The military commissioners arrived in our village and that was the worst thing
ever. Because of them there were so many massacres...[32]

In 1981, the number of military commissioners reached unprecedented levels.
In a speech delivered in Joyabaj, Quiché, General Benedicto Lucas, head of the
army Joint Chiefs of Staff said, "These are voluntary forces. In Rabinal there are
already 1,000 men and 800 in Joyabaj."[33]...

In most cases leaders of the PAC were also military commissioners and played
a double role, especially in the municipalities and departmental capitals. The
trust conferred to them by members of the armed forces was directly connected
to the creation of the PAC...in which weapons were provided to the rural residents and where PAC leaders played a decisive role in ensuring that the people
would reject the insurgency...

Military commissioners participated in army programs of control and surveillance over the population, coordinating and collaborating with military and
civilian authorities...

If a person had to move from one village to another, he had to have a permit or safe-conduct in order to move, like a passport. When he was going to leave, it was stamped, upon entering the other village, the military commissioner also stamped it and upon his return as well. This is how one could be sure that the people wouldn't run off to the guerrillas...[34]

Military commissioners actively participated in denouncing members of their communities. Faced with the task of "maintaining calm in the interior" and fearful that, should they fail, they would be punished by the army, commissioners frequently informed on people that had not participated in the conflict. These denunciations led to detentions, disappearances, and extrajudicial executions...Military commissioners reached the point where they informed on innocent people simply to earn small sums of money.

> The leader of the military commissioners was known for accusing his neighbors "since they gave him money, he sold out." They would give him Q50 for each person he informed on...He killed many people.[35]

Many of those accused by military commissioners of being collaborators or members of the guerrilla did not participate in the insurgency in any way. Some testimonies described how commissioners had to denounce or arrest a certain number of people:

> The leader of the commissioners in San Pablo said, "Give me a few people and I'll promote you to be a leader of the commissioners." To get that job, he started pointing out many people to be handed over as guerrillas. He prepared a list of sixty people to be kidnapped during the night.[36]

Military commissioners used torture when interrogating victims to find out about their support for guerrilla activities. Members of *campesino*, social, political, and student organizations were persecuted and subjected to these violations...

From the mid-1980s on, as the military operations of the armed confrontation decreased, military commissioners were gradually less responsible for human rights violations. However, this did not mean that their power within the communities disappeared. The level of authoritarianism created during the bloodiest phase of the confrontation continued for years:

> The former heads of commissioners remain secure. They know they can do whatever they want. They are the authorities. So what kind of peace is this?...[37]

Patrullas de Autodefensa Civil (Civil Defense Patrols)

The *Patrullas de Autodefensa Civil* (Civil Defense Patrols, PAC) were legally created on April 14, 1983 through Governmental Decree 222–83. However, from 1981 on, civil self-defense groups had been organized in various regions throughout the country. And, from 1982 on, they acted in coordination with the army's campaign plans *Victoria 82* and *Firmeza 83*, under the name *Patrullas de Autodefensa Civil*…

The PAC forced civilians to participate in military actions…leading to the militarization of Mayan communities, confrontations among communities, and human rights violations. Civilians were required to engage in military operations and were exposed to combat. The PAC also destroyed the system of indigenous authority and became a mechanism of exercising total control over Mayan communities.

From 1981 on, members of the army began to force civilians to accompany them on military operations. These people were closely tied to the army and were usually *confidenciales* or military commissioners that would later become patrol leaders. In some municipalities, they took their leaders' names or surnames as the group name, for example, the *Zapones* or the *Arones*, who operated in the municipalities of Santa Cruz and Uspantán, in the Department of Quiché…

The army created the patrols in response to the growth of the guerrilla groups' social base in the countryside and as a means of extending its control. They carried out operations in which the population itself would watch over and manage their neighbors' activities, delivering reports whenever they discovered something suspicious. The involvement of civilians was part of a carefully planned counterinsurgency strategy. One of the objectives was to create a network of informants that would provide, at a low cost, enough coverage to dismantle the guerrilla movement…

The army declared that the creation of the PAC

> was a response by honorable Guatemalans to defend their lives and homeland in the face of criminal terrorist Marxist-Leninist organizations.[38]

In April 1982, the army implemented the *Plan Nacional de Seguridad y Desarrollo* (National Security and Development Plan) in the country. It described the importance of organizing the civilian population to participate in the counterinsurgency struggle. In June 1982, the army developed the campaign plan *Victoria 82,* which included instructions on organizing more self-defense patrols within each military command's area of control…

Beginning at this time, the PAC were officially recognized as armed groups involved in the struggle against insurgent organizations in rural communities…The army's 1982 campaign plans define the main goals regarding the creation of the PAC:

> One of the objectives of organizing the PAC is to unite the Guatemalan family so that they all participate together in the protection of their common interests, with no exceptions of any kind, so that absolutely everyone participates…[39]

The forced involvement of the civilian population in the internal armed confrontation through the PAC was significantly greater in those departments with larger Maya populations…The creation of the PAC represented a new way of using indigenous labor in a widespread and low-cost manner. This was similar to what was done during colonial times and at the start of the Republic, although in this case, indigenous people were used for military purposes.

The PAC were also a means of disrupting community ties, trust between neighbors, and networks of solidarity, making it difficult for the guerrillas to rely on community organizations for support. By dismantling indigenous peoples' own systems of authority and control, the PAC forced communities to become dependent on military organization and command...

The campaign plan *Firmeza 83*...established that the PAC should:

> psychologically influence the inhabitants of each region so that the population rejects the enemy, feeding a sense of unity between the people and the Army, directed toward locating those members of the enemies' organized groups that remain active.[40]

The PAC created divisions between those who favored or opposed the parties in the confrontation as well as between the *patrulleros* and those who didn't want to be involved in armed activities. These divisions were found across communities and regions, creating internal opposition between members of different ethnicities, and forming rivalries that sometimes led to the use of force.

In one case, in the village of Chex in the municipality of Aguacatán, Huehuetenango, representatives of the community went to the military zone asking to join the patrols. This occurred after members of the armed forces committed massacres against the inhabitants of the villages of Pajuil Chex and Llano del Coyote (Aguacatán), in which elderly, women, and children were killed, many of them mutilated and burned. The horror of these acts of violence had such an impact and created such a strong response on the part of the residents of neighboring areas that joining the PAC seemed to be the only practical way to survive in their communities:

> In other villages, for example in Pajuil Chex, the military came and burned entire families. They not only came to burn their homes, but the people as well. Men, women, and children were burned to death, incinerated. This terrified us. It made us very frightened. It was said that those who were burned were guerrilla collaborators...Then, we were even more afraid because we wanted to save our own lives. It was said that if we collaborated with the guerrillas, the military would come after us and if we did the opposite, the guerrillas would come after us. Ultimately, we were between a rock and a hard place. There were men from here, from our *aldea* that came up with a strategy to save us. They went to the [military] zone and asked to be considered for an organization called the *patrullas civiles*... [41]

The *patrulleros'* hierarchy was based on the authority of the leader or commander of the patrol. On the municipal level, the first and second commanders were responsible, and on the departmental level, there was departmental leader. In most cases, patrol leaders were selected by the commanders of the military bases that controlled the area, although communities sympathetic to the army sometimes selected their patrol leaders. In both cases patrol leaders had to be authorized by the commander of the respective military zone.

The patrol leaders held positions of considerable trust and had to be registered in the military zone. In the ongoing recruitment of young people from the communities, preference was given to those who had served in the military or were military commissioners...

The age for participating in the PAC varied by region...The CEH recorded cases in which boys as young as twelve years old patrolled as well as men over seventy years old...

The *patrulleros* were forced to undergo different types of military instruction provided by specialists from the military bases or by patrol leaders with prior army training.

A significant component of the PAC training was internalized through fear...The Army forced *patrulleros* to observe interrogations in which torture was used to obtain lists of suspects, to make suspects suffer before killing them, to punish relatives or witnesses of presumed guerrillas, and to terrorize entire populations so that they would not support the insurgency. Later, they were forced to do the same on their own or under the supervision of military forces. If they refused, they were punished by death or torture...

PAC leaders were gathered by the officers of the military bases and given orders regarding patrol schedules. The schedules were designed so that the communities could monitor the presence of anyone suspicious and guard against insurgent activities. They were also mechanisms of internal social control and a means of extending military power over daily life, twenty-four hours a day. The patrol schedules allowed the military to control the *patrulleros* and the community as a whole. Prolonged shifts were also used as a mode of punishment and repression. These responsibilities impacted the *patrulleros'* daily lives and affected their work, as well as the economic, social, religious, cultural, and other activities of the community...

The *patrulleros* imposed different punishments for their members, from detention to acts of cruelty to the extreme of execution...Punishments were applied for various reasons including disobeying the orders of patrol leaders, refusing to participate in their shifts, or as a result of personal disputes.

The army developed a punishment chart that was distributed to the patrol leaders, who were supposed to carry it with them at all times. The chart referred exclusively to problems associated with a failure to meet their obligations. The *patrulleros'* own punishment system covered many additional issues and their punishments were far more severe....

> In 1988, I refused to continue in the PAC. The members of the patrol grabbed me and put me in a well three meters deep, keeping me there for forty-eight hours. The well had dirty water that came up to my waist. During those two days, I didn't receive any food or water. They threatened to kill me.[42]

The *patrulleros'* actions during the armed confrontation varied based on the time period, region, and their relationship with the army. The army forced the PAC to participate jointly with them in many operations. They had to act alone in others, either under orders or with the military's tacit support. Belonging to the PAC provided many of its members with positions of power, including privileges that allowed them to commit abuses while patrolling and to resolve personal disputes...

Among those violations committed by the PAC against members of their own communities, it is important to consider how the *patrulleros* captured their victims, submitted them to intense interrogations and physical torture, and committed massacres... These acts were sometimes committed in front of neighbors from the community, as *patrulleros* ignored relatives' pleas...

> On that day, in the month of August 1982, the PAC from the six neighborhoods in Mactzul met together. It was in the afternoon when they grabbed thirteen men, both adults and young men. They tied their hands behind their backs. They beat their chests with their weapons, kicked them and, when they fell, they stood on top of them. They put plastic hoods on their heads, interrogated them. The next day in the afternoon, they took them to a hill where a mass was being said. The families of those that were taken arrived. The women were asking the reasons why [they were detained]. The *patrulleros* told them to return to their homes if they didn't want to die as well... The PAC said they were going to hand them over to the soldiers, but they killed them in a ravine... Thirty *patrulleros* participated in the massacre. The PAC leaders and the commissioners said that the order to kill came from the Army and that they had to follow that order to rid the *cantón* of "bad people"...[43]

The scope of the civilian population's involvement reached unimaginable levels. According to the numbers provided by the army, in 1982, there were one million *patrulleros*. Since the 1981 national census established the country's population at around 6 million people and approximately two-thirds of the population were women and children, this leads to the conclusion that, in 1982, close to half of all adult Guatemalan men were *patrulleros*...

PAC Members Forced to Kill Other PAC Members

On May 24, 1982, almost a month after the PAC was established in San José Sinaché, a lieutenant accompanied by about forty soldiers, gathered the *patrulleros* of the municipality of Zacualpa in front of the San Antonio Sinaché church... Around 800 *patrulleros* from various neighboring villages, including the Ladino communities of Chinique, Capuchinas, Rincón de los Leones, and Zacualpa, attended this meeting. Eighty *patrulleros* from San José Sinaché were there.

They were all gathered together in the middle of the day, around twelve-thirty. The lieutenant, referring to the guerrillas, asked:

> Have you found those scum yet? Because they're here. If you don't hand them over, we'll kill everyone here.[44]

At one in the afternoon, the lieutenant ordered the *patrulleros* from San Antonio and San José to do a "search" in the nearby mountains. At three in the afternoon, the *patrulleros* returned to San Antonio without having found any guerrillas. Meanwhile, members of the army and *patrulleros* had executed four members of San Antonio's PAC and two women from San José Sinaché.

Then, the lieutenant addressed all the *patrulleros* and the residents of San Antonio who were there. Pointing at the corpses, he said:

> The "bad people" are here. They are here. You're all supporting them. You're giving them food, that's why they never die. Let them die in the mountains. Let them die in the ravines. They must die from hunger. If you see them, grab them, and take them with me to Zacualpa.[45]

The lieutenant then ordered the *patrulleros* from San José Sinaché to form a line. The soldiers were facing them and behind them were the rest of the... *patrulleros*. They took away their sticks and machetes.

"Which of you spoke the other day?" asked the lieutenant, referring to a meeting in the first week of May 1982.

The *patrulleros* from San José Sinaché remained silent.

"Well, I know you," said the lieutenant, pointing at Manuel Tol Canil, one of the patrol leaders. He said, "It's you."

The *patrulleros* from San José, Martín Panjoj Ramos and Antonio Castro Osorio denied that he was a guerrilla.

They said they had no reason to kill the first patrol leader, Manuel Tol Canil, because he hadn't done anything.[46]

Then, the Lieutenant pointed at them and said, "You also, and you too."

The lieutenant ordered the soldiers to tie each of the three *patrulleros* to the cypresses in front of the church with their hands behind their backs.

The lieutenant gave a machete to the rest of the *patrulleros* from San José Sinaché. He threatened the first *patrullero* in line, "Kill this one. If you don't kill him, I'll kill you."...

The lieutenant insisted that it had to be done "very slowly because they have to suffer a lot." When Martín Panjoj Ramos died, the lieutenant said that it was a "shame that he couldn't take it, that he went after just three blows of the machete."

Manuel Tol Canil died after four strikes from a machete.

Antonio Castro Osorio was struck with a machete six times. One of his relatives took a turn, but as he was taking a long time to die, the soldier said to the lieutenant, "What are we going to do? This shit won't die."

The lieutenant ordered them to break open his head. Then, "the soldier knocked his head off, but not quite all of it. It hung from the skin in the back."

Twelve *patrulleros* had to take their turns cutting him with a machete before their three *compañeros* died. Once they were dead, around seven at night, the lieutenant ordered the *patrulleros* from San José Sinaché to bury them and, pointing at the corpses, he said,"If you don't hand over everyone from the guerrilla, that's what we're going to do to you."

The lieutenant selected a new PAC leader in San José Sinaché, ordering him to tell everyone in his community what happened that day. Later he left with the soldiers. One group had to dig a hole and another had to carry the bodies. When they finished burying their *compañeros*, the *patrulleros* of San José Sinaché returned to their community. As one survivor explained:

> They were cold. They were very scared. Some of them were already very old and they were crying as they came along on the road. The fact is we all cried.

Upon arriving at the community of San José Sinaché, they met at the checkpoint with the fifteen or twenty *patrulleros* that had remained in town. There, the new PAC leader, reviewed what happened that afternoon and ordered four *patrulleros* to grab one of them, Pedro Tol. He also made the *patrulleros* who had not gone to San Antonio form a line...

The PAC leader said, "Since we suffered so much back there [referring to San Antonio], we're going to get it out of our system here."

Many of the *patrulleros*, taking advantage of the fact that it was already dark and the patrol leader couldn't see what they were doing, held back from beating their *compañero*. Later, the patrol leader ordered them to dig a hole, while four *patrulleros* killed Pedro Tol, "The poor man died by machete. They say his head looked like a stew."

The *patrulleros* buried him. After that, all of the *patrulleros* went home...

9

Guerrilla Organizations

The *Partido Guatemalteco del Trabajo* (Guatemalan Labor Party, PGT), *Fuerzas Armadas Rebeldes* (Rebel Armed Forces, FAR), *Organización del Pueblo en Armas* (Organization of the People in Arms, ORPA), and *Ejército Guerrillero de los Pobres* (Guerrilla Army of the Poor, EGP) engaged in a process of unification that resulted in the creation of the *Unidad Revolucionaria Nacional Guatemalteca* (National Guatemalan Revolutionary Union, URNG) on February 7, 1982...

The armed struggle was led by a number of guerrilla organizations that committed acts of violence against the fundamental rights of many people during the confrontation. The insurgency killed people, violated physical integrity and freedom, involved civilians in the confrontation, and attacked personal and state property.

Although they all followed the strategy of *Guerra Popular Revolucionaria* (Revolutionary People's War) and shared the objective of defeating the army, the four organizations did not have the same basic principles or structures. They were distinct in how they managed their actions, where they operated, and the composition of their ranks.

They also had significant political and military differences that fundamentally impacted the pace of the unification process...Above all, their visions differed regarding two main aspects of political-military strategy, that is, distinctions regarding what constituted the motivating forces of the revolution and how to best coordinate the relationship between the armed vanguard and the social base.

The PGT and the FAR followed orthodox Marxist tradition, understanding society in terms of social classes. They defined their guerrilla strategy within the framework of class struggle in which the working class played the lead role in the revolution. Indigenous people were not considered revolutionary actors, as such, but could become so through the process of proletarianization and semiproletarianization as a result of their seasonal movements from the *altiplano* to the *latifundios* of the *Costa Sur*.

According to the ORPA's point of view, Guatemalan society was founded on a racist system and the indigenous people had to be understood as the driving force of the Guatemalan revolution. Their strategy was conceived within the framework of ethnic demands.

The EGP tried to find a third way, reconciling the two perspectives with an ethnic-national understanding. Yet, they remained bound to a class-based framework linking indigenous people with poor Ladinos...

As a result of these differences, the guerrilla movement divided into four groups in the 1960s and began the first attempts at unification in the 1970s. From 1977 to 1978, they formed *la Tripartita* (the Triad) involving the three groups following a Marxist-Leninist orientation: the EGP, the FAR, and the PGT that followed Mario Sánchez known as the Núcleo de Dirección (PGT-ND). A bit later, ORPA was invited to join *el Cuatripartita* (the Quartet). In subsequent years, the PGT, which had been divided into three parts, joined the URNG.

Towards the end of 1980, for regional geopolitical reasons (the Sandinistas' 1979 victory in Nicaragua and the growing revolutionary movement of the Frente Farabundo Martí in El Salvador), Cuba and Nicaragua began to pressure the Guatemalan guerrillas to unify...

They proclaimed their unification through a five-point plan for the future, "Revolutionary Government, Patriotic, Popular, and Democratic":

> First, the Revolution will finally end repression against the people guaranteeing citizens' life and peace and the supreme rights of human beings. Second, the Revolution will create the foundation for resolving the necessities of the great majority of the people, ending the economic and political domination of the very wealthy nationals and foreigners that have governed Guatemala. Third, the Revolution will guarantee equality between the indigenous people and Ladinos, putting an end to cultural repression and discrimination. Fourth, the Revolution will enable the creation of a new society in which the government will be represented by all patriotic, popular and democratic sectors. Fifth, the Revolution will ensure the policies of non-alignment and international cooperation that poor nations need in today's world, based on people's self-determination.[1]

Partido Guatemalteco del Trabajo (Guatemalan Labor Party, PGT)

The Guatemalan guerrilla movement owes its historical and theoretical origins to the PGT...The party's role in the guerrilla movement was debated internally throughout the confrontation, leading to a division within its membership between those that chose armed struggle and those that wanted to follow the official party line.

The controversy was most significant in the early 1960s when, despite accepting the possibility of armed struggle in the Third Congress of 1960, the PGT did not directly become involved, although it continued to view itself as the movement's political vanguard. These contradictions were heightened with the 1966 death of Luis Turcios Lima, commander of the Edgar Ibarra Front, who served as a liaison between the party's leadership and the guerrilla commanders, which led to the final break between the PGT and the FAR.

Between 1966 and 1967, the PGT tried several times, unsuccessfully, to organize itself to participate in the armed struggle with its own military structures and by creating its own fronts. In this period there was much discussion as to whether armed struggle was appropriate...

> It was impossible to resolve the tension between advocating for a democratic struggle of the masses and the military option...which led to division...[2]

Between 1966 and 1967, counterinsurgency operations [against the FAR] increased in Zacapa, Izabal, Chiquimula, and the capital. Guerrilla units in those regions were virtually destroyed.The demobilization of members created a serious leadership crisis and an ideological division within the guerrilla movement that led the PGT to break with the *Fuerzas Armadas Rebeldes* (FAR) in January 1968. In March of that year the PGT decided to create its own armed group called the *Fuerzas Armadas Revolucionarias* (Revolutionary Armed Forces, FAR), "Then, there were the FAR rebels and the FAR revolutonaries"[3]...

The FAR revolutionaries never engaged in significant combat or attacks against the army, since their guiding principle was that they were involved in a process of training and military preparation.

Intense counterinsurgency repression against members of the party weakened them practically from their inception. In January 1968, state agents killed two important members of the party, Alejandro Silva Falla and Ricardo Garrido Samayoa. In the same month, they tortured and brutally killed Rogelia Cruz, another member of the group. That act captivated public opinion, because she was a former national beauty queen. The response of the FAR revolutionaries to these acts was the execution of the North American military attachés Colonel John D. Weeber and Captain Ernest A. Munro.

The attacks against the PGT continued and on September 26, 1972, six members of the political bureau and a domestic worker were captured and executed by state security forces. In 1974, Huberto Alvarado, the party's secretary general, was assassinated. These actions against the leadership created a crisis of direction and weakened the organization:

> By '72, the military units has all but disappeared, some of our operatives had joined other revolutionary organizations, especially the FAR rebels...[4]

Fuerzas Armadas Rebeldes (Rebel Armed Forces, FAR)

For the FAR, revolutionary war was a class struggle in which the issue of ethnicity was secondary and the primary role was played by workers whose participation could be expressed in different forms of struggle, whether political, rights-based, or military. Armed struggle was to be managed through guerrilla warfare, in other words, through the placement of small guerrilla units in different regions of the country. They hoped that this would motivate the population to join the revolutionary struggle, weaken the army, and bring down the government...

Between 1962 and 1965, the FAR spread from the capital to four large regions where the PGT had supporters involved in political work. They gained the backing of the population in the Eastern region (Zacapa, Izabal), the Western region (San Marcos, Retalhuleu, Quetzaltenango), the Southern region (Escuintla, Suchitepéquez), and the Central region (Guatemala, Baja Verapaz).

At this time, the social base of support in the eastern part of the country was composed of small-scale tomato producers and tobacco workers, workers at the United Fruit Company (UFCo) and International Railways of Central America (IRCA) as well as stevedores from Puerto Barrios. On the *Costa Sur*, the main supporters were small landholders who had backed Arbenz, as well as members of agricultural and railroad unions. In the Central region, they had the support of workers, students, and professionals from communist backgrounds...

From 1963 to 1965, the guerrilla organization used the tactic of occupying towns and *aldeas* and engaging in attacks and ambushes in Petén, La Ceibita, and Sunzapote where they "anihilated eleven army soldiers with a group of 60 guerrillas." In those years, they also engaged in *ajusticiamientos* against military commissioners and those supporting ultra-right wing groups...

From 1963 on, the Urban Resistance Front operated as commandos in the capital and were in charge of supplies and logistical support for the guerilla *focos* (a common Latin American guerrilla strategy based on small armed groups) in the east. They supported these efforts financially through attacks on banks and foreign businesses. They also began the practice of kidnapping businessmen and landowners, who they considered to be their enemies...

The 1966 presidential elections created great expectations within the guerrilla movement. The PR promised that the government of Méndez Montenegro would be the third revolutionary government. The PGT and the FAR decided to support Méndez's candidacy and engaged in a unilateral cease-fire...The election of Méndez Montenegro was followed by the forced disappearance of various members and leaders of the PGT, the FAR, and the MR13.

The counterinsurgency policies of the government of Méndez Montenegro in the eastern part of the country under Coronel Carlos Arana Osorio severely impacted the political actions of the guerrillas in rural areas, forcing them to move their operations to the capital. The majority of its leaders were killed in the eastern region and the movement was destroyed in the south where most of its supporters were unarmed.

From January 1968 on, under the control of commander Camilio Sánchez, the FAR unleashed a wave of violence through assassinations, kidnappings, and attacks that created terror among the wealthy sectors of society...Camilio Sánchez was captured and killed by the army in August 1968. The main guerrilla *focos* in the east, the Edgar Ibarra Front and the Alejandro de León Front, ordered their combatants to go to the capital to support the Urban Front.

The period before the 1970 presidential elections was also plagued by violence. The FAR continued to engage in political kidnappings. They kidnapped the minister Alberto Fuentes Mohr, the U.S diplomat S. M. Holly, and the German ambassador Karl von Spreti...

In 1968, the FAR agreed to create a main column in Alta Verapaz, "with the goal of creating a guerrilla *foco* that would lead the *campesino* population to join the guerrillas."[5] The two attempts to operate in the region failed as a result of a lack of support on the part of the population. In 1969, they engaged in a third attempt to create a main column. They decided to concentrate their forces in the department of Petén and then to proceed from there to the south, to the departments of Alta Verapaz and Quiché. The exploratory mission was entrusted to one of the FAR's leaders, Pablo Monsanto…

> In 1971, the small group that was part of the main column went public to show the world that we were alive, we decided to begin actions, and we launched our first ambush in the mountains of Yaltutú, municipality of Dolores.[6]

Although they carried out various ambushes, they were not very successful. The army responded quickly to the guerrilla offensive…and the FAR largely ended its public actions and focused on political work in the Petén region…

In 1979, based on the decision to unify the insurgent forces and create a plan for widespread guerrilla warfare, the FAR established its first main column in Petén, called the Turcios Lima Front. From 1981 on, this group began carrying out ambushes, harassing and attacking the army in the municipality of Melchor de Mencos, and, given the region's importance to tourism, on the road linking Flores to Tikal…

The FAR decided that its guerrilla units should not operate over a wide territory or be involved in too many disconnected actions. Their objective was to use military action and political work to involve an increasing number of people into an expanding guerrilla struggle…

Beginning in 1981, the FAR's strategy was to activate its military forces in eastern Petén while using the west of the department as the rearguard…From 1984 on, when state operations decreased, the FAR lacked adequate social support, since the population was too frightened to be willing to collaborate or even to provide supplies. This significantly weakened the guerrillas…

Organización del Pueblo en Armas (Organization of the People in Arms, ORPA)

ORPA was formed based on prior experiences with the armed struggle and grounded in an understanding that indigenous people should be at the center of the Guatemalan revolution. ORPA rejected *foquismo* (a revolutionary strategy based on multiple *focos*) as its political-military strategy and instead supported the idea that the revolutionary movement should concentrate on armed groups. It insisted on secrecy during the guerilla training phase that was to be developed in parallel with social and rights-based movements as part of a vision of a long-term struggle.

They focused on guerrilla units in the field and had a major advantage by deciding to operate in the densely populated, indigenous majority *Costa Sur* where they attacked the interests of the agro-export oligarchy.

ORPA's did not try to create "liberated zones" and had a local impact, "We were a small but highly skilled combat force."[7] ORPA dismantled their urban front in 1981…They never managed to rebuild their units to prior levels. Still, their ongoing presence in a highly strategic area within the nation's economy was a significant factor in the peace negotiation process.

ORPA was the guerrilla organization most concerned with the role of the Mayan people, or the "*pueblo natural*" (original people) as they were called within the revolutionary process...ORPA viewed "Marxism as an instrument for analysis, but not as dogma."[8] They considered indigenous people, not class, to be the core of the revolution: "the *pueblo natural* were the driving force of the Guatemalan revolution."[9]

ORPA tried to implement a mode of analysis that was very different than the traditional Marxist-Leninist orthodox thinking of the Guatemalan left...They used this approach to train new members and, at times, they presented a millenialist vision of the life of the ancient Mayans...

> We studied the past to comprehend the greatness of our ancestors, the Maya, in order to understand how the conquest changed everything about the lives of this great people...The *pueblo natural* of Guatemala are the descendants of a great people that created an extraordinary culture...The Maya didn't go hungry like we do. They didn't die of malnutrition...They ate better than the inhabitants of Europe in that time...The Maya people were a well-organized and hard-working people.[10]

Many joined the ranks of the ORPA out of a belief that armed struggle was a way to combat racial discrimination. A former combatant explained that his joining "was motivated by the outrage and indignation over how indigenous people were treated."[11] According to its leaders, this antiracist vision was a part of the internal workings of the organization:

> One of the most important principles of the Organization is ending the false division that exists between the poor as a result of racism. On the guerrilla fronts we should carry out this principle to the utmost and we cannot allow any degradation or humiliation to our *compañeros naturales* (indigenous comrades) On the contrary, we should respect them, take an interest in the origins of our true roots, our culture, our language, religion, and clothing. Likewise, fraternity, equality, and love should exist for our *compañeros* who are not *naturales*... [12]

In its strategic vision, ORPA thought that the masses should organize themselves independently from the armed movement:

> Only a small group of the people has to join the clandestine struggle...The clandestine organizations will gain greater strength and significantly weaken the enemy. Then, in the final struggle, the organizations of the masses will join their efforts with ours to defeat the army and the government...We should support and enable the legal struggles of the masses, but we should never control them or lead them. If we did this, we would put our work and our lives at risk...[13]

ORPA's strategic priority involved building an organization that focused not on political struggles, but on creating a guerrilla vanguard:

> We believed that in the beginning of an armed struggle we should focus ourselves on developing a guerrilla force that was very professional and very well-trained...[14]

Based on this idea, ORPA did not try to encourage mass organizations to follow the political-military vanguard or to become involved with the guerrilla war as did the EGP...

ORPA's goal was to control a contiguous space from the Mexican border to the capital, passing through Quetzaltenango along the Sierra Madre with a base of social support from the north of the indigenous *altiplano* to the south of the large and most valuable landholdings...They tried to control the economic nerve center of the country. ORPA developed its operations in some of the most populous regions of the country that were majority indigenous, including the southwest of the department of San Marcos, the southern part of the department of Sololá, and the departments of Quetzaltenango and Chimaltenango...

ORPA developed in two stages: the first, a preparatory stage (1971–1979) and the second, a combat stage (1979–1996)...The primary goals of the preparatory stage were to get to know the terrain, develop a recruiting campaign for the organization, and to train new members...After eight years of preparation, in 1979, ORPA had 600 supporters in the capital and a secret political and military organization with activities in rural and urban areas...

ORPA used a nationalist rather than class-based approach and an anti-imperialist vision that reflected on 500 years of oppression. ORPA focused its attacks against the oligarchy, that is, the landowners and the army that supported them ORPA's policy was to "break the agrarian block" that defined the *Costa Sur*...

ORPA used a variety of tactics. The most common were ambushes...Starting in May 1980, the organization began its operations against the PMA that provided security on coffee plantations and cattle ranches:

> "After the guerrilla actions, they withdrew the PMA and the Army assumed responsibility for the security of the *fincas*"...[15]

ORPA understood the guerrilla front as "a form of *campesino* organization and permanent military force"[16] and for this reason the fronts had to have as close a link as possible with the population...Yet, the relationship was kept secret...

> From the beginning, we were very careful because we had examples of the repression, destroying *aldeas* and whole areas. We were careful not to create any camps or to leave any evidence of the participation of the people...[17]

Ejército Guerrillero de los Pobres (EGP)

The *Ejército Guerrillero de los Pobres* (EGP) was created on January 19, 1972, the date when the first fifteen combatants arrived in Ixcán in northern Quiché. The group was linked to the Edgar Ibarra Guerrilla Front of the FAR whose member, Rolando Morán, began organizing the EGP in 1968 and became its commander-in-chief.

The main characteristics of the EGP's strategy were the participation of the civilian population, an engagement with ethnic-national issues, and an attempt throughout the conflict to balance military and political factors. The EGP's vanguard was composed of permanent military units that planned to take control of the country by developing a coordinated strategy involving guerrilla warfare and social movements. Civilians were expected to play a leading role in the struggle alongside the guerrilla forces.

The population organized in the mountains were responsible for providing logistical support to the guerrillas and served as a source for recruiting while also playing a role in self-defense. They were supposed to expand the organization to take over local structures, destroying them from within by replacing them with revolutionary leadership.

In the cities and in the lowlands...the EGP's link with the population was mainly through popular organizations. By establishing guerrilla cells within these groups, the EGP supported rights-based movements, channeling these efforts toward paralyzing the economic system and trying to elevate their struggles toward revolution. Its plan was that once the guerrillas had advanced to larger battles and liberated territory, its advance toward the city would be combined with mass insurrection that would lead to the overthrow of the government...

The EGP's strategy considered indigenous people not only in relation to their socioeconomic condition—part of the poor *campesinos* that along with the working class made up the driving force of the revolution—but also in relation to their sociocultural identity. Within this strategic vision, their role in the revolutionary process was to act alongside Ladinos:

> The revolution is impossible if the indigenous people are not part of the revolution. If *el indio* is not part of this revolution, not only as an element of the driving force, mechanisms, and numbers, but also as part of the human, cultural, and ethnic element that provides support to the formation of the body of revolutionary Guatemala. In other words, the indigenous people need to be present in every way...[18]

In order to extend guerrilla warfare across the nation, the EGP divided it in three strategic areas: the mountains; the city; and, the lowlands, which it saw as the expression of the three part agrarian, anti-imperialist and anticapitalist character of the people's revolutionary war.

In actuality, the EGP could not maintain a balance among the operations in those three areas. In the mountains, they developed the basic core of their strategic plan out of which the other two areas operated. In the city and the lowlands, they faced a question regarding the degree to which rights-based struggles and guerrilla warfare were complementary. Nevertheless, the determining factor that prevented them from achieving their strategic objectives for the city and the *Costa Sur* was the systematic repression of social movements and the assassination of of leaders and of the organized guerrilla cells...

In 1975, the EGP decided that the moment had arrived that they should be publicly known...On May 28, 1975, in the La Cuchilla de Xalbal center, Ixcán, they made their presence known through the *ajusticiamiento* of Guillermo Monzón. A few days later, on June 7, they executed the landowner Luis Arenas Barrera. He was the owner of the La Perla and San Luis Ranches, in municipality of Chajul, Quiché and was known as the Tiger of Ixcán. On the *Costa Sur*, the EGP's first actions occurred in 1976 through sabotage such as the burning of planes used for aerial spraying and burning cane fields. That same year, they were involved in *ajusticiamientos*, bombings, and worksite occupations in the capital.

One of the objectives of these actions was to educate the population regarding the importance of being trained to defend clandestine political groups and the organized population in general. Self-defense was presented as way for people to participate in the conflict. This idea led to the creation in 1979 of the *Fuerzas Irregulares Locales* (Irregular Local Forces, FIL). As people gained experience with defense, they could later participate in more aggressive actions with the goal of creating a people's army...

In 1978, the EGP had defined its political and popular program, and its vision of the front was being developed based on geographical factors. Also, the first steps were made to unite with the FAR and with the central leadership of the PGT...

From that year on, the EGP began offenses against the army, carrying out attacks and ambushes against roving patrols and some military bases to capture weapons. They also engaged in acts of sabotage involving Claymore mines and other explosives:

> By 1980, the plan was in place to overthrow Lucas' government...We were already trying to advance quickly at a time in which there was a heightened sense of mass struggle, full of enthusiasm, full of combative spirit...[19]

Motivated by a combination of factors and reacting to the January 31, 1980 massacre at the Spanish embassy, people joined the EGP in large numbers...starting in the departments of Quiché and Huehuetenango.

> Then, the displacements no longer occurred only at night, but also during the day. Helicopters passed over and watched huge columns of displaced people moving from one place to another. The people as well as the guerrilla couldn't bear it anymore. All of that gave us the feeling, the sense of tremendous growth. We were able to sign up 5,000 *compañeros* for squads [FIL] in Huehuetenango.[20]

In 1981, the EGP had expanded its reach to a large part of the country...This is when it appeared that the situation had reached the final stage...The army command reacted to the peak of the guerrilla movement in the Ixcán, "The subversion is a cancer that won't stop."[21]

> On November 12, 1981, the army pulled out all its units and took them to Chimaltenango because the guerrilla was at the point of declaring the *Altiplano* to be liberated. All that remained was the base at Playa Grande...[22]

> So, the seed of triumphalism began, the seed of overestimating our own capacity and underestimating the capacities of our adversaries, those were the greatest errors that were committed...[23]

> The victory of the Sandinistas showed that it was possible to gain power in this way, but that created a lot of expectations... [24]

The lack of weapons was "the most powerful reason"[25] for the EGP's inability to take combat to a higher level at that peak moment:

> When we would have meetings with the officers from the army, they would say, "And you all in the 80's, why didn't you move forward instead of stopping at that point, you surprised us that you didn't advance." We didn't have any arms or munitions, in '81 we had only 12 bullets per rifle and so the situation was really difficult.[26]

> It was a point of such great excitement, a pre-insurrectional moment... the people began demanding that the organization give them arms to fight; if we could they all wanted to join, but without arms, no... [27]

The rapid and mass involvement destroyed the clandestine apparatus that the EGP had built based on the principle of compartmentalization, which protected the organized members of the population. As a consequence, those people not only lacked arms, but were also exposed to repressive actions...

Between July and August 1981, military intelligence attacked the EGP's main safe houses, destroying the urban front whose members fled to Chimaltenango to the Augusto César Sandino Front where some members from the *Costa Sur* had also gone to escape severe repression... The EGP tried to concentrate its forces there... At the end of 1981, the army began its major offensive... first in Chimaltenango, later expanding its operations to the whole area covered by the Augusto César Sandino Front, who were forced to retreat to the Ho Chi Minh Front in Quiché. This is when the stage of indiscriminate violence began, the large massacres and the scorched earth military operations...

The confusion created by the army's offensive was overwhelming, as the fronts were left isolated, without any means of communication and receiving contradictory information about what was happening...

> The EGP concentrated in that area, in the Ixcán... we had nowhere to go and so we stayed and decided to resist and began rebuilding as best as we could... [28]

From 1981 on, poor coordination between the fronts, a lack of weapons, and internal power struggles that polarized the EGP's national leadership led to dissatisfaction and rebellion on the part of some leaders of the fronts while many abandoned the group and dozens left for Nicaragua...

In response to the massacres, the people fled in large numbers seeking refuge in Mexico where they kept their ties with the EGP. Thousands of others stayed within the country hidden in the mountains where they formed the *Comunidades de Población en Resistencia* (Communities of Populations in Resistance, CPR) with the CPR-I in Ixcán and the CPR-S in the mountains...

After their defeat in 1982, the EGP failed to reestablish significant offensive capabilities. Its work to recapture the masses, territory, and power was gradually channeled into political activities and it focused its strategy on issues such as safe havens, the return of the displaced and the CPRs for which they sought support and international recognition...

By the second half of 1981, the civilian population was systematically destroyed by the army, and the previously established systems of self-defense proved to be inadequate...

> We didn't have the strength to face those offensives. We didn't think that this would happen in our country...We thought that our defenses would be enough to face the attacks, thinking that the attacks would be directed against the guerrilla forces, we never thought they'd be against the people...[29]

> The guerrilla didn't have the capacity to defend the population. It didn't have the forces or the weapons to fight a war, all they had were a few rifles, sometimes shotguns.[30]

Many of those that joined the organization felt abandoned by the armed vanguard that withdrew to the north and left them facing the army's scorched earth operations:

> When the most severe violence began, the guerrilla wasn't around anymore...We just stayed here and when the soldiers arrived, we were alone...[31]

Arbitrary Execution of Six Members of the Guerrilla Army of the Poor (EGP) by Their Own Organization

In 1981, the EGP experienced its period of greatest expansion...reaching a point where its leaders began considering the idea of creating a future "liberated zone." Nevertheless, the apparent withdrawal of the army from the areas where the EGP had the largest presence was followed by actions by the intelligence service. By the end of that year, this led to the military destruction of the EGP's urban front.

That year, while the EGP's withdrawal to the north of Quiché continued, a large number of militants were captured by the security forces, especially in the capital As a result, the group's leadership sent a number of important militants from the capital to Mexico and especially to Nicaragua.

Guisela Irasema López was among the militants imprisoned in 1982. She had also been detained in 1979 when she was a member of the Robin García Student Front, an organization of leftist high school and university students. After she was freed, Guisela Irasema became involved in the clandestine activities of the EGP. She joined the urban military force, as a core member of the Otto René Castillo Front where she was known by the pseudonym "Beatriz." In February 1982, she was captured again, this time with another militant known as "Paula," by armed men dressed in civilian clothes...She was detained for three months in the *Antigua Escuela Politécnica* (Old Polytechnic School) a place where many people were detained, some of whom were killed. In this secret prison, she met another EGP militant, Aída Marilú Castillo Estrada, known as "Carolina" who had been captured on March 28, 1982, on the border between Guatemala and Mexico.

The captors abused those detained while also engaging in acts designed to gain their trust. Guisela Irasema and Marilú Castillo were often taken to a house located in the Vista Hermosa neighborhood in Guatemala City where the captors had sex with them. On May 23, 1982, when they were both at the house, they took advantage of the men's distraction, and escaped...

Another prisoner was Eugenio Contreras, the former president of the Psychology Students Association of San Carlos University and a member of the EGP who used the pseudonym "Mariano." Contreras was detained by the security forces in May 1982 in Guatemala City. He was held in detention on the *Antigua Escuela Politécnica* until November of that year when...he managed to escape...

After escaping from the house in Vista Hermosa, Guisela Irasema and Marilú Castillo reestablished ties with the EGP. Based on what they had seen and heard during their detention in the *Antigua Escuela Politécnica*, Guisela prepared a ninety-page report that was given to the National Directorate of the insurgent group that included the names of those detained, identifying those that collaborated with the security forces and those that had resisted.

At the end of June, they were both transported to Nicaragua and set up in a house in Casares, in the department of Carazo by the Pacific Ocean. The real purpose of this move was to investigate if their version of the facts was true or if, in fact, they had been "won over" by the army and freed so they could spy on the EGP…

On orders of the National Directorate of the EGP in Nicaragua, both women were interrogated various times about their stories. Following these interrogations, the majority believed that their version was false, "they had obviously negotiated their release with the primary goal of infiltration…and what followed was *fusilamiento*…"[32]

The members of the National Directorate in Nicaragua decided to execute the two militants…both victims were taken from the house by another EGP militant and told to pack their bags because they were both to be moved to Cuba. In a gasoline station near the new road to León, the two women were placed in a vehicle driven by a male militant. They were both executed, in complete secrecy, inside a building provided by the government of Nicaragua…

Once he was free, Eugenio Contreras recorded various tapes regarding his account of captivity that were sent to the members of the National Directorate of the EGP in Nicaragua. However, as with Guisela Irasema and Marilú Castillo, the leaders did not believe his description of the escape and determined that Contreras had negotiated his freedom and betrayed the organization. They decided to execute him. This was done on the road to Aguacatán, in the department of Huehuetenango.

Carlos Ranferí Morales López, the first cousin of Guisela Irasema, had also been a member of the Robín García Revolutionary Front that later joined the Augusto César Sandino Front of the EGP, where he used the pseudonym, "Otto René." On August 26, 1982, Carlos Ranferí left Guatemala for Nicaragua to receive political training under orders from the EGP leadership.

The next day he was in contact with his mother, Marta López, and told her that he had problems with the organization that he thought would be resolved through a meeting with the National Directorate. On November 15, 1982, at four in the afternoon, his mother left him at the intersection of Siete Sur in Managua where members of the EGP were going to pick him up. They took him in what appeared to be the direction of Guatemala. They were with Eugenio Contreras's wife, Ligia…who had traveled to Nicaragua to find out what happened to her husband, They were also accompanied by a third unidentified person, a young man who had joined the César Augusto Sandino Front and who, according to an EGP leader, "was presumed to be a spy."…

None of these three knew that, several days earlier, they had been condemned to death by the National Directorate of the EGP…A member of the National Directorate…told the CEH that en route from Managua to the Honduran border:

> They stopped the car and, with the help of others and the Sandinistas, what they did is cover their noses and mouths with a cloth or towel that was soaked in chloroform. Then, when they were calm and sleeping, in that state, they were executed, the three together in the same place and buried in a grave in the country…[33]

In 1998, the leaders of the URNG that were part of the EGP's last National Directorate publicly acknowledged their organization's responsibility for two of the executions...A member...at that time stated that the *fusilamientos* were

> ...the most terrible acts, the worst expression of a situation of defeat...of a desperate attempt to preserve the little that was left. What was especially difficult was the idea that we had been infiltrated, that we were being beaten because of infiltration.[34]

The CEH determined that the Guisela Irasema López, Aída Marilú Castillo Estrada, Eugenio Contreras, Ligia de Contreras, Carlos Ranferí Morales López, and an unidentified young man were killed by members of the EGP based on a decision of its national leaders. These acts constituted cases of extrajudicial execution for which the leadership is responsible.

No military or political situation provided the legal or moral justification for these crimes...The CEH views this crime as an illustration of the lack of discipline and internal justice within the guerilla organization as well as a failure to protect basic human rights that allowed a loss of trust to lead to the killing of unarmed militants.

Part III

Consequences and Effects of *La Violencia*

10

Terror and Its Consequences

Analyzing the consequences of the armed confrontation requires engaging with the multiple tragedies of this entire period: the loss of so many men, women, and children, and of their dreams and potential; the impoverishment of the country as a whole and of Mayan communities in particular; the collapse of the country's democratic institutions; and the destruction of basic norms of life and coexistence. These issues lead to a fundamental question for the construction and consolidation of peace: what are the consequences of the conflict on society and on its people, communities, and institutions?

During the process of investigation and analysis, the CEH found itself facing the deep and far-reaching impact of the armed confrontation. Some of these issues influenced the dynamic of the CEH's investigation. Terror created an invisible, but tangible barrier that was an obstacle for the presentation of cases and produced gaps and silences within the testimonies. The absence of thousands of displaced people that could no longer return to their communities made it difficult to fully reconstruct of the complete story of what occurred. The lack of networks of social organization in many regions of the country, urban as well as rural, made it difficult to access affected communities and individuals

The analysis of the consequences of *la violencia* required an expansive reading of the testimonies that went beyond documenting violations, extending towards an engagement with the human emotions of the experiences described as well as their psychosocial, cultural, political, and economic impact. This was very complex work, especially since the majority of the testimonies dealt only with the narration of death, disappearance and specific accounts of the violations suffered by the particular person.

For example, if a case involved a student leader who was arbitrarily executed, many times the person presenting the testimony did not know or did not say what had happened to the organization as a result of the loss of its leader. Or, while it was possible to document in detail a massacre in a particular Mayan community, it was difficult for those interviewed to describe in depth the impact that this event had on community life or on their culture. In general, with the passage of time and the natural mechanisms of memory, the testimonies tended to emphasize deeply traumatizing acts over their larger impact; the horror of a concrete moment or period over future consequences...

To complement the testimonies, the CEH used a variety of other sources that it collected, placing special emphasis on interviews with key witnesses, many of whom provided useful reflections on the impact of the confrontation. The CEH also used reports from its regional field offices, documents that often included more interpretative and detailed material on the experience of communities where the research was conducted. In this way, it was possible to use a diverse collection of different documentary sources regarding these issues...

During the investigation, certain themes emerged that repeated themselves over and over: the terror and trauma left by the armed confrontation; the weakening of the country's institutions; the destruction of the social fabric; and material losses. These represent the most common and significant consequences of the long and bloody confrontation. In addition, they present an important part of the fundamental problem in that in order for society to rebuild itself, it must not only address the structural problems that led to the confrontation as well as material and political questions, it must also engage moral and spiritual issues. In addition, it is clear that in the middle of the destruction and chaos that took place, in spite of everything, significant efforts were made toward regeneration and rebuilding. Through these ongoing struggles, especially on the part of those most affected, there has been a reaffirmation of life, dignity, identity, and solidarity...

Terror

The thousands of dead, disappeared, tortured, and displaced, and the hundreds of Mayan communities erased from the map during the armed confrontation, have left a lasting imprint on the minds and hearts of the Guatemalan people. The impact of *la violencia* varies by ethnicity, social origins, economic position, gender, age, place of residence, political affiliation, and religious beliefs...and includes fear, terror, sadness, depression, physical and psychosomatic illnesses, altered mourning, distrust, silence, inhibition, and powerlessness. Other consequences frequently described by those the interviewed by the CEH include alcoholism, recurring nightmares, serious mental illnesses, apathy, suicides, and feelings of anger and loneliness...

Terror in Guatemala was bound to strategies whose greatest impact is associated with the periods of maximum violence and the places where the repression was most severe. However, one cannot reduce terror to a succession of violent incidents or military operations, nor were these actions the only means used to create and maintain terror during the armed confrontation. Rather, terror is a complex process created through its multiple expressions and broad social impact. For this reason, terror did not simply disappear when the levels of violence were reduced. Its effects were cumulative and lasting so that addressing terror requires time, effort, and new types of experiences that allow those affected to overcome the past...

It is important to understand that not all Guatemalans lived with the same degree of terror. Certainly, the extreme fear that is a key element of terror was experienced with great intensity by those most affected by political violence in those areas where *la violencia* was most severe. However, there were more subtle facets of terror that affected people and places less directly impacted by the armed confrontation. These include passivity and conformity, feelings of powerlessness, and the decision, sometimes unconscious, not to see, not to hear, and not to talk about the atrocities that devastated the country. The social consequences of terror are still felt throughout society, especially through the loss of community values that provide the foundation for social life:

> The consequence of the armed confrontation is that we can no longer trust. It's as if the people have gotten worse, that they have no longer have any respect. The people who were around during the time of the patrols—how they liked to carry weapons—were doing bad things. Before the violence, we were closer, we communicated more with each other. We came together to work in the community…Now it's difficult. We don't respect each other anymore…There are lots of divisions. There's no more friendship…[1]

The institutionalization of state violence against its opponents—assumed or real—was combined with policies of psychological warfare, one of the key means of disseminating terror. These actions extended beyond physical harm, to negatively impact all of society. Through the implementation of various strategies and the creation of mechanisms to communicate terror, the state tried to destroy within people's hearts the potential and will for change, in the present as well as for the future. In this way, the state sought to make it clear that, regardless of one's actions or intentions, it was impossible to change the established order and any attempt to do so would lead to death, "they wanted the population to feel how powerless, how defenseless they were"…[2]

The extreme nature of *la violencia* clearly revealed that state terror was not solely directed toward physically destroying its presumed opponents. They wanted everyone to know that those who participated in rights-based activities, as well as their relatives, ran the risk of being killed and subjected to all sorts of atrocities. In the face of the fear that repression created among survivors, many chose to keep quiet or to adapt to the situation through submission or by playing roles forced upon them…

> The people in the community became very afraid. They locked their doors tightly. You could feel a sense of panic. There was no longer much communication among people.[3]

> This created a type of amnesia within the family…they only spoke among themselves about the most basic things, everything became monotonous, waiting for when the men would return, and asking themselves who would be the next victim.[4]

The impact of state terrorism was to silence individuals and society. In this way, the state was able to structure social relations to a greater and lesser degree such that all of society was impacted by the mechanisms of terror. The state gained an ability to control and dominate society, destroying the possibility and will for change among the people by creating a form of psychosocial trauma.

> Here is a sense of apathy, a lack of care…I would say, inertia, there is a general sense of inertia that is a product of the repression.[5]
>
> There is disintegration, disintegration in every sense, disintegration of social organization, and ethical principles…There's enormous mistrust. People no longer have much hope for the future. I know of villages, for example, where people used to have fun playing sports…Now, there are no sports. The only sport is drinking…[6]

In the face of the mechanisms of repression, the people experienced a sense of powerlessness, fear, and conformity that has been further strengthened through impunity, the criminalization of victims, the forced implication in committing atrocities, and silencing. These mechanisms are interconnected and have created social and moral problems at many levels of society.

Impact of Forced Disappearances

During the armed confrontation, there were many situations that prevented thousands of people from carrying out the normal rituals of death and burial. Forced disappearance was an especially destructive practice in this regard because of the uncertainty it created and the fact that it was impossible [for families and friends] to know what happened to victims or even to have the relative comfort of knowing that the person was no longer suffering:

> The worst part of a disappearance is the uncertainty. You don't know if your relative is alive or dead or what they are doing to them.[7]
>
> My mother still thinks my father is alive. We think he is not. If we could find his remains, this would lessen our sorrow…[8]

It was often impossible to bury the dead, especially in the 1980s, because of the generalized mood of terror, the presence of the military, and other issues associated with the massacres such as people fleeing their communities and the persecution of the survivors in the mountains. Violent death and displacement often made it impossible to provide a respectful burial…Relatives and neighbors suffered deep feelings of guilt because they could not prepare the dead [for burial], or bury and mourn them according to the customs of the Mayan communities or Ladino families' religious rituals. Mourning the dead is part of the cycle of life. One of the ongoing consequences of terror is what is known as "disturbed" or "suspended mourning."

> It has hurt us a lot because Francisco died in a bombing and because we had to run away we weren't able to cry well.[9]

In addition, the impossibility of ritualizing a loved one's death makes it difficult to resolve grief through symbolic processes of managing loss through acts shared among families and within the community...

> We haven't been able to bring my daughter's remains to bury her in the cemetery in the village of El Naranjo. My grandchildren and I dream of the day when we can bury my daughter in the cemetery since that brings us comfort as Christians...Also, there is my husband. We don't even know where he is...We have to live thinking and suffering because we had to leave my daughter's remains behind in the place where they left her...All of the things that happened to me left me feeling as if I were floating...Ever since then, I have a nervous condition and have many nightmares.[10]

For the cultures and religions that coexist in Guatemala, it is almost inconceivable to fail to provide dignified burial to those deceased, violating values and offending the dignity of all. For the Maya, this problem is especially important because ongoing connections uniting the living with the dead are central to their culture...

In this sense, clandestine and hidden cemeteries represent an open wound. One can sense the uncertainty with which many Guatemalans suffer as a result of not knowing the whereabouts of their relatives or what happened to them...

For this reason, those providing testimony to the CEH frequently requested exhumations as a means of reparation. Healing the particular wounds of suspended mourning requires exhuming clandestine cemeteries and clarifying the whereabouts of the disappeared. This would provide relatives with the opportunity to reconnect with their dead and to honor them through specific ceremonies...

> We want to know where he is. Not even dogs are left thrown aside like that...We want to give him a Christian burial, even if it's just with some of his bones, because we don't expect anything else anymore.[11]
>
> A dead person should be in the cemetery, because it wasn't an animal that they killed. Why do they deny us the knowledge of where he is so that we can bury him as God commands?...[12]

The Impact of Fear

The absence of justice and the flaunting of impunity created a sense that no offense would be punished, that no one would pay for what they had done, and that there were no limitations to abuse. Impunity was a key mechanism for expanding the impact of repression since it meant that there could be no effective response to *la violencia*. This created a sense of apathy among the people, inhibiting citizens' defense of their basic rights, especially the right to justice:

> I feel that the most difficult thing in Guatemala is to see that so much injustice has been committed and, yet, it goes completely unpunished. Everything is as it was.

No one can do anything. I feel that the murderers, the oppressors that are in the country continue living undisturbed. That is what is most difficult to accept[13]

All the people of Panzós, and those of all the neighboring *aldeas* that were massacred in Panzós, were left completely terrorized and couldn't do anything other than suffer. They couldn't do anything because to whom would they turn? Since it was the same authorities, the same defenders of the people that killed our brothers, then, at that time, what could we do?[14]

As terror was institutionalized and the law proved ineffective, a sense of fear and powerlessness spread across society...At the same time, it was dangerous to express opinions about what was occurring since the simple act of doing so could lead to repression. This created a mood of resignation in the face of repression. Feelings of anger, injustice, or humiliation regarding what occurred were silenced and kept private. These emotions, while hidden, were nevertheless present in many of the victims and their relatives, especially those forced to witness these acts without being able to do anything. The persistence of impunity and injustice means that these harms continue impacting society at the individual, family, community, and national level.

> I think that it has a strong impact, because everything about the situation that we lived through really affects you, you get used to living with it, but still it creates resentment within you. You live all your life with this resentment inside. And it affects you more because you haven't had the opportunity to have a calm life, even if you have all sorts of material things, inside you are destroyed.[15]

> To deal with our ghosts, our monsters, the pain, the suffering, people now kill themselves with drinking, because no one has been able to process their experiences. Those that do not have the capacity to cry, hold their tears and cry inside...So, from there comes a need to tell truth as it is. It is not to awaken vengeance, but rather to know who it is that needs to be forgiven because that is still not known.[16]

During the confrontation, institutionalized violence did not only go unpunished, but it was justified through campaigns aimed at delegitimizing, criminalizing, and blaming the victims. The repression transformed people, groups, organizations, and entire communities into "legitimate" targets, treating their members as "subversive criminals." The accusations were directed against social organizations and those that played important roles in the communities. These mechanisms of criminalization and delegitimization operated throughout the armed confrontation as a form of latent threat. Repression against many people was justified as a result of simple acts such as supporting community development, holding a position of leadership, or encouraging awareness regarding injustice...

> That is what Ríos Montt suggested and told the public that the university is a nest of communists, a breeding ground for guerrillas.[17]

> They also put it into the heads of our people that defending our rights, trying to struggle for our lives, made us bad people. They wouldn't let us lift up our heads and now, what can we do to rebuild?[18]

Rural Mayans experienced the most dramatic consequences of these actions, especially in the northwest of the country. There, entire communities were accused of being part of the guerrillas which often led to the death of all their members, even children.

> The analysis was that they were all guerrillas. That was the analysis. The orders here were, "a known guerrilla is a dead guerrilla" and being indigenous meant being a guerrilla. They were the same for the Army; there was no difference.[19]

In addition to blaming the victims, systematic accusations were created to ideologically co-opt the population while creating a negative and criminal image of social organizations and their representatives. This stigmatization was based on the idea that if something happened to someone it was because "he was up to something." In that way, the repression was justified, In many cases, relatives even blamed victims within their own families...

Phrases such as "he must have done something" or "why did he get involved with *babosadas*" were repeated throughout the country, reflecting the loss of the ability to feel outrage in the face of atrocities. Victims, simply because they were victims, were automatically viewed as guilty, stripped of their right to seek social change and of their dignity as people. The campaigns to criminalize social activists significantly impacted the collective subconscious, at every level:

> In the deepest part of their consciousness, people had it drilled into them that there are things that are forbidden, things that cannot be done such as, getting involved with student groups, because they say that they are communists, that [by participating in them] they would be killed. This is something that younger generations have embedded in their subconscious.[20]

> Now it is very hard to get people together. The youth say, "Those that get involved do so because they want to die."[21]

In this context, many people chose at some point to deny or "forget" their participation in rights-based activities or social organizations. They did this to avoid risking their lives or the lives of their relatives, friends, and *compañeros*, and to avoid being judged or socially stigmatized and suffer persecution. Many people, groups, and even entire communities tried to eradicate their memories of being associated with activities considered to be subversive:

> La violencia changed us. We had to forget about the organization we had in our community before *la violencia*, our experience in the cooperative. Well, we can't remember anymore...We can only remember what we suffered during all those years, as if that erased everything that came before...[22]

For many people, denying participation in social struggles continues to be a mechanism of self-protection. Many of those who provided testimony to the CEH clearly expressed fear of being branded as guerrillas and the possibility that the nightmare of repression might return...

The experience of terror communicated to the people the idea that struggling or dreaming of a better life was a "sin" and would lead to torture, death, or disappearance:

> Digging around in the past like that can produce fatal results. Suppose that, at a given moment, they find out that we're talking about this here, then, something could happen...[23]
>
> Now that I am free, I thank God. I don't want my children to suffer what I did because it was terrible. That is why I advise some of my relatives not to get involved with any *babosadas*... It was a big commitment... it's better to work.[24]

Forced Complicity

Alongside the criminalization of victims, forcing the civilian population to commit violations heightened the sense of terror. Because of their scope and size, the PAC were the main instruments in this process... *Patrulleros* were forced to commit crimes, sometimes against their own neighbors. This practice, especially in the *altiplano* reached extremes, as in those cases where *patrulleros* had to participate in massacres, the destruction of villages, public torture, and the mutilation of corpses.

Because all men were required to patrol, they became participants in the patrols' repressive acts. In this sense, the victims became victimizers...

Recognizing that the majority of the violence committed by the *patrulleros* was the result of coercion reconfigures the human significance of these acts. Although they committed serious violations, in the end their actions were structured by a counterinsurgency strategy planned and executed by the state.

> And they brought the *patrulleros* so that they would kill them... They didn't want to and the army told them, "If you don't kill them, we'll kill everyone." And, then they gave machetes to the *patrulleros* that were there and some of them had children and brothers and sisters among those who were there and they killed them...[25]

Through their participation in violations against their own and neighboring communities, the danger of repression was not only a threat from outside, but arose from within local society. This severely affected social relations, particularly in Mayan communities:

> They were the kings. It is still difficult for us to understand how they made us all submit to them, how it is that we had to bow our heads. What does it matter? They had the backing of the Army, of other Ladinos in the community... The sad thing is that later there were conflicts among our own people, the Mayan people... They forced us to patrol, to take up arms against our will, we were forced against our own people.[26]

This first phase of the PAC—as with the military commissioners and the recruits forcibly trained by the army—led many people to change their ways of thinking.

Some accepted the discourse of counterinsurgency and became active participants in the repression, often gaining economic or political benefits. They began to boast of the impunity under which they worked, exalting violence, and making light of the pain they caused. In this way, they turned into cold and ruthless murderers...

The intensification of authoritarianism and the arbitrary exercise of power—two consequences of this situation—continue to affect victims that live in the same communities as their victimizers. Pain and suffering are heightened when each day they see the faces of their victimizers, whose acts have gone unpunished and who, in many cases, continue to abuse their power. Living together in this way prevents victims from speaking out or engaging in coordinated activities to respond to what occurred, out of fear of reprisals and because of the impunity that protects the perpetrators:

> The people themselves are aware of what this group did and how these killers walk around freely as if nothing happened. How can you possibly ask people to talk about what happened to them?...This group has a lot of power throughout the municipality of El Tumbador. They dominate the entire population through terror, through fear and by threat...[27]

Mistrust and fear regarding complaints have strengthened silence and social isolation, destroying the tradition of solidarity that existed in the Mayan communities.

> Now there is a lack of trust and fear, it all started with the conflict because the army used neighbors against neighbors to provide information to the base.[28]
>
> Before, they attended the ceremonies. They don't anymore. We have become mistrustful among ourselves. We ask ourselves where is that one from because many people took the Army's side as *orejas*. That is how it was in so many in the *aldeas*. Those people were envious of us, of our work, land, because of vendettas. They all took revenge at that time against someone who had money or a bull. That is what happened...[29]

Culture of Silence and Feelings of Guilt

Terror created a climate of generalized fear. Faced with the magnitude and ruthless nature of the violence, silence defined a new mode of living. Many acquired the ability "not to see" and "not to speak." These responses were a means of resistance and survival. People tried to create a semblance of normality by staying at the margins of the confrontation, remaining silent, even when they saw things that they opposed. Both responses heightened people's isolation and reduced the possibilities of creating a social response to *la violencia*.

The acts of terror silenced victims and those affected, negating the possibility of sharing their experiences and denouncing those responsible, which made the social recognition of trauma difficult. Violations were reduced to individual and isolated experiences, stripped of their larger sociopolitical significance.

It became difficult to know the truth and to take a position in the face of *la violencia*.

> Then, some people in the community were certain that they were members of the G-2 but no one wanted to testify, well, they're very afraid of what could happen. I also asked a woman to explain some of what happened, but she refused because she was very afraid. The army did so many things to us, to the people in the *aldea* and other places as well...but the people, out of pure fear, wouldn't say a thing.[30]
>
> People don't want to talk about what happened to them. They prefer to be silent. Why? What can be gained? There is still fear of the Army's presence, although it's not as strong anymore. But, the *campesinos* prefer not to create any more problems for themselves. They prefer to tell a lie, so as not to offend anyone...[31]

The inhibitions of taking action to face human rights violations created feelings of individual guilt that, in many cases, are still present. Some of those that were powerless witnesses of violations told the CEH about their feelings of guilt as a result of their inaction. They are tormented by the idea that perhaps they could have done something to prevent those acts and their fatal results.

Some of those who presented testimonies to the CEH expressed guilt over not having been killed. Others continue to suffer because, as a result of their intense fear, they didn't bury murdered relatives or didn't make more of an effort to look for a disappeared loved one...

> Her sadness remains. Her pain is very strong and now she thinks that it was her duty to have fought so they wouldn't take her son.[32]

Some women, in particular, feel guilt that, when it was time to flee, they couldn't prevent the deaths of their children. Or, they believe that they directly "caused" what happened by allowing their children to fall from their hands or by suffocating them in an attempt to silence their cries in situations of great danger:

> Another woman was hiding with her small children. She couldn't run because of her children, so she hid in the mountains. And, as the soldiers were passing very close by, yelling, her youngest would not stop shrieking. So, she pressed him forcefully against her chest so that they wouldn't hear his cries. When the soldiers left she discovered that the boy had suffocated to death...[33]

The CEH also gathered testimonies from some former soldiers and former members of the PAC who expressed feelings of guilt for having actively participated in atrocities. Sometimes guilt arose from having been forced to carry out acts of extreme cruelty and, on other occasions, for having committed these acts because that is what their *compañeros* were doing. In both situations, this guilt, to a greater or lesser degree, has led to depression and, in some cases, to suicide or attempts at suicide.

> [About las Dos Erres] I feel that it was a pity. It hurts. I will never forget that, it is a weight that bears down on me. No one likes to kill unjustly. I feel depressed. I spent

the whole night thinking... I decided to tell everything in order to be calm and have a clear conscience...[34]

Ever since the day they forced him to kill a *compañero*, one of the *patrulleros* decided that he preferred to die over having to live with the guilt of having killed one of his neighbors and fellow *patrulleros*. From then on, he began to drink a lot of liquor and he became sick and died around three years after the act.[35]

Being unable to denounce or oppose the violence created collective guilt and, to a degree, this had the effect of making society complicit with the perpetrators. However, the social silencing of what occurred—silence that has been maintained for many years—created a situation that enabled social consensus to deny and discredit what had happened. In many sectors of society, complicity and denial became the foundation of an indifference that made living with fear acceptable. This then became a condition of apparent normality, inhibiting and desensitizing those who did not identify with the victims or who preferred to consciously keep themselves at the margin of the conflict...

Guerrilla Violence and Terror

The military actions of the guerrillas included attacks, ambushes, and confrontations, as well as arbitrary executions, forced recruitment, massacres, and other acts of violence. In many cases, this led to an increase in the impact of state terrorism on the people, causing greater suffering in the communities.

To understand the impact of guerrilla violence, it is important to review the initial reaction of certain sectors of the population regarding the insurgent organizations and the armed struggle. The guerrillas' discourse touched on themes that were important for large segments of the population: land, salaries, discrimination, and repression...

We really liked the guerrilla's message, they were very good politicians. They explained to us that in Guatemala only the rich had land, while it was the poor that worked the land. "We will take the land from the rich and divide it among the poor," they told us, "When we win the war we will all drink milk and eat cheese and meat every day. The cotton will be distributed among you and it will be the indigenous people that will live in the beautiful houses of the *finqueros* and drive their vehicles." That is how the guerrilla spoke. According to them, it would only be a little while before they won the war. They said that Lucas García would be the last president for the rich. When they asked us to join them, there were only a few people that didn't want to. Well, we were all poor and all wanted to live better...[36]

Within the framework of what was known as "revolutionary justice," the guerrillas conducted arbitrary executions against representatives of empowered groups, informants, army collaborators, and against supporters they considered to be deserters or "traitors"... These executions created feelings of uncertainty and defenselessness, increasing the sense of vulnerability before guerrilla violence... Other guerrilla actions that increased fear among the civilian population included attacks with military objectives that often led to army repression directed against the people. While the army was clearly responsible for this repression, many people blamed the guerrillas for exposing them to the potential violence of the military...

> For me one of the reasons that led the army...to massacre communities is that the guerrillas at that time had scattered their forces to gain greater control of the area, that is supposedly to protect a larger zone...They didn't have a concentration of forces and only left one, two or three *compañeros* in each *aldea* to respond when the army arrived. Then, the response of the army to each guerrilla act, however minor, was to massacre the nearest community...[37]

With the growing army repression, the guerrilla violence increased. Beginning in 1981, with the creation of the PAC, and out of fear of losing their social base, the guerrilla began to pressure the civil population to work with them, especially in the northwestern departments of the country. This strengthened the idea within the region that this was a war that did not allow for neutrality. Over time, many people, motivated by fear and the need to protect themselves, saw themselves forced to collaborate with both sides as a strategy of survival, which further provoked increasing division.

> Yes, I believe that our role was very polarizing. We said, "Whoever is not with us is against us. If you don't want to fight with us, it's because you're on the other side." In some cases it was very political [how we convinced them] but in other cases it was totally brutal...[38]

The incapacity of the guerrilla to protect the communities from the massacres and the scorched earth, much less to put into practice their proclamations of justice, created feelings of abandonment and resentment against the insurgent organizations. Many of those who presented testimonies to the CEH described this issue, mentioning it as a justification for changing allegiances in those areas most impacted by the repression, as a response to the defenselessness and abandonment that they felt during *la violencia*. The resulting sense of deception was strengthened by the army's systematic indoctrination, which consistently blamed the guerrillas, emphasizing their responsibility for the suffering of the civilian population. As a strategy of survival, little by little, people accepted the official story...

> After the massacre of Cuarto Pueblo, many people wanted to throw the guerrillas out because what had they done to defend the people of Cuarto Pueblo? They harassed [the military] but that didn't help defend the people and only provoked more harm. Where are the arms that they spoke about? There was nowhere to go. If we stayed the army would capture us and if not and we went into the mountains, the guerrillas would kill us. We had to think about how to save our lives. The guerrillas didn't have the capacity to defend the people...[39]

Another expression of the sense of abandonment and deception is seen in the conclusion by many of those that spoke with the CEH that both sides created harm so that now they do not want to have anything to do either group...

> I don't want to see either one of those soldier-assassins or one of the guerrillas because both brought a lot of suffering.[40]

Consequences of Torture and Rape

Torture and rape were two of the human rights violations that most contributed to generating and maintaining terror during the armed confrontation. These violations always involved an intention to destroy the victim's identity and dignity in the most profound and intimate ways. Their systematic use in Guatemala reflects a profound moral degradation of the direct perpetrators as well as those that ordered and enabled these practices.

For the survivors of torture and rape, suffering did not end when they were freed. These experiences produced multiple and severe physical and psychological consequences that changed victims' lives forever and, in extreme cases, became disabling. At the same time, the consequences extended beyond the individual and affected the family as well as the social environment, leaving a profound imprint of the trauma that was experienced.

Many survivors have suffered serious physical consequences resulting from wounds, large bruises, having nails pulled out, teeth broken, fractures, vaginal tears, torn eardrums, and so on...Burns and mutilations left permanent marks...Torture by suspension led to chronic joint pain, especially of the back and shoulders...Many suffer from migraines caused by various factors such as repeated strikes to the head as well as psychological stress, jaw problems, and depression...In many cases, internal damage has led to chronic diseases, and the CEH documented multiple situations in which those tortured died years later...

The most common psychological consequences of torture are low self-esteem, body perception problems, anxiety, memory loss, a lack of confidence, and depression. After being tortured, the survivors almost always suffer permanent fatigue...as well as of a sense of disorientation and heightened irritability. They don't understand their reactions, which contributes to their anxiety...Torture severely violates the victim's personality, their sense of themselves, their values, and their convictions..."I could only think, why would I want to live? I was disgusted with myself"...[41]

The experience of torture has caused permanent pain for many of those that survived and has left a lasting imprint causing intense suffering. For years, victims of torture often have trouble sleeping. They wake up repeatedly and experience horrible nightmares in which they relive the torture, over and over. An encounter with a person, place, or object can also bring back the experience...

> One day [in 1998] I saw that man [one of the torturers]. Since that day I began another struggle...I go out onto the street and feel as if that man is watching me.

At night, I close my eyes and see the face of that man, I sense his laughter, his eyes. I feel it all. I go to the street and every Ladino I see seems like him. I feel like he is following me. As a result of all of this, I am here being treated for migraines... I depend on medications as a result of all the pain that those people have caused for us... [42]

For the relatives of those tortured, the consequences are deeply painful and ongoing. Many times, a spouse witnessed the arrest of their partner under violent circumstances and the victim may have been beaten, raped, or mistreated in some other way. Children often witnessed victims' arrest and were forced to watch terrible things...

To see the torture of your loved ones, terrible... In that moment you feel so humiliated because there is absolutely nothing you can do. In fact, they make you look, they are laughing, torturing. They enjoyed the moment when (one of our brothers) screamed, "Papa, tell them what you know so that they will leave you alone"... [43]

These visions often stay with them and may torment them for the rest of their lives.

Well, I believe that as a result of everything that we lived through in Guatemala, the future for us has not changed, nor have we been cured of all that we lived through there... My siblings will never forget... how they tortured my father and my sister and my pregnant sister-in-law. I think that they will never be able to erase that from their minds because they were young, and their future has been affected up until now... I cannot explain the resentment that they feel towards those people and towards everything that happened in Guatemala... [44]

The consequences of torture extend to victims' children, even those born after the mother's or the father's experience of torture:

I saw [his torturer]... After so many years... finding him here [outside of Central America], doing so well, so at peace. That made me think about how it is that these people are still around. And, another thing I think about is that even if I reported him, even if I did everything possible to identify him, I don't know what guarantee there would be that one could say that justice will done. I felt disempowered seeing that those people that caused so much harm—and who might still be doing so here—could continue to ruin lives. Because right now, they are not just ruining the lives of four brothers, but now this could impact the lives of my children because my daughter has to share my painful nights, seeing me cry, seeing me suffer and asking me what's wrong. And, I have to make her understand at her young age what is happening. I think that is very hard... [45]

There are two main social consequences of the systematic way in which torture was practiced in Guatemala. First, is the preparation and training of generations of assassins, expert in the most efficient and disturbing ways of applying pain to human beings in order to break them both physically and spiritually.

Second, torture became something "normal" within the operation of the state security forces and within society, including among judicial functionaries and others charged with applying the law.

In order to be used in a systematic manner, it was necessary to create torturers...Torturers are not distinct types of people, but are members of the ordinary population, men and women. According to the available evidence, the torturer is able to engage in his "work" and then go to mass, play with children, and behave like anyone else...Once torturers are trained to do their work, they become some of the most dangerous members of society. They become accustomed to killing, kidnapping, and causing pain, later shifting to seek increased power and wealth through violence and crime. They are used to imposing themselves upon others in society through force.

Torture committed on a mass scale as occurred in Guatemala requires an ideological justification to legitimize the physical and psychological destruction of its victims. It is necessary for society as a whole, or at least those groups in power, to affirm the use of torture. In Guatemala, torture was widely used as an expression of a particular social reality, based on positions and rationalizations that served to maintain the political order and the socioeconomic system...

As with torture, the systematic practice of raping women as one of the weapons of the counterinsurgency strategy has had a profound impact on those victims that survived as well as their families and society...The impact of sexual violence is bound to the consequences of terror: pain, silence, shame, mistrust, guilt, rejection, humiliation, and a loss of dignity.

A large number of survivors suffered immediate and long-term physical consequences...as a result of having been raped....Many of the women that survived rape also suffer psychological trauma, including an inability to remember, denial of what occurred, profound nervous tension, mistrust, insecurity, and loss of a desire to live...

The country's social and cultural context has increased the suffering and emotional impact of these crimes on women that were raped. In general, much of the blame over what happened is placed on the victim. She is viewed as a "used" or "worn out" woman. The repressive context in which rape took place is not considered, and rapes are not understood as violent acts forcibly committed against women. Many times the women were made to feel guilty by their own *compañeros*, by their relatives, by state agents, and by the very same people who committed the violations.

> When the soldiers arrived at my house I was alone, there were seven men...They beat me, the wanted to hang me, they suspended me from a beam and while I was hanging they raped me, tearing my clothes, I bled a lot...Thank God I didn't become pregnant. Now, I am not well, I have pain in my waist and I can't get any rest and I am always ill. Up until now, no one has asked me to get married because I was raped...[46]

The stigma that marks women who suffered rape is seen in their silence and the ways that these acts are hidden for an entire lifetime, eventually impacting their children. The feelings of shame and guilt are so strong for these women that, from the time of the rape onward, many prefer to remain silent about what happened, even among their closest loved ones. These violations are so bound to privacy that they humiliate the women, who have been conditioned not to talk about what happened because to do so is not "proper":

> Now I am old and, because of the war and having suffered so much. I can no longer work because I am so ill. The rape left me really affected. I have never again been able to be with a man. The humiliation was so great. So, I tried to forget. I never talked about this before. Because of the shame, I don't want people to know.[47]

This sense of shame was especially severe among Mayan women...

> Many were left in silence with their pain...They wouldn't even tell their mothers, or their brothers...so as not to feel the shame of the community or of their own family.[48]

Shame implies rejection. Women who survived rape, even those who fled their communities, had to separate themselves from their families, to live from that moment on with the fear of "being discovered" as if they had committed a "crime" without being able to contextualize "what happened to them" within the framework of *la violencia*.

Sexual violence against women affected not only individuals but also deeply impacted close family and damaged family relations...

> I couldn't run because I was carrying my five small children, the soldiers grabbed me near the church. The children piled on me and they were crying the whole time. The little girl hugged the baby. They put them in a room in the social center and five soldiers raped me. I will never forget what they did to me. I was never able to return to my husband, Still, when I gather together with my children, we look at each other and we begin crying...[49]

In addition to the loss of dignity for Mayan women, for whom rape is viewed as one of the most severe offenses, survivors and their leaders remain concerned about the impunity through which those responsible have been protected...

> Those who raped us grew accustomed to raping women. There's no respect. There are no punishments for the rapists. The youth have also learned this; a woman isn't worth anything. A woman can't defend herself. If she doesn't speak Spanish, she can't file a complaint. And, if she tries to fight back, they threaten her, they insult her, they call her a bad woman. There is always fear. They tell us that peace was signed, but they [those responsible for the rapes] are left alone. They know they can do whatever they want. They're the authorities. So, what sort of peace is this?...[50]

The presence of sexual violence within the collective memory of the communities has become a source of shame and suffering, as well as a call to take urgent action to prevent the repetition of these acts in the future.

Weakening of State Institutions

Just as the mechanisms of terror used in the armed confrontation have profound and lasting consequences for Guatemalan society the elevated role of impunity and militarization impacted the state's institutional structure, as well as people's attitudes towards the government...

By tolerating or directly participating in the impunity for perpetrators of human rights violations, the organs of justice became dysfunctional in terms of their capacity to protect individuals from the state. They thereby lost all credibility as the guarantors of basic legality. In this way, the functioning of a democratic state based on the rule of law became impossible since, by definition, it requires a judicial system that guarantees rules and norms for coexistence that are recognized and applicable to all... Restoring the effectiveness and credibility of these institutions will require time, coordinated will, and new approaches by all of the actors.

Impunity enabled the domination by the military of the public, social, and cultural spheres, destroying state institutions by subordinating them to National Security Doctrine. In this way, impunity dismantled the autonomy of these institutions and undermined their ability to respond to the needs of different sectors of society...

The judicial system's role in the armed confrontation—involving multiple actions and omissions—led Guatemalan society to have good reasons to question the degree to which laws represent an appropriate and efficient mechanism for regulating social life... The legacy of impunity creates, in turn, consequences in other areas. For example, it prevents a reversal of the dominance of executive power over other state powers, a situation that undermines the basic principles of a democratic regime. It impedes parliamentary discussions regarding the preparation of laws that respond to reasonable social needs, further aggravating the legislative system's crisis. This then impacts political parties, which are further weakened as individuals and social groups do not believe that through them they can actively participate in discussions regarding a normative system based on citizens' rights and the obligations of the state and its functionaries. The democratic political system, based on the rule of law was dismantled. Rebuilding it from its foundations is one of the great challenges for the future...

Impunity came to dominate the very structure of the state and became an end in itself. It was a means of enabling the repressive actions of the state while it was also the result of the methods used to destroy and eliminate its enemies... Closing off opportunities for dissent through forms of mediation essential to democratic systems supported the systematic instability of the social order. In this way a vicious cycle was created in which social injustice provoked political instability, which was then repressed by the state. In this way the use of National Security Doctrine during the armed confrontation to view social organizations as enemies fundamentally contradicted the democratic principle of the use of legitmate force within a legal system, placing security and order above any other common value or social function. This aberration in the functioning of a democratic state produced effects at every level that continue in society to this day.

The CEH documented over 57,536 violations in which responsibility was attributed to diverse forces and agents of the state, serving as evidence of the magnitude of persecution and illegal punishment applied against those viewed as enemies of national security...The impunity protecting particular sectors of society has decisively contributed to the spread a culture of violence and the abuse of power. This issue impacts the minds of many Guatemalans, those that experienced the war as well as younger generations who have grown accustomed to resolving conflicts through violence or by acting outside of the law...

One of the central elements of the research methodology involved allowing those providing testimony with the opportunity to respond to questions such as, "What do you expect from the CEH?"; and, "What recommendations do you think that the CEH should make?"...The majority of those presenting testimonies that sought criminal punishment came from urban centers, such as the capital or the departmental centers, and many of these were linked to some type of social organization. In rural areas, the most common demands were for an investigation of what occurred, the discovery of the causes motivating the violence, and public acknowledgment of those responsible.

In reference to forced disappearances, those providing testimony insisted that the state should clarify the whereabouts of the victims. There were also demands for exhumations of clandestine and hidden cemeteries where many believe the remains of their disappeared relatives can be found...

> Don't let the acts go unpunished. Let there be justice and let the Army's responsibility be recognized. And, let the bodies be found so they can be given Christian burial.[51]

There was also a tendency to link justice with the moral demand of identifying those responsible for the violations. Many of those who provided testimony saw the work of documenting these acts and [identifying] those responsible as the beginning of the path toward justice:

> The first steps are to reveal what happened and from these first steps, let's delve deeper...[52]

Many of those who spoke to the CEH discussed the importance of knowing and spreading the truth, as a means of guaranteeing that *la violencia* will not return.

Beyond judicial sanctions, or perhaps precisely because of a lack of confidence that this will ever happen, a number of those who provided testimony recommended that the CEH publicly denounce the perpetrators and establish some type of mechanism to prevent them from occupying elected positions within the government.

For many Guatemalans, these responses suggest that, beyond legal action, historical clarification is, in and of itself, an act of justice. It is also a way to guarantee that the acts of violence will not recur:

> If those responsible are not put on trial, then at least there should be publicity so that these acts of violence never occur again in Guatemala. So that military governments do not return...[53]

In general, there was support for a commitment to justice, although they expressed doubts that the law would ever be applied... It is not that the Guatemalan people do not want a functioning judicial system or that they have given up or have no confidence in the law. On the contrary, their interest is a response to the fact that the judicial system failed in its essential mission of protecting citizens, especially the weakest members of society, from the abuse of power...

Forced Transfer of Children Who Survived the in Río Negro Massacre, Municipality of Rabinal, Baja Verapaz

On March 13, 1982, Guatemalan Army forces and *patrulleros* from Xococ killed 70 women and 107 children from the village of Río Negro... [Then], the soldiers and the *patrulleros* headed toward Xococ, taking eighteen children with them, the only survivors of that operation.

They walked all night. The children were listening to what the *patrulleros* said about what happened, "that they died for being bad people, some said they killed ten, others fifteen."[54]

At one in the morning of the next day, they arrived at Xococ:

> We entered the church and they gave us food. They were waiting for us. They asked if we were the only survivors or if they let the women live. They said they killed the women.[55]
>
> It was like a party, they killed livestock, ate meat and tortillas. I didn't eat because I was sad about everything that had happened.[56]

One of the children's first reactions was a deep sense of powerlessness:

> I was crying and everything because I saw them kill my mother.[57]
>
> I was crying, I wanted to go back to Río Negro... only through threats were they able to convince me [to stay].[58]

That same day, at dawn, the soldiers authorized the *patrulleros* to take the children, "each *patrullero* took an orphan to his house."[59]

During the time that the children lived in the *patrulleros'* houses, they were forced to do hard labor... In Guatemala's rural communities, this type of work is assigned to children at a very young age... However, the testimonies gathered by the CEH describe how they were treated differently than the children [of the *patrulleros'* families]:

> ... She didn't treat me the same as her own children. She gave them food. She didn't scold them. She didn't hit them.[60]

They were also forced to do work that was very difficult given their age, and when they didn't do it, they were abused:

> Then one day, when I was unable to work the oxen, he got very mad and put two cords around my neck... I began to vomit blood. As he beat me, as always, he said it would be better to send me to my end because there were plenty of holes and it wouldn't cost him anything to bury me.[61]

Some of the children were also brutally beaten and threatened with death:

> ... One of the animals went missing. He threatened that he was going to kill me... He brought some rope, tied one end to the ceiling and placed the other end around my neck. His wife wouldn't let him kill me...[62]

In addition to having been direct witnesses to the execution of their relatives and neighbors, the eighteen Río Negro children…from three to fourteen years old…were forced to live with the perpetrators…

They changed the names of some of the children, substituting the *patrulleros* last names for theirs, "…They changed my name and got me an identity card with this last name [that of the *patrullero*]."[63]

They also tried to make the children feel guilty by stigmatizing the inhabitants of Río Negro and their relatives:

> …They asked me where my parents were, I told them I didn't know. They said they were buried because that is what they do to guerrillas…The woman's children treated me like the daughter of guerrillas.[64]

But the older children looked for ways to face the situation, either by asking about what had happened or by trying to escape:

> …Because we were getting older and were thinking about whether this was our mother or if this was our father. One day, a man from there told me that I wasn't living with my parents.[65]

Two years later, the relatives who weren't in the *aldea* on the day of the massacre returned to their community and learned that the children that hadn't been killed in Río Negro were living in Xococ. When they found this out, they began filing papers to recover them in the municipality of Rabinal and the court in Salamá. The proceedings were supported by the military base in Rabinal.

> One day I came with the *patrulleros*' wife. I always stayed seated in the plaza. I said that I had to go urinate and went to the park. As I was walking, my sister suddenly appeared, like a miracle, and hugged me. She started asking me about my siblings, and I told her that they were all dead. She told me that I should stay with the *patrulleros* for another few months while she started legal proceedings with the authorities.[66]

Finally, the children were handed over to their relatives. Nevertheless, the *patrulleros* of Xococ used coercion to try to avoid handing them over. They told the children that their relatives were guerrillas and that they were going to return to kill them:

> The *patrulleros* started threatening me and told me that if I went with my sister, they were going to kill us again since they had already proven that they were capable of this…[67]

The small children, that had never really known their families, had doubts about the true identity of their relatives:

> I was scared because I didn't know if this one was not my father or if this one was my father…I felt was sadn because I didn't know for sure who my father was…[68]

Currently some live in Pacux and some in Cobán or Guatemala City.

II

Facing *La Violencia*

Solidarity was among the most important responses to *la violencia*, representing an important means of rebuilding community ties and family support. Solidarity allowed victims to speak and seek comfort and came to play a central role in the practical reconstruction of the social fabric. It also enabled other modes of defense and organization during the armed confrontation...

After the initial emergence of survival strategies, little by little, people established movements to defend life and rebuild the social fabric...The defense of human rights, the search for the disappeared, and the struggle against militarization and impunity were all efforts to respond to *la violencia* arising from the suffering of victims. Although the organizations created to address these issues were frequently the targets of repression, they responded to *la violencia* through actions grounded in the rule of law...

The same period saw the rebirth of an indigenous movement that, while different in its goals and methods, shared common objectives. In particular, indigenous activists focused on ending the racism that justified the repression of Mayan communities during the confrontation and allowed the basic rights of indigenous people to be violated for centuries. In their struggle, they emphasized the necessity of profound changes to support peace and create a new vision for the nation.

Human Rights Movement and the Struggle against Impunity

Political violence did not only create terror, passivity, and silence. It also led to the parallel creation...of organizations to defend people's fundamental rights. Largely composed of victims' families, these groups were dedicated to defending life even when this implied inevitable repression and death threats...

Faced with the critical orientation of these groups, the army and various governments at the time responded with intimidation, including publicly accusing activists of being part of the guerrillas and, in the most serious cases, assassinating and disappearing their members...From the perspective of counterinsurgency and National Security Doctrine, these activists were viewed as a part of the internal enemy. And, the systematic practice of delegitimizing, intimidating, and repressing these groups and their leaders continued even under the civilian governments.

This commission recognizes the difficult work of those who struggled to create meaningful responses to *la violencia* for different sectors of society, who moved beyond the paralysis and terror, through life-affirming acts, gestures, and demands throughout the conflict, even during its worst moments. It is important to acknowledge the work of the *Comité de Familiares de Desaparecidos, Grupo de Apoyo Mutuo* (GAM), *Familiares de Detenidos-Desaparecidos de Guatemala* (FAMDEGUA), *Consejo de Comunidades Étnicas Runujel Junam* (CERJ), *Coordinadora Nacional de Viudas de Guatemala* (CONAVIGUA), *Defensoría Maya, Conferencia de Iglesias Evangélicas de Guatemala* (CIEDEG), *Comisión de Derechos Humanos de Guatemala* (CDHG) *Oficina de Derechos Humanos del Arzobispado de Guatemala* (ODHAG), and the social assistance offices of many of the Catholic Church dioceses. In addition, the commission recognizes other groups including the *Centro de Acción Legal para los Derechos Humanos* (CALDH), *Fundación Myrna Mack, Instituto de Estudios Comparados en Ciencias Penales de Guatemala* (ICCP), *Centro de Investigación, Estudio y Promoción de los Derechos Humanos* (CIEPRODH), *Alianza Contra la Impunidad* (ACI), *Convergencia por la Verdad, Fundación Rigoberta Menchú, Fundación de Antropología Forense de Guatemala* (FAFG), and *Coordinadora Nacional de Derechos Humanos de Guatemala* (CONADEGUA).

In particular, the CEH highlights the decisive role played by Guatemalan women in many of the groups that led the struggle against impunity and militarization and in support of victims and the respect of human rights in Guatemala, especially from the mid-1980s on.

The Struggle against Forced Disappearance

Throughout the armed confrontation, in different places and times, mothers, brothers, husbands, wives, and children consistently sought to establish the whereabouts and fates of their loved ones. These activities began in the 1960s and reveal the courage of victims' relatives.

In response to terror, whose scope was constantly expanding, student groups provided solidarity, giving support and ongoing assistance...

> At the AEU we were committed... We called every person whose relatives had been disappeared to meet together. We brought a banner to the May First [celebration] and our banner stated, "Families of the Victims of Repression"... It was 1968 and I was willing to do anything to find out about Pepe. Those were terrible years.[1]

In the late 1960s, the *Bufete Popular* (Popular Clinic) and the *Asociación de Estudiantes Universitarios* (Association of University Students, AEU) began supporting the *Comité de Familiares de Desaparecidos* (Committee of the Families of the Disappeared). The *Comité* was composed of the fathers and mothers of professionals and students that were detained and later disappeared. They filed legal actions in search of loved ones that ultimately proved useless…Those were the first steps of the groups that organized to defend the rights to liberty and life…

Another early public response came in support of Juan Luis Molina Loza, disappeared on January 13, 1971. He was the son of a radio actress and public servant that was very popular in the media in the capital. On March 9, 1971, the actress placed herself in the Central Park in front of the National Palace with a sign that read, "I am the mother of Licenciado Juan Luis Molina Loza and today I am starting an ongoing fast until the government pays attention and my son appears…" The government of the time led by Colonel Arana Osorio sent a National Police ambulance that took her off to the psychiatric hospital…

In the interior of the country, relatives and friends of those disappeared sometimes engaged in spontaneous acts. For example, on March 19, 1980, when searching for Nehemías Cúmes—an important community leader kidnapped several days earlier in Pachaj in the municipality of Comalapa, Chimaltenango—a dumping ground full of corpses was discovered. A group of students went to the bottom of the pit and found the first six corpses. After two days of intense labor by voluntary firemen, they found twenty-six corpses. The news was covered by the media for a week, drawing dozens of people from around the country that were trying to find the remains of their disappeared relatives.

> Many families showed up, among them the wives of the Obregón brothers, kidnapped in San Antonio Suchitepéquez…Others arrived from the capital, others from Escuintla…The relatives of Señor Oscar Leonel Córdoba also arrived, [he was] a radio host on *Nuevo Mundo*, kidnapped twelve days earlier in Huehuetenango…[2]

Another important case involved parents that responded to the disappearance of seven young people on January 20, 1982, in the community of Natividad de María, in the municipality of la Reforma, San Marcos…They made many efforts to find out what had happened to their children including speaking with General Efraín Ríos Montt, who told them…that if they were alive when they entered [detention] they would still be alive…The young people never reappeared.

In the 1980s, relatives of the disappeared met in various places in search of family members, in hospital emergency rooms, morgues, detention centers, and dumping grounds for bodies. Some began to call on the support of the nation's respected institutions, such as the Catholic Church and the USAC. This led to collective responses in an effort to overcome the powerlessness and passivity brought on by terror:

> They changed me. I was a very peaceful person, but whoever took my brother made me very angry and I no longer felt any fear, but rather courage to keep fighting…I would have liked to have been bad so I could take revenge, particularly when I listened to the military, especially Mejía Víctores…We saw each other at the morgue, at the police station, in different places. But, we never spoke. Then, there we were, waiting for the Monsignor to see us and we started talking. The most painful thing was that I visited morgues every day and saw what they did to people…I saw men whose genital organs had been removed and put in their mouths, other people

were there without eyes, without ears, without noses...Yet, this made one strong to keep on struggling, to keep going on and to say, that's enough, no more kidnappings, no more murders...That is how I got involved with the struggle, working, trying to denounce, being the big finger pointing to so many kidnappings, so much brutality, and so much evil. There's no fear of God, no fear of justice, no fear of anything.[3]

Mutual Support

These and other efforts gave rise to GAM. It made its public debut on June 4, 1984, led by a small group of women from the capital that were looking for disappeared relatives...They gathered together the families of disappeared people from around the country, alongside international humanitarian organizations. GAM grew very quickly as Mayan women from all over the country joined:

> When we got together, we were all the same. We were all from the metropolitan area and were middle-class...[it was] a surprise for us...when suddenly...we began to receive visits from many indigenous women...(who) would tell us..."It's so good that you are organized"; "They not only kidnapped my husband, but also my brother, my son, my son-in-law." "And when was it, in 1984?" "No, in 1980." "Why didn't you report it?" "Because there was no one to report it to, there was no organization and we were scared." It was surprising to us, there were so many...That is how many of the indigenous women began joining. We began with a group of twenty-five women, all *Ladinas* and it helped us raise our awareness of ourselves as Guatemalans because we had failed to understand our identity. In truth, our very world, our work, didn't allow us to know about the reality of such painful and dramatic cases, perhaps even more painful and severe than our own. Alongside their suffering they experienced the pain and powerlessness of living in the countryside with barely a penny...And, seeing these women with a bunch of children, it was like saying, well...we need to understand ourselves...There, we learned about the massacres, the genocide, the scorched earth policy...[4]

The growth of the group occurred under very dangerous conditions. Social movements had been destroyed through severe repression and there were no opportunities for rights-based claims...Activists and their organizations were accused by the army of being manipulated by the guerrillas:

> Suddenly they called us communists, subversives, enemies of the state. We, the women, before we were workers, mothers of families and we had been suffering. We were victims of *la violencia*...Mejía Víctores told us, "Look, señoras, do you know what you're doing? You're doing what the mothers of the Plaza de Mayo are doing in Argentina. You're doing the same thing, Do you know that they are guerrillas?...You will ruin the Guatemalan State.[5]

During the first months of its existence, GAM received very little coverage in national media. Facing the state's indifference and lack of interest, the emerging group...occupied the *Asamblea Nacional Constitiyente* (National Constitutional Assembly, ANC, which was drafting the new constitution)...

> Our goal was to make sure that the new constitution included the issue of political prisoners, because it would be impossible to build a future by ignoring the past...When we occupied the ANC they took away our megaphones so that we couldn't interrupt the session. But, I was inspired and I went and bought whistles at the first store [I found] to make noise. There were 300 of us blowing whistles...[6]

Slowly, the movement started gaining strength as it revealed the nation's most profound suffering. GAM gained a position among the different social organizations and it became a refuge for persecuted activists belonging to various groups....

The existence of GAM, their vigils and complaints drew attention to human rights violations. The state responded immediately and forcefully with the usual methods of intimidation and terror...as a commitment to life was met with a violent response...GAM activists were assassinated during the time of General Mejía Víctores; first Héctor Gómez Calito and a few days later María del Rosario Godoy Aldana de Cuevas, along with Mynor René Godoy Aldana, and Augusto Rafael Cuevas...

During the presidency of Vinicio Cerezo, another GAM activist, María Rumualda Camay, was disappeared...And, there were other attacks, such as the kidnapping and assassination of Eleodoro Ordón Camey, Aurelio Lorenzo Xicay, Martín Chitay, Eusebio Camey, and Victoriano Camey...There were death threats and constant surveillance against Nineth Montenegro and Mario Polanco, among others. Although these acts affected the activists, GAM continued with its campaign related to disappearances.

Exhumations

Toward the end of the 1980s, the search for the disappeared entered a new phase. The first exhumation of a clandestine cemetery occurred in June 1988. From then until the end of the CEH's investigation, at least sixty-three other exhumations were conducted. These actions were supported by diverse human rights organizations and proved that forced disappearances had occurred, while also revealing undeniable evidence of many massacres.

A significant number of the testimonies presented to the CEH called for exhumations of the hundreds of clandestine and hidden cemeteries. This is one of the most important elements in the process of supporting collective memory. Exhumations contribute to repairing the communal social fabric and generating possibilities for justice, as well as creating new sociocultural norms of understanding...

The struggle related to the disappeared involved various types of independent and complementary actions. On June 16, 1992, FAMDEGUA arose out of this process, and one its main activities was to press for exhumations...

These efforts supported the investigation of specific cases, recovering the dignity of victims and highlighting the importance of providing reparations to address the harm caused by the violations. While presenting his testimony, an interviewee took some bones out of his bag and part of a set of teeth belonging to one of the victims and said:

> It's very painful for me to carry these...It is like carrying death...I am not going to bury them yet...Yes, I want him to rest. I also want to rest, but I cannot yet...They are the proof of my statement...I am not going to bury them yet. I want a document that tells me, "The patrols killed him because of the Army and he committed no crime. He was innocent."...Then, we will rest.[7]

The Struggle against Militarization

The struggle against militarization was led by different groups and achieved significant gains especially through the work of organizations...responding to repression and impunity. Alongside GAM, it is important to acknowledge the important work of CERJ, the *Defensoría Maya*, Consejo Nacional de Desplazados de Guatemala (National Council on the Displaced of Guatemala, CONDEG), and CONAVIGUA. These were essentially indigenous organizations created to rescue their communities from military control and to support a respect for human rights. As the years went by, they formed part of the Mayan movement, which went on to play an important role in the peace process.

The intensification of the internal armed conflict extended the military presence throughout the entire country through the creation of zones, bases, command posts, and military patrols. The mass military presence and its destructive effects on communities, particularly through human rights violations, led communities to respond and react. These actions took place at various times through different forms of organization, mobilization and complaints, acts that required great individual and community courage.

In the beginning, the organizations involved in the struggle against militarization worked under very dangerous conditions. Grounded in their communities, they rejected forced participation in the PAC as well as forced military recruitment and its discriminatory nature.

One of the most important group criticisms of the army's presence occurred in December 1990 in Santiago Atitlán, Sololá. following a massacre committed by the military. The people of Santiago Atitlán had a tradition of social organizing and had experienced ongoing abuse, particularly after the establishment of a military base in Panabaj in 1980.

They created a community response system...and, in the early morning on December 2, the church bells rang, calling the people to come out...Hundreds responded to the call, expressing their anger at the ongoing harassment from the military base. They were then shot at by troops from the base. Following the massacre of fourteen people that morning, the residents of Santiago organized themselves and sent delegations to the capital to denounce what had occurred and to seek support for their decision to expel the army from their municipality.

They presented a memorandum to the president of the Republic in which they described their capacity to protect themselves collectively...

Faced with the deep indignation of the Guatemalan people as well as international pressure, the civilian government ordered the withdrawal of the base from Santiago...The struggle for demilitarizing the municipality also led to the withdrawal of the National Police. In addition, community members rejected the presence of guerrilla forces operating in the zone and demanded that they respect the population's decision to exclude the presence of all armed parties from the municipality...

The struggle against militarization was also directed against the institutions of military commissioners and civil patrols, especially within the country's Mayan communities. These organizations rejected forced participation in the PAC and the abuses committed by many of their leaders as well as by commissioners. In many places, these actions were linked with a refusal to participate in forced and discriminatory military recruitment. Although opposition to forced recruitment had its roots in the 1970s, the community struggles against militarization gained new significance, especially during that least decade of the conflict within the context of the larger process of political transition.

Some of these resistance efforts took place within the context of the mobilization of many Kaqchikel municipalities in Sololá in 1993. With the clear goal of preserving their communities, they sought to eliminate the position of military commissioners...One witness who spoke with the CEH remembered the campaign...

> [We told them] "Look *señores* starting now you're no longer military commissioners."...Some said, "You can't pull me out because I volunteered with the leader"...Then we made a note in every *cantón*, we said, "If you don't want to leave that is ok, but when the army says that you have to recruit young people, to bring your son or bring your nephew, or when the army tells you to have your wife bring firewood, or your daughter, or your niece bring the army firewood...Be careful if you grab a young person...or force a woman to prepare tortillas [for them]. If you force them here, we will expel you from the *cantón*. That is the rule that we have proposed throughout this area."[8]

CUC, GAM, CONDEG, CERJ, and CONAVIGUA led many of these efforts. The work of CONAVIGUA, directed by Rosalina Tuyuc, a Kaqchikel woman, was especially innovative, largely because it was an organization of Mayan women who came from hundreds of villages in the country's interior. After its creation in 1988, it focused on denunciations, actions against the militarization of communities and responses to the discrimination of indigenous women.

> What makes us very proud is that for the first time in five centuries we have created a strong organization of rural and indigenous women. We ourselves are the ones who came to lead this organization, to plan our own structure and objectives because it was almost always men who were speaking for women, for our pain, our discrimination. At that time, we were the ones who took up the struggle...although it is unspoken, in practice, it is completely a gender struggle...[9]

From the mid-1980s on, the groups that emerged out of repression and impunity were joined by other organizations involved in humanitarian work and efforts to exercise democratic rights. Again, the army responded to the work of these groups by presenting them as criminals. The minister of defense and the army press secretary publicly accused activists of following the insurgents' ideology, thereby identifying them for repression within their communities...

Another important element of the struggle against the PAC was the support of human rights bodies not associated with the social movements in Guatemala that provided legal assistance and support through the courts. In addition, the new constitution of 1985 created government bodies to protect citizens' rights, such as the *Procurador de Derechos Humanos* (Human Rights Ombudsman) and the Constitutional Court. The Ombudsman supported the many accusations against the PAC made by social organizations and the Catholic Church.

In February 1994, the Human Rights Ombudsman presented a plan before Congress that requested the repeal of the law that created the civil patrols... As a result of these efforts, as well as advances in the peace process, the PAC was dismantled in some areas in the early 1990s. Still, the official demobilization of the PAC did not occur until 1996...

The political transition that involved several civilian governments and opened dialogue between the government and the guerrillas envisioned the creation of state institutions that would safeguard human rights, enable due process protections, and establish a democratic state based on the rule of law...

The struggle against impunity... became a new collective mission that challenged the militarization of the country in favor of a democratic state based on the rule of law. This included a demand that the formally constituted rules and procedures of the judicial system be used to address legal complaints.

> One could see a difference, it wasn't just filing a complaint for the sake of filing a complaint, but rather documenting how the law could function as it always should have. What we saw was a whole system. The laws weren't bad, the problem was their application, that is, the fact that they were not applied out of fear... All of this came out of a movement which had the support, for example, of international organizations. The energy was contagious, whether or not one was a human rights activist. The simple fact that those from the military were beginning to be punished, that they were questioned, broke the silence and changed attitudes towards an understanding that the military really deserved to be brought before the courts because almost everyone had suffered from their abuses.[10]

While actions to combat impunity developed in the capital, there were also important activities in Mayan communities. These efforts sought judicial punishment for those responsible for massacres, kidnappings, sexual violence, and extrajudicial executions. When the domestic courts proved incapable of imparting justice, activists turned to international mechanisms, such as the Inter-American Court of Human Rights...

Signing the Oslo Accord that established the mandate for the CEH opened another aspect of the debate regarding justice and impunity. This provoked serious discussions within the core of civil society organizations regarding the possibility of a general amnesty. This was presented by some political interests as a necessary mechanism for national reconciliation and was rejected by groups that had been working to combat impunity in the country. The *Alianza contra la Impunidad* (Alliance against Impunity) was born out of these discussions and brought together a diverse set of organizations that sought consensus on these issues at the same time as the peace accords were being negotiated.

This process led to the creation of the *Ley de Reconciliacíon Nacional* (National Reconciliation Law) which allowed for protection from criminal responsibility for certain crimes committed during the armed confrontation but did not apply... "to the crimes of genocide, torture, forced disappearance..."[11]

The Indigenous Movement

During the period of the armed confrontation, the Maya people gradually emerged as political actors and were recognized as such, although with reservations on the part of both the state and society...

In the 1970s, Mayan organizations were formed in the area of the western *altiplano* including Maya cultural associations, groups of indigenous professionals and youth organizations. These were almost totally destroyed. Their regional and national links were dismantled, such as the *Seminarios Indigenas* (Indigenous Seminars), *Coordinadora Indígena Nacional* (National Indigenous Coordination) and the monthly bulletin *Ixim*. The CUC was also subjected to severe repression, after managing to bring together thousands of indigenous *campesinos* in only a few years, campaigning for their labor claims and taking a strong position against discrimination.

During the second half of the 1980s, the situation led to the creation of new indigenous organizations and the rebuilding of other groups that together, developed diverse strategies and adopted different positions in relation to the state and the armed confrontation. Some groups were affiliated with the URNG, while others directed their efforts toward taking advantage of emerging political opportunities and focusing their work on their communities to create development strategies grounded in the Mayan belief system...

The indigenous movement was defined by the fact that the Mayan people and their communities were both the primary victims of the armed confrontation and among the most significant actors... The severity of the wounds and losses suffered created a process of rigorous reflection among the Maya about the central role of racism within the longstanding social conflicts that enabled the armed confrontation, the importance of building new social ties among the different peoples in the country, and the need for a new relationship between indigenous people and government institutions. This process led to a variety of proposals and initiatives, with varying orientations, claims, and ideologies. Yet, all had common objectives including the formal recognition of the Mayan people and their distinct rights.

Some organizations and leaders, especially those with support in urban areas, were convinced that none of the parties represented their interests. They sought to distance themselves from the framework of the confrontation with the goal of developing proposals regarding the specific rights and culture of indigenous peoples. They set themselves apart from traditional forms of political protest and mobilization, choosing other mechanisms to create and develop proposals...

Their plans and claims placed fundamental importance on a respect for Mayan languages and strengthening culture, positioning cultural identity at the center of political identity. These important initiatives were advocated by a number of groups including the *Academia de la Lenguas Mayas de Guatemala* (Academy of Maya Languages in Guatemala, ALMG), the *Consejo de Organizaciones Mayas de Guatemala* (Council of Mayan Organizations of Guatemala, COMG), the *Consejo Nacional de Educación Maya* (National Council of Maya Education, CNEM) and the *Mesa Nacional Maya de Guatemala* (National Maya Board of Guatemala, MENAMGUA)...

At the same time, in the heart of Mayan communities, other organizations developed to address demands associated with the terrible, devastating violence. With a social base that included victims of *la violencia* and their relatives, groups such as CONAVIGUA, CONDEG, and CUC worked to confront the army's systems of control in their communities and to rebuild community structures based on their own culture...

In this regard, special attention should be given to the work of Rigoberta Menchú, a K'iché' woman from a rural family, who, from 1982 on, worked as a representative of the CUC in various international forums... According to research conducted by the CEH, Menchú's historic denunciation about the situation of her people accurately reflected the country's reality. Her talent, ability, and commitment to human rights and the rights of indigenous people in Guatemala as well as in other countries was recognized in 1992 when she was awarded the Nobel Peace Prize...

From 1990 on, groups that were formed to advocate for the rights of *campesinos* and the defense of human rights increasingly promoted Mayan political and cultural rights. The commemoration of the five hundredth anniversary of the arrival of the Spanish in the Americas played a significant role in these struggles. During the two years prior to the anniversary celebrated in October 1992, Guatemalan indigenous organizations and leaders participated in national and international meetings to clarify their analyses and claims. For those indigenous organizations that focused on human rights issues, the anniversary stimulated renewed interest in the specific nature of their cultural needs...

The recent development of the indigenous movement is grounded in the political transition from de facto military governments to constitutional governments and the opening of a process of dialogue and negotiation that culminated with the signing of the peace accords... The 1985 Constitution of the Republic, created as part of the transition, provided, to a degree, a political recognition of the role of indigenous people in society... Although it was created within a paternalistic framework and with limited focus on specific indigenous rights, it signalled the beginning of a process of creating normative legal support to end the exclusion of indigenous peoples and state and social discrimination.

The new constitution explicitly reflected, for the first time, the country's multiethnic reality:

> Guatemala is composed of diverse ethnic groups, among which indigenous groups of Mayan descent are prominent. The State recognizes, respects and promotes their ways of life, customs, traditions, ways of social organization, the use of indigenous dress for men and women, languages, and dialects.[12]

Alongside constitutional recognition, conditions were created during this period that gradually assisted indigenous people in developing improved social cohesion and opportunities to address basic historic claims. In this regard, it is worth noting the initiatives of Mayan leaders, including various linguists, to define the ALMG as an autonomous state entity responsible for supporting and strengthening Guatemala's indigenous languages... There were various other groups that emerged in 1990 such as COMG. They expressed the interest of indigenous leaders and intellectuals in promoting the development of the Mayan culture, as well as addressing the most urgent needs of their communities... In the same time period, another coordinating group, *Majawil Q'ij* (New Dawn), was formed by leaders of the CUC, CONAVIGUA, CONDEG, and the CPR. They sought to create an organization based on ethnic demands and initiatives, unifying processes that added to the growing numbers of Mayan organizations...

Mayan organizations and groups created throughout this period took advantage of national opportunities for debate and participation linked to the peace process, including the *Comisiones del Diálogo Nacional* (National Dialogue Commissions) and the *Coordinadora de Sectores Civiles* (Coordinator for Civil Sectors) both created by the *Comisión Nacional de Reconciliación* (National Commission for Reconciliation), and later the *Asamblea de Sociedad Civil* (Civil Society Assembly) that was involved in the direct negotiations between the parties.

The consensus documents that were produced through these organizations provided the foundation for the *Acuerdo de Identidad y Derechos de los Pueblos Indígenas* (Accord on the Identity and Rights of Indigenous Peoples) signed by the parties on March 31, 1995,... The accord established a series of commitments designed to achieve three fundamental objectives: eliminating the historic discrimination against indigenous people; permitting the participation of indigenous people in all public decisions that affect them; and recognizing "the Guatemalan nation as a national, multiethnic, multicultural, and multilingual."[13]

Arbitrary Execution of Myrna Elizabeth Mack Chang

Myrna Elizabeth Mack Chang, anthropologist and founding member of the *Asociación para el Avance de las Ciencias Sociales* (Association for the Advancement of Social Sciences, AVANCSO), led a small team that, from 1987 on, carried out investigations in communities of the internally displaced in the mountains in northern Alta Verapaz. Her goal was to develop and present a study about the living conditions of victims... and governmental policies regarding the displaced...

On September 11, 1990,... after leaving the AVANCSO office... Myrna Mack was attacked by two individuals who stabbed her twenty-seven times, killing her...

Firemen and the National Police arrived and secured the area. The general director of the National Police and the chief of the National Police's Bureau of Investigation conducted the first review of the case. In addition, according to a report presented to the IACHR, "Various members of Military Intelligence (G-2) showed up at the scene... These people were not uniformed but were wearing street clothes."[14]

From the start, the investigation following the crime involved irregularities. The police did not preserve the crime scene in the appropriate manner. They failed to dust for fingerprints... take blood samples... or examine clothing.

José Mérida Escobar and Julio Pérez Ixcajop were the National Police investigators assigned to the case. On December 29, 1990, they presented a sixty-page report in which they concluded that Myrna Mack had been killed for political reasons. The report mentioned Army Sergeant Major Noel de Jesús Beteta Alvarez, member of the Departamento de Seguridad Presidencial (Presidential Security Department, DSP) of the EMP as a suspect...

Mérida and Pérez's report was replaced by a thirteen-page version signed by the then-chief of the Homicide Section of the Department of Criminal Investigations (DIC). It was that report, dated November 4, 1990, that was sent to the courts. All references to military's involvement in the murder were removed and its final conclusions stated that the motive for the crime had been robbery.

On October 10, 1990, Helen Mack appeared as an *acusador particular* (private prosecutor) in the case. On January 6, 1991, the court called on the investigators to confirm the November 4 report, but the National Police responded that the agents were not available. Later, on June 26, 1991, investigators Mérida and Pérez appeared before the judge. Mérida confirmed the sixty-page report and, after testifying, admitted that his statement equaled a "death sentence." Pérez, on the contrary, refused to acknowledge the report.

At the end of July 1991, Mérida made preparations to leave Guatemala, since he had already received two death threats and knew that armed men were watching him. On August 5, 1991, Mérida was murdered by gunshots, less than 100 meters away from a National Police station. The incident has not been taken to court. In September of that same year, the National Police took Pérez's weapon and withdrew his bodyguards. In October, he and his family fled Guatemala after noticing that armed men were watching them.

On November 29, 1991, Noel de Jesús Beteta Alvarez was detained in Los Angeles by U.S. Immigration and Naturalization Service agents. On December 4, he was deported to Guatemala. The Ministry of Defense told the courts that Beteta had worked in the EMP until November 30, 1990... and that he was removed "on the advice of the service." Beteta, on the contrary, insisted that his duties were criminal investigations of kidnappings and robberies personally directed by the head of the EMP who gave him verbal orders...

On October 29, 1992, two young witnesses, Juan Carlos Marroquín Tejeda and José Tejeda Hernández, agreed with a third witness whose statement was recorded in the nonpublic phase of the investigation about the physical description of Beteta, who was identified as one of Myrna Mack's two assailants.

On February 12, 1993,... Beteta was sentenced to twenty-five years in prison, without commutation, for murder... A few months earlier... Beteta confided to another convict, in statements that were tape recorded and filmed, that the murder of Myrna Mack

> was a planned operation... I received the direct order from... yes... it was politically motivated. She was investigating things that, I think, questioned what one calls the security and stability of the government and that was why they ordered the crime... [15]

The *acusadora particular* appealed the case to the Fourth Appellate Chamber asking that the case should remain open to pursue the intellectual authors of the anthropologist's murder...

There were a significant number of irregularities in the judicial process. [The case] was the responsibility of twelve different judges, from the justice of the peace who carried out initial procedures to the Supreme Court. The process was delayed due to the presentation of multiple motions as well as violations of timeliness of legal procedures. In the initial phase, the process was delayed from September 1990 to December 1994.

In the criminal process, there were acts of obstruction and the manipulation of evidence by the military authorities. The EMP denied information, invoking state secrets... It denied the existence of any file on Myrna Mack... although the CEH reviewed a copy that corresponded to a military intelligence file.

In the beginning, it also denied any investigation of the murder, despite there being many witnesses who stated that they had been visited by or interrogated by a "Captain Estrada" belonging to the military. In addition, the EMP provided false data regarding the date on which Beteta was relieved of his position and functions, as well as relating to treatment he received at the Military Hospital. Likewise, it refused to hand over the EMP's daily news report and refused to honor a request for the records of the entry and exit of DSP vehicles... It did not want to provide the EMP's organizational chart and refused to provide the names of departments and sections within the EMP. It also did not provide information about the Ministry of Defense's Personnel Department or previous records regarding those accused, the names of the commanders of the military zones, and units where Myrna Mack carried out her research, or [information] about the group to which Beteta belonged and the D-2...

Throughout 1998, the Ministry of Defense continued to refuse to cooperate, so much so that one of those standing trial failed to honor the requirement of the precautionary measures to appear before the judge every fifteen days to register. Nevertheless, the judge rejected a request by the prosecutor from the *Ministerio Público* (Public Ministry, MP) to revoke precautionary measures in favor of pre-trial detention.

On June 23 of that same year, the prosecutor presented a case against the three officers. At the time of this report, the trial has been delayed as a motion questioning jurisdiction is under review by the Supreme Court...

However, the IACHR opened the case based on a petition by Helen Mack in September 1990...Considering all of these facts, the CEH determined that the murder of Myrna Elizabeth Mack Chang was committed by an agent of the state in his role as an active member of the EMP, following orders received from other officers of that entity within the military.

Part IV

Conclusions and Recommendations

12

The Tragedy of the Armed Confrontation

With the outbreak of the internal armed confrontation in 1962, Guatemala entered a tragic and devastating stage of its history, with enormous human, material, and moral cost. In documenting human rights violations and acts of violence connected with the armed confrontation, the CEH registered a total of 42,275 victims, including men, women, and children. Of these, 23,671 were victims of arbitrary execution and 6,159 were victims of forced disappearance. Eighty-three percent of fully identified victims were Mayan and 17 percent were Ladino.

By combining this data with the results of other studies of political violence in Guatemala, the CEH estimates that the number of persons killed or disappeared as a result of the fratricidal confrontation reached a total of over 200,000…

Human Rights Violations Committed by the State

Human rights violations and acts of violence attributable to actions by the state represent 93 percent of those registered by the CEH…85 percent of all cases of human rights violations and acts of violence registered by the CEH are attributable to the army, acting either alone or in collaboration with another force, and 18 percent, to the civil patrols, which were organized by the armed forces…

The responsibility for a large part of these violations, with respect to the military chain of command as well as political and administrative responsibility, reaches the highest levels of the army and successive governments. According to the CEH's investigation, the excuse that lower-ranking army commanders were acting with a wide margin of autonomy and decentralization without orders from superiors, as a way of explaining that "excesses" and "errors" were committed, is an unsubstantiated argument. The well-known fact that no high-level commander, officer, or person in the mid-level command of the army or state security forces has been tried or convicted for their acts violating human rights during all these years reinforces the conclusion that the majority of these violations were the result of an institutional policy…

Acts of Violence Committed by the Guerrillas

The armed insurgent groups that participated in the internal armed confrontation had an obligation to respect the minimum standards of international humanitarian law that apply to armed conflicts, as well as the general principles common to international human rights law. Their high command had the obligation to instruct subordinates to respect these norms and principles.

Acts of violence attributable to the guerrillas represent 3 percent of the violations registered by the CEH. This contrasts with 93 percent committed by agents of the state, especially the army. This quantitative difference provides new evidence of the magnitude of the state's repressive response. However, in the opinion of the CEH, this disparity does not lessen the gravity of the unjustifiable offenses committed by the guerrillas against human rights.

Historical Roots of the Armed Confrontation

The CEH concludes that the structure and nature of economic, cultural, and social relations in Guatemala are marked by profound exclusion, antagonism, and conflict—a reflection of its colonial history. The proclamation of independence in 1821, an event prompted by the country's elite, led to the creation of an authoritarian state which excluded the majority of the population, was racist in its precepts and practices, and protected the economic interests of a privileged minority. The evidence for this, throughout Guatemala's history, and especially during the armed confrontation, lies in the fact that the violence was fundamentally directed by the state against the excluded, the poor, and above all, the Mayan people, as well as against those who fought for justice and greater social equality.

The antidemocratic nature of the Guatemalan political tradition has its roots in an economic structure which is marked by the concentration of productive wealth in the hands of a minority. This established the foundations of a system of multiple exclusions, including elements of racism, which is, in turn, the most profound manifestation of a violent and dehumanizing social system. The state gradually evolved as an instrument for the protection of this structure, guaranteeing the continuation of exclusion and injustice.

The absence of an effective state social policy, with the exception of the period from 1944 to 1954, accentuated this historical dynamic of exclusion. In many cases, more recent state policy produced inequality, or, at the very least, endemic institutional weaknesses have accentuated it. Proof of this can be seen in the fact that, during the twenty years of Guatemala's most rapid economic growth (1960–1980), state social spending and taxation were the lowest in Central America.

Due to its exclusionary nature, the state was incapable of achieving social consensus around a national project to unite the whole population. At the same time, it abandoned its role as mediator between divergent social and economic interests, thereby...making direct confrontation between them more likely. The CEH is especially concerned with the way that successive constitutions of the

Republic, and the human and civil rights guarantees they define , became formal instruments that were violated by the various elements within the state itself.

The legislative branch and participating political parties also contributed at various times to increasing polarization and exclusion by establishing legal norms that legitimized regimes of exception and the suppression of civil and political rights while also hindering and obstructing any process of change. There was a lack of appropriate institutional mechanisms for channeling concerns, claims, and proposals from different sectors of society. This deficit of mechanisms for constructively directing dissent through mediation, typical of democratic systems, further consolidated a political culture of confrontation and intolerance and provoked ongoing instability that permeated the whole social order.

Thus a vicious circle was created in which social injustice led to protest and subsequently political instability to which there were always only two responses: repression or military coups. Faced with movements proposing economic, political, social, or cultural change, the state increasingly resorted to violence and terror in order to maintain social control. Political violence was thus a direct expression of structural violence.

Repression as a Substitute for the Law

The CEH has concluded that during the armed confrontation, the incapacity of the Guatemalan State to provide answers to legitimate social demands and claims led to the creation of a complex repressive apparatus that replaced the legal activities, operations and focus of the courts...Military intelligence established and directed an illegal and secretive system of punishment. The state relied on this system, which operated with the direct or indirect support of dominant economic and political sectors, as its main form of social control throughout the internal armed confrontation.

The Ineffectiveness of the Judicial System

The country's judicial system failed to guarantee the application of the law through both inadvertent and deliberate mismanagement thereby tolerating, and even facilitating, violence. The judiciary contributed to heightening social conflicts at various times in Guatemala's history both through purposeful actions and by failing to act. Impunity permeated the country to such an extent that it defined the very structure of the state and became both a means and an end...

The Closing of Political Spaces

After the overthrow of the government of Colonel Jacobo Arbenz in 1954, there was a rapid reduction of the possibility for political expression. New legislation that was inspired by fundamentalist anticommunism, outlawed broad and diverse social movements and consolidated the restrictive and exclusionary nature of the political system. The country's empowered interests agreed to these limitations on political participation, which were supported by the civil and political forces at the time. This process constituted one of the most overwhelming pieces of evidence of the close relationship that emerged in 1954 between the military, the economic elite, and the political parties. Then, from 1963 on, alongside legal restrictions, the state expanded repression against its real or suspected opponents creating another decisive factor in limiting political options in Guatemala...

The Cold War, the National Security Doctrine, and the Role of the United States

The CEH recognizes that the movement of Guatemala toward polarization, militarization, and civil war was not only an element of national history. The Cold War also played an important role. While anticommunism, promoted by the United States within the framework of its foreign policy, was generally supported by right-wing political parties and various other powerful actors in Guatemala, the United States demonstrated its commitment by supporting strong military regimes in its strategic backyard. In the case of Guatemala, military assistance was directed toward reinforcing the national intelligence apparatus and training the officer corps in counterinsurgency techniques, key factors that significant impacted the human rights violations committed during the armed confrontation.

Anticommunism and National Security Doctrine formed part of the anti-Soviet strategy of the United States in Latin America. In Guatemala, these were first expressed as antireformist policies, then as antidemocratic policies, and eventually they became criminal counterinsurgency policies. National Security Doctrine fell on fertile ground in Guatemala where anticommunist thinking had already taken root and, from the 1930s on, had merged with the defense of religion, tradition, and conservative values, all of which were allegedly threatened by the worldwide expansion of atheistic communism. Until the 1950s, these views were strongly supported by the Catholic Church, which viewed any position that contradicted its philosophy as communist, thus contributing even further to division and confusion in Guatemalan society...

The Catholic Church

It is only recently within Guatemalan history...that the Catholic Church abandoned its conservative position and prioritized work with excluded, poor and underprivileged sectors by promoting the construction of a more just and equitable society. This shift in attitude and practice was based on the decisions of the Second Vatican Council (1962–1965) and the Episcopal Conference of Medellin (1968). These doctrinal and pastoral changes clashed with counterinsurgency strategy, which considered Catholics to be allies of the guerrillas and therefore part of the internal enemy, subject to persecution, death, or expulsion. However, the guerrilla movement saw the practice of what was known as "liberation theology" as common ground on which to extend its social base, seeking to gain the support of its followers. A large number of catechists, lay activists, priests, and missionaries were victims of *la violencia* as their suffering served as a testimony to the cruelty of the armed confrontation.

The Guatemalan Insurgency, the Armed Struggle, and the Cuban Influence

The Guatemalan insurgency arose as the response of one sector of the population to the country's diverse structural problems. Faced with injustice, exclusion, poverty, and discrimination, it proclaimed the need to take power by force in order to build a new social, political, and economic order. Throughout the armed confrontation, insurgent groups adopted Marxist doctrine in its diverse international forms. Although they had common historical roots in the communist PGT, several guerrilla organizations emerged as a result of their criticism of the party's reluctance to follow the path of armed struggle.

Cuba's influence and its promotion of armed struggle impacted these processes in Guatemala as in the rest of Latin America. The CEH concludes that political, logistic, instructional, and training support provided by Cuba for the Guatemalan insurgents during this period was an important external factor that affected the evolution of the armed confrontation. In the context of an increasingly repressive state, sectors of the left, specifically those that followed Marxist ideology, adopted the Cuban perspective of armed struggle as the only way to protect the rights of the people and to take power.

As state repression intensified and broadened its range of potential victims, the rebel position that held a guerrilla victory to be the country's only political solution, gained strength. During most of the confrontation, the cohesion of the Guatemalan insurgency was not bound to a common ideological-political platform, but instead was grounded in the idea of the need for, and the primacy of, armed struggle as the only solution.

During its investigation, the CEH determined that the political work of the guerrilla organizations within the different sectors of society was increasingly directed toward strengthening their military capacity to the detriment of the type of political activity characteristic of democratic groups. Likewise, attempts by other political forces to take advantage of the limited opportunities for legal participation were radically dismissed by some sectors of the insurgency as "reformist" or "dissident," while people who sought to remain distant from the confrontation were treated with profound mistrust and even as potential enemies. These attitudes contributed to political intolerance and polarization…

More Than Just Two Parties

Although the most visible actors in the armed confrontation were the army and the insurgents, the CEH investigation has clearly revealed the involvement of the entire state, through the unification of various coercive institutions and mechanisms. Likewise, although of a different nature, the CEH has drawn attention to responsibility and participation of economically powerful groups, political parties, universities, and churches, as well as other sectors of civil society.

For this reason, the CEH concludes that a full explanation of the Guatemalan confrontation cannot be reduced to the sole logic of two armed parties. Such an interpretation fails to explain or establish the basis for the persistence and significance of the participation of political parties and economic forces in the initiation, development, and continuation of the violence; nor does it explain the repeated efforts at organization and the continuous mobilization of those sectors of the population struggling to achieve their economic, political, and cultural demands.

A Disproportionately Repressive Response

The magnitude of the state's repressive response was totally disproportionate in relation to the military force of the insurgency and can only be understood within the framework of the country's profound social, economic, and cultural conflicts. Based on the results of its investigation, the CEH concludes that from 1978 to 1982 citizens from broad sectors of society participated in growing social mobilization and political opposition to the continuity of the country's established order. Some of these movements maintained ties of varying types with the insurgency. However, at no time during the internal armed confrontation did the guerrilla groups have the military potential necessary to pose an imminent threat to the state. The number of insurgent combatants was too small to be able to compete in the military arena with the Guatemalan Army, which had more troops and superior weaponry, as well as better training and coordination. It has also been confirmed that during the armed confrontation, the state and the army had knowledge of the level of organization, the number of combatants, the type of weaponry, and the strategy of the insurgent groups. They were, therefore, well aware that the insurgents' military capacity did not represent a real threat to Guatemala's political order.

The CEH concludes that the state deliberately magnified the military threat of the insurgency, a practice justified by the concept of the internal enemy. The inclusion of all opponents under one banner, democratic or otherwise, pacifist or guerrilla, legal or illegal, communist or noncommunist, served to justify numerous and serious crimes. Faced with widespread political, socioeconomic, and cultural opposition, the state resorted to military operations directed toward the physical annihilation or absolute intimidation of this opposition, through a plan of repression carried out mainly by the army and national security forces. On this basis the CEH explains why the vast majority of the victims of the acts committed by the state were not combatants in guerrilla groups, but civilians...

Children

The CEH has concluded with particular concern that a large number of children were among the direct victims of arbitrary execution, forced disappearance, torture, rape, and other violations of fundamental rights. Moreover, the armed confrontation left a large number of children orphaned and abandoned, especially among the Mayan population, who saw their families destroyed and lost the possibility of living a normal childhood based on their cultural values.

Women

The CEH's investigation has revealed that women represented approximately a quarter of the direct victims of human rights violations and acts of violence. They were killed, tortured, and raped, sometimes because of their ideals and political or social participation, and sometimes in massacres and other indiscriminate actions. Thousands of women lost their husbands, becoming widows and the sole breadwinners for their children. They were often left with no material resources after the scorched earth policies led to the destruction of their homes and crops. Their efforts to reconstruct their lives and support their families deserve special recognition.

At the same time, the CEH recognizes the fact that women, the majority of them relatives of victims, played an exemplary role in defending human rights during the armed confrontation, promoting and directing organizations for relatives of the disappeared, and struggling against impunity.

The Mayan Population as the Collective Enemy of the State

In the years when the confrontation was most severe (1978–1983), as the guerrilla support base and area of action expanded, the army identified Mayans as a group in several different parts of the country as guerrilla allies. Occasionally this was the result of the effective existence of support for the insurgent groups and of pre-insurrection conditions in the country's interior. However, the CEH has ascertained that, in the majority of cases, the identification of Mayan communities with the insurgency was intentionally exaggerated by the state, which, based on traditional racist prejudices, used this identification to eliminate any present or future possibility among the people for providing assistance or joining the insurgent project.

The consequence of this manipulation, extensively documented by the CEH, was massive and indiscriminate aggression directed against communities independent of their actual involvement in the guerrilla movement and with a clear indifference to their status as a noncombatant civilian population. The massacres, scorched earth operations, forced disappearances, and executions of Mayan authorities, leaders, and spiritual guides were not only an attempt to destroy the social base of the guerrillas, but were above all, [an effort] to destroy the cultural values that ensured cohesion and collective action in Mayan communities.

Racism as a Component of Violence

Through its investigation, the CEH also concludes that the undeniable existence of racism expressed repeatedly by the state as a doctrine of superiority, is a basic explanatory factor for the indiscriminate nature and particular brutality with which military operations were carried out against hundreds of Mayan communities in the west and northwest of the country, especially between 1981 and 1983, when the scorched earth operations and more than half of the massacres occurred.

Militarization

The CEH has confirmed that the militarization of the state and society was a strategic objective that was defined, planned, and executed institutionally by the Guatemalan Army, based on National Security Doctrine and the institution's particular interpretation of the country's reality. The process of militarization passed through different stages during the years of the armed confrontation. It began during the 1960s and 1970s with the army's domination of the structures of the executive branch. The army subsequently assumed almost absolute power for half a decade during the 1980s, by penetrating all of the country's institutions, as well as its political, social, and ideological spheres. In the final stage of the confrontation, the army developed a parallel, semivisible, low profile, but high impact, control of national life.

Militarization was one of the factors that provided the incentive for and fed the armed confrontation as it profoundly limited the possibilities for citizens to exercise their rights. Subsequently, it became one of the most damaging consequences of the confrontation. Militarization became a pillar of impunity. Moreover, in a broad sense, it weakened the country's institutions, reducing their potential to function effectively and contributing to their loss of legitimacy, since for years people lived with the certainty that it was the army that retained effective power in Guatemala...

Terror

The CEH confirmed that throughout the armed confrontation the army designed and implemented a strategy to provoke terror in the population. This strategy became the core element of the army's operations, including those of a strictly military nature as well those of a psychological nature and those that were called "development" operations.

The guerrilla organizations committed violent and extremely cruel acts, which terrorized people and had significant consequences. Arbitrary executions, especially those committed before relatives and neighbors, accentuated the already prevalent climate of fear, uncertainty, and defenselessness...

A high proportion of the human rights violations that were committed by the army or security forces and presented to the CEH were perpetrated publicly and with extreme brutality, especially in the Mayan communities of the country's interior. Likewise, in considering the training methods of the armed forces, and especially the *Kaibiles*, the CEH concludes that extreme cruelty was an intentional strategy used to produce and maintain a climate of terror among the population.

The terror created was not only a result of military operations and acts of violence; it was also generated and sustained by other related mechanisms, such as impunity for the perpetrators, extensive campaigns to criminalize the victims, and the forced involvement of civilians in the processes that led to the commission of atrocities. For these reasons, terror does not automatically disappear when the levels of violence decrease; on the contrary, there are cumulative and lasting effects, which can only be overcome through time, effort, and the direct experience that things have changed.

The investigation has established that beyond the physical elimination of opponents, either alleged or real, state terror was applied to make it clear that those who attempted to assert their rights, and even their relatives, ran the risk of death by the most hideous means. The objective was to intimidate and silence society as a whole in order to destroy the will for transformation in both the short and long term.

Criminalization of Victims

The state tried to stigmatize and blame the victims and the country's social organizations, defining them as criminals in the public eye and thus making them "legitimate" targets for repression…The CEH considers that this systematic indoctrination has profoundly marked the collective consciousness of Guatemalan society. Fear, silence, apathy, and lack of political participation are some of the most important effects of having criminalized the victims, and present a serious obstacle to the active participation of all citizens in the construction of democracy.

Forced Complicity in the Violence

The CEH considers that forcing large sectors of the population to be accomplices in the violence represents among the most damaging effects of the confrontation. This is especially true as regards participation in the PAC which operated in most of the Republic. The CEH is aware of hundreds of cases in which civilians were forced by the army, at gun point, to rape women, torture, mutilate corpses, and kill. This extreme cruelty was used by the state to create social disintegration. A large proportion of the male population over the age of fifteen, especially in the Mayan communities, was forced to participate in the PAC. This deeply affected values and behavioral patterns, as violence became a normal method of confronting conflictive situations, promoting contempt for the lives of others.

Local Arbitrary Power

Of deep and special concern to the CEH is the fact that these processes created a group of civilians who…committed atrocities against their own neighbors and even against close relatives. This created an uncontrolled armed power that acted arbitrarily in villages, often pursuing private and abusive ends.

The fact that victims and perpetrators continue to live together in the same villages reproduces the climate of fear and silence. For the victims, daily confrontation with their victimizers has kept the painful memory of their violations alive. The CEH has confirmed that a large number of people continue to remain silent about their past and present suffering out of fear of reprisals as the internalization of trauma prevents their wounds from healing...

The Weakening of Social Organizations

The CEH has determined that social organizations were an important target of the state's repressive action during the armed confrontation. Considered as part of the "internal enemy," hundreds of leaders and grassroots members from a wide spectrum of groups were eliminated. These actions left civil society weakened and still affect its full participation in Guatemala's political and economic debates. The loss of professionals, academics, and researchers, the "creative powers" who died or went into exile, not only created a vacuum during a specific period of political and cultural history, but also resulted in the loss of an important element of the pedagogic and intellectual capacity to educate several generations in Guatemala.

Alongside repression and exile, the state used various mechanisms instituted during the armed confrontation to weaken and fragment social organizations.These mechanisms continue to be present in the collective memory. Stigmatization, fear, mistrust, and the perception among some sectors that the signing of the peace accords has not yet changed the repressive state, remain obstacles that prevent the full participation of society, even though the process of peace and national reconciliation indicates an encouraging reversal of this tendency.

Acts of Genocide

After studying four selected geographical regions, (Maya-Q'anjob'al and Maya-Chuj, in Barillas, Nentón, and San Mateo Ixtatán in North Huehuetenango; Maya-Ixil, in Nebaj, Cotzal, and Chajul, Quiché; Maya-K'iche' in Joyabaj, Zacualpa, and Chiché, Quiché; and Maya-Achí in Rabinal, Baja Verapaz), the CEH confirmed that between 1981 and 1983 the army identified groups of the Mayan population as the internal enemy, considering them to be an actual or potential support base for the guerrillas...In this way, the army, inspired by National Security Doctrine, defined a concept of internal enemy that went beyond guerrilla sympathizers, combatants, or militants to include civilians from specific ethnic groups.

Considering the series of criminal acts and human rights violations that occurred in the regions and periods indicated and which were analyzed for the purpose of determining whether they constituted the crime of genocide, the CEH concludes that the reiteration of destructive acts, directed systematically against groups of the Mayan population...demonstrates that the only common denominator for all the victims was the fact that they belonged to a specific ethnic group and makes it evident that these acts were committed "with intent to destroy, in whole or in part" these groups...

With great consternation, the CEH concludes that many massacres and other human rights violations committed against these groups obeyed a higher, strategically planned policy, manifested in actions that had a logical and coherent sequence. Faced with several options to combat the insurgency, the state chose the one that caused the greatest loss of human life among non-combatant civilians. Rejecting other options, such as a political effort to reach agreements with disaffected noncombatant civilians, moving people away from the conflict areas, or arresting insurgents, the state opted for the annihilation of those they identified as their enemy.

In consequence, the CEH concludes that agents of the State of Guatemala, within the framework of counterinsurgency operations carried out between 1981 and 1983, committed acts of genocide against groups of Mayan people that lived in the four regions.

Acts of Violence Committed by Private Individuals

The CEH concludes that private individuals also committed acts of violence in connection with the armed confrontation to defend their own interests, either by instigating these actions or directly participating in them. In general, the perpetrators were economically powerful people at the national and local level.

Many human rights violations were committed in rural areas with the participation of large landowners. Some of these violations were committed jointly with agents of the state in order to use force to resolve conflicts with *campesinos*. On other occasions, violations to protect landowners' interests were committed directly by agents or hired assassins of the state,

In urban areas, diverse human rights violations were committed against trade union members and labor advisors. These acts were perpetrated by agents of the state or those acting with its protection, tolerance, or acquiescence and involved close cooperation between powerful business people and security forces. They were committed to protect business interests in accordance with openly antitrade union policies of the government.

The Denial of Justice

The courts were incapable of investigating, trying, judging, and punishing even a small number of those responsible for the most serious human rights crimes, or of providing protection for the victims. This conclusion can be applied both to military tribunals charged with the investigation and punishment of crimes committed by individuals within their special jurisdiction, as well as to the ordinary justice system...[which had] given up exercising its functions of protecting and safeguarding the rights of the individual.

Acts and omissions by the judicial branch, such as the systematic denial of habeas corpus, continuous interpretation of the law favorable to the authorities, indifference to the torture of detainees, and limitations on the right to defense demonstrated the judges' lack of independence. These constituted grave violations of the right to due process and serious breaches of the state's duty to investigate, try, and punish human rights violations. The few judges that kept their independence and continued to act in a professional manner were victims of repressive acts, including murder and threats, especially during the 1980s...

Impunity

The justice system, nonexistent in large areas of the country before the armed confrontation, was further weakened when the judicial branch submitted to the requirements of the dominant national security model. The CEH concludes that, by tolerating or participating directly in impunity, which concealed the most fundamental violations of human rights, the judiciary became functionally inoperative with respect to its role of protecting the individual from the state, and lost all credibility as guarantor of an effective legal system. This allowed impunity to become one of the most important mechanisms for generating and maintaining a climate of terror.

These factors combined to thwart the existence of the rule of law in Guatemala. Likewise, a deep-rooted skepticism developed in society regarding the value of improving Guatemala's legal system and of believing that the administration of justice could be an effective option for the construction of a society of equally free and respected individuals. Thus, one of the most challenging and complex tasks in the establishment of peace consists of restoring the basic legal system, making it available to and functional for all citizens, so that social groups as well as individuals may channel their demands and conflicts through competent state institutions.

Curtailed Freedom of Speech

Freedom of speech goes hand in hand with the free exercise of civil rights. When opportunities for social and political participation are closed, then, implicitly, so are opportunities for freedom of speech. During the long period of the armed confrontation, even thinking critically was a dangerous act in Guatemala, and writing about political and social realities, events, or ideas, meant running the risk of threats, torture, disappearance, and death. In exercising freedom of speech, citizens, writers, artists, poets, politicians, and journalists were subjected to the dangers of repression and ideological polarization. Although there were people who spoke out despite these risks, the major news agencies generally supported the authoritarian regimes through self-censorship and distorting the facts. The price paid for this was very high, not only in terms of the number of lives lost, but also because Guatemala became a country silenced.

Altered Mourning and Clandestine Cemeteries

The testimonies received by the CEH bear witness to the wide range of circumstances that prevented thousands of Guatemalans from observing the rites that normally accompany the death and burial of a person during the armed confrontation. This has caused deep and persisting anguish among the affected sectors of the population. Forced disappearance was the most destructive practice as a result of the uncertainty it produced regarding the whereabouts and fates of the victims. The climate of terror, the presence of military forces, as well as other circumstances related to the massacres, flight and persecution in the mountains, often prevented people from burying the dead...

The CEH has concluded that the existence of clandestine and hidden cemeteries, as well as the anxiety suffered by many Guatemalans as a result of not knowing what happened to their relatives, remains an open wound in the country. They are a permanent reminder of the acts of violence that denied the dignity of their loved ones. To heal these particular wounds requires the exhumation of secret graves, as well as the definitive identification of the whereabouts of the disappeared.

The Economic Costs of the Armed Confrontation

In its investigation of the economic costs of the armed confrontation, focusing only on the ten-year period between 1980 and 1989, the CEH estimates that the total direct quantifiable costs were equivalent to zero production in Guatemala for almost fifteen months or 121 percent of the 1990 Gross Domestic Product (GDP)...

Based on its investigation, the CEH concludes that the increase in military spending during the armed confrontation diverted necessary investments of public resources away from health and education, resulting in the abandonment of social development. This accelerated the deterioration of health and educational conditions in those areas most severely affected by the confrontation.

The armed confrontation also exacerbated the traditional weakness of the state regarding tax collection and intensified private sector opposition to necessary tax reform. This was reflected by the fact that from 1978 to 1984 taxes as a percentage of GDP dropped constantly, reaching 7.1 percent in the final year, the lowest level registered over the previous fifty years. The effects were decisive as the gap between income and spending widened, leading to a macroeconomic imbalance that further weakened the state's capacity to promote development...

The CEH has concluded that society as a whole, and not just those people directly affected, has had to assume the high costs that resulted from the confrontation.

Solidarity and the Defense of Human Rights

Simultaneously, and with varying intensity at different stages of the armed confrontation, there were individual and collective responses to the dehumanizing and denigrating effects of violence. The organizations that emerged from this process were dedicated to defending life, even as they faced enormous obstacles including death threats. These groups were mainly composed of the surviving communities and relatives of victims whose primary motivation was solidarity, the defense of basic human rights and the desire to respect dignity and justice. At the same time, they contributed to reclaiming people's rights as citizens within the country's legal system.

Human rights organizations made decisive contributions toward establishing new principles of social relations and reconstructing the social fabric. Although these organizations emerged from those most affected by the confrontation, their claims immediately extended to other sectors of society. Particularly during the final years of the armed confrontation, various civil society groups developed strategies to limit the army's power and preeminence in Guatemalan social and political life by focusing on the close links between impunity for those who used systematic violence and the persistent militarization of society. The CEH concludes that these efforts promoted a new awareness of the need for justice, respect for the law, and the validity of the rule of law as basic requirements of democracy.

The Mayan Movement

The CEH concludes that the Mayan movement affirmed its role as a key political actor during the later years of the armed confrontation. The Mayan people have made important contributions toward multicultural understanding and peace through their struggle against the exclusions they have suffered since the foundation of the Guatemalan State. These actions provide the essential basis for society as a whole to review its history and commit itself to building a new project of nationhood consistent with its multicultural nature as inclusive, tolerant, and proud of the wealth implicit in cultural differences.

Peace and Reconciliation

The intensity of the armed confrontation diminished considerably during the long process that began in 1987 of searching for a political solution to the conflict. However, during this period, violence, impunity, and the militarization of society still prevailed in Guatemala. Considering the complexity of the situation and the fact that there were hostile groups that opposed the peace process for different reasons, the CEH recognizes the admirable effort and courage of those men and women who contributed to the signing the accords after nine years of rapprochement and negotiation between the parties including the presidents of the Republic over this period and the public officials of the administrations that participated in the negotiations and initiation of the first conciliatory initiatives; the URNG Command; the citizens who participated in the National Reconciliation Commission and the Assembly of Civil Society; and the religious sector, especially the Catholic Church. It is also worth noting the significant contribution of army representatives to this process...

The armed confrontation has left deep wounds in individuals, in families, and in society as a whole. Due to this undeniable fact, making the peace accords a reality and achieving true national reconciliation, will be a long and complex process. The immediate key tasks that will facilitate Guatemala's full transition to reconciliation and the observance of the rule of law in a democratic state include: furthering the process of demilitarization of both the state and society; strengthening the judicial system; opening up increased opportunities for effective participation; and ensuring reparations for the victims of human rights violations.

To achieve true reconciliation and construct a new democratic and participatory nation, which values its multiethnic and pluricultural nature, the whole of society must assume the commitments of the peace process. This doubtless requires a profound and complex effort, which Guatemalan society owes to the thousands of brave men and women who sought to obtain full respect for human rights and the democratic rule of law and so laid the foundations for this new nation. Among these, Monsignor Juan Gerardi Conedera remains at the forefront.

With humility and profound respect, the CEH dedicates its work to the memory of the dead and other victims of over three decades of fratricidal violence in Guatemala.

13

Recommendations

The Oslo Accord establishes one of the three objectives of the CEH as

> Formulate specific recommendations to encourage peace and national harmony in Guatemala. The Commission shall recommend, in particular, measures to preserve the memory of the victims, to foster a culture of mutual respect and observance of human rights and to strengthen the democratic process...

The violence and horrors described in the report should leave no room for despair. Subsequent generations in Guatemala have the right to a brighter, better future. Guatemalans can, and must, encourage a common project of nationhood. To bring about a reconstruction of Guatemala's social fabric, based on lasting peace and reconciliation, it is vital to foster an authentic sense of national unity among the diversity of peoples that make up the nation. By means of its recommendations, the CEH aims to help strengthen the hope of the people of Guatemala that its violent history will never be repeated.

Measures to Preserve the Memory of the Victims

The Oslo Accord emphasizes the need to remember and dignify the victims of Guatemala's fratricidal confrontation. The CEH believes that historical memory, both individual and collective, forms the basis of national identity. Remembrance of the victims is a fundamental aspect of this historical memory and enables the recuperation of the values of human dignity and the validitation of this struggle. On the basis of these considerations, and considering the appeal for forgiveness made by the president of the Republic on December 29, 1998, and the partial appeal for forgiveness made by the URNG on February 19, 1998, the CEH recommends:

Dignity for the Victims

That, in the name of the state of Guatemala and with the primary aim of restoring dignity to the victims, the president of the Republic recognize, before the whole of Guatemalan society, before the victims, their relatives, and their communities, those acts described in this report, ask pardon for them and assume responsibility for the human rights violations connected with the internal armed confrontation, particularly those committed by the army and the state security forces.

That the Congress of the Republic issue a solemn declaration reaffirming the dignity and honor of the victims and restoring their good name and that of their relatives.

That the ex-command of the URNG, with the primary aim of restoring dignity to the victims, ask forgiveness, solemnly and publicly, before the whole of society, before the victims, their relatives and their communities, and assume responsibility for those acts of violence committed by the ex-guerrillas connected with the armed confrontation that have caused suffering for the Guatemalan people.

Remembrance of the Victims

That the Guatemalan State and society commemorate the victims by means of various activities carried out in coordination with organizations from civil society, among which the following measures are essential:

- Designation of a day of commemoration of the victims (National Day of Dignity for the Victims of the Violence).
- The construction of monuments and public parks in memory of the victims at national, regional, and municipal levels.
- The assigning of names of victims to educational centers, buildings, and public highways.

That the commemorations and ceremonies for the victims of the armed confrontation take into consideration the multicultural nature of the Guatemalan nation, to which end the government and local authorities should promote and authorize the raising of monuments and the creation of communal cemeteries in accordance with Mayan collective memory.

That the sacred Mayan sites violated during the armed confrontation are reclaimed and their importance highlighted in accordance with the wishes of the communities affected.

Reparatory Measures

The CEH considers that truth, justice, reparation, and forgiveness are the bases of the process of the consolidation of peace and national reconciliation. Therefore, it is the responsibility of the Guatemalan State to design and promote a reparation policy for victims and their relatives. The primary objectives should be to dignify the victims, to guarantee that the human rights violations and acts of violence connected with the armed confrontation will not be repeated, and to ensure respect for national and international standards of human rights.

On this basis, the CEH recommends:

National Reparation Program

That the Guatemalan State, by means of appropriate measures taken by the government and the Congress of the Republic, urgently create and put into effect a National Reparation Program for the victims of human rights violations and acts of violence connected with the armed confrontation and their relatives.

That, to this end, the government present to the Congress of the Republic, with the utmost urgency, a legislative bill on reparations for victims of the armed confrontation to create the National Reparation Program. The said bill should set out the general principles and the structure of the program, the categories of beneficiaries, the measures, the procedures for identifying beneficiaries, the manner, and the financial mechanisms, to be set forth below.

Principles and Measures

That the National Reparation Program include a series of measures inspired by the principles of equality, social participation, and respect for cultural identity, among which at least the following should figure:

- Measures for the restoration of material possessions so that, as far as is possible, the situation existing before the violation be reestablished, particularly in the case of land ownership.
- Measures for the indemnification or economic compensation of the most serious injuries and losses resulting as a direct consequence of the violations of human rights and of humanitarian law.
- Measures for psychosocial rehabilitation and reparation, which should include, among others, medical attention and community mental health care, as well as the provision of legal and social services.
- Measures for the satisfaction and restoration of the dignity of the individual, which should include acts of moral and symbolic reparation.

That, depending on the type of violation, the reparatory measures be individual and collective. Collective reparatory measures should be implemented in such a way as to facilitate reconciliation between victims and perpetrators, without stigmatizing either. Therefore, collective reparatory measures for survivors of human rights violations and acts of violence, and their relatives, should be carried out within a framework of geographically based projects to promote reconciliation, so that in addition to addressing reparation, their other actions and benefits also favor the entire population, without distinction between victims and perpetrators.

That, for the process of reparation to become one of the principal bases for national reconstruction and reconciliation, it is vital that Guatemalan society participate actively in the definition, execution, and evaluation of the National Reparation Program. This participation is especially important in the case of the Mayan population, which was affected with particular severity by the violence. In the specific case of measures for collective reparation it is essential that the beneficiaries themselves participate in defining the priorities of the reparation process.

Beneficiaries

That the beneficiaries of the moral and material reparatory measures must be the victims (or their relatives) of human rights violations and of acts of violence connected with the internal armed confrontation.

That for the purposes of the program, victims are considered to be those persons who have personally suffered human rights violations and acts of violence connected with the internal armed confrontation.

That in those cases where individual economic indemnification is appropriate, the prioritization of beneficiaries must be established, taking into consideration the severity of the violation, their economic situation, and social vulnerability, and paying particular attention to the elderly, widows, minors, and those who are found to be disadvantaged in any other way.

That the identification of program's beneficiaries should be guided by criteria of clarity, justice, equality, speed, accessibility, and broad-based participation.

Program Structure

That the board of directors of the program be composed of nine members: (1) two persons appointed by the president of the Republic; (2) two persons appointed by the Congress of the Republic; (3) one person designated by the Human Rights Ombudsman; (4) a representative from victims' organizations; (5) a representative from human rights organizations; (6) a representative from Mayan organizations; and (7) a representative from women's organizations.

That, with the aim of facilitating the appointment process for the representatives of the aforementioned organizations, the person designated by the Human Rights Ombudsman convene and facilitate appointment processes of the respective sectors.

That the program's board of directors should have the following functions:

- Receive individual and collective applications from potential beneficiaries.
- Assess, according to the circumstances of each case, whether the potential beneficiary has the status of a victim or relative of a victim. Victims of cases contained in the case annexes of this report should be automatically qualified as victims without the need for another case study.

- Assess the socioeconomic status of potential beneficiaries previously identified as victims.
- On the basis of the former, decide who the beneficiaries are.
- Decide on the relevant reparatory measures.

Financing

That the state fund the National Reparation Program by putting into effect the universally progressive tax reform established by the peace accords. To achieve this, a redistribution of social spending and a decrease in military spending would be appropriate. These measures should constitute the principal source of financing.

That, to the same end, the state solicit international cooperation from those countries that, during the internal armed confrontation, lent military and financial aid to the parties.

Period of Operation

The National Reparation Program should cover the time period necessary for it to achieve its objectives. This should not be less than ten years, considering the period determined for the presentation of the applications and the time necessary for allocating and delivering the benefits.

Forced Disappearance

Given the extent of the crime of forced disappearance, developed as an ongoing practice in Guatemala during the period of armed confrontation, and considering that forced disappearance not only causes those close to the detained person long-term distress due to the uncertainty of the fate of their loved one, but also generates a series of legal and administrative problems, it becomes vital to rectify these problems so that the suffering and complications occasioned by the disappearance are not prolonged. Therefore, so that it may be included in the National Reparation Program, the CEH recommends:

Search for the Disappeared

That the government and the judiciary, in collaboration with civil society, initiate, as soon as possible, investigations regarding all known forced disappearances. All available legal and material resources should be utilized to clarify the whereabouts of the disappeared and, in the case of death, to deliver the remains to the relatives.

That the Guatemalan Army and the former Guatemalan National Revolutionary Unity provide whatever information they may have in relation to the disappearances of people that occurred during the period of internal armed confrontation...

Specific Recommendations Concerning Children
Who Have Been Disappeared, Illegally Adopted, or
Illegally Separated from Their Families

That the government urgently activate the search for children who have been disappeared including, at the very least, the following measures:

- Establishment of a National Commission for the Search for Disappeared Children whose aim should be to look for children who have been disappeared, illegally adopted, or illegally separated from their parents and to document their disappearance...This commission should be composed of the Human Rights Ombudsman and representatives from national NGOs working on human rights and children's issues, with the advice and technical and financial support, as available, of UNICEF, the ICRC, and international NGOs specializing in children's issues...
- The promotion of legislative measures by which, at the request of interested parties, the courts and tribunals of the judiciary and the bodies charged with the protection of unaccompanied children, allow access to their files, facilitating the acquisition of information regarding the identity, ethnic origin, age, place of birth, current whereabouts, and real name of the children given up for adoption or taken into care during the armed confrontation.
- The implementation of a wide-reaching general information campaign in Spanish and all the native languages, across every region of the country and in refugee sites located in other countries, concerning the activities and measures connected with the search for these children.

That the media actively assist the initiatives in the search for disappeared children.

That the government promote extraordinary legislative measures that, on the request of the adopted person or his/her relatives, allow for the review of adoptions brought about without the knowledge, or against the will, of the natural parents. The said review should always take into consideration the views of the person who was adopted in such a way as to promote cordial relations between the adoptive and natural families to avoid subsequent trauma for the adopted person.

Recognition of the Legal Status of Absence Due to
Forced Disappearance

That the government prepare and present a legislative bill to the Congress of the Republic by which the declaration of absence due to forced disappearance is recognized as a legal category with the purpose of validating for legal purposes inheritance, rights reparations, and other associated civil issues.

Active Policy of Exhumations

The CEH believes that the exhumation of the remains of the victims of the armed confrontation and the location of clandestine and hidden cemeteries, wherever they are found, is in itself an act of justice and reparation and is an important step on the path to reconciliation. It is an act of justice because it constitutes part of the right to know the truth and it contributes to the knowledge of the whereabouts of the disappeared. It is an act of reparation because it dignifies the victims and because the right to bury the dead and to carry out ceremonies for them according to each culture is essential for all human beings.

On this basis, and taking into consideration the large number of clandestine cemeteries referred to in this report, as well as those still not publicly known, the CEH recommends:

That the government prepare and develop an active policy of exhumation and urgently present to the Congress of the Republic legislation for a Law of Exhumation, which establishes rapid and effective procedures for this and which takes into account the three following recommendations.

That the process of exhumation is carried out with full respect for the cultural values and dignity of the victims and their families, considering the process of exhumation not only as a judicial procedure, but above all as means for individual and collective reparation.

That the bodies and remains of the victims be handed over to their relatives for a dignified burial according to their particular culture.

That the work of the NGOs specializing in forensic anthropology and the investigation and identification of human remains be promoted and supported. The said specialist organizations should work in association with the Human Rights Ombudsman, whose office should serve as the depository for the relevant data.

Measures to Foster a Culture of Mutual Respect and Observance of Human Rights

Culture of Mutual Respect

As reflected in the previous chapters of the report, a culture of violence has developed in Guatemala which has resulted in mistrust and a lack of respect among its people. This clearly needs to be transformed into a culture of tolerance and mutual respect.

The CEH believes that the peace accords are a basic foundation for the development of peaceful and tolerant relations between the various sectors of Guatemalan society. Consequently, the knowledge and assimilation of the past, an understanding of the causes and the scope of the uncontrolled violence, as well as of the basic principles of respect for human rights, the mechanisms for their defense, and the peaceful solution of disputes are essential elements for the consolidation of a peaceful future.

The CEH believes that to achieve national harmony and reconciliation, a concerted effort at cultural change is required and that this can only be achieved through an active policy of education for peace.

The relationship between the state and the indigenous population of Guatemala—particularly the Mayan people—has existed within an environment of racism, inequality, and exclusion. As this can be considered to be one of the historical causes of the armed confrontation, measures guaranteeing the protection of the individual and collective rights of the indigenous population, the respect for cultural plurality, and the promotion of intercultural relations become vital.

On this basis, the CEH recommends the following:

The Dissemination and Teaching of the Contents of the Report

That the state, as a moral imperative and as a duty, embrace the contents of this report and support all initiatives put into effect for its dissemination and promotion among all Guatemalans.

That, to this end, and in coordination with civil society organizations in Guatemala and particularly with indigenous and human rights organizations, the government promote a campaign for the general dissemination of the report, which takes into consideration the social, cultural, and linguistic reality of Guatemala.

That, respecting the multilingual character of Guatemala, the Guatemalan Academy of Mayan Languages carry out the translation of the report, with public financing, into the following languages:

- the entire report should be translated into, and published in, at least five Mayan languages: K'iche, Kaqchikel, Mam, Q'eqchi' and Ixil; and,
- the report's conclusions and recommendations should be translated into the twenty-one Mayan languages and disseminated in both written and oral forms.

That the government provide for and finance the translation of the report's conclusions and recommendations into Garífuna and Xinca.

That the curricula of primary, secondary, and university-level education include instructions on the causes, developments, and consequences of the armed confrontation and likewise of the content of the peace accords with the depth and methodology relevant to the particular level.

Education for a Culture of Mutual Respect and Peace

That the state, along with the national human rights' NGOs, cofinance an educational campaign to promote a culture of mutual respect and peace, to be developed by the aforementioned NGOs and aimed at the country's diverse political and social sectors. The said campaign should be based on principles such as democracy, tolerance, respect for human rights, and on the use of dialogue as an instrument for the peaceful solution of disputes. Likewise, it should promote the development and free circulation of information, with particular emphasis on the content of the Universal Declaration of Human Rights and on the fundamental principle of peace. That the government, by means of the educational reform envisaged by the peace accords, foster an environment of tolerance and respect and promote self-awareness and awareness of the other, so that the dividing lines created by ideological, political, and cultural polarization may be erased.

Observance of Human Rights

With the aim of strengthening a culture of mutual respect and observance of human rights and of effectively protecting those working for their defense, the CEH recommends the following:

Mechanisms for International Protection

That the executive and legislative branches take all necessary steps to allow the Guatemalan State to ratify those international human rights instruments still pending, as well as the corresponding implementation mechanisms. The CEH particularly recommends giving priority to the following:

- International Convention on the Elimination of All Forms of Racial Discrimination, with recognition of the competence of the Committee for the Elimination of All Forms of Racial Discrimination to receive individual complaints.
- First optional Protocol to the International Covenant on Civil and Political Rights.
- Convention against Torture and Other Cruel, Inhuman, or Degrading Treatment or Punishment, with recognition of the competence of the Committee against Torture to receive individual complaints.
- Additional Protocol of the American Convention on Human Rights for the Question of Economic, Cultural, and Social Rights ("Protocol of San Salvador").
- Inter-American Convention on Forced Disappearances.
- Statute of the International Criminal Tribunal.

International Humanitarian Law

That the government take the necessary measures to fully incorporate into national legislation, the standards of international humanitarian law and that it regularly provide instruction regarding these norms to the personnel of state institutions, particularly the army, who are responsible for respecting, and in turn engendering respect in others for these norms.

Human Rights Defenders

That the government promote, with prior consultation of the organizations for human rights, legislative measures specifically orientated toward the protection of human rights defenders.

Administrative Measures Related to Public Officials
Responsible for Human Rights Violations

At the same time as reiterating the importance of the measures and commitments assumed by the signatories to the Comprehensive Agreement on Human Rights, and as a solely preventative rather than repressive or punitive measure, the CEH recommends:

That a commission should be established by the president of the Republic using his constitutional prerogative, to be under his immediate authority and supervision, which will examine the conduct of the officers of the army and of the various bodies of state security forces active during the period of the armed confrontation. Its purpose is to assess the adequacy of their conduct in the execution of their duties during the said period, in regard to the minimum standards established by the instruments of international human rights and humanitarian law.

That the said commission be composed of three independent civilians of recognized honesty and irreproachable democratic trajectory.

That the aforementioned commission should carry out its tasks by the procedure it deems most appropriate, but in any case should listen to the interested parties, bearing in mind the CEH's Report and the personal record of the officers.

That consequently, and in view of the magnitude and severity of human rights abuses, administrative measures be adopted that take into account the content of the draft document, "Set of Principles for the Protection and Promotion of Human Rights through Action to Combat Impunity" of the United Nations Commission on Human Rights.

Measures to Strengthen the Democratic Process

Administration of Justice

In various sections of the peace accords there are clear references to Guatemala's system for the administration of justice. Specific references are made in the Agreement on the Strengthening of Civil Power and the Role of the Armed Forces in a Democratic Society, in which it is described as "one of the greatest structural weaknesses of the Guatemalan State." In fulfilling the said agreement, the Commission on the Strengthening of the Justice System produced a final report including various recommendations. As a result of its own investigations, the CEH has also come to the conclusion that the weakness and dysfunction of the judicial system has contributed decisively to impunity and the misapplication of criminal law during the period covered by the CEH's mandate. Also, as a result of the peace accords, the Congress of the Republic approved the National Reconciliation Law, which, according to Article 1, is considered to be a "basic instrument for the reconciliation of those people involved in the internal armed confrontation."

Considering the former, the CEH recommends the following:

Commitments Pertaining to the Peace Accords

That the powers of the Guatemalan State regard the fulfillment of their commitments on justice contained in the Agreement on the Strengthening of Civil Power and the Role of the Armed Forces in a Democratic Society, as of utmost importance. The recommendations contained in the final report produced by the Commission on the Strengthening of the Justice System, and which the CEH assumes and reiterates as it own, should be carried out in full.

National Reconciliation Law

That the powers of the state fulfill, and demand fulfillment of, the Law of National Reconciliation, in all of its terms and in relation to the rest of Guatemalan law. Those crimes for whose commission liability is not extinguished by the said law, should be prosecuted, tried, and punished, particularly following Article 8, "Crimes of genocide, torture and forced disappearance, as well as those crimes that are not subject to prescription or that do not allow the extinction of criminal liability, in accordance with domestic law or international treaties ratified by Guatemala."

That, in applying the Law of National Reconciliation, the relevant structures take into account the various degrees of authority and responsibility for the human rights violations and acts of violence, paying particular attention to those who instigated and promoted these crimes.

Right to Habeas Data

That a legislative bill be presented by the government to the Congress of the Republic that quickly and effectively establishes the right of *habeas data* as a specific mechanism of protection and activates the constitutional right, recognized in Article 31 of the constitution, of access to information contained in archives, files, or any other form of state or private record. It should also penalize the gathering, storage, or concealment of information about individuals, their religious or political affiliation, their trade union or social activism, and any other data relating to their private lives.

Traditional Forms of Conflict Resolution

The Commission on the Strengthening of the Justice System included a series of recommendations in its final report that uses as its starting point the fact that it is "necessary to proceed with the search for formulas that encompass traditional methods of conflict resolution and the state judicial system, capable of complementing both components."

As outlined in its report, the CEH has noted that disrespect for the traditional methods of conflict resolution, and for the authorities charged with applying them, to the point of committing acts aimed at eliminating them, has been an almost constant characteristic from 1980 until the end of the armed confrontation.

Considering all the former, and reiterating the need to fulfill the recommendations made by the Commission on the Strengthening of the Justice System, the CEH especially recommends the following:

Legal Integration

That what is known as customary law is recognized and integrated into the Guatemalan legal framework, formalizing and ordering a respectful and harmonious relationship between the judicial system and the traditional forms of conflict resolution, with their principles, criteria, authorities, and procedures, as long as the rights recognized in the Guatemalan Constitution and in international treaties on human rights are not violated.

Instruction

That universities and other state educational bodies that teach law include knowledge of the norms of the traditional forms of conflict resolution as a distinct subject in their curriculum.

That the Ministry of Education support the publication of materials that contain the latest advances in the research into the practices that constitute what is known as customary law.

Primacy of civilian power and the role of the Armed forces

Legal reform

Considering the grave human rights violations committed by army agents during the armed confrontation and the marked weakening of the social fabric as a direct consequence of militarization, the CEH believes that it is vital to enact legislative measures that establish the foundation for the correct relationship between the army and civil society within a democratic system, and the necessary subordination of the army to civilian rule. These measures should include an adaptation of military norms to fulfill the army's constitutional mandate to promote respect for human rights, the exercise of discipline in accordance with the law, the apolitical nature of the military, and to restrict its role to external defense.

The CEH also recognizes the pernicious effect of the activities of military intelligence on the human rights situation and on civilian-military relations. Equally, it recognizes the severe abuse of authority committed in the past through antidemocratic behavior and the serious violation of human rights by forces directly linked to intelligence services and often carried out by means of covert actions.

The CEH believes that unquestioning obedience to any kind of order is one of the most significant and most dangerous factors generating human rights violations.

On the basis of the former, the CEH recommends:

That the government present to the Congress of the Republic the necessary legislative reforms including measures to implement the recommendations presented below. These bills should be based on, and complement, what was established in the Agreement on the Strengthening of Civilian Power and the Role of the Armed Forces in a Democratic Society.

Reform of the Constitutive Law of the Army

That the Presidential and Vice-presidential Joints Chief of Staff structures be abolished, being unnecessary in a democratic state.

Reform of Military Legislation

That a new military code be drafted and put into effect based on legal, moral, and doctrinal criteria in accordance with the Constitution of the Republic and the reforms outlined in the peace accords.

That the military code include the correct concept, already contained in the Constitution of the Republic, of discipline and obedience solely within the law and never outside it, and that reference be removed in the military code to obedience being owed to any type of order.

That the death penalty for the military offence of disobedience be abolished.

New Legislation Regarding the State Intelligence Apparatus

That the government present to the Congress of the Republic corresponding legislation that

a) Precisely define the structures, tasks, and limits of civil and military intelligence, restricting the latter to exclusively military affairs; and
b) Establish clear mechanisms of effective control in Congress regarding all aspects of the apparatus of state intelligence.

That the commitments regarding intelligence contained in the Agreement on the Strengthening of Civilian Power and the Role of the Armed Forces in a Democratic Society be fulfilled as soon as possible, particularly those relating to the approval of the following: the Law on Methods of Supervision of the Organs of State Intelligence; the Law Regulating Access to Information on Military or Diplomatic Affairs relating to National Security; the limitation of the jurisdiction of the Intelligence Office of the Army General Staff, reconciling this with the new role of the army; the configuration of the Department of Civil Intelligence and Information Analysis and of the Secretary for Strategic Analysis.

New Military Doctrine

That the government promote a new military doctrine for the Guatemalan Army that should result from a process of internal reflection and consultation with civil society organizations. This doctrine should establish the basic principles for the appropriate relationship between the army and society within a democratic and pluralist framework. At a minimum, the following should figure among these fundamental principles:

a) The function of the army is the defense of the sovereignty and independence of the state and the integrity of its territory. Its organization is hierarchical and based on the principles of discipline and obedience within the law.

b) The army should accept that sovereignty resides in the Guatemalan people. As a consequence, the army should respect whatever social reforms and changes that result from the exercise of this sovereignty, reconciling itself to the mechanisms established in the constitution.

c) The army will base its legal standards, as well as its conduct, on systematic respect for human rights.

d) The army will be subordinate to political power, which emanates from the ballot box through the procedures established by the constitution.

e) The army will show respect for the constitution in every way.

f) The army is apolitical. It should remain at the margins of party politics and respect all legally constituted political forces. None of these may be persecuted or submitted to surveillance or the control of any of their legal activities.

g) Members of the military accept the limitations inherent in their career, specifically intended to preserve the apolitical nature of the institution, that, while they are in military service, they may not affiliate to, nor become a member of, any party or trade union.

h) Members of the military may exercise their right to vote freely and secretly in national and local elections. Nevertheless, while they remain in active service they may not reveal their political preferences in any public act or through any medium of social communication.

That the basic values of members of the military must conform to the following concepts and fundamental principles:

a) that members of the military are citizens in the public service of national defense;

b) that military discipline has to be based on the concept of strict obedience within the law, and never outside it;

c) that the concept of military honor must be inseparable from respect for human rights; and,

d) that the group morale must conform to a high standard of ethics and be based on principles of justice and public service.

Reform of Military Education

That the government take measures for the revision of the curricula of the Guatemalan Army's various training centers, in such a way as to include, as basic subject material, the points previously mentioned.

That the CEH's Report be studied as part of the Guatemalan Army's educational curriculum.

That the Guatemalan Army's various educational centers promote a review of the teaching staff and remove military personnel involved in present or past human rights violations from educational functions. Maximum professional and ethical rigor from the teaching staff is required.

That the civilian faculty of the Guatemalan Army's training centers be composed of people with a recognized commitment to democracy.

Other Recommendations Pertaining to the Army

Civil Service: Military and Social

Considering that forced and discriminatory recruitment has been a continuous and abusive practice throughout the armed confrontation, having affected almost every Mayan community, and considering the future approval of the Civil Service Law contemplated in the Agreement on the Strengthening of Civilian Power and the Role of the Armed Forces in a Democratic Society, which will regulate military and social service, the CEH particularly recommends the following with regard to this law:

That the regulations of military service maintain strict respect for the principle of equality before the law in the mechanisms and process of recruitment.

That the option of conscientious objection be established and registered for those whose religious, ethical, or philosophical convictions do not permit them to carry arms, so that they are not obliged to do so, but instead are allowed to perform other types of civic service to the community.

That young men of military service age who themselves, or whose family members within the first degree of consanguinity, were victims of human rights violations and acts of violence connected with the armed confrontation, remain exempt from military service and be directly assigned to civil service.

Special Forces

That, in conformity with the principles of military doctrine and education stated previously, the training programs of the armed forces be subject to drastic and profound revision, especially those conceived specifically for counterinsurgency, such as the program known as the *Kaibil* School.

Respect for Mayan Cultural Names and Symbols

That, with the aim of respecting the Mayan people's cultural identity, which was severely violated during the armed confrontation, the army should no longer use names of particular Mayan significance and symbolism for its military structures and units.

Civic Defense of Peace

In a world in which national and international peace is the responsibility of all and in which the fundamental duty of the armed forces should be the defense of peace, the CEH recommends:

That, as one of its priorities, the army promote participation in peace initiatives and international security under the authority of the United Nations and the Organization of American States.

That military professionals make every effort to create a Guatemalan Army dedicated to the service of peace and to the citizens of Guatemala, of which every Guatemalan may feel proud.

Public Security

The principal aim of the restructuring of the security forces, their professionalization, and their instruction regarding the law, democracy, human rights, and a culture of peace, as stipulated in the Agreement on the Strengthening of Civilian Power and the Role of the Armed Forces in a Democratic Society, is to convert the role of the police into one of genuine public service. This implies the exclusively civilian character of the police force and respect for the multiethnic nature of the Guatemalan nation in the recruitment, selection, training, and deployment of the police.

Given the discrediting of former police institutions through their responsibility for grave human rights violations and their general failure to provide the community with public security, the new National Civilian Police (PNC) must ensure its professional conduct. In addition, in developing a professional and modern police force, the PNC should also implement the minimum principles contained in the relevant international instruments regarding respect for human rights, public liberties, rule of law and democracy.

On this basis and with a view to guaranteeing the suitable future development of the duties of the police, the CEH particularly recommends the following:

Security Forces Doctrine

That under the guidance of the Ministry of the Interior, the PNC begin a process of internal reflection in consultation with civil society organizations, with the aim of producing and defining the doctrine of the civilian security forces, whose bases should be

a) service to the community, without discrimination of any type and with respect for the multiethnic character of the Guatemalan nation;
b) development of the civilian nature of the police force and the demilitarization of its organization, hierarchy, and disciplinary procedures;
c) complete respect for human rights and the consequent investigation, prosecution, and conviction of any members who have committed human rights violations;
d) respect for democracy and the rule of law; and
e) the continuous professional training and instruction of the police at every rank.

Internal Control

That under the supervision of the Ministry of the Interior, the directorate of the PNC take relevant measures to ensure the removal from the police of those elements who have acted, or act, against its doctrine of public service and create a new unit for internal control and inspection, which may be accessed by the public and the Human Rights Ombudsman, and which has autonomy to investigate and sanction both individual and institutional professional misconduct.

Indigenous Participation

That the directorate of the PNC promote measures that genuinely open the way for participation by indigenous peoples in public security service, such as

a) taking into consideration bilingualism in the academic evaluation, as well as eventual deployment of a police candidate;
b) the elimination of discrimination in the summoning and selection processes and their adaptation to the realities of a multiethnic country;
c) the education in the PNC Academy on the multicultural nature of Guatemala and intercultural harmony; and
d) the organization of the police service in such a way that indigenous members are able to use their native language skills in contact with the public, promote positive relations with indigenous institutions and authorities, and respect forms of conflict resolution characteristic of their cultures.

Resources

That, when determining the national budget, the government and the Congress of the Republic increase the financing of the National Civilian Police, guaranteeing adequate training and equipment with modern means and installations and dignified working conditions.

Civilian Nature of the PNC

That the new Public Order Law, referred to in the Agreement on the Strengthening of Civilian Power and the Role of the Armed Forces in a Democratic Society, considers the civilian nature of the police during emergency situations of any type, and does not require the police to participate in duties that are the responsibility of the army. That, in case the reforms proposed in the peace accords are unsuccessful, Congress take the necessary legislative action to separate the functions of the army and the police, limiting the participation of the army in the field of public security to an absolute minimum.

Other Recommendations to Promote Peace and National Harmony

The CEH believes that for the promotion of peace and national harmony it is necessary to know and face the causes of the armed confrontation and its consequences in such a way as to put an end to the social, ethnic, and cultural divisions in Guatemala.

Equally necessary are social participation and the contribution of all Guatemalans without discrimination in the fulfillment of public duties.

Although the CEH's Report should serve as a fundamental reference point in the investigation of Guatemala's past, it does not in itself bring to a close the investigation and analysis that must be carried out regarding the armed confrontation, its causes, the extent of the violence, and its effects. The report CEH should serve as a platform for continuing investigations within Guatemala.

On this basis, the CEH recommends the following:

Investigation and Analysis of the Past

That the Guatemalan people continue the investigation and analysis of the events of the past, so as to construct firm foundations for the future based on their knowledge of the past, and thereby avert a repetition of the mistakes that provoked the confrontation.

Political Participation of Indigenous Peoples

The CEH, without prejudice to the commitments already established in the Agreement on Identity and Rights of Indigenous Peoples, would like to reiterate the importance of the obligations assumed by the government to promote social and political participation by the indigenous population and to enable regional administration associated with ethnic identity. For this reason the CEH particularly recommends:

That among the public officials and other personnel employed by the state, room is given, in sufficient number, to indigenous professionals with the qualifications and experience relevant to the demands of various positions.

That, to the end expressed in the previous paragraph, the state establish and finance a system of grants for the training and specialization of the aforementioned indigenous professionals.

Elimination of Racism and of the Subordination of Indigenous Peoples

Given that the relationship between the state and the indigenous population of Guatemala—particularly the Mayan people—has existed within an environment of racism, inequality, and exclusion, and that this is one of the historical causes of the armed confrontation, measures guaranteeing the protection of the individual and collective rights of the indigenous population, respect for cultural plurality, and promotion of intercultural relations, become vital.

On this basis, the CEH reiterates:

That the Agreement on Identity and Rights of Indigenous Peoples be implemented, in its entirety.

Fiscal Reform

Considering the Agreement on Social and Economic Aspects and the Agrarian Situation and the need for all Guatemalans to contribute to social development and the improvement of public services, the CEH reiterates:

That the government promote measures designed to encourage the mobilization of national resources, carrying out urgent fiscal reform that is just, equitable, and progressive, as established in the Agreement on Social and Economic Aspects and the Agrarian Situation.

Body Responsible for Promoting and Monitoring the Implementation of the Recommendations

The CEH believes that it is vital that these recommendations be fulfilled so that the mandate entrusted to the CEH within the framework of the peace process achieves its objectives. To accomplish this, the joint participation of the state and civil society is needed, as every Guatemalan without distinction should benefit from the recommendations.

Therefore, the CEH recommends the establishment of a follow-up body in which both state and civil society are represented, to aid, promote, and monitor the implementation of the recommendations. Consolidation of the peace and reconciliation process in Guatemala requires that the state and civil society work together to achieve their common objectives.

Although the monitoring and implementation of the recommendations regarding the consolidation of peace and reconciliation falls to Guatemala, continuing support from the international community will be necessary.

On this basis, the CEH considers it necessary and, therefore, recommends:

That the Congress of the Republic, through the initiative of its Commission on Human Rights, approve, no more than 60 days from the publication of the CEH's Report and through the corresponding legislative measure, the establishment of a body responsible for implementing and monitoring the recommendations of the CEH under the name "Foundation for Peace and Harmony" (hereinafter, "the Foundation"), whose mandate, composition, appointment procedure, constitution, installation, period of operation, human and material resources and financing are outlined below.

Mandate

The foundation's principal objective will be to facilitate the implementation of the recommendations made by the CEH, regarding the five principal areas of activity covered by the mandate:

a) Direct implementation of specific recommendations;
b) Backing and assistance in the implementation of the recommendations;
c) Monitoring the adequate implementation of the recommendations;
d) Promotion of and support for historical research;
e) Assistance in seeking funds to finance projects for the implementation of the recommendations.

Composition

The foundation shall be composed of seven members who will be appointed for a period to be determined by the corresponding legal resolution. Their distribution shall be as follows:

- Two persons appointed by the Congress of the Republic, who shall be of different political affiliations.
- One person appointed by the government.
- An independent person, with a recognized commitment to democracy and to the peace process.
- Two representatives from Guatemalan NGOs working on human rights and supporting victims.
- One representative from Guatemalan Mayan organizations.

The appointment by the relevant institutions shall be made no later than two months from the date of the congressional resolution.

Appointment Procedure

The Congress of the Republic and the government respectively shall appoint the relevant persons. It is suggested that the person appointed by the government should be the secretary of peace.

The independent person of recognized commitment to democracy and the peace process shall be appointed by the Secretary-General of the United Nations, by the procedure he deems most appropriate.

The representatives of the human rights NGOs and the Mayan organizations shall be chosen by the organizations of each sector through an election, to be convened and facilitated by the independent person appointed by the Secretary-General of the United Nations.

Constitution

The foundation shall hold its constitutive meeting as soon as the members have been appointed.

Installation

The foundation shall be fully installed and operational, at the latest, five months after having been initially integrated and constituted.

Period of Operation

The foundation shall have an initial operational period of three years from the date of its installation, which can be extended by Congress in view of advances made in the implementation of the recommendations.

Human Resources

The personnel shall be Guatemalan, and include qualified individuals with experience in the field of investigating and defending human rights.

Material Resources

The CEH has left instructions with United Nations Office for Project Services (UNOPS) enabling the latter, in consultation with the donors to the CEH and on viewing the foundation's draft budget and plan of operation, to determine the material resources and the computing and communications assets of the CEH to be transferred by UNOPS to the foundation as a donation.

National and International Support

It is suggested that the foundation seek both the national and international support necessary to achieve the aforementioned objectives.

Request to the United Nations

The CEH requests that the Secretary-General of the United Nations lend his support, through the United Nations Verification Mission in Guatemala (MINUGUA) and within the framework of the mission's mandate, so that the recommendations laid out above may be implemented and may achieve their objectives.

The CEH also requests that the Secretary-General of the United Nations appoint the foundation's independent member and that, through the UN body deemed to be most appropriate, he establish an international mechanism to provide the foundation with technical support and to channel donations from the international community.

Afterword

"No Room for Despair": The Impact of the Guatemalan Truth Commission

Daniel Rothenberg

Despite the tragic nature of *la violencia,* the CEH viewed its mission as ultimately positive, stating, "The violence and horrors described in the Report should leave no room for despair." The spirit motivating the CEH's research and analysis—and of transitional justice more generally—is ultimately constructive, an effort to redeem society from its own barbarism. Or, as the CEH claimed, "Subsequent generations in Guatemala have the right to a brighter, better future. Guatemalans can, and must, encourage a common project of nationhood."

Since, the majority of the report provides a detailed and rigorous review of decades of brutality, the CEH's mission to "strengthen the hope of the people of Guatemala" is largely found in its recommendations. These were included in the executive summary that was widely distributed when the report was first presented in Guatemala. Great care went into drafting the recommendations that cover a variety of interrelated issues, including honoring the nation's victims; providing reparations; creating a national policy for investigating the whereabouts of the disappeared; exhuming clandestine cemeteries; developing policies to limit the public role of perpetrators; and developing government programs to support democracy and promote peace.

The commission began its recommendations by suggesting that the Guatemalan president issue a formal apology "before the victims, their relatives, and their communities" to "ask pardon for them and assume responsibility for the human rights violations connected with the internal armed confrontation." In fact, prior to the release of the report, the president of Guatemala and the URNG had issued apologies, but the commission viewed these as partial and inadequate, largely because they failed to accept full responsibility for past violations.

In March 1999, inspired by the release of the CEH report, President Bill Clinton, while on a state visit to the country, apologized to the Guatemalan people for the U.S. government's role in the armed conflict. Two days later, the URNG formally apologized to the nation's victims. In 2001, President Alfonso Portillo of the FRG party (whose leader at the time was General Ríos Montt, dictator from 1981 to 1983, and a member of the Guatemalan Congress) asked for forgiveness at an event honoring the victims of the Las Dos Erres massacre. Given his general political position on *la violencia* and the limited nature of the apology, few considered this act as complying with the CEH's recommendation.

In 2008, almost a decade after the release of the CEH report, President Álvaro Colom asked for forgiveness from the Guatemalan people. As the first left-leaning head of state since Arbenz and a prior director of the *Fondo Nacional para la Paz* (National Fund for Peace, FONAPAZ, a government mechanism supporting postconflict development projects), his apology has generally been accepted by many victims and civil society organizations. He emphasized a personal understanding of the impact of *la violencia* as someone who had worked closely with affected communities and as the nephew of a former mayor of Guatemala City who was assassinated by the military.

The commission also recommended symbolic acts to commemorate victims including a national day of remembrance, naming streets and public sites for victims and others, and creating monuments and memorials. In 2000, the Guatemalan Congress declared February 25—the day the CEH released its report—as the *Día Nacional de la Dignidad de las Victimas* (National Day for Victims' Dignity). Although the date has been used by the government in various ways, such as announcing new programs to assist victims, many criticize its relatively low national profile. In general, the government has invested limited resources on memorials and other public acts of remembrance. However, many civil society groups and communities in various parts of the country have created monuments, small museums, and symbolic sites, some of which have been supported by state funds.

As part of the growing institutionalization of transitional justice, the international community has come to recognize that victims of political violence have fundamental rights to reparations. This is evidenced by the United Nation's approval of specific guidelines on the issue and the integration of reparations within postconflict reconstruction programs around the world.

The CEH recommended that the Guatemalan government create a special body—the *Programa Nacional de Resarcimiento* (National Reparations Program, PNR)—to define and implement a comprehensive set of formal reparations. From the release of the commission's report on, there were a number of attempts by the government and civil society groups to create such a program. Nevertheless, it took until 2003 for the PNR to be created through a presidential decree.

The PNR is an element of the *Secretaría de la Paz* (Peace Secretariat, SEPAZ), an office of the presidency created in 1999 to coordinate government policies related to the peace agreements. The PNR's mission was defined in the 2003 *Libro Azul* (Blue Book), which outlined the government's commitment to providing monetary compensation to victims; material restitution for lost land and housing; psychosocial rehabilitation; support for exhumations and acts of remembrance; and the creation of mechanisms for cultural reparations. In line with evolving international standards, the PNR used a broad interpretation of victims that covered both direct victims of violence as well as indirect victims.

The PNR is managed by the *Comisión Nacional de Resarcimiento* (National Commission for Reparations, CNR), an autonomous body created to ensure that reparation policies were independent of political interests and manipulation. Between 2003 and 2005, the CNR was mainly composed of representatives of human rights and victims' advocacy groups. These organizations often disagreed with each other and with the government on key policy issues, such as whether to include genocide as a violation for which reparations would be provided. In response, the government amended the CNR to be composed solely of representatives of state institutions.

The PNR began its work in 2004 with a limited financial support. From 2005 on, its activities increased significantly as the PNR managed an annual budget of around $38 million. The PNR has a main office in Guatemala City and multiple regional offices where thousands of victims have presented complaints and requests for assistance. To date, the majority of funding has been spent on distributing land, building housing, and supporting a variety of development programs.

In 2006, the PNR began providing economic compensation to victims with survivors of torture, sexual violence, and rape receiving a single payment of $2,700; families of victims of extrajudicial execution, death through massacres, or forced disappearance receiving a single payment of $3,200; and families with multiple deaths and violations receiving up to $5,900. The PNR also created a *Registro Nacional de Victimas* (National Victims' Register, RNVO) and has forwarded thousands of files related to past crimes to the *Ministerio Público* (Public Prosecutor) for investigation and possible legal action.

Despite spending tens of millions of dollars on reparations in the form of land, housing, individual payments, services, and programs, the PNR has been widely criticized by human rights groups, victims' organizations, and indigenous communities. The majority of victims' claims have yet to be processed and many thousands of people throughout the country are still waiting for individual compensation and other reparations. The PNR is known for excessive bureaucracy and a failure to engage affected populations in a sensitive manner. Civil society groups commonly claim that the PNR presents victims with a variety of administrative barriers that are particularly difficult for the most vulnerable Guatemalans, such as rural residents that are illiterate and are only fluent in indigenous languages. Given the fact that *la violencia* disproportionately impacted these populations, the criticisms are significant and viewed by many as a sign of the state's inability to substantively address the social divisions that marked the conflict. The tensions associated with the obstacles that victims face in receiving reparations are heightened by the fact that the PNR has sometimes failed to spend all of the money it has been allocated, leading to attempts to significantly reduce its budget.

In 2003, alongside calls for victims' reparations, former *patrulleros* began demanding compensation for their efforts as members of the PAC. While *patrulleros* were required to spend substantial unpaid time involved in PAC activities, the CEH found that 18 percent of serious violations were committed by this group and they represented a key element of the state's counterinsurgency strategy. Nevertheless, at the time, the government and Congress were dominated by the FRG party, which drew substantial support from former *patrulleros*. Soon after the first payments to former PAC members began, the policy was successfully challenged in court. The government responded by creating a new mechanism of providing compensation to the former *patrulleros*, not for past services but through work on a program known as "*Bosques y Agua para la Concordia*" ("Forests and Water for Harmony"). In this program, former PAC members received around $700 each for providing assistance in reforesting areas of the country. Through this program and other related policies, the Guatemalan government paid over $200 million to former *patrulleros*, an amount for greater than what has been paid to victims.

In its report and recommendations, the commission emphasized the importance of exhuming mass graves and clandestine cemeteries. These policies were designed to support psychosocial healing, help resolve thousands of cases of disappearances, gather evidence for possible legal action, and provide closure for victims and their families. While the Guatemalan government never implemented is own exhumation policies, hundreds of exhumations have been conducted by various civil society groups. These efforts have recovered the remains of over 5,000 bodies. Most of this work has been financed by international donors, although some exhumations have been supported by PNR funds.

The CEH also recommended that the Guatemalan government create a special commission to investigate the estimated 50,000 cases of disappearances. While a law to create this commission was proposed in 2007, the commission was never established.

The CEH also recommended a government commission to review the status of children that were disappeared, including those that may have been illegally adopted, a practice associated with repressive regimes in other countries in Latin America. This commission was never created. While there has been a lack of government action in these areas, civil society organizations have formed a working group on disappearances and gathered substantial information on many cases, often working with victims and communities to determine the whereabouts of loved ones. Many of the groups participating in these efforts were among the first human rights advocacy organizations in the country, having begun their struggle to account for the disappeared in the 1980s and 1990s.

For many Guatemalans, the most pressing legacy of *la violencia* is the nation's extraordinary level of impunity. Despite the widespread nature of atrocities and the fact that thousands of individuals at all levels of authority—military leaders, officers, soldiers, *Kaibiles,* intelligence agents, *patrulleros*, military commissioners, and others—committed severe human rights violations, only a handful of legal cases have been processed in the Guatemalan courts. Unlike other postconflict countries, such as neighboring El Salvador, this is not the result of a blanket amnesty banning prosecutions for past atrocities. In fact, Guatemala's Law of National Reconciliation prevents individuals from receiving amnesty for major human rights violations, such as forced disappearances, torture, and genocide. In addition, the law requires that each request for amnesty be assessed individually, making it impossible to quickly provide protection from prosecution to large numbers of alleged perpetrators.

There are, however, a small number of well-known cases against perpetrators of human rights violations, including the successful prosecution against Myrna Mack's assassin and later against the intellectual authors of the crime (the CEH case study is included in this book); cases against several *patrulleros*; and the complicated case of the murder of Bishop Gerardi that led to the conviction of three army officers, one of whom was killed in jail. In general, these cases have advanced only as a result of substantial domestic and international political pressure, often because of the high-profile nature of the cases.

Civil society groups have pressured the Guatemalan government to take action on the thousands of potential criminal cases arising from the decades of brutality documented by the CEH. In general, advocacy groups have sought prosecutions against high-ranking members of the Guatemalan military regimes that ran the country during the worst period of *la violencia*. In 2000 and 2001, several organizations developed legal cases accusing the leaders of the military regimes under General Lucas García and General Ríos Montt of genocide. In 1999, Nobel Laureate Rigoberta Menchú Tum and massacre survivors (including one of the children forcibly transferred in the Rio Negro massacre; the CEH case study is included in this book) presented a complaint alleging genocide in the Spanish courts.

The claim was based on the doctrine of universal jurisdiction through which Spanish courts can process cases involving actions that occurred outside of the nation's normal jurisdiction because of the especially severe nature of the crimes, such as torture and genocide. This doctrine has been used for cases arising from other countries in Latin America as in a Spanish court case against General Augusto Pinochet, the former military dictator of Chile. The legal actions led to his detention and house arrest in the United Kingdom and eventually stimulated multiple domestic cases against other military officials. After receiving testimony and reviewing documents, including the CEH report, a Spanish judge requested the extradition of former president General Mejia Víctores and others, including a former minister of defense, former head of the police, and police officials. In 2006, a local trial court judge in Guatemala responded to the Spanish request by issuing arrest orders for these former officials. This decision was followed by a complex series of legal processes that ended when the Guatemalan Constitutional Court decided to reject the Spanish arrest warrants, claiming that they violated basic principles of national sovereignty. Nevertheless, the Spanish courts continued to gather testimony and process these cases, which remain delayed, but may ultimately influence legal actions in Guatemala and elsewhere.

In 2005, the attorney general's office created a special group, *Unidad de Esclarecimiento Histórico* (Historical Clarification Unit) to review cases arising from the armed conflict. While it has opened files and reviewed many cases, including those presented by the PNR, there has been limited progress on actual prosecutions.

While few cases related to *la violencia* have advanced in Guatemalan courts, there are signs that the domestic legal system may be expanding its actions against those responsible for past human rights violations. In 2009, the country successfully prosecuted its first criminal case of forced disappearance against a former military commissioner. This was followed by a successful prosecution of a retired colonel and three former paramilitaries, also for forced disappearance. Several other cases have advanced in domestic courts, such as indictments against high-ranking officials, including the former head of the *Estado Mayor* (Joint Chiefs of Staff). In addition, the government convicted several of the *Kaibiles* involved in the massacre at Las Dos Erres (the CEH case study is included in this book). If the recent histories of other Latin American countries, including Argentina and Chile, are any indication, it is quite possible that, over time, more legal cases against perpetrators of past violations will be processed by national courts.

To date, the Inter-American Human Rights System—composed of a series of regional treaties, a commission, and a court—have proved to be the most successful forum for legal claims by victims of *la violencia*. The Inter-American Commission on Human Rights seeks to resolve disputes through friendly settlements between petitioners and the state, and the Inter-American Court of Human Rights issues legally binding judgments on a select number of cases that the commission is unable to resolve. The Inter-American Human Rights System has processed over two dozen cases regarding past violations in Guatemala, including high-profile assassinations (Myrna Mack, Jorge Carpio Nicolle, Efrain Bámaca Velásquez, Irma Flaquer Azurdia) as well as massacres of entire communities (Plan de Sánchez and Las Dos Erres).

While the Inter-American system cannot issue criminal penalties or sanctions against individuals, it allows for far-reaching decisions against states involving compensation for victims, including awards for amounts far greater than what has been provided by the PNR. In addition, the judgments of the Inter-American Court of Human Rights have required the Guatemalan government to provide psychosocial services, acknowledge state responsibility for human rights violations, create videos and other modes of informing the public about past atrocities, and build monuments. Through these processes, hundreds of Guatemalan victims have received reparations totaling over $16 million. In addition, settlements achieved by the commission and legally binding judgments by the court have consistently required the Guatemalan government to engage in serious investigations of many cases including pursuing domestic criminal cases against those responsible (as seen in the Las Dos Erres case).

The government's dealings with the Inter-American Human Rights System are managed by the *Comisión Presidencial Coordinadora de la Política Ejecutiva en Materia de Derechos Humanos*, (Presidential Commission for the Coordination of Executive Policy on Human Rights, COPREDEH). COPREDEH is responsible for developing and implementing the government's human rights policies and managing friendly settlements with the commission and responding to the court's judgments.

The CEH clearly understood its mission as part of an ongoing process of investigating the past, "Nor should one consider this Report to be the final word on the history of the armed confrontation... In the future, generations of scholars will struggle to explain, in its depth and complexity, all the factors and mechanisms of terror that were used to brutalize the people of Guatemala for over three decades." With this in mind, the CEH recommended national legislation to encourage improved access by citizens and civil society groups to government documents, including those held in state security archives. While in 2008, the government passed a law designed to improve transparency of state documents, the records of the security services remain largely inaccessible. The Ministry of Defense has kept its files closed and has repeatedly refused to provide documents related to legal cases regarding past atrocities. It is believed that key archives such as those of the EMP have been destroyed. However, there is one notable exception to the difficulty of accessing the archives of Guatemalan security forces. As a result of an accidental discovery, the archives of the former National Police dating back over a hundred years were found, preserved and are in the process of being analyzed by the *Proyecto de Recuperación del Archivo Histórico de la Policía Nacional* (Project for the Recovery of the Historical Archive of the National Police, PRAHPN). The initial focus of the research is on police surveillance activities and human rights violations during the conflict.

The commission recommended that the Guatemalan government engage in substantial institutional reform of the judicial system alongside a more robust commitment to international law and human rights. Following the formal end of the conflict, the government has approved substantial legislative reforms. It has adopted a new criminal code that includes human rights violations, strengthened protections against racism and discrimination and created new law on the functioning of the judicial system. The Guatemalan government also ratified a number of key human rights treaties including those designed to combat racism and protect women and children, although it has not accepted the jurisdiction of the International Criminal Court (which, nevertheless, cannot address past abuses such as those related to *la violencia*).

The CEH also recommended that the government create a special civilian commission to review the conduct of army officers and others in the security forces to asses individual responsibility for human rights violations. This commission was never created.

Unlike many other postconflict countries, Guatemala never instituted a vetting system to ensure that perpetrators of past atrocities would be barred, either for life or for a set period of time, from positions of responsibility within the army, the National Police, the judiciary, or other government institutions. In fact, many individuals that played key roles in planning, coordinating, and managing the brutal policies of *la violencia* remain in the police and the army. In addition, others associated with past repression play key roles within political parties, serve in Congress, and hold positions of significant influence in government ministries.

One of the most basic goals of the CEH, and of all truth commissions, involves communicating its findings to the larger society to encourage an awareness and acknowledgment of past political violence. Truth commissions around the world are based on the idea that knowing and acknowledging the reality of atrocities represents a profound social good and plays an essential role in the creation of a more respectful and responsive society. The commission distributed thousands of copies of its executive summary to the public and distributed a limited number of copies of the full report to libraries and other institutions. The Guatemalan government also translated the executive summary into seven Mayan languages and local civil society groups produced popular versions of the report for use by those with limited literacy.

One of the commission's key recommendations for communicating its work to the Guatemalan people and improving awareness of *la violencia* involved integrating its findings within the country's public education system. This is especially significant given the fact that Guatemala, like most developing world nations, has a young population, with a median age of around twenty and with nearly 40 percent of the country under the age of fifteen. As such, most Guatemalans were born or grew up after the conflict ended and many remain unaware of the relationship between current problems—corruption, high levels of crime, government dysfunction, and social mistrust—and past political violence.

Nevertheless, when the government began a process of widespread educational and curricular reform in 2007, very little attention was focused on the work of the CEH. New curriculum plans include substantial references to human rights, indigenous rights, and the peace process, yet present limited specific reviews of past systematic repression. Public school materials make only cursory mention of torture, disappearances, massacres, and the forced complicity of civilians in committing atrocities against their own neighbors. Textbooks, teaching guides, and other educational material generally ignore the basic statistics regarding the conflict presented by the CEH or its analysis of the causes and impact of *la violencia*. The failure to connect educational reform with a more serious engagement with the nation's recent, violent history has been widely criticized by civil society groups, particularly since the new programs include a significant focus on the national anthem, the flag, and various patriotic rituals.

Along with many Latin American countries, Guatemala has been engaged in broad process of legal reform which began in 1992 and, over time, has integrated a number of key CEH recommendations. While legislative and institutional reforms have produced many benefits, the system remains inefficient, poorly coordinated, and dysfunctional and polls reveal that courts are widely mistrusted by the Guatemalan people. The failure of the judicial system is related to a general security crisis involving organized crime, drug trafficking, street gangs, and corruption. Since the end of the conflict, crime rates in Guatemala have increased substantially. Property crimes, kidnappings, and murder are among the highest in Latin America. Violence against women has been especially severe and rising levels of gendered murder have led to the creation of a new term in the country, femicide.

The general sense of uncertainty and insecurity is heightened by the fact that most cases are inadequately investigated and remain unsolved. Human rights defenders and those challenging empowered interests as well as prosecutors, witnesses, and others have been threatened and even killed. Guatemala faces a new type of impunity that tracks a shift in the responsibility for violence from state agents to organized crime, gangs, and related groups.

In response to this situation, the government supported the creation in 2006 of the *Comisión Internacional contra la Impunidad en Guatemala* (International Commission against Impunity in Guatemala, CICIG), a United Nations–sponsored independent body charged with investigating criminal cases involving what has come to be known as "clandestine groups." CICIG develops cases and then supports the attorney general's office with prosecutions. It was created in response to a general concern regarding the failure of domestic legal institutions to combat impunity for current violations. While the quality of its investigations has been widely acknowledged, the head of CICIG resigned in mid-2010 protesting the Guatemalan government's lack of commitment to pursuing serious cases.

The CEH did not recommend the creation of CICIG. However, in many ways, it represents a direct response to the commission's work. High levels of criminality in Guatemala, ongoing impunity, and the rising influence of clandestine groups that link violence, illegal activities, and political and economic inequality are connected to patterns established and institutionalized by *la violencia*. Many individuals involved in these groups—as leaders and as direct perpetrators of killing and other crimes—were involved with past repression. Similarly, Guatemalan society's reliance on violence to resolve disputes and its failure to create a strong, independent system of governance has allowed these groups to prosper.

The CEH remains the most comprehensive review of *la violencia* to date and represents a foundational document for Guatemala, the region, and the world. While the commission issued its report over a decade ago, implementing its forward-looking recommendations and embracing its commitment to truth represent ongoing processes. If a reflection on other transitional nations is a guide for Guatemala, it is likely that the nation will require many years to process the CEH report, and address the complex impact and consequences of *la violencia*. It is important to understand that the harsh realities of contemporary Guatemala do not decrease the importance of the work of the commission and its focus on past atrocities. In fact, to a large degree, the country's ongoing struggles for stability, security, and the rule of law are related to the necessity—and, often failure—to honestly face the tragedy of the recent past. The corruption, dysfunction, disempowerment, and violence that characterize contemporary Guatemala are closely linked to institutionalized impunity following decades of state repression.

Over the last number of years, it has become increasingly clear that the CEH's commitment to acknowledging and responding to difficult truths within a highly contested political climate is of great significance for Guatemalan society. Not long ago, it was common in Guatemala to deny the severity of *la violencia*, even to suggest that massacres and other serious violations never took place, or were the acts of rogue units or cases of occasional and uncharacteristic excess. Similarly, the severity and brutality of the state's strategics of repression were questioned, minimized, and justified as a necessary means of protecting national security. Also common were the claims that whatever abuses may have occurred were equally committed by the state and the URNG. As a result of the work of the CEH as well as many groups within the nation's courageous human rights community, it is impossible now to seriously present these claims. In this way, the commission succeeded in establishing a basic foundation of truth for understanding Guatemala's past.

The work of the CEH is also of great value for drawing attention to the larger significance of engaging the difficult truths of our world. In the United States, the terrible suffering of Guatemalans remains almost entirely unknown. This is particularly troubling given the central role played by the U.S. government in developing and promoting the national security ideology that justified past atrocities while also supporting the Guatemalan government and its repressive institutions. The systematic violations that characterized *la violencia* expressed a Cold War vision that valued regional geopolitical alliances over an embrace of democratic principles and support for basic human rights. Looking back on this period, from the mid-1950s through the 1980s, the decision to support brutal regimes that protected highly inequitable and discriminatory societies appears difficult to support and of little actual value for the people of the United States.

Similarly, throughout Central America, Latin America, and around the world, the story of the Guatemalan armed conflict is relevant for an improved understanding of the mechanisms of authoritarian rule and the central role of documenting human rights violations in order to delegitimize repressive regimes. While many aspects of the conflict are particular to Guatemala and the late-twentieth century, the basic themes of the *la violencia*—in particular, the justification of severe state repression in the name of national security—are relevant for making sense of past authoritarian rule within the region as well as current repressive practices throughout the world. The commission's work stands as a tragic warning of the devastating implications of privileging security above core values and the practical and moral necessity of protecting fundamental human rights. Yet, as the report suggests, its work is ultimately constructive, providing a set of recommendations to help Guatemala honor its many victims and engage in a broad process of national reconstruction and reconciliation.

Further Readings

Michelle Bellino

There are many excellent books, monographs, articles, and reports on Guatemala. This section provides suggestions on useful sources for readers interested in the themes covered in the commission's report, including Guatemalan history; the nature and impact of *la violencia*; other large-scale human rights projects in Guatemala; the peace process and reconstruction; testimony, truth-telling, and transitional justice; and indigenous rights and political movements. It also provides some guidance for further reading linked to local and international organizations working on human rights and accountability in Guatemala.

The sources suggested here—published in both English and Spanish—do not represent a complete list of valuable material. Instead, they represent suggestions for learning more about the country, its recent tragic history, and the struggle for truth and accountability in the aftermath of decades of devastating political violence.

Guatemalan history—According to the commission, the armed conflict should be understood in relation to a long history of colonial and postcolonial inequality in which social and political violence played a central role. For some useful sources on Guatemala's asymmetrical power structure, see Richard N. Adams, *Crucifixion by Power: Essays on Guatemalan National Structure, 1944–1966* (University of Texas Press, 1970) and Jim Handy, *Gift of the Devil: A History of Guatemala* (Between the Lines Press, 1984). Other valuable sources include the following: Carol A. Smith, *Guatemalan Indians and the State, 1540 to 1988* (University of Texas Press, 1992) on the history of political inequality of indigenous people and a review of repressive State practices; John D. Early, *The Structure and Evolution of a Peasant System: The Guatemalan Case* (University of Florida Press, 1982) on issues of land, labor, class, and conflict; and David McCreery, *Rural Guatemala, 1760–1940* (Stanford University Press, 1994) for a useful review of the development of rural society.

There are a number of important historical analyses that situate recent conflict within the context of indigenous struggles for power, recognition, and justice, including Yvon Le Bot, *La Guerra en Tierras Mayas: Comunidad, Violencia y Modernidad en Guatemala (1970–1992)* (Fondo de Cultura Económica, 1995), which reviews the repression against various indigenous social movements; Greg Grandin, *The Blood of Guatemala: A History of Race and Nation* (Duke University Press, 2000), which provides excellent insight into the complexity of race and power in the country; and Victoria Sanford, *La Masacre de Panzós: Etnicidad, Tierra y Violencia en Guatemala* (F&G Editores, 2009), analyzing an early massacre within the context of larger strategies of repression.

The ideology and formation of a "guerrilla generation" across Central America is described in Dirk Krujit, *Guerrilla: Guerra y Paz en Centroamérica* (F&G Editores, 2009), which may be usefully read alongside Walter LaFeber, *Inevitable Revolutions: The United States in Central America* (W.W. Norton, 1993), a key work on the rise of regional insurgencies within the context of governments' inability to address structural inequality. There are also useful studies on particular groups within Guatemalan politics, such as Deborah Levenson-Estrada, *Trade Unionists against Terror: Guatemala City, 1954–1985* (University of North Carolina Press, 1994).

There are many important works on external influences on Guatemalan history, especially actions by the U.S. government. For a detailed review of the U.S. government's role in overthrowing the Arbenz regime and its implications, see the classic work by Stephen Schlesinger and Stephen Kinzer, *Bitter Fruit: The Story of the American Coup in Guatemala* (Harvard University Press, 1999), as well as Piero Gleijeses, *Shattered Hope: The Guatemalan Revolution and the United States, 1944–1954* (Princeton University Press, 1992). For other discussions of U.S. involvement with the nation, see Richard H. Immerman, *The CIA in Guatemala: The Foreign Policy of Intervention* (University of Texas Press, 1982) and Michael McClintock, *The American Connection: State Terror and Popular Resistance in Guatemala* (Zed Press, 1985). In addition, for a more general review of the development of the Guatemalan security state as linked to U.S. foreign policy, see Susanne Jonas, *The Battle for Guatemala: Rebels, Death Squads, and U.S. Power* (Westview Press, 1991).

La violencia—There are many important studies of the terrible violence that devastated Guatemala involving multiple disciplines and a variety of different documentary and analytic approaches.

Two early and pathbreaking studies include Robert Carmack's edited collection of essays, *Harvest of Violence: The Maya Indians and the Guatemalan Crisis* (University of Oklahoma Press, 1988) and Beatriz Manz, *Refugees of a Hidden War: The Aftermath of Counterinsurgency in Guatemala* (State University of New York Press, 1988). There are a number of detailed and contextually grounded reviews of human rights abuses, including Ricardo Falla, *Massacres in the Jungle: Ixcán, Guatemala, 1975–1982* (Westview Press, 1994) an account by a priest and anthropologist who worked closely with local communities; Victor Perera, *Unfinished Conquest: The Guatemalan Tragedy* (University of California Press, 1993), an informative and personal perspective on *la violencia*; Linda Green, *Fear as a Way of Life: Mayan Widows in Rural Guatemala* (Columbia University Press, 1999), a detailed ethnography on how repression produced a culture of silence and quiet resistance among Mayan women; and David Stoll, *Between Two Armies: In the Ixil Towns of Guatemala* (Columbia University Press, 1994), an ethnography presenting indigenous communities as caught between the URNG and the military. There are also useful reviews of how *la violencia* impacted specific local communities, such as Daniel Wilkinson's compelling *Silence on the Mountain: Stories of Terror, Betrayal, and Forgetting in Guatemala* (Houghton Mifflin, 2002) and Robert S. Carlsen, *The War for the Heart and Soul of a Highland Maya Town* (University of Texas Press, 1997). For a review of how the regional human rights system was used to address violations, see a useful collection of reports by the Inter-American Commission of Human Rights, *Compilación de Informes publicados sobre la situación de los derechos humanos en Guatemala, 1980–1995* (IACHR, 1993).

Jean-Marie Simon's *Guatemala: Eternal Spring, Eternal Tyranny* (W.W. Norton & Company, 1988) is an extraordinarily moving book of photographs and text documenting Guatemalan life in the 1980s. For a valuable review of literary responses to *la violencia* see, Marc Zimmerman, Raul Rojas, and Patricio Navia (Eds.), *Voices from the Silence: Guatemalan Literature of Resistance* (Ohio University Center for International Studies, 1998)

Readers interested in the issue of genocide in Guatemala may want to reference the very helpful, full English translation of the CEH's genocide section in Etelle Higgonet's *Quiet Genocide* (Transaction Publishers, 2009). Other works on genocide include Miguel Dewever-Plana, *La Verdad Bajo la Tierra: Guatemala, el Genocidio Silenciado* (Blume, 2007), and Prudencio García, *El Genocidio de Guatemala: A la Luz de la Sociología Militar* (Sepha, 2006), which contextualizes the military campaigns that targeted indigenous people.

For investigations of political violence, targetting agents of social and political reform, see Carlos Figueroa Ibarra's, *Los Que Siempre Estarán en Ninguna Parte* (Espiral Editores, 1999) as well as Francisco Goldman, *The Art of Political Murder: Who Killed the Bishop?* (Grove Press, 2007) an exceptional account of the assassination of Bishop Gerardi days after he publicly presented the REMHI report.

Forensic exhumations of mass graves and other evidence of atrocities have played a key role in the struggle against impunity and have aided a more accurate understanding of *la violencia*. One of the key groups working on these issues, the *Fundación de Antropología Forense de Guatemala*, (Guatemalan Forensic Anthropology Foundation, FAFG, previously the *Equipo de Antropología Forense de Guatemala*, or EAFG) has presented its work in several publications including *Las Masacres en Rabinal: Estudio Histórico-Antropológico de la Masacres de Plan de Sánchez, Chichupac y Río Negro* (EAFG, 1995) and *Informe Especial de la Fundación de Antropología Forense de Guatemala, 1996–1999* (FAFG, 2001). For an excellent review of the relationship between forensic investigations, historical memory, and atrocities, see Victoria Sanford's *Buried Secrets: Truth and Human Rights in Guatemala* (Palgrave Macmillan, 2003).

Other large-scale human rights projects in Guatemala—Before the Commission began its work, there were two major projects that gathered and analyzed extensive numbers of testimonies from around the country and related information regarding political violence in Guatemala. Data from these projects was used by the CEH in its analysis.

The first was an initiative run by the *Centro Intrernacional para Investigaciones en Derechos Humanos* (International Center for Human Rights Investigations, CIIDH) whose innovative analysis was based on fieldwork gathered under very difficult circumstances by various human rights organizations. An overview of this research can be found in Patrick Ball and Paul Kobrak's *State Violence in Guatemala, 1960–1996: A Quantitative Reflection* (American Association for the Advancement of Science, 1999).

The second large-scale human rights data collection and analysis initiative was the *Proyecto de Recuperacion de Memoria Histórica* (Recovery of Historical Memory Project, REMHI) project of the *Oficina de Derechos Humanos del Arzobispado de Guatemala* (Human Rights Office of the Archbishop of Guatemalan, ODHAG). This exceptionally important and sensitive work created a nationwide network of local researchers linked to the Catholic Church that were trained to gather thousands of first-person narratives. Their work was then reviewed and analyzed by teams of human rights professionals who prepared a detailed four-volume report that is available in English as *Guatemala: Never Again!* (Orbis Books, 1999). This text can be usefully read alongside the work of the CEH. It is worth noting that ODHAG continue to use its research and analysis as an advocacy tool to encourage Guatemalan society to face the tragedy of past repression. These efforts have included the creation of a popular version of the REMHI report and an extensive educational program including teacher training and workbooks to help schools integrate these issues into the curriculum at various educational levels.

A related initiative is the *Proyecto de Recuperación del Archivo Histórico de la Policía Nacional* (Project for the Recovery of the Historical Archive of the National Police, PRAHPN), which is engaged in the detailed analysis of extensive police archives accidentally discovered in 2005. This enormous collection of materials is being qualitatively and quantitatively analyzed with a focus on the period investigated by the CEH.

Peace process and reconstruction—There are a number of publications that document the years following the war's official end as the nation struggled with its peace initiative, culminating in the peace agreements between the Guatemalan state and the URNG. The agreements have been collected in several publications, such as *Acuerdos de Paz* (Fundación Friedrich Ebert, 1997). Other useful sources on the peace process include the following: Susanne Jonas and Marrack Goulding, *Of Centaurs and Doves: Guatemala's Peace Process* (Westview Press, 2000), which presents a detailed and contextually grounded review of the negotiations; Gabriel Aguilera Peralta, *Realizar un Imaginario: La Paz en Guatemala* (FLACSO, 2003) reviewing theories motivating the peace process as well as challenges and limitations of the process; Gudrun Molkentin, *Los Difíciles Senderos de la Paz en Guatemala: Resultados de un Estudio Empírico con Énfasis Local* (FLACSO, 2001), which links the national processes to their local impact; Raúl Zepeda López's *El Espacio Político en que se Construye el Paz* (FLACSO, 2004), discussing the evolution, actors, and objectives of the "culture of peace"; and Rachel M. McCleary, *Dictating Democracy: Guatemala and the End of Violent*

Revolution (University Press of Florida, 1999) for an analysis of the challenges of the peace process and its complex relation to achieving substantive democracy.

For material presenting the role of the military in the democratic transition see, Jennifer Schirmer, *The Guatemalan Military Project: A Violence Called Democracy* (University of Pennsylvania Press, 1998). For a review of the positions of key figures in the military regarding the transition and peace process, see Julio Balconi and Dirk Kruijt, *Hacia la Reconciliación: Guatemala, 1960–1996* (Piedra Santa, 2004) in which a former general describes his role in the conflict and chronicles the peace talks as well as Héctor Alejandro Gramajo Morales, *De la Guerra... a la Guerra: La Difícil Transición Política en Guatemala* (Fondo de Cultura Editorial, 1995) by a former minister of defense.

There are several reviews of the conflict and peace process from the perspective of former guerrillas including Mario Payeras, *Days of the Jungle: The Testimony of a Guatemalan Guerrillero* (Monthly Review Press, 1984), an account of life during the conflict; and Gustavo Porras Castejón, *Las Huellas de Guatemala* (F&G Editores, 2009), which reflects on past experiences from a post-conflict perspective. Of special note is Jennifer K. Harbury's *Searching for Everardo: A Story of Love, War, and the CIA in Guatemala* (Grand Central Publishing, 1997), which tells the story of an American woman's search for the whereabouts of her husband, a guerrilla leader captured and killed by the military.

For a review of some aspects of the role of religion during the peace process and religious conflict following the democratic transition, see Ian MacLean, *Reconciliation, Nations and Churches in Latin America* (Ashgate Publishing, 2006) and Paul Jeffrey *Recovering Memory: Guatemalan Churches and the Challenge of Peacemaking* (Life and Peace Institute, 1998).

There is a growing literature devoted to assessing and critiquing the fulfillment of promises made in the peace accords, including Rachel Sieder, *Guatemala after the Peace Accords* (Institute of Latin American Studies, 1998), an excellent discussion of the accords shortly after formal peace was signed; *Cinco Años de la Firma de la Paz: Un Balance Crítico* (FLACSO, 2002), a useful review by Rubén Zamora and others from a major Guatemalan think tank on the first five years following the formal end of the conflict; and Humberto Flores Alvarado's *Los Compromisos de Paz: Sinopsis de su Cumplimiento* (Secretaría de la Paz, 2003), a discussion of the postconflict period from within the government body charged with overseeing policy actions linked to the peace agreements. For a review of issues related to ongoing impunity and the challenges to justice in postwar Guatemala, see the Human Rights Ombudsman's report, *Seguridad y Justicia en Tiempos de Paz: Cumplimiento e Institucionalización de los Compromisos Contraídos por el Estado en los Acuerdos de Paz* (Procurador de los Derechos Humanos, 2006).

To learn more about the tension between postwar reconstruction and hope in the face of ongoing violence, trauma, and fear, see Beatriz Manz, *Paradise in Ashes: A Guatemalan Journey of Courage, Terror, and Hope* (University of California Press, 2005), which focuses on the traumatic experiences of a single village; George Lovell, *a Beauty That Hurts: Life and Death in Guatemala* (University of Texas Press, 2000), a personal account of *la violencia;* Frank M. Afflitto and Paul Jesilow, *The Quiet Revolutionaries: Seeking Justice in Guatemala* (University of Texas Press, 2007), a review of how survivors have worked jointly on popular movements for accountability; Diane Nelson, *Reckoning: The Ends of War in Guatemala* (Duke University Press, 2009), an imaginative engagement with the impact of conflict on the country and its social relations; and Walter Little and Timothy Smith, *Mayas in Postwar Guatemala: Harvest of Violence Revisited* (University of Alabama Press, 2009), an overview of the situation of Guatemala's Mayan people in the years following the end of the conflict.

Testimony, truth-telling, and transitional justice—There is a growing literature linking testimonies, truth-telling, and transitional justice in Guatemala and throughout Latin America.

Testimonies of victims, bystanders, perpetrators, and activists have been essential in understanding the impact of the conflict in Guatemala, as well as for motivating political responses to atrocities. The most famous and significant of these works is the first-person narrative of Nobel Peace Prize winner Rigoberta Menchú Tum in Elisabeth Burgos-Debray, *I, Rigoberta Menchú: An Indian Woman in Guatemala* (Verso, 1984). There are a growing number of first-person accounts and testimony-based work, such as Guatemalan anthropologist Victor Montejo's description of the massacre of a village in *Testimony: Death of a Guatemalan Village* (Curbstone Books, 1995).

Those interested in issues of transitional justice across Latin America may want to review the growing literature on truth commissions, justice, and accountability, including Cynthia J. Arnson, *Comparative peace processes in Latin America* (Stanford University Press, 1999); Dinorah Azpuru, Ligia Blanco, Ricardo Córdova Macías, Nayelly Loya Marín, Carlos G. Ramos, and Adrián Zapata, *Construyendo la Democracia en Sociedades Posconflicto: Guatemala y El Salvador, Un Enfoque Comparado* (F&G Editores; IDRC, 2007); and Rachel Sieder, Line Schjolden, and Alan Angell *The Judicialization of Politics in Latin America* (Palgrave Macmillan, 2009). For an analysis of the role of the courts and the limitations of legal responses to address past atrocities, see the Rigoberta Menchú Tum Foundation, *Una Mirada Crítica de la Resolución de la Corte de Constitucionalidad sobre Justicia Transnacional* (Fundación Rigoberta Menchú Tum, 2008).

A number of nongovernmental organizations (NGOs) have prepared useful research and analysis on transitional justice policies and public opinion in Guatemala. For an excellent overview of the ongoing problem of impunity and the status of implementing CEH's recommendations see Impunity Watch, "Recognising the Part: Challenges for the Combat of Impunity in Guatemala" (Impunity Watch, 2008). In addition, findings of a revealing poll on public attitudes toward transitional justice issues by the *Equipo de Estudios Comunitarios y Acción Psicosocial de Guatemala* (Guatemalan Community Study and Psychosocial Acrion Team, ECAP) and the *Grupo de Acción Comunitaria* (Community Action Group, GAC) can be found in *"Exhumaciones, verdad, justicia y reparación en Guatemala"* (ECAP and CAC, 2009).

The tension between the urgency of social memory and the desire to move on through selective forgetting is questioned by one of the CEH commissioners, Edgar Alfredo Balsells Tojo, in *Olvido o Memoria: El Dilema de la Sociedad*

Guatemalteca (F&G Editores, 2001). For discussions of individual and community reconciliation, see ODHAG, *Lucha, Dolor y Esperanza del Campesinado Guatemalteco* (ODHAG, 2007), and AVANCSO, *Memorias Rebeldes Contra el Olvido, Paasantzila Txumb'al ti' Sotzeb' al K'u'l* (AVANCSO, La Cuerda, Plataforma Agraria, 2008), in which Ixil female ex-combatants recount their experiences. Several towns have taken on local memory projects to reconstruct the experience of *la violencia* through images and narratives, such as Arnoldo Curruchich Cúmez, *Nuestra Historia, Nuestra Memoria: San Juan Comalapa* (PNUD, 2006) and Bert Janseen, *Oj K'aslik, Estamos Vivos: Recuperación de la Memoria Histórica de Rabinal (1944–1996)* (Museo Comunitario Rabinal Achí, 2003).

Indigenous rights and political movements—There is a substantial body of literature on indigenous identity politics and activism and the rise of Mayan movements in the aftermath of the war. For an overview of general issues of race and power in Guatemala, see Marta Casaús Arzú, *Guatemala: Linaje y Racismo* (FLACSO, 1995), and for a review of Maya political thought see Demetrio Cojti Cuxil, *Configuracion del Pensamiento Político del Pueblo Maya* (Asociación de Escritores Mayances de Guatemala, 1991).

There are also many useful studies of the growing significance of Maya politics, including Richard Wilson, *Maya Resurgence in Guatemala: Q'eqchi' Experiences* (Oklahoma University Press, 1999), an excellent review of indigenous political activism in a key region in the highlands; Kay Warren, *Indigenous Movements and Their Critics* (Princeton University Press, 1998), a fine overview of the intellectual and political debates surrounding the indigenous movement; Edward F. Fisher and R. McKenna Brown, *Maya Cultural Activism in Guatemala* (University of Texas Press, 1996), a very useful overview of indigenous politics in the country; and Santiago Bastos, *Abriendo Caminos: Las Organizaciones Mayas desde el Nobel hasta el Acuerdo de Derechos Indígenas* (FLACSO, 1995), which reviews the rise of indigenous political movements in relation to the peace process.

Local and international organizations working on human rights and accountability—Guatemala has many local NGOs working on human rights, community assistance, and social justice. In addition the country has been the focus of serious research and advocacy on the part of many international NGOs and related organizations.

For valuable reports on past and current human rights issues by key international organizations, see the work of Amnesty International (AI); Guatemala Human Rights Commission (GHRC); Human Rights Watch (HRW); Impunity Watch (IW); International Crisis Group (ICG); Robert F. Kennedy Center for Justice and Human Rights, and the Washington Office of Latin America (WOLA).

Regarding the struggle to document human rights violations, assist victims, and press for accountability for *la violencia*, there are many Guatemalan civil society groups that often produce research, publications, press releases, and related information, including *Alianza Contra la Impunidad* (ACI); *Centro de Acción Legal para los Derechos Humanos* (CALDH), *Centro de Investigación, Estudio, y Promoción de los Derechos Humanos* (CIEPRODH), *Comisión de*

Derechos Humanos de Guatemala (CDHG); *Conferencia de Iglesias Evangélicas de Guatemala* (CIEDEG), *Consejo de Comunidades Étnicas Runu`jel Junam* (CERJ), *Convergencia por la Verdad*; *Coordinadora Nacional de Derechos Humanos de Guatemala* (CONADEGUA); *Coordinadora Nacional de Viudas de Guatemala* (CONAVIGUA); *Equipo de Estudios Comunitarios y Acción Psicosocial de Guatemala* (ECAP); *Familiares de Detenidos-Desaparecidos de Guatemala* (FAMDEGUA), *Fundación de Antropología Forense de Guatemala* (FAFG); *Fundación Myrna Mack*; *Fundación Rigoberta Menchú*; *Fundación Sobrevivientes, Defensoría Maya, Grupo de Apoyo Mutuo* (GAM), *Oficina de Derechos Humanos del Arzobispado de Guatemala* (ODHAG); *Asociación para el Estudio y Promoción de la Seguridad en Democracia* (SEDEM); and *Unidad de Defensores y Defensaras de Derechos Humanos de Guatemala* (UNDEFEGUA).

In addition, there are a number of important research institutions in Guatemala that review social, political, economic, and historical issues, including *Asociación de Investigación y Estudios Sociales* (ASIES); *Asociación para el Avance de las Ciencias Sociales en Guatemala* (AVANCSO); *Facultad Latino Americano de las Ciencias Sociales* (FLACSO); and *Instituto de Estudios Comparados en Ciencias Penales de Guatemala* (ICCPG).

Taken together, the sources referenced here by scholars, journalists, analysts, organizations and others provide a wealth of information on Guatemalan society, politics, the armed conflict, and its aftermath. These suggested materials should help to contextualize the CEH's report and to highlight its significance within a large and diverse literature on political violence in Guatemala. Ideally, the CEH report as well as these related materials regardingGuatemala's recent history will continue to stimulate and encourage ongoing reflection and inquiry regarding the meaning and impact of *la violencia* and the challenge ofpeace and national reconciliation.

Appendix I

Tables

Table 1 Responsibility for human rights violations and acts of violence (1962–1996)

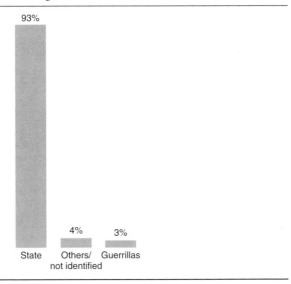

Table 2   Principal human rights violations and acts of violence (1962–1996)

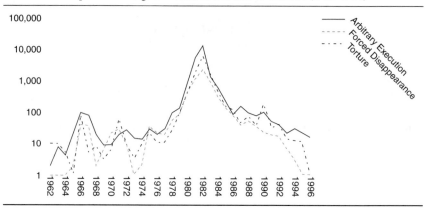

Table 3   Percentage of identified victims by ethnic group (1962–1996)

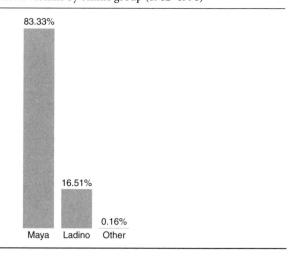

Table 4   Number of massacres by department

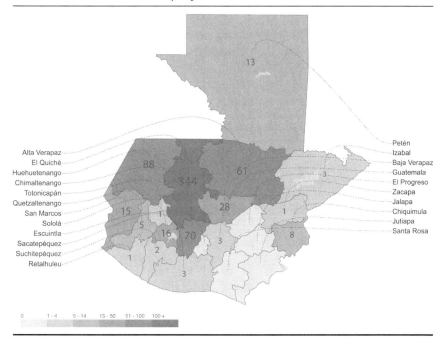

Table 5   Forces responsible for human rights violations and acts of violence (1962–1996)

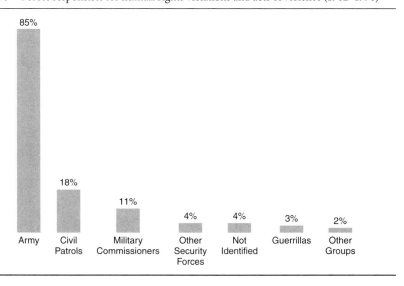

Table 6 Total number of human rights violations and acts of violence, by ethnic group (1962–1996)

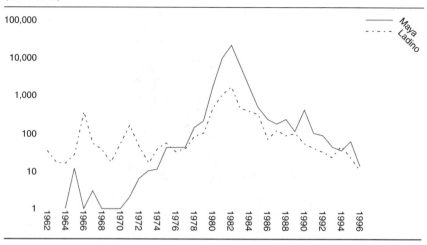

Table 7 Total percentage of human rights violations and acts of violence, by department (1962–1996)

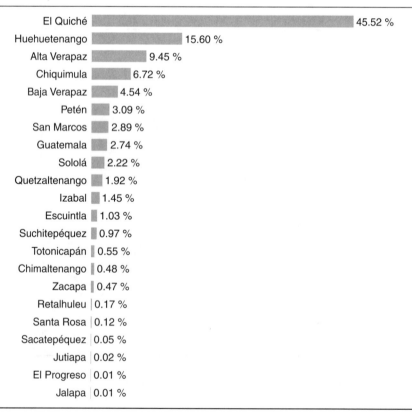

Department	Percentage
El Quiché	45.52 %
Huehuetenango	15.60 %
Alta Verapaz	9.45 %
Chiquimula	6.72 %
Baja Verapaz	4.54 %
Petén	3.09 %
San Marcos	2.89 %
Guatemala	2.74 %
Sololá	2.22 %
Quetzaltenango	1.92 %
Izabal	1.45 %
Escuintla	1.03 %
Suchitepéquez	0.97 %
Totonicapán	0.55 %
Chimaltenango	0.48 %
Zacapa	0.47 %
Retalhuleu	0.17 %
Santa Rosa	0.12 %
Sacatepéquez	0.05 %
Jutiapa	0.02 %
El Progreso	0.01 %
Jalapa	0.01 %

Appendix 2

CEH Mandate and Methodology

I. Establishing the CEH and Work Plan

Once the Agreement on a Firm and Lasting Peace was signed, the secretary-general of the United Nations...began the process of selecting the CEH's three members...On February 7, 1997, with the approval of the parties, the secretary-general appointed Professor Christian Tomuschat as the first member of the CEH...[and] on February 22, he selected Otilia Lux de Cotí and Alfredo Balsells...as the other two commissioners...

Once appointed, the commissioners, with the assistance of the United Nations, carried out the necessary preparations so that the CEH could formally begin the time period for its work...

The commissioners held meetings with the parties and civil society representatives—especially from human rights, victims, and indigenous organizations—which allowed them to listen to suggestions and proposals regarding the procedures that would allow them to best fulfill their mandate. They also considered procedures used by other commissions and the accumulated experience of the United Nations...

The CEH was formally installed and began its mandated work on July 31, 1997...The CEH was assisted by 269 professionals, support personnel, and security officials—142 were Guatemalans and 127 were foreigners representing 31 different nationalities...

From the start, the commission decided to organize the support office in a way that would make it possible for the greatest number of Guatemalan citizens to gain easy access to voluntarily present their testimonies. For this reason, the commission chose a system of broad territorial coverage with substantial presence throughout the countryside. The commission's researchers were able to cover the entire country by setting up field offices around the nation and using mobile teams. When deciding where to place the offices, special priority was given to those areas most affected by human rights violations and acts of violence related to the armed confrontation, as well as to the most isolated regions of the country. Considering these factors, the largest number of offices were opened in the western part of the country.

On September 1, 1997, the commission began its work around the country by creating four main offices—Guatemala City, Cobán, Santa Cruz del Quiché, and Huehuetenango—and ten regional offices in Barillas, Cantabal, Escuintla, Nebaj, Poptún, Quetzaltenango, San Marcos, Santa Elena, Sololá, and Zacapa. From these offices, researchers traveled to municipalities and communities in all the country's departments...

The field offices visited municipal centers in order to inform the public about the CEH's mandate both directly and through NGOs, local officials, and traditional authorities. As a result of these visits, the public information campaign and the participation of diverse civil society organizations, thousands of citizens visited the commission's offices, either to request visits to their communities or to present their testimonies directly to the CEH.

Between September 1997 and April 1998—and in some cases up until May— CEH investigators visited nearly 2,000 communities. Many were visited more than once and some up to ten times. In this way the CEH compiled around 500 collective testimonies for a total of 7,338 testimonies. The commission interacted with more than 20,000 people who participated with the research by providing information. Among these there were over 1,000 key witnesses including: members and former members of the army and other state institutions, former members of the PAC, military commissioners, former guerrilla combatants, politicians, leaders of unions and civil society groups, intellectuals, and so on.

The commission also collected testimonies in Canada, the United States, Mexico, and several European countries. With the exception of Mexico, these testimonies were gathered by nongovernmental organizations that generously provided their support...

Once the field offices closed on April 15, 1998, additional research was conducted from the central office using mobile teams that traveled to throughout the country.

When the fourteen field offices finished their work, personnel worked in the central office as staff levels were reduced after the main stage of gathering testimonies had been completed. Nevertheless, the central office continued receiving testimonies and information up until July 31, 1998, in accordance with the commission's mandate.

After that date, the support office was restructured to focus on three areas: systematizing data, thematic analysis, and recommendations...The process of data systematization involved a case studies team; an ordinary case team; a database team; a documentation center team; a context and history team; a key witnesses team; a special team; an administration of justice team; a foreign governments' document team (with a liaison in Washington, DC); and a legal advisory team. The thematic analysis area was composed of three teams that dealt with causes and origins of the internal armed confrontation; strategies and mechanisms of the violence; and consequences and effects of the violence. The recommendations area was comprised of a single team.

Beginning August 17, 1998, the central office teams were gradually reduced as they completed their work. Beginning November 15, as other teams were closing down, the coherence section was created, consisting of a coherence team; a text review team; and a text editing team. In the final phase, a team was created to organize the public presentation of the report and another for its printing and publication. The support office of the CEH continued to operate until the presentation of the report on February 25, 1999,...

Legal Framework

It is important to understand that the reference to human rights in the Oslo Accord is essentially a reference to international norms. Only international rules and principles allow for an objective analysis of the distortions, if not perversions that the country's system of legal order suffered...under various military governments.

The fundamental base of the commission's legal framework is the Universal Declaration of Human Rights, adopted on December 10, 1948, by the UN General Assembly via resolution 217 A (III), which formalized the member states' commitment to promote and protect human rights. While the resolution, by itself, was not binding on member states, the "essential core elements" of the declaration quickly gained legal significance as customary law. This applies especially to the right to life and personal integrity, including the prohibition of torture. The prohibition of genocide also forms part of customary law. There is no doubt that these norms were in effect at the beginning of the Guatemalan internal armed confrontation.

The commission also took into account international human rights treaties. The majority of these treaties were ratified by Guatemala after the worst horrors of the armed confrontation, with the exception of the Convention on the Prevention and Punishment of the Crime of Genocide. However, they all contain legal norms that have been established by humanity in the course of the second half of the twentieth century with the goal of ensuring that rights of people are respected in all countries. For this reason, they constitute a precise legal framework for classifying the acts that the commission was created to investigate.

The Oslo Accord does not mention international humanitarian law. However, in the broadest sense, humanitarian law also forms part of the international system to protect human rights. It covers all of the rules that govern the conduct of an armed conflict. Humanitarian law seeks to maintain a minimal level of civilization, even during war. This is the main reason that the commission has referred to this body of law as part of the legal framework of its work...

International rules applying to internal conflicts are outlined in Common Article 3 of the four Geneva Conventions of 1949, all of which were ratified by Guatemala. Their applicability is based on minimal requirements, such as the party in conflict with government forces is an armed movement with some level of clear organization seeking political ends though not necessarily controlling a portion of national territory.

In addition, the Additional Protocol II adopted in 1977 improved international rules regarding internal armed conflicts and was ratified by Guatemala on October 18, 1987, that is, quite late in the armed confrontation. While the government has consistently denied its applicability to the internal armed confrontation, the CEH considers it as part of its legal framework given that most of the rules outlined in the protocol form part of international customary law.

As a result, and in response to the distinction made in the Oslo Accord between human rights violations and acts of violence, the CEH has established that during the internal armed confrontation, both parties were obliged to respect the minimum standards outlined in Common Article 3 of the Geneva Conventions. Therefore, this was the general criteria that the CEH applied to both parties and formed the basis for its findings on their respective responsibilities. This was done without impacting the application of international human rights law to state agents, in order to determine the responsibilities of the Guatemalan State.

In addition, the commission applied the common principles of international human rights law and international humanitarian law to the acts of violence committed by the guerrillas to ensure that both parties were treated in a fair and equal manner... The commission also considered domestic law in analyzing the parties' conduct, specifically Guatemala's various constitutions. It is undeniable that even in the most difficult periods of the nation's history there was no suspension of basic guarantees, such as the obligation of the state to respect and protect the right to life. As a result, these guarantees were obligatory for all authorities, including the army... Therefore, when the report refers to "human rights violations", it references those acts committed by state agents as well as acts committed by private individuals with the knowledge or acquiescence of state agents. "Acts of violence" refers to those acts committed by members of the URNG as well as to all other acts of violence committed by private individuals, including those that took advantage of... the conditions created by the armed confrontation, with the goal of serving or favoring individual interests without the state's consent, collaboration, tolerance, or acquiescence.

Period of Investigation and Connection to the Armed Confrontation

According to the Oslo Accord, the commission was to investigate human rights violations and acts of violence "connected to the armed confrontation." Therefore, the period to be investigated starts with the beginning of the internal armed confrontation, which the CEH established as January 1962 and ends with the signing of the Firm and Lasting Peace Accords.

Because the Oslo Accord did not specify the type of connection between the acts to be investigated and the armed confrontation, and in an attempt to fulfill its mission of historical clarification, the CEH has used a broad interpretation of this phrase, one that does not limit it to those acts committed strictly in the framework of the internal armed confrontation...

Therefore, the report presents all acts connected to the armed confrontation including those that: were motivated by or related to the armed confrontation; were an element of its conflicting strategies and ideologies; were committed by those who took advantage of their role in the confrontation; or involve victims of the confrontation or in relation to its ideologies.

Participation of the Parties

According to the Oslo Accord, "The Parties undertake to collaborate with the Commission in all matters that may be necessary for the fulfillment of its mandate." According to Article 10 of the Law of National Reconciliation, the CEH is responsible for "designing necessary measures to facilitate knowledge and acknowledgement of the historic truth regarding the internal armed confrontation in order to prevent such acts from being repeated. To this end, State bodies and entities shall provide the Commission with the support that it may require."...

State Support for CEH Research

The CEH sought support various times from the president of the Republic, ministers, and the judiciary system to provide information related to its research...

The CEH views the support provided by the nation's army to be inadequate and unsatisfactory. Although a liaison mechanism established by the army with the commission allowed for cordial relations, the centralized nature of the process made it difficult to gain access to information. The army's responses to the commission's requests for specific information were slow, incomplete, and insufficient. The majority of requests for information went unmet or were responded to in a partial manner, and then with delays of up to four months.

For example, the army failed to respond or responded in a completely insufficient manner to the commission's requests for information regarding the deployment of military units throughout the country during the armed confrontation as well as for information about URNG prisoners of war and military casualties.

In addition, the documents the army provided to the CEH were incomplete. For example, CEH requests to review the operational plans of military units were dealt with by providing only some plans for a few military zones. Even those were incomplete and pages and appendices were missing. The army did not provide the CEH with a single operational plan for the military zones in regions most affected by the armed confrontation. Nor was the commission provided with any operational reports prior to 1987. In addition, the CEH was not allowed to review any official documents related to the Presidential Chief of Staff

At the same time, those CEH requests that received partial responses from the army were handled through slow and complicated mechanisms. With the exception of some military instruction manuals, none of the documents requested by the CEH were provided in the original form or as photocopies. In some cases, documents were made available for review by CEH investigators at the Center for Military Studies, but photographs or photocopies of those documents were prohibited.

During the course of the commission's work, the executive branch—through a variety of offices including the army and the president's private secretariat—gave different explanations for not providing the requested documents. Initially the executive claimed that the documents were classified under the constitution.

Later, the executive changed its position and claimed that these documents never existed or had been lost or destroyed. Nevertheless, the commission has verified that documents—whose existence the executive consistently and repeatedly denied—do, in fact, exist and are stored in army installations. For example, before the army structured its relationship with the CEH through a special liaison group, the commission had access to various military operational plans and intelligence reports whose existence was later denied.

The commission also calls attention to the extreme gravity regarding the supposed misplacement of certain documents belonging to different elements of the executive and judiciary. In many cases the misplaced documents contain key information regarding important procedures including sentences involving the death penalty.

The information provided by the Ministry of the Interior, the National Police, and the judiciary regarding investigations in particular cases were extremely inadequate, revealing the lack of investigation into grave human rights violations, which should have been prosecuted...

URNG Collaboration with CEH Investigations

The URNG established a liaison mechanism with the commission in November 1997, after some delays.

The working relationship and methods established by the URNG for providing information to the CEH proved to be effective. The CEH found that all of URNG member organizations displayed a collaborative attitude. In particular, members of the FAR and the EGP provided relevant documents and war reports. In many cases, this information allowed the commission to determine the URNG's responsibility for acts of violence under investigation.

Within this generally collaborative context, the commission calls attention to the fact that one request for information regarding presumed URNG responsibility went unanswered. In addition, ORPA failed to submit war reports requested by the commission, and many ORPA members' responses to commission questions regarding responsibility for acts of violence acts were either evasive or unclear.

The commission considers that the URNG collaboration was satisfactory, with the exception of those problems mentioned above...

II. Research and Methodology

The historical clarification of human rights violations and acts of violence related to the internal armed confrontation presented in this report are supported by the commissioners' determination that each case actually occurred and was either a human rights violation for which the state was responsible or an act of violence for which the guerrillas were responsible. To meet this basic objective, the commission relied fundamentally on legal categories within international human rights law and international humanitarian law...

In addition to applying these legal categories, the commission achieved its goals by using insights provided by other disciplines such as history, anthropology, sociology, economics, and military science, which assisted the commission in understanding complex issues related to Guatemalan reality...

From the start, the commission encouraged many national and international actors to provide information regarding situations that might later be classified as human rights violations or acts of violence connected to the internal armed confrontation. It also sought information at all levels—local, national, and international—on the historical, political, socioeconomic, and cultural contexts in which these events occurred...

It is important to emphasize that the commission worked with absolute independence in deciding the usefulness and value of different sources, and that this independence was respected by all actors, both national and international. Neither the parties to the conflict, nor civil society organizations, nor any Guatemalan or foreign individual or institution ever sought preferential treatment for their information or viewpoints...

Sources of a Personal Character

The commission's primary and most relevant source of data came from the testimonies of people who suffered human rights violations or acts of violence. The CEH used a variety of media to invite all victims and their families, without preference, to present testimonies describing the events that affected them. Their testimonies, collected under the norms established by the commission, represent indispensable data for research on each of the cases presented. Taken together, they serve as an invaluable source, both qualitatively and statistically, for the general analysis of the themes covered in the main chapters and for developing the report's conclusions.

Collective testimonies presented by communities affected by human rights violations or acts of violence also had special value. Taken together, these testimonies presented by survivors allowed the commission to reconstruct very complex cases, some of which occurred fifteen or more years earlier. These testimonies were also useful for reconstructing local historical situations, given that there are few relevant documentary and bibliographic materials.

Direct witness testimony by nonvictims was another key source of information for the investigation and clarification of cases as well as for more comprehensive analysis. There were also people who provided supporting testimonies such as those familiar with the victims' or other direct-witnesses' versions of events, or whose social position allowed them privileged access to knowledge of the context of these events. These sources provided the CEH with important information for verifying complaints and contributed to the analysis of specific local and national issues related to the internal armed confrontation.

At a certain stage in the investigations, the commission received information regarding the identities of individuals who may have participated directly in human rights violations and acts of violence connected to the armed confrontation or who, in one way or another, may have been involved in these acts. Given the importance of the testimonies that these people could provide, the commission established a specific procedure to invite them to present their versions of events and used special procedures for preparing and conducting these interviews.

The testimonies given by these individuals provided key elements for clarifying many individual cases as well as invaluable input for analyzing the strategies and mechanisms of human rights violations and acts of violence. As with all of the testimonies gathered, the identity of these witnesses was and will be guarded with the strictest confidentiality, except where they agreed that their names could be made public. It is important to note that refusing the commission's request for an interview did not prevent the commission from clarifying a case by using the other sources at its disposal.

In addition, there were more than 1,000 "key witnesses" who were important sources for the different aspects of historical clarification. People were defined as key witnesses when, as a result of their characteristics or circumstances, they were privileged witnesses to general or particular situations related to grave human rights violations or acts of violence connected to the armed conflict; or, if they had knowledge of the structures, organizations, or strategies of the parties to the conflict, or of groups and institutions that participated in some way in the internal armed confrontation. For example, key witnesses included former presidents, state ministers, former and current military officers, former guerrillas, and other individuals with the previously mentioned characteristics either at a local or national level. Key witness testimony contributed to confirming the occurrence of particularly serious acts as well as toward developing criteria for understanding the parties' specific strategies or prevailing policies in the country at a particular time.

The main source for reflections on the historical elements of the report came from the contributions of a select group of Guatemalan historians who spent months analyzing the causes, origins, and development of the internal armed confrontation.

Similarly, the commission greatly valued the substantial assistance of consultants from the United Nations system on issues such as the impact of the confrontation on children and on the economy...

The variety of testimonies provided by these various sources allowed the CEH to have direct contact with thousands of Guatemalans who trusted the commission, many of whom spoke about their experiences for the first time. Their testimonies served as the foundation for preparing this report.

Documentary Sources

Many of those mentioned, whether victims or key witnesses, provided the CEH with private and public documents whose contents were used to confirm specific events and for the analyses presented in this report.

Many national institutions, including social organizations, business associations, professional societies, Mayan organizations, student associations, groups of retired military, and others affected by human rights violations or acts of violence, came voluntarily to the commission to provide invaluable documentary materials, which, in some cases, contained denunciations of acts that affected members of their organization. While these denunciations did not meet the criteria of either being associated with an individual witness or being connected to a particular testimony, the information was essential for analyzing different stages of the confrontation and was also used in the clarification of particular case studies.

The commission also examined and gave special attention to information provided by national and international nongovernmental human rights organizations, including organizations of victims and family members, particularly when they included databases and lists of victims. These could be checked against and used to verify information compiled by the CEH during field investigations and then cross-checked and compared with the commission's own statistics.

The investigations and analyses were also enriched in many ways by the databases, lists of cases, and special reports on human rights abuses committed in Guatemala that were presented to the commission by organizations that are part of the international and Inter-American human rights system…

Registered Cases

The CEH defined "registered cases" as those for which the commission decided, with justification, that there was sufficient evidence to determine, with varying degrees of certainty, the identity of the perpetrators and the fact that the events occurred. The CEH presented summaries of these cases in the Appendix of Presented Cases.

The term "case" was applied to the description of an action that occurred in a specific place on a determined date, consisting of one or more human rights violations or acts of violence committed against one or more victim(s) and connected to the internal armed confrontation…

In order to clarify the 7,517 cases, the commission compiled an enormous amount of information from multiple sources with field research by the commission as the primary basis for its conclusions. Especially, relevant sources included victims' testimonies, testimonies by direct or supporting witnesses, key witness testimony, testimony from current and former state agents, former members of the guerrilla, and the results of exhumations.

For exhumations related to particularly serious or significant cases, the commission relied on assistance from the FAFG to provide forensic anthropology reports on victims' remains regarding four massacres. Exhumations were conducted in Panzós, Alta Verapaz; Belen, Suchitepéquez; and Acul and Chel, in Quiché. CEH investigators were also present at and collaborated with other exhumations conducted by CALDH and ODHAG conducted during the same period as CEH fieldwork. The results of their reports were provided to the CEH and presented important data for the clarification of certain cases.

During the first stage of investigation, the commission's primary responsibility involved gathering victims' testimonies through the efforts of field researchers.

Researchers in all of the CEH field offices traveled throughout the areas covered by their respective offices to respond to the many individuals that wanted to provide testimony...

In order to open investigation on a case, the acts described in the testimonies needed to meet certain minimal requirements, such as having occurred during and in relation to the armed confrontation; being classified as a human rights violation or as an act of violence in relation to the CEH's mandate; and being clearly shown to be directly linked to the armed confrontation.

During this initial stage, the commission determined that guaranteeing the objective and impartial nature of its investigations required an evaluation of the likelihood and credibility of the testimonies and of the informants while, at the same time, seeking relevant information from other sources. As such, significant emphasis was placed on the descriptions of the events. For example, the mere affirmation of a killing was insufficient to register a case. In order to register a case, the informant had to provide concrete descriptions of the event and its circumstances.

In addition to an insufficient description of the events, a testimony's credibility was also questioned when its content was inconsistent with the patterns of events in the location and during the corresponding period.

The general rule was that each statement presented to the CEH would be signed by the person presenting the testimony as a way of guaranteeing its seriousness and conveying the solemnity of the process, while maintaining the confidentiality of the source whenever requested. Those who could not write signed their testimony with a fingerprint.

Information in the CEH database used for all of the statistics contained in the report was compiled exclusively from testimonies that fulfilled these requirements.

For this reason, the events described in documents submitted by a number of institutions, all of which had been informed of the commission's procedures, could not be considered "registered cases" by the CEH unless witnesses met the requirement of personally signing their statement...

In addition, whenever the commission was presented with a denunciation, investigators collected further information about the situation to assist with the legal analysis and to determine its connection to the armed confrontation. In general, the CEH collected the most information possible for each case, which was later submitted to the commissioners for their consideration...

The long period of time that passed since many of the events had occurred presented a significant challenge for the research, especially because at the beginning of the data collection process the only available evidence came from the victims' recollections. However, as their testimonies were cross-checked with other sources, it was possible to determine the degree of certainty regarding each case.

The comparison with other sources was complex, in part, because the vast majority of the victims of the most serious acts were indigenous *campesinos*, many of whom could not read or write, and spoke in their maternal language, having great difficulty communicating in Spanish. In addition, their narrative style did not use the terms necessary for establishing and clarifying what occurred with the precision required by the commission's methodology. To facilitate the collection of testimonies from everyone, the CEH contracted translators and interpreters, allowing people to speak more comfortably in their native language.

Despite these difficulties, the great value of this report, whose pages are alive with the memories of many Guatemalans, is the collection of a large number of testimonies gathered in the field...

Determining responsibility was a fundamental component of analyzing the acts under investigation. In many cases, the commission gathered reliable information regarding the material or intellectual authors. However, the commission prioritized the determination of institutional responsibility, not only because of the mandate—which prevented the attribution of individual responsibility—but also because of the larger goal of historical clarification.

Nevertheless, while the commission could not present information regarding the identities of responsible individuals in the report, it was useful for identifying people to invite them to provide their versions of what occurred. This also helped in reconstructing complex situations involving several cases...

Degrees of Certainty

The goal of investigating cases was to establish if human rights violations or acts of violence connected to the internal armed confrontation had occurred, and not to achieve the level of certainty required for police or judicial action, nor to determine criminal responsibility. The commission was not a tribunal with the purpose of collecting material proof of a crime in order to attribute individual responsibility, nor did it have the authority to subpoena witnesses or engage in evidentiary proceedings...

The cases investigated and analyzed by the commission are included in the commission's statistics and the Appendix of Presented Cases. They were evaluated based on all of the information collected on the case and are arranged according to degrees of certainty regarding the occurrence of the act(s), and according to those responsible.

In evaluating the information on these two issues, the commission considered, among other things, whether the witnesses providing testimony were direct or indirect, their credibility, and the existence of additional evidence.

Three different degrees of certainty were used to evaluate a case:

- Complete certainty—This level referred to cases with direct witnesses whose testimonies left the commission with no doubt as to their credibility regarding the events and perpetrators, or where there existed documentary evidence confirming the act and its author.
- Well-founded probability—This second level of certainty referenced cases when not all of the testimonies regarding what occurred or those responsible were from direct witnesses, but where the commission had no doubts regarding credibility.

- Reasonable likelihood—This third level of certainty described cases in which there were no direct witnesses regarding the act or those responsible, yet where there were elements of analysis such as supporting witnesses whose testimonies corroborated each other, collective public knowledge of those responsible, or where the commissioners considered in good conscience that the information was sufficient to affirm the legitimacy of the case.

This third level of certainty was the minimum requirement for cases to be used in the statistical analyses or included in the Appendix of Presented Cases.

Of the total cases registered by the CEH: 33 percent were classified as being of complete certainty regarding occurrence and perpetrator(s). 43 percent of all registered cases were classified as being of well-founded probability of occurrence and perpetrator(s); and, 25 percent of all registered cases were classified as being of reasonable likelihood of occurrence and perpetrator(s).

It is important to reiterate that the commissioners have established and affirmed with the same level of rigor that all of the cases in these three categories occurred and have had the responsible parties identified...

Case Validation

In order to be included in the report, each case needed to be validated, first by field investigators, who sent all relevant information to the central office. There, database analysts reviewed the testimonies, documentary support, and other information and then classified cases according to type of violation or act of violence and the responsible party.

Before registering a case in the database, it was cleaned by reviewing the list of victims to detect any repetitions of dates or locations, errors in the legal classification of what occurred, or possible technical errors.

Once the cases were registered in the database, they were reviewed again, this time by a team of legal experts. These experts drafted the summaries that are included in the Appendix of Presented Cases. Their conclusions were submitted to the commissioners, who made the final determination regarding the level of certainty and decided on their publication.

Case Studies

Almost 100 of the cases investigated by the commission were selected to be reviewed in greater depth, providing special value for the comprehensive analysis of issues covered in the report. Eighty-five of these cases are presented in the Case Studies appendix.

Case studies were chosen using the following criteria: they highlighted an important change in the strategies or tactics of one of the parties to the conflict; they had special impact on the national conscience, due to their severity; or, they illustrated patterns of human rights violations or acts of violence connected to the internal armed confrontation in a particular region or period...

Each case study was analyzed and reviewed by a special team of professionals at the central office, then submitted for the commissioners' final approval.

Systematizing and Analyzing Information and Drafting the Final Report

Beginning with the registered cases, as well as the case studies, together with all of the available sources and statistical support from the database, the staff began the process of systematizing and analyzing all of the information that had been collected to draft the report.

The degrees of certainty assigned to each case were essential for this comprehensive and general task.

Because of the enormous number of testimonies about what occurred as well as the additional information compiled from other sources and compared to the versions provided by the parties, the commission was able to establish clear conclusions regarding the nature of human rights violations and acts of violence connected to the armed confrontation, their causes and origins, and their consequences, which then served as the basis for the conclusions and recommendations.

Specialized teams systematized this information, in order to facilitate the work of analysts in charge of drafting the report. These were the "input" teams, which covered the database, presented cases, case studies, key witnesses, and the documentation center.

All of the inputs used by the teams in charge of drafting the report's three main chapters were indispensable. However, certain sources, such as testimony given by important actors in the armed confrontation, in particular those who were part of institutions or groups that perpetrated human rights violations or acts of violence, as well as the declassified documents provided by the U.S. government, often took on special importance.

In the stage prior to drafting the report, the commissioners decided that it was not only necessary to examine human rights violations and acts of violence, but also to study their historical context, particularly the causes and origins of the violence. This task was mainly the responsibility of the Historical Analysis Group, which was comprised of high-level academics from various disciplines...

The progressive systematization and analysis of all of the information culminated in the final drafting of the chapters included in the report, which were reviewed, discussed, and approved by the commissioners in lengthy work sessions.

The commissioners developed their final conclusions and formulated their recommendations based on the acts and phenomena described in the three central chapters.

The Database

The CEH Database was created to electronically manage cases of human rights violations and acts of violence that the CEH gathered throughout the country's different regions. The systematization was designed to organize information according to certain previously defined criteria to produce statistics regarding frequencies of acts and their specific characteristics such as dates, places, responsible forces, victim characteristics, and types of violations...

The database was the source for the commission's statistical analyses. It was structured around a set of interrelated, dependent concepts, and basic criteria, which should be understood in relation to the overall structure...

Information contained in the CEH database was exclusively comprised of information compiled from individual or group testimonies...

Information the CEH obtained from other sources was classified and systematized separately by the documentation center or by the investigative teams... Based on the nature of the information in the cases, the database utilized both quantitative and qualitative information.

Quantitative information referred to concrete data systematically collected in previously designed formats or forms, in order to quantify and obtain a corresponding statistical base. This type of data referred to the case (date, place); victims (name, age, gender, type of victim); perpetrators (name, age, gender, group or organization); type of violation or act committed; and finally, those testifying (name, age, gender).

Glossaries were developed to classify this information through typologies of human rights violations and acts of violence. Care was taken to assure that equivalent categories were used for both parties to the conflict based on international human rights instruments and international humanitarian laws as well the common principles contained in both legal classifications...

The qualitative information available in the database comes from the narrative case summaries based on the information provided by those giving testimony and refers to descriptions of the acts, their circumstances, and context.

In order to classify this information, a glossary of thematic key words was compiled to assist analysts. In this way, cases could be classified according to key words contained in the glossary.

Appendix 3

Oslo Accord

Agreement on the Establishment of the Commission to Clarify Past Human Rights Violations and Acts of Violence That Have Caused the Guatemalan Population to Suffer

Whereas the present-day history of our country is marked by grave acts of violence, disregard for the fundamental rights of the individual and suffering of the population connected with the armed conflict;

Whereas the people of Guatemala have a right to know the whole truth concerning these events, clarification of which will help avoid a repetition of these sad and painful events and strengthen the process of democratization in Guatemala;

Reiterating its wish to comply fully with the Comprehensive Agreement on Human Rights of 29 March 1994;

Reiterating its wish to open as soon as possible a new chapter in Guatemala's history which, being the culmination of a lengthy process of negotiation, will put an end to the armed conflict and help lay the bases for peaceful coexistence and respect for human rights among Guatemalans;

Whereas, in this context, promotion of a culture of harmony and mutual respect that will eliminate any form of revenge or vengeance is a prerequisite for a firm and lasting peace,

The Government of Guatemala and the Unidad Revolucionaria Nacional Guatemalteca (hereafter referred to as "the Parties") have agreed as follows:

To establish a Commission whose terms of reference shall be as follows:

Purposes

I. To clarify with all objectivity, equity and impartiality the human rights violations and acts of violence that have caused the Guatemalan population to suffer, connected with the armed conflict.

II. To prepare a report that will contain the findings of the investigations carried out and provide objective information regarding events during this period covering all factors, internal as well as external.

III. Formulate specific recommendations to encourage peace and national harmony in Guatemala. The Commission shall recommend, in particular, measures to preserve the memory of the victims, to foster a culture of mutual respect and observance of human rights and to strengthen the democratic process.

Period Covered

The Commission's investigations shall cover the period from the start of the armed conflict until the signing of the firm and lasting peace agreement.

Operation

I. The Commission shall receive particulars and information from individuals or institutions that consider themselves to be affected and also from the Parties.

II. The Commission shall be responsible for clarifying these situations fully and in detail. In particular, it shall analyse the factors and circumstances involved in those cases with complete impartiality. The Commission shall invite those who may be in possession of relevant information to submit their version of the incidents. Failure of those concerned to appear shall not prevent the Commission from reaching a determination on the cases.

III. The Commission shall not attribute responsibility to any individual in its work, recommendations and report nor shall these have any judicial aim or effect.

IV. The Commission's proceedings shall be confidential so as to guarantee the secrecy of the sources and the safety of witnesses and informants.

V. Once it is established, the Commission shall publicize the fact that it has been established and the place where it is meeting by all possible means, and shall invite interested parties to present their information and their testimony.

Composition

The Commission shall consist of the following three members:

I. The present Moderator of the peace negotiations, whom the Secretary-General of the United Nations shall be asked to appoint.

II. One member, a Guatemalan of irreproachable conduct, appointed by the Moderator with the agreement of the Parties.

III. One academic selected by the Moderator, with the agreement of the Parties, from a list proposed by the University presidents.

The Commission shall have whatever support staff it deems necessary, with the requisite qualifications, in order to carry out its tasks.

Installation and Duration

The Commission shall be set up, installed and shall start to work as of the day the firm and lasting peace agreement is signed. The Commission shall work for a period of six months starting from the date of its installation; this period may be extended for a further six months if the Commission so decides.

Report

The Commission shall prepare a report which shall be handed over to the parties and to the Secretary-General of the United Nations who shall publish it. Inability to investigate all the cases or situations presented to the Commission shall not detract from the report's validity.

Commitment of the Parties

The Parties undertake to collaborate with the Commission in all matters that may be necessary for the fulfillment of its mandate. In particular, they undertake to establish, prior to setting up the Commission and during its operations, the necessary conditions so that the Commission may fulfill the terms of reference established in the present agreement.

International Verification

In conformity with the Framework Agreement of 10 January 1994, implementation of this Agreement shall be subject to international verification by the United Nations.

Measures for prompt execution following the signing of this Agreement

The Parties agree to ask the Secretary-General to appoint the Moderator of the negotiations as a member of the Commission as soon as possible. When he is appointed, he shall be authorized to proceed forthwith to make all necessary arrangements to ensure that the Commission functions smoothly once it is established and installed in conformity with the provisions of this Agreement.

Oslo, 23 June 1994

For the Government of the Republic of Guatemala

(Signed) Héctor ROSADA GRANADOS
(Signed) General Carlos Enrique PINEDA CARRANZA

(Signed) Antonio M. ARENALES FORNO
(Signed) General Julio Arnoldo BALCONI TURCIOS
(Signed) Mario PERMUTH
(Signed) General José Horacio SOTO SALAN
(Signed) Amilcar BURGOS SOLIS

For the *Unidad Revolucionaria Nacional Guatemalteca*

General Command

(Signed) Carlos GONZALES
(Signed) Commander Rolando MORAN
(Signed) Commander Gaspar ILOM
(Signed) Commander Pablo MONSANTO

Political and Diplomatic Commission

(Signed) Luis Felipe BECKER GUZMAN
(Signed) Miguel Angel SANDOVAL
(Signed) Francisco VILLAGRAN MUÑOZ
(Signed) Luz MENDEZ GUTIERREZ

Advisers

(Signed) Mario Vinicio CASTAÑEDA
(Signed) Miguel Angel REYES
(Signed) Jorge ROSAL

For the United Nations

(Signed) Jean ARNAULT
Moderator

A Note on the Translation

The majority of the material from the CEH report presented here has been translated for this book by Anna Kushner. The book also uses the CEH's English translation for material drawn from the report's prologue, conclusions, and recommendations (found here in sections I and IV). In addition, the section on genocide uses some of the translations found in *Quiet Genocide* (Estelle Higonnet, Ed. Transaction Publishers 2009), portions of which were translated by the editor of this book. For reference, the complete CEH report can be found online in Spanish at http://shr.aaas.org/guatemala/ceh/mds/spanish/.

Translation is always complex, and some terms, concepts, phrases, and ideas are difficult to express in a different language. With this in mind, a number of terms are italicized and left in the original Spanish (these are listed and defined in the list of acronyms and abbreviations and the glossary of key Spanish terms). Other terms have been translated directly, such as "department," which refers to the Guatemala's administrative divisions and corresponds to the idea of a province or state.

The book uses the phrase "internal armed confrontation" to reference the armed conflict. This is the English translation preferred by the commission although in some parts of the report other terms are used.

There are also a number of adjustments and minor changes in the text which have been included to conform to the publisher's style and grammar guide. For example, numbers upto one hundred are written out, the word "percent" is used instead of the percent sign (%), and some terms that are capitalized in the original (such as Civil Patrols or Military Intelligence) are not capitalized here. In addition, U.S. rather than U.K. spellings are used.

In some cases, this book uses words, terms and phrases that differ from the commission's English translations. Some long sentences that read well in Spanish, where multiple clauses are appropriate, have been broken up into shorter sentences that read more clearly in English. And, some particular terms have been adjusted for clarity. The translation also presents some grammatical adjustments, such as regularizing verb tenses for clarity and consistency.

In all cases, the goal of the translation has been to ensure that the text is as readable and accessible as possible with the overall objective of broadening access to the important work of the CEH.

Acknowledgments

This book has benefited enormously from the comments, ideas, suggestions, and support of many colleagues, contacts, and friends over a number of years. The original idea for the project began when I worked at the CEH during its initial stages. Then, over time, as Guatemalans and others told me of the need for a more accessible version of the commission's report, the project matured into a proposal and, eventually, to this book.

As outlined in the introductory essay, the original Spanish language edits were reviewed by a skilled, critical, and insightful group of Guatemalan and international consultants, including Roddy Brett, Michelle Bellino, Iduvina Hernandez, Gustavo Meoño Brenner, Victoria Sanford, Arturo Taracena Arriola, Christian Tomuschat, Edelberto Torres Rivas, and Manolo Vela Castañeda. Their insights and suggestions have been invaluable. In addition, Michelle Bellino provided exceptional research assistance and help in editing and formatting the text.

Many friends and colleagues read and commented on this book at different stages in its development. Several individuals reviewed multiple versions of the text and deserve special mention for their excellent suggestions, helpful ideas, good humor, patience, and ongoing support, including Julia Lieblich, David Rothenberg, and Bill Wyman. The book also benefitted from Emoline Fox's careful textual review and from very insightful and sensitive comments from Nassim Assefi, David Gartner, and Michael Heller. Also, special thanks to Karin Badt and Daniel Wilkinson for their edits and ideas.

The book began with a grant from the Moriah Foundation where Lael Parish provided steady, patient assistance, and a sustained interest in social justice.

The evolution of the project—including travel, meetings, and research—benefited from generous support from the Jeanne M. and Joseph P. Sullivan Foundation. The commitment of Jeanne Sullivan, as well as the late Joseph Sullivan, deserve special mention. As engaged global citizens and benefactors of many important projects, they worked tirelessly for years to give voice to the voiceless and to support the less powerful among us.

At various stages in the evolution of this book, I have benefitted from the institutional and academic support of many wonderful colleagues. While at the Orville H. Schell, Jr. Center for International Human Rights at Yale Law School, I was fortunate to work with Oona Hathaway, Deena Hurwitz, Paul Kahn, Harold Koh, Ben Kiernan, and James Silk, whose ideas, creative scholarship, and commitment to justice are inspiring. In addition, Barbara Johnson and Barbara Mianzo provided significant assistance with project management.

At the DePaul University College of Law, I was honored to trade ideas and share reflections about human rights and Latin American politics with Alberto Coll, while also benefiting from the input of colleagues with whom I taught in Central America, including Alicia Alvarez, Len Cavise, Bruce Ottley, and Victor Rodriguez. Over a number of years, this project was enriched from conversations, input, and intellectual exchanges with Susan Bandes, David Franklin, Jerry Friedland, Michelle Goodwin, Brian Havel, Stephan Landsman, Andrea Lyon, Roberta Kwall, Song Richardson, Stephen Siegal, and Glen Weissenberger.

I am indebted to DePaul's International Human Rights Law Institute, and especially the organization's founder, M. Cherif Bassiouni. My work on this project was supported by the ideas and input of many colleagues there, particularly Mohamed Abdel Aziz Ibrahim, Meredith Barges, Martin Cinnamond, Kurdistan Daloye, Michael Wahid Hanna, Etelle Higonnet, Kelly McCracken, Charles Tucker, and Elizabeth Ward. The project would not have been possible without the assistance of Molly Bench, T. J. Chernick, Kandy Christensen, Allison Rudi, and especially Angel Graf.

More recently, my colleagues at the Sandra Day O'Connor College of Law at Arizona State University have provided many useful insights regarding international law, human rights, Latin American politics, and transitional justice. In some cases, they have helped resolve specific academic and policy questions and, in other cases, their collegiality, support, and spirit of engaged inquiry has supported this book and many related projects. Special thanks go out to key partners at the Center for Law and Global Affairs—Ken Abbott, David Androff, Dan Bodansky, Charles Calleros, Laura Dickinson, Aaron Fellmeth, David Gartner, LaDawn Haglund, James Hodge, Orde Kittrie, Jonathan Koppell, Victor Peskin, Douglas Sylvester, Rebecca Tsosie, and Margaret Walker—as well as to other fine colleagues, including Paul Berman, Bob Bartels, Sarah Buel, Adam Chodorow, Patty Ferguson-Bohnee, Dale Furnish, Joel Garreau, David Kader, Marcy Karin, Gary Marchant, Ruth McGregor, Michael Saks, and George Schatzki.

For their invaluable assistance, patience, and support, thanks to Farideh Koohi-Kamali, Sarah Nathan, Richard Bellis and Sara Doskow at Palgrave Macmillan for their hard work and dedication.

Also a very big thank-you to Anna Kushner for being such a wonderful translator, to Mark Fowlie Beasley for preparing the tables used in this book, and to Luis Gonzalez Palma for allowing his photograph "Fidelidad del dolor" to be used on the cover.

For their help in preparing for the book's reception in Guatemala, thanks to Raúl Figueroa Sarti of F&G Editores and to Edelberto Torres-Rivas, Manolo Vela, and FLACSO.

In Guatemala, many thanks to friends and colleagues for years of advice and support and for opening their hearts and sharing difficult stories of *la violencia*.

Finally, my deepest gratitude and respect to Ilissa Lazar, who has helped me with this book and with so much more.

Notes

In this book, endnotes are only included where they reference direct quotations, either from interviews or documents. The reference system used here is that of the CEH and is presented in the same format as in the original report. Documents referenced indicate the author (where this is available), the title, the source and the date. Quotations from interviews reference the particular case with the letter "C" followed by the case number. Quotations from witnesses are indicated by the terms "witness" or "direct witness" often presenting the witness' status in parentheses (former soldier, former G-2, etc.). Some references use the letters T.C. which sometimes means *testigo clave* ("key witness") and other times means *testigo colectivo* (collective testimony), with corresponding codes related to the CEH database. A quotation taken from a case study is referenced with the letters C.I. for *caso ilustrativo* ("case study", some of which are included in the book) and the number references that particular case study. Most references include information regarding when the issue or event occurred, using the month and year, as well as the location, listing the community, town, and department. In addition, some quotations are from research conducted by entities other than the CEH, like the REMHI project or human rights groups, such as FAMDEGUA, as indicated.

1 Extrajudicial Executions and Forced Disappearances

1. Witness (high-level government official) CEH. (T.C. 13).
2. C 3705. December, 1981. San Juan Cotzal, Quiché.
3. C 5807. May, 1981 San Ildefenso Istahuacán, Huehuetenango.
4. Direct witness REMHI. (T. 53).
5. Ibid.
6. C 197. August, 1981. Guatemala City, Guatemala.
7. Direct witness (university administrator) CEH. (T.C. 3).
8. Witness (EGP high command) CEH. (T.C. 154).
9. C 16685. 1974. Santa Cruz del Quiché, Quiché.
10. C 6097.1981. San Miguel Acatán, Huehuetenango.
11. Witness REMHI. Perpetrator testimony.
12. Witness (former EGP combatant) CEH. (T.C. 8).
13. Direct witness (former soldier) CEH. (T.C. 53).
14. C 19002. October, 1984. Guatemala City, Guatemala.
15. CI. Forced disappearance of José Arnoldo Guilló Martínez, speaker and teacher, July 1967, Escuintla.
16. C. 276. June, 1982, San José Poaquil, Chimaltenango.

17. C 284. May, 1982. Patzún, Chimaltenango.
18. CI 87. September, 1981. Guatemala City, Guatemala.
19. C 13129. 1964. Escuintla, Escuintla.
20. C 1022. January, 1982. Los Amates, Izabal.
21. Frente Estudiantil de Reforma Universitaria (Student Front for University Reform, FERU), "Breve cronología de los actos represivos en contra del Movimiento Estudiantil," p. 9. ("Brief chronology of the repressive acts against the student movement")
22. C 1112. February, 1978. Olapa, Chiquimula.
23. C 3054. December 1981. Nebaj, Quiché.
24. CI 8. December, 1981–1997.
25. Direct witness CEH.
26. Ibid.
27. Ibid.
28. Direct witness CEH.C 331. June, 1980.
29. U.S. embassy in Guatemala, Report of the Department of State, June 1980, pp. 3–59; U.S. embassy in Guatemala, Report of the Department of State, June 1982, pp. 3–82; CIA, Report to the Department of State, June 1980, pp. 12–37.
30. File No. 1445, Judiciary of Guatemala, Criminal Division, Guatemala, 1989.

2   Torture

1. C 7218. December, 1981. Tejutla, San Marcos.
2. Witness CEH. (T.C. 31).
3. C 2485. March, 1983. San André Sajcabajá, Quiché.
4. C 5355. September, 1982. Jacaltenango, Huehuetenango.
5. C 13042. 1983. Yepocapa, Chimaltenango.
6. CI 17. 1981 y 1982. Ixcán, Quiché.
7. Translation of declassified U.S. document, HR/9.8.
8. C 7313. December, 1981. Ixchiguán, San Marcos.
9. C 11418. 1985. Ixcán, Quiché.
10. C 15253. 1981–1982. Cahabón, Alta Verapaz.
11. C 2798. December, 1981. Quiché.
12. C. 7221. December, 1981. Tacaná, San Marcos.
13. El Imparcial. July 4, 1966.
14. C 7091. April, 1984. San Pablo, San Marcos.
15. C 11351. January, 1982. Ixcán, Quiché.
16. C 11185. July, 1982. Ixcán, Quiché.
17. Direct witness (former army confidencial assigned to the Playa Grande military base) CEH.
18. Direct witness (torture survivor) CEH.
19. Direct witness (torture survivor) CEH.
20. Ibid.
21. C 11496. December, 1981. Playa Grande military base, Ixcán, Quiché.
22. Direct witness (torture survivor) CEH.
23. Direct witness (torture survivor) CEH. C 11166. January, 1981. Ixcán, Quiché.
24. C 11351. January, 1982. Ixcán, Quiché. C 11352. January, 1982. Ixcán, Quiché. C 11353. February, 1982. Ixcán, Quiché.
25. Direct witness (former specialist assigned to the Playa Grande military base from 1980 through 1983).

3   Forced Displacement

1. C 11196. 1982 Ixcán, Quiché
2. C 16117. May, 1981. Uspantán, Quiché.
3. C 2756. March, 1982. Zacualpa, Quiché.
4. C 16117. May, 1981. Uspantán, Quiché.
5. Héctor Alejandro Gramajo, *De la guerra…a la guerra: La difícil transición política en Guatemala*, Fondo de Cultura Económica, 1995, p. 181.
6. T.C. 51. Collective testimony from women survivors of *la violencia*. Comalapa, Chimaltenango.
7. C 9054. November 1981. Chisec, Alta Verapaz.
8. C 2699. March 1983. Uspantán, Quiché.
9. C 9229. 1984. San Cristóbal, Alta Verapaz.
10. T.C. 857. Collective testimony, Najtilabaj. 1981–1985. San Cristóbal Verapaz, Alta Verapaz.
11. T.C. 346. Nebaj, Quiché.
12. C 9061. 1982. Saraxoch, Alta Verapaz.
13. C 9229. 1983. San Cristóbal, Alta Verapaz.
14. Collective testimony, CEH. C 928. March, 1982. San Martín Jilotepeque, Chimaltenango.
15. Direct witness CEH. C 893. February, 1982. San Martín Jilotepeque, Chimaltenango.
16. Key witness CEH. (T.C. 873).
17. Direct witness CEH. C 893. February, 1982. San Martín Jilotepeque, Chimaltenango.
18. Key witness CEH. (T.C. 873).
19. Key witness CEH. (T.C. 872).
20. Collective testimony CEH. C 928. Marzo, 1982. San Martín Jilotepeque, Chimaltenango. The source did not specify the name of the foreign commission.

4   Massacres

1. C 6075. July, 1982. San Mateo Ixtatán, Huehuetenango.
2. C 9001. October, 1982. Cobán, Alta Verapaz.
3. C 3141. May, 1981. San Juan Cotzal, Quiché.
4. C 304. April, 1981. Nebaj, Quiché.
5. CI 43. January, 1982. Santa Cruz del Quiché, Quiché.
6. CI 43. January, 1982. Santa Cruz del Quiché, Quiché.
7. C 5536. August, 1982. Aguacatán, Huehuetenango.
8. C 6080. January, 1981. Barillas, Huehuetenango.
9. CI 51. March 1982. San Martín Jilotepeque, Chimaltenango.
10. C 2756. March, 1982. San Antonio Sinaché, Quiché.
11. C 9078. August, 1982. Senahú, Alta Verapaz.
12. Direct witness (former *Kaibil*) FAMDEGUA. November 14, 1996.
13. Direct witness (former *Kaibil*) Public Ministry. Court document 541–94.
14. Ibid.
15. Direct witness (former *Kaibil*) FAMDEGUA. November 14, 1996.
16. Ibid.
17. Direct witness (former *Kaibil*) FAMDEGUA. November 14, 1996.
18. Direct witness Public Ministry. Court document 541–94.

19. Ibid.
20. Direct witness FAMDEGUA. July, 1994.
21. Direct witness (former *Kaibil*). Public Ministry. Court document 541–94.
22. Direct witness FAMDEGUA. July, 1994.
23. Direct witness (former *Kaibil*). Public Ministry. Court document 541–94.
24. Ibid.
25. Direct witness (former *Kaibil*) CEH. (T.C. 262).

5 Rape and Sexual Violence

1. C I77. July, 1983. Uspantán, Quiché.
2. C 2620. January 1981. Cotzal, Quiché.
3. CI 91. March, 1981. Quiché.
4. CI 10. March, 1982. Rabinal, Baja Verapaz.
5. C 2593. February, 1983. San Miguel Uspantán, Quiché.
6. CI 77. 1980–1996. San Miguel Uspantán, Quiché.
7. Witness CEH. (T.C. 106).
8. C 2502. January, 1982. Joyabaj, Quiché.
9. C 11630. September, 1981. Panzós, Alta Verapaz.
10. Direct witness REMHI.
11. C 16246. March, 1982. Chinique, Quiché.
12. Direct witness CEH. C 2311. October, 1982. Cotzal, Quiché.
13. C 2419. March, 1981. Uspantán, Quiché.
14. C 2596. November, 1982. Uspantán, Quiché.
15. Direct witness REMHI.
16. C 3515. April, 1982. Chajul, Quiché.
17. Direct witness REMHI.
18. Direct witness (female guerrilla combatant who was raped at the age of fifteen) CEH.

6 Genocide

1. Ben Whitaker, *Revised and updated report on the question of Prevention and punishment of the crime of genocide;* UN document E/CN.4/Sub.2/1985/6, par. 29, p. 16.
2. Centro de Estudios Militares, *Manual de guerra contrasubversiva,* 1982, p. 6.
3. Centro de Estudios Militares, *Manual de Inteligencia G-2,* 1972, p. 217.
4. 887 Ejército de Guatemala, plan de campaña *Victoria 82,* anexo F, literal A, numeral 2-c.
5. Asociación de Veteranos Militares de Guatemala (AVEMILGUA), *Guatemala, testimonio de una agresión,* 1998, p. 77.
6. *The New York Times,* July 20, 1982.
7. Accord on the Identity and Rights of Indigenous Peoples. In 1982, the issue of the exclusion of indigenous peoples was even recognized by the military regime that established the "14 Essential Points for Immediate Action," "Achieve the reestablishment of a nationalist spirit and create a base for the participation and integration of the different ethnic groups that comprise our nation." *"El Imparcial,"* April 6, 1982.
8. Marta Casaús Arzú, *Guatemala: linaje y racismo,* 1995, p. 274.
9. Guatemalan Army, Campaign Plan *Victoria 82,* Annex. H, Number I, subsection G-2.
10. Guatemalan Army, "Apreciación de asuntos civiles (G-5) para el área Ixil" ("Review of civilian issues (G-5) in the Ixil area"), *Revista Militar,* September–December 1982,

p. 31. This document was published in the *Revista Militar* alongwith "Una solución a la operación Ixil. Plan de AACC operación Ixil" ("A solution to operation Ixil. AACC plan operation Ixil"), pp. 25–54. Witness (army official) CEH. (T.C. 103), confirmed its authenticity.

11. Guatemalan Army, Campaign plan *Victoria 82,* Annex. G, Number II, subsection C-1.

12. Guatemalan Army, "Indígenas que han sido históricamente hostiles al Ejército", ("Indigenous people have been historically hostile to the Army") declassified U.S. government document, CIA; G5-41, p. 41 released 002/98, February 1982, p. 37.

13. "Una solución a la operación Ixil. Plan de AACC Operación Ixil" ("A solution to operation Ixil. AACC plan operation Ixil"), p. 55.

14. Witness (retired military) CEH. (T.C. 92).

15. Guatemalan Army, "Apreciación de asuntos civiles (G-5) para el área Ixil" ("Review of civilian issues (G-5) in the Ixil area"), p. 32.

16. C 3161. 1987. Nebaj, Patulul, Suchitepéquez.

17. Collective testimony, Bicalamá, Nebaj, Quiché (T.C. 287).

18. Witness CEH. (T.C. 346).

19. Collective testimony CEH, San Juan Cotzal, Quiché, regarding scorched earth policies in Asich. (T.C. 341).

20. Witness (religious figure) CEH. (T.C.136).

21. C 11385, May 1982. Rabinal, Baja Verapaz.

22. C 9075. July, 1982. Rabinal, Baja Verapaz. Plan de Sánchez massacre.

23. C 16646. April, 1982. Zacualpa, Quiché.

24. C 16358. February, 1983. Zacualpa, Quiché.

25. Guatemalan Army, *Resumen de Inteligencia al plan de operaciones, Gran Ofensiva del área militar de Huehuetenango* (Overview of Intelligence for the operational plan, Major Offensive in the military area of Huehuetenango), Annex. B, 1981.

26. Ibid.

27. Ibid.

28. Ibid.

29. C 6096. July, 1981. San Miguel Acatán, Huehuetenango.

30. C 6022. July, 1982. San Mateo Ixtatán, Huehuetenango.

31. Testimony REMHI, C 0839.

32. Witness CEH (survivor).

33. Ibid.

34. Ibid.

35. Ibid.

36. Direct witness CEH.

37. Ibid.

7   Acts of Violence

1. Witness (former EGP leader) CEH. (T.C. 184).

2. C 905. November, 1981. Tecpán, Chimaltenango.

3. C 810. August, 1982. Patzún, Chimaltenango.

4. Witness (former EGP leader) CEH. (T.C 157).

5. EGP, "Sobre nuestro concepto de la propaganda armada como forma principal de lucha en la nueva fase" ("Regarding our understanding of armed propaganda as the main mode of struggle in the new phase"), August, 1975.

6. Witness (former EGP combatant) CEH. (T.C. 80).

7. Witness (former EGP high command) CEH. (T.C. 152).
8. War Reports No.7, southern region, Capitán Santos Salazar, November, 1983.
9. FAR, "Complemento a la información de accionesdel Regional Sur de March," ("Additional information on the actions in the Southern Region in March"), December 7, 1981.
10. Witness (former FAR combatant) CEH. (T.C. 225).
11. FAR, "Comunicado de la Dirección Nacional de las Fuerzas Armadas Rebeldes" ("Statement by the National Directorate of the Armed Rebel Forces"), June 20, 1980.
12. Witness (former ORPA leaders) CEH. (T.C. 165).
13. Ibid.
14. C 7191. June, 1985. La Reforma, San Marcos.
15. Ibid.
16. Ibid.
17. Witness (former ORPA high command) CEH. (T.C. 164).
18. Witness (former EGP high command) CEH. (T.C. 146).
19. Witness (former EGP combatant) CEH. (T.C. 256).
20. Witness (EGP member) CEH. (T.C. 79).
21. C 11243. 1981. Ixcán, Quiché.
22. Witness (former FAR combatant) CEH. (T.C. 235).
23. Frente Guerrillero Tecún Umán, 1982.
24. FAR, War Report no. 7, Regional Sur Capitán Santos Salazar, November 1983.
25. Witness (former EGP high command) CEH. (T.C. 152).
26. Witness (former EGP high command and leader) CEH. (T.C. 207).
27. Witness (former EGP combatant) CEH. (T.C. 159).
28. CI 20. 1982. Nicaragua and Huehuetenango.
29. FAR, Military Rules, June, 1990.
30. Ibid.
31. Witness (former FAR combatant) CEH. (T.C. 223).
32. Witness (former regional head of the EGP) CEH. (T.C. 247).
33. C 683. July, 1982. Comalapa, Chimaltenango.
34. C 5003. 1982. Aguacatán, Huehuetenango.
35. Witness (former FAR high command) CEH. (T.C. 224).
36. Fuerzas Armadas Rebeldes, "Situación y perspectiva del movimiento revolucionario guatemalteco" ("Situation and perspective of the Guatemalan revolutionary movement"), March, 1967.
37. CI 088. 1970. Guatemala City.
38. CI 089. December 1977. Guatemela City.
39. FAR, Verdad Proletaria (the propaganda publication of the FAR), No. 6, July, 1980.
40. Ibid.
41. Prensa Libre, Guatemala, March 5, 1982.
42. Witness (member of the PGT) CEH. (T.C. 430).
43. Witness (former FAR high command) CEH. (T.C. 224).
44. Witness (former FAR combatant) CEH. (T.C. 220).
45. Witness (former FAR combatant) CEH. (T.C. 221).
46. Witness (former ORPA high command) CEH. (T.C. 165).
47. Witness (former indigenous political organizer, EGP) CEH. (T.C. 61).
48. Collective testimony CEH. How the EGP began operating in Xoxlac, Barillas, Huehuetenango.
49. Testimony (community leader) CEH.(T.C. 287).
50. Collective testimony CEH. (T.C. 96). Zacualpa, Quiché.

51. Collective Testimony CEH. (T.C. 107).
52. Witness (former EGP high command) CEH. (T.C. 207).
53. Witness (former EGP high command) CEH. (T.C. 207).
54. FAR, "Press release," Guatemala, April 20, 1983.
55. C 5126. February, 1982. San Antonio Huista, Huehuetenango.
56. EGP, *Compañero*, EGP publication for international distribution, No. 6, July, 1982.
57. FAR, "Nuestras tareas fundamentales en la actual situación política y nuestra preparación para su inminente cambio futuro" ("Our fundamental work within the current political situation for its imminent and future change"), internal FAR document, January, 1968.
58. FAR, National Propaganda Section, June 1970, pp. 8–9.
59. Witness (former EGP leaders) CEH. (T.C. 145).
60. EGP, *Informador Internacional*, No. 1, December, 1981, pp. 9–10.
61. Witness (former EGP high command) CEH. (T.C. 150).
62. EGP, *Informador Guerrillero*, bi-weekly publication, No. 30. January 10, 1984.
63. EGP, *Informador Guerrillero*, bi-weekly publication, No. 2. January 16, 1982.
64. EGP, *Informador Guerrillero*, bi-weekly publication, December 16, 1981.
65. Witness (former ORPA high command) CEH. (T.C. 163).
66. *El Imparcial*, May 6, 1966, pp. 1 and 4.
67. Julio César Macías, *La guerrilla fue mi camino*, Editorial Piedra Santa, S.A. (Guatemala, 1977), pp. 128–29.

8   Army, Security Institutions, and Civilians Acting under State Control

1. Guatemalan government, Ministry of Defense, document No. 001-MDN-acom/98. January 5, 1998, from minister of defense, Héctor Mario Barrios Celada to Christian Tomuschat, coordinator of the CEH.
2. Guatemalan Army, Campaign plan *Victoria 82*, paragraph IV.
3. Center for Military Studies, Guatemalan Army, *Manual de guerra contrasubversiva* (Manual of counterinsurgency war), 1983, p. 3.
4. Witness CEH. (T.C. 91)
5. C 11418. 1985. Ixcán, Quiché.
6. Guatemalan Army, *Revista Militar*, No. 21, June 1980.
7. Ibid.
8. Witness (former member of the PMA) CEH. (T.C. 104).
9. Ibid.
10. C 15253. August, 1982. Cahabón, Alta Verapaz.
11. Translation of a declassified U.S. document, PG 2550, p. 67.
12. Guatemalan Army, campaign plan *Victoria 82*, paragraph VIII, mission. Guatemala 1982.
13. Witness (officer of the Guatemalan Army) CEH. (T.C. 102).
14. C 7091. 1987 and 1990, San Pablo, San Marcos.
15. C 11431. April, 1983. Ixcán, Quiché.
16. C 11411. December 1981, Ixcán, Quiché.
17. Carlos Osorio Avaria, "¿Buenos Vecinos? La Doctrina de Seguridad Nacional en América Latina" in Anuario de Ciencias Sociales, Universidad Autónoma de Aguascalientes, Mexico, Year 2, Vol. II, May 1997, p. 58.
18. Eduardo Galeano, *Guatemala: país ocupado*, 1967, p. 49.

19. Witness CEH. (T.C. 119).
20. Flyer "Junio Rojo! Comunistas de Guatemala" ("Red June! The Communists of Guatemala"), 1967.
21. Translation by the CEH of a declassified document, HD/10.4.
22. Witness CEH. (T.C. 137).
23. "Testimony by a former refugee, a former soldier and a former member of the G-2," in Víctor Montejo, *Brevísima relación testimonial de la continua destrucción del Mayab'*, Guatemala, pp. 46–47.
24. Witness CEH. (T.C. 85).
25. Guatemalan government, Decree 23–54, Article 2.
26. *Nuevo Diario*, November 16, 1979.
27. Guatemalan Army, "Reservas Militares, Síntesis histórica de los comisionados militares" ("Military reserves, Historical overview of military commissioners") p. 49.
28. CEH translation of a declassified document from the United States, HD/10.4, May 12, 1967.
29. CEH translation of a declassified document from the United States, HD/10.9, October 23, 1967.
30. Witness (retired army general) CEH. (T.C. 24).
31. C 9371. October, 1981. Cahabón, Alta Verapaz.
32. C 1036. 1984. Dolores, Petén.
33. Inforpress, November 26, 1981.
34. Direct witness CEH. (T.C. 155).
35. C 7164. January, 1982. La Reforma, San Marcos.
36. C 7087. 1982. San Pablo, San Marcos.
37. C 2800. February, 1982. San Bartolomé Jocotenango, Quiché.
38. In "Procurador de los Derechos Humanos: Los comités de la defensa civil en Guatemala" ("Human Rights Ombudsman: The committees for civil defense in Guatemala"), Office of the Human Rights Ombudsman, Spanish Agency for International Cooperation and the *Asociación para la Autogestión del Desarrollo Integral*, Guatemala, July, 1994, p. 33.
39. Guatemalan Army, "Guía para la organización de las Patrullas de Autodefensa Civil" ("Guide for organizing the Civil Defense Patrols"), Appendix I to section J of the Campaign plan *Victoria 82*.
40. Guatemalan Army, Campaign plan *Firmeza 83*, Objective II, Appendix 5 to Section B.
41. C 15665. July, 1982. Aguacatán, Huehuetenango.
42. C 11177. 1988. Ixcán, Quiché.
43. C 2990. 1982. Chichicastenango, Quiché.
44. Direct witness (former *patrullero*) CEH.
45. Direct witness (former *patrullero*) CEH.
46. Direct witness (former *patrullero*) CEH.

9 Guerrilla Organizations

1. EGP, *Bajo las banderas de la unidad revolucionaria*, April, 1983.
2. Witness (former director of the PGT's university section) CEH. (T.C. 436).
3. Huberto Alvarado, *Apuntes para la historia del Partido Guatemalteco del Trabajo*, Guatemala, University collection, 1994, p. 69.
4. Witness (former PGT leader) CEH. (T.C. 568).

5. Witness (former FAR military leader) CEH. (T.C. 293).
6. Ibid.
7. Witness (former ORPA high command) CEH. (T.C. 209).
8. Witness (former ORPA high command) CEH. (T.C. 161).
9. Witness (former ORPA high command) CEH. (T.C. 163).
10. ORPA, "Qúe sabemos de nuestros antepasados", ("What we know about our ancestors") propaganda material, no date.
11. C 7036. June, 1981. Colotenango, Huehuetenango.
12. ORPA, "Manual del buen combatant, material de campaña" ("Manual of a good combatant, campaign material"), 1984.
13. ORPA, *Guía para el desarrollo de las pláticas de estudio*, 1988.
14. Witness (former ORPA high command) CEH. (T.C. 163).
15. Witness (former ORPA leader and founding member) CEH. (T.C. 31).
16. "Pueblos en Armas", ("People in Arms") interview of Gaspar Ilom by Marta Harnecker, originally published in the magazine *Punto Final Internacional*, Mexico, August 1982 and September 1985.
17. Witness (former ORPA high command) CEH. (T.C. 165).
18. "El EGP en la prensa" ("The EGP in the press"), interview with former commander-in-chief of the EGP Rolando Morán by Mario Menéndez Rodríguez, 1981.
19. Witness (former EGP high command) CEH. (T.C. 150).
20. Witness (former EGP high command) CEH. (T.C. 152).
21. Witness (Army high command) CEH. (T.C. 213).
22. Ibid.
23. Witness (former EGP high command) CEH. (T.C. 23).
24. Witness (former EGP high command and leader) CEH. (T.C. 146).
25. Witness (former EGP high command and leader) CEH. (T.C. 207).
26. Witness (former EGP high command) CEH. (T.C. 152).
27. Witness (former EGP high command) CEH. (T.C. 156).
28. Witness (former EGP high command) CEH. (T.C. 160).
29. Witness (former EGP leader) CEH. (T.C. 244).
30. Witness (former member of the CCL in the EGP) CEH. (T.C. 72).
31. Witness (community leader in Quiché) CEH. (T.C. 280).
32. Key witness (member of EGP National Directorate in 1982) CEH. (T.C. 23); direct witnesses (current URNG leaders) CEH. 30 de marzo de 1998.
33. Key witness (member of EGP National Directorate in 1982) CEH. (T.C. 23).
34. Ibid.

10   Terror and Its Consequences

1. Witness CEH. Chiché, Quiché.
2. Witness CEH. March, 1982. Sibinal, San Marcos.
3. Witness CEH. C 7311. January, 1981. San Pedro Sacatepéquez, San Marcos.
4. Witness CEH. C7308. August 1980. San Pedro Sacatepéquez, San Marcos.
5. Witness (former USAC staff) CEH (T.C. 3).
6. Witness (Kaqchikel survivor of *la violencia* and missionary) CEH. (T.C. 82).
7. Witness (GAM founder) CEH. (T.C. 382).
8. Witness CEH. C 7149. September, 1983. La Reforma, San Marcos.
9. Witness CEH. C 7157. 1981 Tajumulco, San Marcos.
10. Witness (Ladina widow) CEH. C 7109. 1984. San Rafael Pie de la Cuesta, San Marcos.

11. Witness CEH. C 7316. 1986. Nuevo Progreso, San Marcos.

12. Witness CEH. C 7315. 1983. Nuevo Progreso, San Marcos.

13. Witness (survivor of *la violencia* in Escuintla) CEH. (T.C. 194).

14. Witness CEH. C 1628. May 1978. Panzós, Alta Verapaz.

15. Witness (victim who was a minor at the time) CEH. (T.C. 195).

16. Witness (survivor, former missionary) CEH. (T.C. 82).

17. Witness (former USAC staff) CEH. (T.C. 3).

18. Witness CEH. C 2961. March, 1982. Chiché, Quiché.

19. Witness (former municipal leader) CEH. Nebaj, Quiché. (T.C. 254).

20. Cited in Byron Barillas y otros, "Dos décadas, tres generaciones. El movimiento estudiantil visto desde la óptica de sus protagonistas" ("Two decades, three generations. The student movement as seen from the perspective of its participants").

21. Witness CEH. C 13013. October, 1979. Santa Lucía Cotzumalguapa, Escuintla.

22. Witness CEH. C 2596. June, 1983. Uspantán, Quiché.

23. Witness CEH. (T.C. 260).

24. Witness CEH. C 7218. December, 1982. Tejutla, San Marcos. CI 43. Quiché. 1982, 1988. CI 53. Quiché. 1982.

25. Witness REMHI. (2246). 1982. Huehuetenango.

26. CI 82. 1981 and 1982. Uspantán, Quiché.

27. Witness (child survivor) CEH. C 9156. 1982. Rabinal, Baja Verapaz.

28. Witness CEH. C 5343. 1982. San Antonio Huista, Huehuetenango.

29. Witness CEH. C 9071. San Cristóbal Verapaz, Alta Verapaz.

30. Witness CEH. C 7111. April 1990. Esquipulas Palo Gordo, San Marcos.

31. CI 70. 1982. San Marcos.

32. Witness CEH. C 425. 1984. Patzún, Chimaltenango.

33. Witness REMHI. 477.

34. Witness CEH. C 16053. 1982. Zacualpa, Quiché.

35. Witness CEH. C 16053. 1982. Zacualpa. Quiché. CI 53. 1982. Quiché.

36. Collective testimony. San Miguel Acatán, Huehuetenango. (T.C. 352).

37. Witness (demobilized, Huista region, Huehuetenango) CEH. (T.C. 131).

38. Witness (former EGP member) CEH. (T.C. 8).

39. Witness CEH. C11437. 1982. Cantabal, Quiché. CI 4. 1982. Quiché.

40. Witness CEH. C6017. 1982. Barrillas, Huehuetenango.

41. Witness CEH. (T.C. 800).

42. Witness CEH. (T.C. 800).

43. Ibid.

44. Witness CEH. C 13375. 1982 to the present. Santa Lucía Cotzumalguapa, Escuintla.

45. Ibid.

46. C 9267. January 1983. Cahabón, Alta Verapaz.

47. C 6164. March, 1982. Barillas, Huehuetenango.

48. Witness (Maya leader) CEH. (T.C. 106).

49. C 9112. 1982. Cahabón, Alta Verapaz.

50. C 2800. February, 1982. San Bartolomé Jocotenango, Quiché.

51. Witness CEH. C 16679. 1983. San Cruz del Quiché, Quiché.

52. Witness CEH. C 521. 1985. Guatemala City.

53. Witness CEH. C 6043. 1982. Barillas, Huehuetenango.

54. Direct witness CEH. March, 1982. (T.C. 851).

55. Direct witness CEH. March, 1982. (T.C. 362).

56. Direct witness CEH. March, 1982. (T.C. 851).

57. Direct witness CEH. March, 1982. (T.C. 848).

58. Direct witness CEH. March, 1982. (T.C. 362).
59. Direct witness CEH. March, 1982. (T.C. 848).
60. Direct witness CEH. March, 1982–1984. (T.C. 853).
61. Direct witness CEH. March, 1982–1984. (T.C. 362).
62. Ibid.
63. Direct witness CEH. Marzo, 1982–1984. (T.C. 853).
64. Ibid.
65. Direct witness CEH. March 1982–1984. (T.C. 850).
66. Direct witness CEH. March 1982–1984. (T.C. 362).
67. Ibid.
68. Direct witness CEH. March 1984. (T.C. 850).

11 Facing *La Violencia*

1. CI 41. June 1967. Escuintla.
2. *La Nación*. March 22, 1980, p. 1 and *Prensa Libre*, March 21, 1980, p. 8.
3. Witness, REMHI. FAMDEGUA activist.
4. Witness (GAM activist) CEH. (T.C. 84).
5. Witness (GAM activist) CEH. (T.C. 84).
6. Witness (GAM founder) CEH. (T.C. 383).
7. Witness CEH. C 16503. May, 1982.
8. Witness (Kaqchikel leader) CEH. (T.C. 266).
9. Witness (Kaqchikel CONAVIGUA activist) CEH. (T.C. 111).
10. Witness (human rights activist) CEH. (T.C. 233).
11. Article 8, LRN, Decree No. 145–96, approved by the Congress of the Republic on December 23, 1996.
12. Guatemalan Constitution, Article 66.
13. Accord on the Identity and Rights of Indigenous Peoples.
14. Georgetown University and the Lawyers Committee for Human Rights, "Supplementary petition presented to the CIDH for Case No. 10.636 against the Republic of Guatemala, under the name Myrna Mack," p. 6.
15. Claims made from November 12 to 13, 1993, recorded by another convict.

Glossary of Key Spanish Terms

acusador particular—"supporting plaintiff" a legal term referencing a mechanism through which private citizens play a role in criminal cases

ajusticiado(s)—victims of *ajustacimiento*, that is, those killed by the guerrillas as part of their political-military strategy.

ajusticiamiento(s)—a guerrilla violation in which individuals were specifically targeted and killed as part of the insurgency's political-military strategy.

alcalde rezador—Maya priest/local leader

aldea(s)—rural village

aldeas modelo—"model villages," referring to a specific military strategy of forcibly resettling those displaced into communities under the direct control of the army.

altiplano—highlands of Guatemala

babosada(s)—"foolishness," a term commonly used to refer negatively to social justice activities or support for the insurgency which might lead to victimization, as in "That's what happens to those who get involved in *babosadas*."

caballerías—a measurement of land

campesino(s)—rural resident/worker, sometimes translated as "peasant"

cantón—neighborhood

carceles clandestinas—"secret prisons," clandestine sites where the security agents would hold detainees

cofradía(s)—Maya religious association/brotherhood

comisionados militares—"military commissioners," locals working for the military often former members of the armed forces

compañero(s)—general term used to refer to a close friend or colleague, used within leftist social organizations and guerrilla movements to indicate membership or association, similar to "comrade"

confidencial(es)—"confidentials," refers to spies and those working secretly for the army

corte(s)—traditional skirt worn by Maya women

Costa Sur—"Southern Coast," Guatemalan Pacific coastal region that runs from Mexico to El Salvador and where sugar, cotton, and other plantations are located

delegados de la palabra—"representatives of the word," those involved in progressive Catholic Church activities

esbirros—"thugs," refers to spies and those working secretly for the army

finca(s)—farm/plantation

finquero(s)—the owner of a *finca*

foco(s)—small, mobile, focused groups of revolutionaries

foquismo—a revolutionary strategy widely used in Latin America in which insurgents create multiple small groups that organize and incite dissent

fusiles y frijoles—"rifles and beans," a counterinsurgency program linking food and assistance with militarization used in the highlands

fusilamiento(s)—A guerrilla violation in which individual members of the insurgency were killed as punishment, usually for acts of betrayal

guerra popular revolucionaria—"revolutionary people's war," a key idea within the insurgency referring mass uprising against the established social order

güipile(s)—traditional shirt worn by Maya women

impuestos de guerra—"war taxes" referring to a guerrilla policy of forcing landowners and others to provide money and goods to support the insurgency

indio(s)—"indian(s)," derogatory term used to refer to indigenous people

judiciale(s)-"judicials", sometimes also referred to as "la judicial" ("the judicial"), used to refer to the detective corps of the National Police, which worked closely with the intelligence services.

justicia revolucionaria—"revolutionary justice," a term used by the insurgency to justify acts of violence designed to punish landowners, spies, army collaborators and others

Kaibile(s)—Guatemalan Special Forces

La violencia—"the violence," a term used to refer to the armed conflict

Ladino(s)/Ladina(s)—a general term used to reference Guatemala's nonindigenous population

latifundios—large landholdings, farms/plantations

muchá—short for "muchacho" or "boy" and used to reference a friend or close colleague

naturales—"naturals," used to refer to indigenous peoples, especially by ORPA

orejas—"ears," refers to spies and those working secretly for the army

panel blanca—"white van" references a famous case involving disappearances

patrón—boss

patrullero(s); patrullero(s) civil(es)—"patrollers"; "civil patrollers," referring to members of the *Patrullas de Autodefensa Civil*, or Civil Defense Patrols

paz, segurida y desarrollo—"peace, security, and development," a counterinsurgency program linking development aid with the control of displaced populations resettled under military control

pintos—slang for soldiers

polos de desarrollo—"development poles," an integrated counterinsurgency program linking forced resettlement in *aldeas modelos* with ideological policies, social assistance, surveillance, and militarization

pueblo—people

shuca—slang for "shit," something/someone of low value

susto—fear or terror, describing a debilitating illness associated with trauma

techo, tortillas y trabajo—"housing, food, and work," a counterinsurgency program linking development programs with militarization used in the highlands

temascal—a traditional bath

traje(s)—general term referring to traditional Maya clothing

Index